THE RAMAYANA TRADITION AND SOCIO-RELIGIOUS CHANGE IN TRINIDAD 1917–1990

THE RAMAYANA TRADITION AND SOCIO-RELIGIOUS CHANGE IN TRINIDAD 1917–1990

Sherry-Ann Singh

Ian Randle Publishers
Kingston • Miami

First published in Jamaica, 2012 by
Ian Randle Publishers
11 Cunningham Avenue
Box 686
Kingston 6
www.ianrandlepublishers.com

© 2012, Sherry-Ann Singh

National Library of Jamaica Cataloguing in Publication Data

The Ramayana Tradition and Socio-Religious Change in Trinidad, 1917–1990/
    Sherry-Ann Singh

    p. ; cm.

Bibliography : p. Includes index

ISBN 978-976-637-361-0 (pbk)

Hinduism – Trinidad and Tobago   2. Hindus – Trinidad and Tobago social life and customs
Title
294.5922   -dc 22

All rights reserved. No part of this publication may be reproduced, stored in a retrieval system, or transmitted in any form, or by any means electronic, photocopying, recording or otherwise without prior permission of the author or publisher.

Cover image: 'The Ramayana: Love and Valor in India's Great Epic – The Mewar Ramayana Manuscripts' courtesy of The British Library.

Cover and book design by Ian Randle Publishers
Printed in United States of America

For my daughter, Jayashree, with all my love

TABLE OF CONTENTS

Acknowledgements / **ix**

List of Abbreviations / **xi**

Introduction / **1**

Chapter One: Socio-Religious Change, 1917–45 / **28**

Chapter Two: The *Ramayana* Tradition / **63**

Chapter Three: The Hindu Textual Tradition / **100**

Chapter Four: Socio-Religious Change, 1945–90: The Private Domain / **139**

Chapter Five: Socio-Religious Change, 1945–90: The Public Domain / **190**

Conclusion / **236**

Appendices / **257**

Notes / **273**

Glossary / **285**

Bibliography / **293**

Index / **313**

ACKNOWLEDGEMENTS

This book is based on my doctoral thesis (Singh 2005), parts of which have been previously published. Through the stages of research, writing and publication I was very fortunate to have received assistance and guidance from a number of individuals who I must thank. My foremost appreciation must go to Dr Kusha Haraksingh who supervised this study as a thesis at the University of the West Indies, St Augustine. His incisive criticism, interpretations and suggestions have been fundamental to this study. Special thanks also to Professor Brinsley Samaroo, Professor Bridget Brereton and to the late Dr Kenneth Parmasad for their invaluable support, insights and recommendations. I express my deepest gratitude also to those individuals who agreed to be interviewed since their contribution was crucial to this study.

I am also very grateful to the secretarial staff of the Department of History, University of the West Indies, St Augustine for their unfailing assistance throughout the years. Special mention must also be made of the staff at the West Indiana Division of the University of the West Indies, St Augustine for their unwavering assistance throughout the entire period of my research. I am indebted to the UWI Board for Graduate Studies and Research for awarding me a three-year UWI postgraduate scholarship which allowed me to pursue this study, and to the University Grants Committee for funding my research on several occasions in London, Toronto, and India. My deepest appreciation also to SEPHIS, the South-South Exchange Programme for Research on History Development for awarding me a one-year fellowship at the Centre for the Study of Culture and Society (CSCS), Bangalore, which contributed immensely to the scope and depth of this book. I am also grateful to the staff of the various institutions where I conducted research, especially at CSCS.

Finally, my warmest appreciation goes to my dear friend Sarah Pereira for her unwavering encouragement and belief in me. Thanks also to the members of my family for their constant encouragement and assistance; especially the babysitting. And to my daughter, Jayashree, thank you so much for all your patience and hugs and for not complaining too much at having to share your mother with this study for so many years.

LIST OF ABBREVIATIONS

APS	Arya Pratinidhi Sabha
BVS	Bharatiya Vidya Sansthaan
DLP	Democratic Labour Party
DLS	Divine Life Society
IOR	India Office Records
KPA	Kabir Panth Association
NAR	National Alliance for Reconstruction
NCIC	National Council for Indian Culture
PDP	People's Democratic Party
PNM	People's National Movement
POSG	Port-of-Spain Gazette
SDA	Sanatan Dharma Association
SDBC	Sanatan Dharma Board of Control
SDMS	Sanatan Dharma Maha Sabha
SWAHA	Society Working for the Advancement of Hindu Aspirations
TG	Trinidad Guardian
ULF	United Labour Front
UNC	United National Congress
VHP	Vishwa Hindu Parishad

INTRODUCTION

During the period of Indian indenture a total of 143,939 Indians migrated to Trinidad (Brereton 1981, 103), approximately 88 per cent of whom practised various facets of Hinduism. Of this number, 12.03 per cent belonged to the 'Brahmans and other high castes,' 36.82 per cent belonged to the 'agricultural castes,' 6.39 per cent belonged to the 'artisan castes,' and 33.16 per cent belonged to the 'low castes' (Vertovec 1992, 33). Despite the trying conditions experienced under the indenture system,[1] about four of every five Indian immigrants chose, at the end of their contracted periods of indenture, to make Trinidad their permanent home (Vertovec 1992, 73). From their very entrance into Trinidad society, Hindus were engaged in the practice of many aspects of their religion. This was especially so of the more private aspects which could be observed within either the home or the immediate Hindu/Indian community. However, although Hindu immigrants, as it has been argued, 'carried a slice' (Haraksingh 1985, 163) of their society and, hence, religion with them, the uprooting from the Indian context necessitated attempts at community and religious reconstruction. In Trinidad, elements of religion were variously truncated, modified, diluted, intensified or excised. Thus, reconstitution and telescoping (Haraksingh 1985, 163), rather than transplanting, were two of the dominant processes that could be observed. This subsequently yielded a form of Hinduism in which some of the more visible and tangible elements were markedly modified. At the same time, however, the Hinduism which emerged was unarguably rooted in the general philosophy and tenets of many of the strands of Hinduism practised in India. This applied to the caste system, Hindu priesthood, the institution of marriage, gender roles, and many of the religious rites, rituals and observances.

Because Indian indentured immigration encompassed a wide sweep of the Indian sub-continent, there was a remarkable degree of social, religious and cultural diversity within the immigrant population in Trinidad. This was evident in such areas as language, kinship ideology, social and economic structures, values, and general attitudes, lifestyle and behaviour. This social and geographical diversity also underscored a 'jumbled medley of beliefs, doctrines, rites, experiences, relationships, restrictions, polities, economies and orientations regarding matters supernatural and spiritual' (Vertovec 1992, 106). Specific regions in India yielded particular religious traditions which, inevitably, were transported – albeit often in highly attenuated forms – to the Trinidad context with the indentured immigrants. The Bengal, Bihar and Orissa regions were dominated by Shaktism (ecstatic type worship of the Mother Goddess) and, to a lesser extent, by Vaishnavism (worship of the various forms of the God Vishnu). Eastern and Western Uttar Pradesh were also primarily Vaisnavite and permeated by the Bhakti tradition. Yet, some of these regions were also strongholds of Shaivism (worship of the God Shiva) (Vertovec 1992, 106).

Regions in south India also provided a high concentration of Shakti traditions. Compounding this religious mélange was the presence of a number of socio-religious sub-groupings specific to the different religious traditions. In his 1893 'Note On Emigration,' Surgeon Major W.D. Comins identified the presence of sects such as the *Ramanund Phunt*, the *Kabeer Phunt*, the *Oughur Phunt*, and the *Sewnarain Phunt*.[2] The diversity among these four groups was very evident. He described the *Ramanand Phunt* and the *Kabeer Phunt* as being very clean and not consuming meat, alcohol or fish. On the other hand, the *Oughur* and *Sewnarain Phunts* were characterised as groups whose adherents ate and drank everything and whose ceremonies often entailed the use of alcohol. All four groups comprised mainly non-Brahmin individuals. Interestingly though, the headmen of both the *Sewnarain Phunt* and the *Ramanund Phunt* were described as 'now a Brahmin' (Comins, 1893). Since their names indicated non-Brahmin origins, it can be speculated that the station of Brahmin was assumed by the headmen to enhance their status as socio-religious leaders of these sects. In addition to the main, there were a host of lesser gods and goddesses, and district or village godlings, saints, spirits and supernaturals (Vertovec 1992, 107). Much of this diversity was situated in the presence of elements of both the Great and Little Traditions of Hinduism[3] in Trinidad. Caste distinctions also added to the religious diversity. However, by the beginning of the twentieth century most of these smaller traditions were being subsumed by the drive for a standardised form of Hinduism, namely the Sanatan Dharma strand of Trinidad Hinduism.

Following the abolition of indentured immigration in 1917 (Laurence 1994, 478–83), the Hindu community was then able to intensify its efforts at community and religious reconstitution. The sporadic and haphazard nature of these efforts during the period of indenture, which was due largely to the limitations of the conditions of indenture, was gradually replaced by more sustained, structured and collective efforts. By the 1920s then, a most discernible feature of Trinidad Hinduism was a move towards homogenisation along with a simultaneous and arguably paradoxical persistence of the many threads of Hinduism brought to Trinidad from the various geographico-cultural regions of India. Other equally observable features included the prominence of the highly personal Bhakti (devotion-oriented) form of worship, the sanctifying and inclusion of many local elements into the Hindu religious realm, the increase in collective religious activity and observances, the proliferation of temples, and the prominence of the *Ramcharitmanas* (a particular written version of the *Ramayana* story) as the most popular Hindu religious text. A highly attenuated caste ideology, ambiguity surrounding the role and requirements of the Hindu priest, and the intensification of socio-religious organisation (Vertovec 1992, 44–61) essentially defined the socio-religious ethos of the time. It is within this framework that this publication embarks on its examination of Trinidad Hinduism during the period 1917–90.

Rationale, Aims and Objectives

Providing a rationale for the chosen topic was possibly the least challenging facet of this entire endeavour. Firstly, although in 1990 Hinduism was the second largest socio-religious denomination in Trinidad and Tobago[4] (see Appendix I), the history of many of its more fundamental aspects remained largely undocumented. This was due to the preoccupation of Hindus with active socio-economic and religio-cultural reconstitution and sustenance rather than with documentation, and to the potential conflict in historicising a religion. This, however, is notwithstanding the commonly held though arguable notion that Hinduism as a religion and Hindus as a people lack a sense of history.[5] The book, therefore fills this void by examining some of the most fundamental dimensions of Trinidad Hinduism which, despite their longstanding presence in Trinidad, remained an enigma for most of the non-Hindu and some of the Hindu population.

Secondly, in addition to documenting the history and dynamics of this socio-religious group, some of the major misconceptions that continued to surround many aspects of Hindu thought and practice in Trinidad are deconstructed. These include such notions of Trinidad Hinduism as essentially static and homogeneous; as unaccommodating and inflexible when faced with seemingly conflicting elements of the wider society; and as exhibiting clannish tendencies amidst Trinidad's cosmopolitan society.

Thirdly, the chosen time frame (1917–90) underscores another major incentive. The year 1917 marked the abolition of indentured immigration, and the intensification of the Hindu community's dialogue with Trinidad society as its homeland. The book charts this period of multi-dimensional transformation, highlighting and analysing along the way the major points, causes and consequences of such transformation. By the late 1980s, one could discern a less defensive and less apologetic attitude of Hindus in terms of both their religious affiliation and their socio-cultural life. The need of some Hindus to justify Hinduism as a worthy and valid socio-religious body was being replaced by a more assertive, progressive desire to advance and transform the religion on its own terms; to meet the needs of Hindus instead of, as previously, being heavily conditioned by the dictates and expectations of the wider society. Thus, one can argue that, by 1990, the Hindu community had achieved a substantial level of stability, national recognition and, hence, had reached a defining juncture in its efforts at community development.

In effect then, this book explores various dimensions of Hindu socio-religious change in Trinidad during the period 1917–90. Chapter one addresses Hindu socio-religious change during the period 1917–45 and encompasses the realms of religious practice and belief, family life, community dynamics and the Hindu community's interaction with the larger Trinidad society. Chapter two examines the various dimensions of the *Ramayana* tradition in Trinidad, emphasising the symbiotic relationship between social change and transformations in this defining aspect of Trinidad Hinduism. Chapter three proceeds to look at the textual dimension of Trinidad Hinduism, with special emphasis on the most widely consulted Hindu religious text in Trinidad, the *Ramcharitmanas*. Chapters four and five both deal with the period 1945–90. Chapter four analyses the more private areas of family life, religious practice and Hindu community dynamics. Chapter five explores the considerable ferment in the public domain of Trinidad Hinduism during the period 1945–90, which was substantially located in the desire for recognition and acceptance as both equal citizens of Trinidad and Tobago and as a valid religious grouping. Standardisation, compartmentalisation, and westernisation are identifid as processes at work in Hindu socio-religious change. It also proves that, though encompassed under the umbrella of 'Trinidad Hinduism,' Hinduism in Trinidad can more aptly be described as an amalgam of various strands of Hindu religious thought and practice. However, while drawing heavily from Hindu religion, tradition and culture located in the South Asian sub-continent, Trinidad Hinduism has been considerably conditioned by the social, economic, cultural and political ethos of Trinidad.

In terms of the institution of the family, the impact that both Hindu social and religious life and the intercourse between the Hindu community and the larger Trinidad society have had on the traditional Indian structures, ideology and values of this institution are examined. The primary areas of focus include marriage, women, kinship structure and ideology, aspects of religion observed in the home and changing definitions and roles of individuals within the family. The internal dynamics of the Trinidad Hindu community are also analysed. This entails an examination of the major traditional, inherently Indian social systems and agents, along with their eventual dilution or demise. The emergence, development and transformation in Hindu socio-religious organisation(s) and their efforts at community mobilisation and enhancement will also be explored. Within this context, the Hindu idea and treatment of politics is examined. The varying shades and degrees of individual and collective attempts at enhancing the status and visibility of the Hindu community within the larger society are also discussed. Both the attempts at co-operation of the many Hindu socio-religious organisations, along with the conflict inherent in such interaction are analysed.

The nature, processes and impact of the intercourse between the Hindu community and the larger Trinidad society is another primary concern of this book. The major issues that have faced Trinidad Hindus in their station as but one community within Trinidad's cosmopolitan society will be examined. The study demonstrates how the unique history, nature, structures and ideology of Trinidad Hindus, largely rooted in the Indian subcontinent, have quite often been at odds with those of the wider society. In the process, (mis) conceptions held by the Hindu community and the wider Trinidad society about each other will be revealed. Special attention will be paid to those issues that have challenged the Hindu community at the official levels, more often than not on account of the discord between Hindu practices and belief and those of the larger non-Hindu society.

Another primary concern of this book is the transformation in Hindu religious thought and practice. This is realised through an exploration of the major Hindu life cycle rituals, Hindu religious texts, the religious forums of the *yagna* and *satsang*, the more prominent Hindu festivals and religious observances, the contribution of individuals and groups, and the dissolution of caste sensibility in Trinidad. The processes of assimilation, omission, dilution and standardisation are analysed within the seemingly paradoxical contexts of both the diversity and the umbrella of Trinidad Hinduism. Elements of the Little Tradition and their ability to endure the more orthodox, or more specifically Brahminic, efforts at diluting or discounting them are also explored.

The arguments come full circle in considering the impact of society and social change in its consideration of the *Ramayana* tradition in Trinidad. It demonstrates that the *Ramayana*, by constantly informing and reflecting the Trinidad Hindu experience, can be deemed both mirror and metaphor of history and society, and thus, Hindu socio-religious transformation. This argument echoes the view of Indian historian Romila Thapar that the 'multiple forms of the Ramkatha [story of Rama] reflect changing historical situations and at the same time, are in themselves an index to change' (Thapar 1978, 2). This book argues for a uniquely Trinidadian recension of the *Ramayana*. This local version can be defined as a collection of both conscious and unconscious remakings and interpretations (rather than one singular version) whose values, ideas and concepts have been influenced to varying extents by the history, experiences and attitudes of both the Hindu and wider Trinidad society. This proposed local recension is informal in the sense that it has not yet assumed a written form, but rather, has its plausibility entrenched largely in the oral and visual modes of diffusion and transmission, which have continuously fed on the written texts. In as much as this collection of remakings is based on one written version of the Rama myth, the *Ramcharitmanas*, this proposed local version can be considered a remaking of the remade. The role of this primary written version of the *Ramayana* in Trinidad, the *Ramcharitmanas*, both as religious writ and as social doctrine is also analysed. Finally, it examines the *Ramayana*'s role in the spheres of Hindu family life, politics, religious life and social interaction. In effect then, a chain of events emerges wherein Hindu social change impacts on the various aspects of the *Ramayana* tradition and yields what can be termed a Trinidad version of the tradition. In turn, this intrinsically Trinidadian form furnishes and advances, not just Trinidad Hinduism as a socio-religious group within a multicultural society, but also the growing idea of a 'Caribbean Hinduism.'

The Story So Far

Thus far, Hinduism in Trinidad has been predominantly analysed as but one secondary dimension of the larger Indian experience, with Hindu socio-religious thought and practice often shaped or eclipsed by the focus on the *Indian* community. This is clearly observable in the works of Klass, Niehoff, Tikasingh and others. The works of Morton Klass and Arthur and Juanita Niehoff are still possibly the most referred for the history of Indians in Trinidad. In his early publication *East Indians in Trinidad. A Study of Cultural Persistence*, Klass, while acknowledging changes within the Indian community during the 1950s, emphasised the retention and reconstitution of culture. He examined such dimensions of Indian life as the family, the community, marriage, kinship, occupation, community organisations and religion. However, since the locus of his study – the village of 'Amity' in north-central Trinidad – was predominantly Hindu, one gets a fairly detailed picture of Hindu life during the period. Although he was more interested in establishing and comparing patterns of cultural persistence in relation to India (Klass 1961, 4), Klass's exploration of the religious life of the village yielded valuable insights into the diversity of Trinidad Hinduism and particularly its sub-groupings, festivals, its private, semi-private and communal ceremonies, and lifecycle rituals. In his later work *Singing with Sai Baba. The Politics of Revitalization in Trinidad*, Klass provided an account of the transformations that were taking place within Hinduism during the 1980s. He explored the dialectics of change and continuity among Hindus in Trinidad through an in-depth examination of the emergence and spread of the Sathya Sai Movement in Trinidad (Klass 1991).

Arthur and Juanita Niehoff admitted that their focus was on 'East Indian society in Trinidad as a means of interpreting cultural patterns and values of India…' (Niehoff 1960). They explained that they

> …treated East Indian society in Trinidad as a 'laboratory' situation where, due to intense strains of acculturation, the basic and necessary aspects of Indian culture would become more apparent than they could in India (Niehoff 1960, 181).

Their study *East Indians in the West Indies* is located in the same time period as Klass's earlier work but examined a different village, 'Boodram,' in the southern part of Trinidad. It explored areas similar to those which Klass had investigated: family, religion, work and community. This provided for a very revealing exposition of both the consistencies and divergences within Trinidad Hinduism. While such anthropological studies attempt to tackle the workings of the Indian community from the inside, their focus and value is with the immediate community and period of the fieldwork. Thus, the historical dimension of the Indian experience is largely superseded by the anthropologist's interest in the contemporary situation. They do, however, provide valuable sources of information from which the historian can draw in examining and analysing the past.

In *Survivors of Another Crossing. A History of East Indians in Trinidad 1880–1946*, Marianne Ramesar examined the growth, location and occupations of the Indian community, education, ethnic integration and changing attitudes among Indians. Some of the factors and manifestations of social change during the period 1920–45 are outlined. However, this was done primarily in relation to the emerging middle classes, and largely ignored the more numerous Hindu group (Ramesar 1994). In E.B. Rosabelle Seesaran's *From Caste to Class, Social Mobility among Indo-Trinidadians*, conversion, the Canadian Mission, economic advancement, and various forms of westernisation were promoted as the major avenues of social mobility among Indians. Social change and mobility were considered and measured along the yardstick of the wider society, and the intrinsically Hindu factors and processes of mobility and social change were minimally considered (Seesaran 2002).

Gerard Tikasingh's thesis, *The Establishment of Indians in Trinidad, 1870–1900*, identified 'the transformation of the Indians from a mere category of immigrants into a community' (Tikasingh 1973). His is a very useful account of the emergence and adjustment of the Indian community in the late nineteenth century. However, he too focused on the entire group as Indian and examined Hinduism but briefly as one aspect of Indian life. The works of Ramesar, Seesaran and Tikasingh rely heavily on material that can be argued as having an essentially Western, middle-class and Christian bias such as official records and reports of the Canadian Mission, Colonial Office Records, Official Reports, Despatches and Letters, Newspapers and Minute Papers. The absence of oral history from within the Indian community further intensified this slant.

In her detailed analysis of gender dynamics among Indians entitled *Gender Negotiations among Indians in Trinidad, 1917–1947*, Patricia Mohammed employed (sometimes questionably) some prominent concepts and aspects of Hinduism such as the caste system, the *Ramayana,* and symbols such as the *Shiva Lingam*. However, this is done within the boundaries and focus of the study, resulting in a somewhat selective approach. While advocating the importance of and operating along the lines of the 'inside' view, and providing valuable insights into several areas, Hinduism is treated as but one of several equally important factors in gender negotiations; not as a separate entity, but, yet again, ultimately enveloped in the all-consuming category of Indian (Mohammed 2002).

Steven Vertovec's 1992 study, *Hindu Trinidad: Religion, Ethnicity and Socioeconomic Change*, comes very close to breaking this trend of subsuming Hindu under the umbrella of Indian. He provided an insightful analysis of the dynamics of social and economic change within the Hindu community by placing Hindus, their major social institutions and their religious practices at the centre of the study. Vertovec demonstrated a good grasp of the internal workings of this community in his consideration of the plurality and diversity among generations, and the variation of individual, domestic and communal activities influenced by both Indian and Caribbean cultures, thereby dispelling the notion of the Hindu community as essentially static, homogeneous and conservative. He asserted that,

> ...since Indians were introduced to the island, there were – or have emerged – among Hindus marked differences in class interests, devotional orientations, caste or regionally derived predilections, rural/urban lifestyles, and local inter-ethnic relations (Vertovec ix).

The limited number and scope of works on the Hindu community are, to an extent, understandable given the nature of the available sources. Official reports and documents based on their own economic, political and social agendas, and not concerned with the diversity or dynamics of this group, tended to classify them as a single entity – Indians. Newspapers adopted a similar attitude and contained their own biases. Before the mid-1930s, newspapers such as the *Port-of-Spain Gazette* (**POSG**) and the *Trinidad Guardian* (**TG**) paid miniscule attention to the Hindu population. While post-1935 saw the weekly and sometimes bi-weekly publication of what can be called an Indian Page in each of these newspapers (*Bharatiya Samachar*, literally *Indian News* in the POSG, and *Indian News And Views* in the TG), the largely middle-class and Western biases were transparent. Emphasis was placed on the unusual, less mundane aspects of Hinduism such as visiting swamis, Indian scholars and dignitaries, Hindu and Vedic philosophy, reports on issues and events in India, and notices of local events pertaining largely to middle-class Indians. Many of these issues did not have a direct bearing on the local Hindu community. When they did, the views and reactions of Hindus were either totally overlooked or subsumed by those of the largely middle-class, considerably westernised and often non-Hindu individuals and organisations. As Shameen Ali noted in her study of 'Africans, Indians and the Press in Trinidad, 1917–1946,'

> [The] Colonial press upheld Christian values in Trinidad. It was very intolerant and sometimes disdainful of non-Christian religions and portrayed Indians as followers of false religions. Indian religious practices were ridiculed by the press which propagated the view of white missionaries that Christian beliefs were the only valid ones (Ali 2001, 11).

Misinterpretations and misrepresentations of the Hindu community were often evident. The following article from the *Port-of-Spain Gazette* March 18, 1937 provided an outstanding example:

> A *Phagwa* known as Indian Carnival is now being observed in the town of Arima by members of the Hindu religion. The ceremony is being conducted by Imam Baksh Moon prominent resident and jeweler. The festival is being conducted daily at his residence....A large number of East Indians can be seen daily seated together listening intently on what is being read. The observance of this festival began on the 26th of February and will come to a close on Sunday. The festival is being observed in connection with the Hindu Year which starts from Wednesday last.

The level of misrepresentation in this article generates absolute confusion. *Phagwa* (a Hindu festive, yet religious observance) is erroneously referred to as an 'Indian Carnival.' An Imam is a Muslim priest and would not have been conducting any Hindu 'festival.' The latter part alludes to the ambience and structure of a *yagna*, while at the same time again invoking *Phagwa* as the festival which marks the beginning of the Hindu New Year. Indian publications such as the *East Indian Weekly* (1928–32), the *Observer* (1941–67), and the *Indian* (1940–46) did focus almost solely on issues directly related to or affecting the Indian community, but their perspective was heavily conditioned by the inclinations and attitude of the largely non-Hindu Indian middle class. One has to resort to varying degrees of extrapolation and reading between the lines, or rather against the grain, to arrive at some conclusion of how the Hindu community was affected by, or reacted to such issues. Thus, the bulk of this type of primary source placed the westernised and Christian (mainly Presbyterian) sections of the Indian community at the centre, and although claiming to be working for the welfare of all Indians, in actuality, relegated the Hindus, the largest Indian group, to the margins.

In the primacy it gives to the Trinidad Hindu community and in some dimensions of its approach to this socio-religious group, this study can be seen as operating along similar lines as Vertovec's work on Trinidad Hinduism. However, there is substantial divergence in the points of emphasis. This study attempts to unravel and analyse a number of facets which fell outside of the scope of Vertovec's work. But possibly the deepest divergence resides in Vertovec's work being essentially anthropological, while this book is situated in the discipline of History. The book seeks to take the anthropology back into history thereby supplementing and historicising Vertovec's highly penetrating but notably contemporaneous work. Herein, the study argues that the Hindu community possessed its own markers and procedures of social mobility, and that these operated alongside, but also independently of the considerations which have usually been highlighted when social mobility is examined through a Western and Christian perspective. In its attempt to realise this argument, the study employs an insider's view of the Hindu community. This stands in contrast to the approach usually taken by the majority of works done on both Hindus and Indians in Trinidad, which can be described generally as views from the outside.

This 'outsider's' view is characterised by an insufficient distinction between Hindu and Indian, with the associated, sometimes erroneous, extrapolating of the former from the latter. In most cases, little regard is paid to the fact that the relationship between both concepts is one of suggestivity and implication rather than synonymity. Thus, when the terms are merged into each other, the distinctiveness of Hindu life is overlooked or ignored, and a tendency emerges to focus on those areas and groups within the Indian community which are more socially visible, on which information is more readily accessible, and where change is more observable. This has helped to promote the view of the bulk of the Hindu community as conservative and resistant to change. By contrast, the view from the inside, which informs this study, acknowledges the distinctiveness and dynamics of the Hindu community, locates the community at the centre of focus, examines and analyses it as an entity in itself, and endeavours to decode (rather than ignore) its many nuances and idiosyncrasies. Accordingly, it is the objective of this book to re-examine the view of Hindu socio-religious stasis, and to substantiate the claim that this group, through its own internal social, political and religious structures, was dynamic and predisposed to change, not unlike any other group in the society.

'Selective Sanskritisation'

Since the major objective of this book is to analyse the Hindu community on its own terms, the adoption of a preconceived theory may prove confining and even problematic. Yet, of the numerous theories on social change within both the Caribbean and Indian contexts, two have proven to be partially reflective of what was taking place within Trinidad Hinduism. In the Caribbean, change among and within cultures has been varyingly examined as acculturation, creolisation, assimilation and homogenisation. However, in her study of Indians in Jamaica, historian Verene Shepherd identified the theory 'Selective Creolisation' as the 'conscious decision to conform to the norms of creole society as a result of the need to be accepted and be permitted to move up the social ladder' (Shepherd 1993, 205–206). While Shepherd's concept may be more useful in places such as Jamaica and Grenada, where the comparably smaller number of Indians and other related factors led to the latter's substantial 'creolisation' (Shepherd 1993, 206), it cannot, by itself, cover the entire range of developments in the Trinidad situation. In addition, this examination of Indians is clearly done from the outside where change is being measured in relation to the larger society, thereby imposing a structure that does not fully fit the Hindu mode.

In examining the dynamics of social change and mobility among Hindus in Trinidad then, the concept coined by Indian sociologist M.N. Srinivas, '*sanskritisation*,' can prove useful. In his analysis of mobility within the traditional caste system, Srinivas defined sanskritisation as the process by which,

> ...a 'low' Hindu caste, or tribal or other group, changes its customs, ritual ideology, and way of life in the direction of a high and frequently, 'twice-born' caste. Generally such changes are followed by a claim to a higher position in the caste hierarchy than that traditionally conceded to the claimant class by the local community. The claim is usually made over a period of time, in fact, a generation or two, before the 'arrival' is conceded. Occasionally a caste claims a position which its neighbours are not willing to concede (Srinivas 1969, 6).

He added that although the Brahminical model of sanskritisation, Brahminisation,[6] (where the Brahmins are the socially dominant caste) is dominant in many parts of India, and by extension, within the Indian diaspora, there are also the Kshatriya, the Vaishya and the Sudra models (Srinivas 1989, 7), both defined by and reflecting the socially dominant group of a specific area. The subdivisions within each major caste also lends to the plurality, fluidity and flexibility of this process, whereby one local section of a caste imitates another. The dominant castes set the model for the majority of people living in rural areas including, according to the specific situation, the *Brahmins*. Where their (the dominant caste's) way of life has undergone a degree of sanskritisation, the culture of the area over which their dominance extends experiences change (Srinivas 1989, 21). Other, newer factors affecting dominance include Western education, jobs in administrative positions, and urban sources of income, which all contribute to the prestige and power of the particular caste group both in the village and in the wider region.

Possibly the most pertinent example of this notion of sanskritisation in India is what is referred to as the Backward Classes Movement based largely in South India, which gained momentum and form by the prospect of the transfer of political power into Indian hands. It has been described as a 'movement to achieve mobility on the part of groups which had lagged behind the Brahmins in Westernisation' (Srinivas 1989, 114). This movement had several crucial implications. It emphasised the role of secular factors in the mobility of caste groups and individuals. There was no longer the desire, on the part of the dominant castes, to pass as Brahmins, Kshatriyas or Vaishyas, but rather, a reversal of the process. In some areas outside South India such as Gujarat, some dominant castes opened their ranks to lower castes in order to strengthen themselves politically (Srinivas 1989, 69). While defining the process within the parameters of the traditional Hindu caste system, Srinivas asserted that sanskritisation is not confined to the Hindu castes, but also occurs among tribal and semi-tribal groups such as the *Bhils* of Western India and the *Pahadis* of the Himalayas (Srinivas 1969, 7).

While applicable in India, Srinivas' concept of sanskritisation by itself, like Shepherd's selective creolisation, cannot fully elaborate and elucidate the dynamics of Hindu social mobility in Trinidad. Here, the elements that came into play, such as wealth, colour, ethnicity, education, land acquisition, and urbanisation, fall, in varying degrees, outside the scope of Srinivas's established notion of sanskritisation. What emerged instead was a combination of both Shepherd's and Srinivas' respective theories; a peculiar form of sanskritisation that seemed to prefer secular over ritual attributes in several areas, ritual over secular in others, and even a leveling of both in certain instances. Essentially then, there was an interplay between Indian and Caribbean processes of socio-cultural transformation. The bilateral and intricate nature of this discourse was recognised by Edward Brathwaite. He asserted that due to the retention of 'their traditional culture (rooted in India), the creolising and anglicising process have affected Indians in ways different from the Africans' (Brathwaite 1974, 46–47). He simultaneously agreed that 'the Indian relates his own notions of cultural norms to the master culture of Euro-America; and selects/adapts in order to modernise' (Brathwaite 1974, 54).

In attempting to fill in the gaps of both concepts of sociocultural transformation discussed, this book argues that what fits the case of Trinidad Hinduism is a hybrid theory of sorts, which it terms *selective sanskritisation*. This proposed theory can be described as a transposing of aspects of the ideology of sanskritisation out of the Indian context into Trinidad's creole society. This, however, is conditioned by a substantial degree of selection from the Indian, Hindu and Caribbean social, religious and cultural contexts. Throughout the study socio-religious transformation will be examined through the lens of this proposed theory. The predominance of the interplay between Hindu/Indian and Caribbean/Western factors in almost all of the investigated areas will ultimately substantiate the proposal of this theory of selective sanskritisation. A most vivid example of this theory is its application to and manifestation in the exploration of the *Ramayana* tradition. What is immediately discernible is the degree and nature of the changes therein, the prominence or subsumption of various aspects of the tradition, and a medley of rituals, values and attitudes – all variously conditioned by the process of selection proposed in this theory.

Methodology and Data

A wide range of written primary material was examined. These include official records, reports and correspondence pertaining to Indians in Trinidad and the other British colonies between 1922 and 1966; Trinidad and Tobago Administration Reports, Colonial Emigration Passes, statistical digests and reports, Debates of the Legislative Council and the House of Representatives, newspapers, journals, magazines, and outstanding contemporary publications on Indians in Trinidad. The majority of this primary material was accessed at the National Archives, Trinidad; the Library at the University of the West Indies, West Indiana Collection; The British Library, London; The Public Records Office, London; The National Archives, Kolkata; The National Library, Kolkata; and The Asiatic Society, Kolkata.

Secondary material comprised books, published and unpublished articles and conference proceedings. These covered such topics as Hinduism; Indians and Hindus in Trinidad and in the larger Indian diaspora; the Ramayana; myth; religious transformation; Indian/Hindu literature; Indian history, culture and society; historical and social studies on Trinidad and Tobago; and theories of social and religious change. The majority of the secondary material was sourced at the Library of the University of the West Indies, St Augustine campus; the School of Oriental and African Studies, London; University of Toronto; the Sahitya Akademi, New Delhi; and the library at the Centre for the Study of Culture and Society, Bangalore.

The proceedings of the 1975, 1979 and 1984 conferences on East Indians in the Caribbean and the 1995 conference on *Challenge and Change: the Indian Diaspora in its Historical and Contemporary Contexts* – all organised by the University of the West Indies, St Augustine – provided an extensive source of incisive and scholarly examinations of numerous dimensions of the Indian experience in both Trinidad and the larger Indian diaspora. Novels spun around the Indian/Hindu experience in Trinidad also yielded invaluable supplementary and background material for many aspects of this study. The works of V.S. Naipaul, Seepersad Naipaul, Harold Sonny Ladoo and Lakshmi Persad were especially pertinent. Relevant PhD dissertations were also of great assistance in substantiating or questioning the arguments of this book.

In order to realise the proposed objective of an 'insider's view' of the Hindu community, emphasis has been placed on oral sources, which encapsulate elements of both the oral tradition and oral history. Since they have been derived directly from within, oral tradition and oral history echo the sentiments and emotions of the respective community, and more faithfully capture the resonances and nuances of daily life. As such, they encapsulate 'the study of the past by means of life histories or personal recollections, where informants speak about their own experiences' (Henige 1982). Works such as Jan Vansina's *Oral Tradition. A Study in Historical Methodology* (Vansina 1961), Richard Price's *The Historical Vision of an Afro-American People* (Price 1983), and George Ewart Evans's *Where Beards Wag All* (Evans

1970), which all rely heavily on oral sources, offer glimpses of the past and provide valuable and valid historical information. Oral sources provide the bulk of the evidence for those areas whereon no, little, or questionable written material was available. Such areas include the *Ramayana* tradition, the Hindu textual tradition, several dimensions of Hindu religious practice and thought, and various aspects of family life and interpersonal interaction. However, where written primary and secondary material were available, these were as equally (and in some instances more so) pivotal in the argument as the evidence derived from oral sources.

Seventy-five persons were formally interviewed throughout a three-year period. This number is not inclusive of the 20 or so informal discussions that also contributed to the arguments of this book. Factors such as age, gender, geographical location, caste sensibility/ affiliation, economic and social status, and ritual specialisation underscored the choice of interviewees, with the aim of giving as comprehensive and precise a representation of the Trinidad Hindu population as possible. Special attention was also paid to the selection of the areas in which the oral interviews were conducted. These included Felicity, Chaguanas, Bejucal, Barrackpore, Tunapuna, El Dorado, Sangre Grande, and Sangre Chiquito which comprise a geographical cross-section of the country. Areas such as Felicity, Bejucal, Barrackpore and Sangre Chiquito were, until the late 1970s, essentially rural agriculture-based communities. The others – Chaguanas, Tunapuna, El Dorado and Sangre Grande – can be classified as more semi-urban communities. In each of these locales there is a notably high concentration of Hindus. It was felt that the collection of data from areas spanning both a geographic and a socio-economic cross-section of the country would help capture distinctions in socio-religious practice, ideology and cultural nuances among the different locations. The variety in locales also allowed for a deeper revelation of the impact of such factors as urban/ rural dynamics, occupational and economic diversity, and variant lifestyles on Hindu socio-religious change. Many individuals were also selected by virtue of their expertise in specific areas such as *Ramayana* recitation, the *Ramleela*, Indian dance, singing and music, and in their station as leaders or prominent members of Hindu socio-religious organisations.

Special attention was paid to the structure and process of the oral interviews. Most of the interviews assumed a semi-structured format wherein the issues to be discussed during a particular session and the general direction of the questioning were identified. However, formulating a set list of questions proved, more often than not, somewhat restrictive. Pre-set lists of questions were most fruitful when interviewing professionals, academics and some leaders of Hindu socio-religious organisations. It was found that, for the bulk of the interviews, the use of questioning to guide, rather than to determine, the direction and pace of the interviews yielded responses which often served to deepen the researcher's perception of the issue. An average interview was about one hour long. However, this was never a pre-established parameter. Whenever it was felt that the information was both forthcoming and valuable, the interview was extended for another half hour or for another hour. This was, of course, after assessing the temperament of the respondents and having acquired their permission to proceed. As the book began taking shape, many of the persons interviewed were revisited for additional or supplementary information.

Most of the sessions were conducted either at the homes or workplaces of the interviewees. Despite occasional interruptions by children, spouses, visitors and the telephone, it was evident that respondents' sense of comfort in their respective personal spaces generated amicable and liberal discussion. Most of the interviews were conducted on a one-on-one basis between the writer and the respondent. This privacy seemed to promote a higher level of veracity and willingness to divulge personal or potentially contentious information. This was especially borne out in those situations where a husband and wife were interviewed together. In one specific case, the wife created the picture of a perfect marriage: a loving husband, an understanding mother-in-law, and a generally comfortable life. However, when the husband left to answer the telephone, the wife immediately requested that the tape be turned off. She then offered quick details of beatings at the hands of both husband and mother-in-law, her husband's earlier alcoholism and philandering and of a life dotted with emotional and economic travails.

As previously mentioned, an attempt was made to include individuals from as varied a spectrum as possible within the Hindu community. Of the 75 persons interviewed, 31 were women and 44 were men. Twenty-five belonged to what can be loosely termed the professional/educated group. These included pundits, teachers, school principals, leaders of socio-religious organisations, and persons in the field of business. The majority of the respondents, however, belonged to what can be termed the working class in Trinidad. These comprised labourers, farmers, housewives, persons in various types of small scale commercial activities, and others at the middle and lower end of Trinidad's socio-economic spectrum. Nine of the respondents were between the ages of 30 and 40 years, 12 were between 41 and 50 years, 15 were between 51 and 60 years, 16 were between 61 and 70 years, and 16 were over 70 years. The ages of seven interviewees could not be ascertained.

There is an evident proliferation of Hindi and Bhojpuri words throughout the book. Those words which have been italicised can be found in the glossary. However, those words which have crossed over into mainstream usage in the English language were neither italicised nor placed in the glossary. Such words can be found in the *Concise Oxford Dictionary, Tenth Edition*.

The Ramayana *Tradition*

In this analysis of Trinidad Hinduism, it was found that the *Ramayana*, in its capacity as both the most subscribed-to Hindu religious text and as one of the most diverse, enduring and fluid Hindu traditions in Trinidad, can function as a lens through which Hindu socio-religious transformation can be examined. Since the very earliest days of Indian indenture in Trinidad, the *Ramayana* had established itself as the most popular Hindu religious text. It evolved from a collection of memorised verses and stories diffused through the oral tradition, to a multitude of dimensions which all simultaneously yielded to and reflected transformation in society. While the basic storyline and the characters are the same, the symbiotic relationship between the society and the *Ramayana* tradition generated changes in interpretation, thematic emphasis, focus, style and modes of presentation. Yet, it still managed to retain its tenets, themes and status as a religious and social doctrine.

The Ramayana *and History*

The level of historicity of the *Ramayana* and the Rama story has always been a point of contention and debate. Some people believe that the story is totally historical in the sense that it actually occurred as told in the text, while others consider it pure myth. Extensive historical and archaeological research has shown, however, that like presumably all mythological works, the basis of the Rama story – namely the banishment of the hero – is indeed historical, with its other elements originating from variant sources, circumstances and at different times (Ramakrishna Mission 1962, 17). The incorporation of interpolations catering to popular local and contemporary needs and inclinations would have been quite a common occurrence during the stage of oral transmission. Additional matter consisting of repetitions and imitations, the motifs of boons and curses, Puranic legends,[7] the supernatural and the marvellous, poetic embellishments and whatever else that appears to go against the historical nature of the work, can almost certainly be regarded as later additions (Ramakrishna Mission 1962, 17) cast and recast in conformity with social assumptions. The *Ramayana* has also been widely held as an allegorical representation of the highly contentious theory of the Aryan conquest of the southern part of India (Vaidya 1972, 51–77). Its transition from poetic epic to divine proportions can be allotted to that inherent propensity of Indian mythology to have its gods incarnate as heroes and to ascribe divine qualities to its human heroes.

This debate on the historicity of the *Ramayana* has extended to the present, both in Trinidad and in other countries of the Indian diaspora. In one account of Fijian Hinduism, several of the interviewees acknowledged that the events in the *Ramayana* may not have happened, yet, 'still the teaching would be there, and would be important to follow even if it were only a parable' (Wilson 1979, 100). One respondent added that 'the *Ramayana* have the truth. It teaches the way to live.'[8] This echoes the popular Hindu view that Rama is God and the *Ramayana* is an actual account of His actions.

The *Ramayana* as Myth

Myth, on a superficial level, can be defined as prose narratives which seek to recount events of the remote past, and which, more often than not, are associated with some aspect of religion, ceremony or ritual of a particular society. The narrative focuses on the exemplary actions of the main characters – often gods in human form – and it is set in either an earlier world or another world such as the sky or the underworld (Dundes 1984, 9). Through the activities and relationships of these gods, myth attempts to account for the origin of the world and mankind, and to explain the numerous complex elements in both nature and culture which contributed to the creation of an order which, to varying degrees, still obtains (Dundes 1984, 9). On a more profound level, myth mirrors and confirms the integrating values and religious norms of society. As historian Romila Thapar says, it '...codifies belief, safeguards morality, vouches for the efficiency of the ritual and provides social norms' (Thapar 1978, 272). It also provides models of behaviour to be imitated.

It can be concluded that the basic mythic idea is part of the conception rather than the actuality of an event. This both distinguishes myth from history and renders it extremely flexible and open to numerous interpretations, especially in cultures that depend on the oral tradition as the primary means of passing on information. The diversity and flexibility of myth allows for a constant recasting, through both conscious and unconscious (re)articulation. It can be argued though, that the latter, since it is more likely to be relatively free of the possible biases of the former, allows for a more reliable reflection of the dynamism of both the society and social change. Undoubtedly, most of the inherent nature, features, functions and interpretations of myth can be applied to the *Ramayana*. However, the popular perception of myth as essentially fantastical fabrication, when applied to as central and revered a tradition/text as the *Ramayana* and the widely held Hindu belief in the historicity of the

Rama story, substantially prohibits the classification of this tradition/text as myth.

Myth and History

Since the *Ramayana* operates on an interplay between myth and history, a brief examination of this relationship is necessary. While myth can never be categorised as true reflections or descriptive sources of history, it can work in harmony with and to the advantage of history by encapsulating the historical struggles and the major crisis situations of society (Rogerson 1984, 68). Thus, an analysis of myth can reveal the more distinctive perspectives and assumptions of a time and society (Thapar 1978, 271). In light of the foregoing

> ...myth is in a sense a proto-type history since it is a selection of ideas composed in narrative form for the purpose of preserving and giving significance to an important aspect of the past (Thapar 1978, 271).

The perspective becomes even more apparent through a comparison of various retellings, and in this vein, contestations aid in historical reconstruction. The forms which these variants assume, the interpretations which they generate, and even the acts of translation and commentary render narrative an agent of cultural history (Thapar 2000, 4). Any kind of relationship between myth and history, however, must be conditioned by the following cautions: myths, their events and characters are manipulated to bestow prestige upon rulers and lineages, and to propagate or counter specific social, political, ideological and economic orders. Imagination, syncretism and confusion, numerous retellings and resulting variations add to the ambiguity (Day 1984).

The *Ramayana* in a Global Setting

A narrative such as the *Ramayana*, brimming with social and moral values, multi-dimensional in nature and enduring for such an extensive period of time is prone to variations, additions and omissions. Indeed, the *Ramayana* tradition since the time of its very inception in India before 500 BC in the form of the Rama stories (Chatterji 1980, 242), has undergone such extensive variation and change that it has spawned two contentious questions: whether the recensions are simply variations of one text, or whether some can be considered independent texts/tellings (rather than variants) on their own (Richman 1991, 2). Due to its intricate and intimate connection with the life of the people, the *Ramayana* tradition can be found in almost every literary genre: heroic, dramatic, lyric, elegiac, tragic, comic and even farcical poems or songs; street and theatre dramas; epics; *kavyas* (ornate poetic compositions); *Puranas* (mythological stories); dance dramas and other performances; sculpture, bas-reliefs, and mask, puppet and shadow plays of both the classical and folk traditions (Richman 1991, 7). In terms of the epic itself, almost 300 tellings have been recorded (Richman 1991, 7). However, Valmiki's version of the Rama story has proven to be fundamental to the *Ramayana* tradition since, in the words of one scholar, 'all past inspiration had flown into this reservoir, and all later tellings have flown from it' (Iyengar 1983, 7–8).

Each recension or literary genre inevitably exhibits numerous variations based on the purposes of the particular composer, the historical and social location, religious affiliation, gender, and political, cultural, chronological and ideological contexts. The plethora of *Ramayana* versions in various Indian languages exhibit regional and local shifts in emphasis, and changes in minor or major situations, actions and characterisation. Recensions outside of India also display variations that cater to and reflect the values, lifestyle and cultural nuances of country and people. Although the structure and sequence of events may be the same, or at least similar, the discourse[9] or actual retelling may differ greatly in relation to such matters as style, detail, tone, texture and the import and working of traditional, regional or folk motifs into the story. Thus, to varying extents, all later *Ramayanas* play on the knowledge of previous versions and can be labeled meta-*Ramayanas*.

While some tellings affirm the social, religious or political status quo, others contest it. In E.V. Ramasami's 1930 interpretation, Ravan, the villain in the *Ramayana* story, is viewed as an epitome of South Indian virtue. Several groups such as the Dalits (a group of militant untouchables) and the *Nadars* (a low sub-caste), as well as a number of Dravidian tribals and lower sub-castes of southern and central India, have claimed variant affiliations with Ravan, whom they view as the real hero of the *Ramayana*. (Richman 1991,15). Diverse tellings render the *Ramayana* an apt vehicle for accusing, justifying, mediating or debating issues pertaining to social or political grievances. Many folk songs of the Telugu women focus on a *Ramayana* tradition that questions the prevailing male dominance. Rama's integrity and actions as a husband are severely questioned, and grander male-dominated events such as war and coronation are sidestepped while prominence is given to more female-oriented events and domestic matters such as childcare and even the queen's morning sickness (Rao 2001).

Metonymy (the selection of one small part of the text as representing the essence of the whole) also adds to the plurality of the *Ramayana* tradition (Richman 1991, 16). Groups such as the *Ramnamis* (a sect of untouchables) recast the Rama story to reflect their beliefs and values, while ignoring other aspects of the story. They peruse the *Ramcharitmanas*, create their own personalised texts by rejecting passages condoning Brahmin supremacy and the caste system, and stress those that assert Rama's love for all (Lamb 1991, 233–55). The Jaina[10] tellings seek to counter Brahminical self-serving extravagances by opening not with Rama's, but Ravan's genealogy and greatness (Richman 1991). In the two classic Buddhist crystallisations of the Rama story, the author, in the sense of the first teller of the tale, is said to be Buddha himself, with each recension being presented as a sermon of Buddha (Reynolds 1991).

In contemporary times, and more specifically, within the context of the Indian diaspora, the *Ramayana* has both reflected and contributed to the transformation of Indian culture and society in the various alien lands. For example, the Southall Black Sisters' 1979 *Ramleela* production reflected their particular circumstances of migration to Britain, and reworked the *Ramayana* tradition through the conceptual categories of race, class, gender and colonialism (Richman 2001, 309–28).[11] Though done within a celebratory atmosphere, it is an example of a united move to combat sexism and racism by satirically questioning patriarchal attitudes, and by using Ravan as a symbol of the British state.

John Kelly explored the notion of the *Ramayana* as Fiji's 'fifth Veda.'[12] He examined the political emergence and role of the *Ramayana* in Fiji's courtrooms, 'the colonial concretisation of the *Ramayana* political imaginary' (Kelly 2001, 349), the *Ramayana* as a vehicle for self-identification, and the relevance of its themes of exile and the quest for *Ramrajya* (utopian state) to the Indian diaspora (Kelly 2001, 349). These diverse tellings indicate that throughout history a variety of voices was heard within the *Ramayana* tradition. This is quite applicable to the *Ramayana* tradition in Trinidad. In this study, it will be argued that, operating on principles parallel to those of the *Ramayana* tradition on a global level, local variations both reflected and generated the transformation of thought, attitude and action in almost all spheres of life.

Undoubtedly, due to the 159-year dislocation from the ancestral homeland, Hinduism in Trinidad and in the Caribbean has developed significant divergences in terms of both practice and ideology from Hinduism in India. Yet despite the divergence in time and space, parallels and similarities are observable. I was afforded the opportunity of experiencing the Indian side of the story during a one year research visit to India. This was facilitated by a postgraduate fellowship funded by SEPHIS, the South-South Exchange Programme for Research on the History of Development. Throughout that year, I was continuously confronted by the vastness and diversity of Hinduism that, thus far, had been experienced just vicariously through literature and the media. Witnessing the numerous Hindu rites and rituals, tracing the variant ideological strands, and attempting to locate them within their respective geographico-cultural contexts greatly enhanced my understanding of the dynamics of Hinduism. Places such as Kolkata, Varanasi, and especially locations in the states of Uttar Pradesh and Bihar (which supplied the majority of immigrants to the Caribbean), not unexpectedly but still amazingly, loudly resonated multiple dimensions of Trinidad Hinduism. One can, thus, better locate and appreciate the paradoxes that seem to characterise Hinduism within the context of the Indian diaspora: the change and the continuity; the sanctifying and the secularising; the diversity and the homogeneity; the sanskritising and the westernising. A year of living in a South

Indian community provided a level of insight into Hindu dynamics which could not have been otherwise acquired. Most interesting was the high degree of ignorance about even the existence of Indian descendants in the Caribbean.

It is evident that the period 1917–90 was a very crucial one for Hinduism in Trinidad characterised by progressive phases of reinstitutionalisation, homogenisation, destabilisation, organisation and revitalisation. Extremely fluid and complex, each phase entailed a number of major socio-religious transformations, which worked cumulatively to create, by 1990, a distinct – though never rigid – entity known as Trinidad Hinduism. The lack of distinction in Hinduism between what can be termed the sacred and the secular created a situation where Hinduism was manifest in almost every aspect of life in Trinidad: in the temples, at the home, at the level of the village, at Parliament, in the Carnival. The *Ramayana* tradition in Trinidad provided a most visible example of this pervasiveness of Hinduism. It is hoped that, by analysing the group largely on its own terms, this book will elucidate the many dimensions of Hindu socio-religious change in Trinidad from 1917–90, especially through the lens of the *Ramayana*.

CHAPTER ONE
Socio-Religious Change 1917–45

The period 1917–45 stands as a relatively hazy one in the history of Indians in Trinidad, with the bulk of existing material focusing on either the previous period of indenture, or on the 25 years immediately post-1945. However, though neither as socially visible as in the period of indenture, nor ripe enough as a community, the period 1917–45 was extremely crucial as a turning point in local Hindu history. By the 1920s, factors such as the acceptance of Trinidad as their homeland by those immigrants who had opted to remain in the colony, the leavening out of the male-female ratio and the age imbalance, and the noticeable increase in the birth rate of Indians contributed to the characterisation of the Indian population as 'a "whole" population, a vehicle and a receptacle for cultural ferment and effort' (Haraksingh 1988, 117). This wholeness would facilitate the establishment of community. It would also, in turn, pave the way for a focus on and acceleration of social change and further integration into the wider society towards the goal of being recognised as a part of Trinidadian society, rather than as a semi-alien entity grudgingly hosted on its margins.

The unfavourable economic conditions that dominated the period collectively impacted on the society, providing both the backdrop and a changing context, which acted as a potent force of social change within the Hindu community. These included the collapse of the cocoa industry in the 1920s (Pemberton 1996), the onset of the Great Depression, the relatively unchanged management-employee relations (of the indenture period) in the agricultural sector, the stagnation in wages for Indian workers in the sugar industry, the presence of the American bases in Trinidad during the Second World War, the upsurge in labour organisation and radical political activity, the emergence of trade unionism, the rise in labour protests, strikes and riots (Brereton 1981, 157–98), the high level of illiteracy and general widespread hardship and poverty.

By 1921, Indians comprised 33 per cent of the entire population, with a rise to 35 per cent in 1946.[1] Interestingly, the figure for Hindus showed a gradual decline during these years. In 1921, Hindus comprised 72.7 per cent of the Indian population; in 1931, 67 per cent; and in 1946, 64.5 per cent (Ramesar 1994). However, by 1938, J.D. Tyson, reporting on the conditions of Indians in Trinidad, was of the opinion that 'the Hindu community on the island...has undoubtedly been "quickened" in its Hinduism during the last few years.'[2] With most of the fundamental, inherently Indian social, religious, economic and political structures in place, the drive towards personal and communal advancement saw a dynamic interplay between the notions of Indian and Trinidadian, the traditional and the modern, the religious and the secular, retention and transformation, between the theory of being free and the reality of restrictions.

Reworking Religion

This period witnessed a number of key developments that contributed to the restructuring of certain aspects of Hinduism. Although by the 1920s, the Hindu community had undergone some amount of homogenisation, the continued influx of Indians from India and the return and visits of Trinidad Indians to India provided a substantial level of transience and variation to the situation. During this time, the Brahmins assiduously attempted to cement their position at the top of the socio-religious hierarchy. The consolidation of a standardised form of *Sanatan Dharma* – literally, eternal duty, order or religion but in this context, the generalised form of Hinduism that evolved in Trinidad (Vertovec 1992, 245) – as a representative body of Trinidad Hindus, was possibly the major struggle in which Hindus were engaged. In addition, faltering steps were made in the direction of organising. Both goals were achieved by 1945. This period witnessed the beginnings of the slow yet prominent move towards the notion of a Trinidad Hinduism.[3] This idea of Trinidad Hinduism can be best defined as the synthesis and retention of the fundamental tenets, beliefs and rituals of the various strands of Hinduism brought and reconstructed by the indentured immigrants. The inevitable adoption, omission or altering of certain dimensions essentially mirrored the conscious or unconscious movement towards a 'Trinidadian idea of religion,' that is to say, what Hinduism could or should constitute in Trinidad. Many of these changes echoed the aspiration for both individual and communal mobility.

This period also came to incorporate what was popularly referred to by the Indian middle class in Trinidad as the 'Indian Renaissance,' and saw the local move to reinterpret and present Hinduism (Sanskritic ideology) as more of a universal religion, whose principles and practices could apply to and, in some aspects, parallel those of the wider society. The concept of universal religion apparently played itself out in Hinduism, not as the acceptance *by* all of one religion, but as the acceptance *of* all the religions by everyone (Sharma 1998, 135). Locally, this concept was evident in the gradual emergence of a more highly simplified and uniform culture, one that tended to incorporate all the varying strands of Hinduism present in Trinidad. Thus, vegetarianism, practised by the priestly caste, was upheld as the ideal for which one should strive in the quest for a more healthful and beneficent way of life, and within the Hindu community, as a signifier of greater ritual purity, and hence, higher religious and social merit. The principle of ahimsa (non-violence) advocated by Gandhi and strongly highlighted by the local press provided another essentially Hindu approach upon which Hindu and Indian leaders and political aspirants could base their arguments.

The worship of a multiplicity of deities was always a characteristic feature of both popular and Sanskritic Hinduism. Since Hinduism was seemingly polytheistic in an otherwise monotheistic society, the pressure for recognition and status saw a move by community leaders, priests, and other local figures to reinforce the idea of a single Supreme.[4] While Hinduism could never fit into the Western definition of monotheism, there was increasing emphasis on the principle of one god with multiple forms and names; this was especially evident in the emergence of various socio-religious groups. Nothing, however, was allowed to detract from the divinity of any of the various deities. Hindus based their choice of special deity on personal preference, while simultaneously worshipping the multitude of others.

Nevertheless, several aspects of Hinduism, usually originating in the little (folk) tradition, were rejected by some of those who aspired for higher status. Practices such as animal sacrifices and the fire pass ritual, and the worship of deities connected to these events were toned down, modified or dropped altogether, and both publicly and privately denounced. Thus, even a folk ritual such as the *Dee puja*[5] began to elicit mixed reactions towards what was heretofore a vital aspect of the performance, namely, the sacrifice of a rooster. In an attempt to emulate the ritually higher Sanskritic practices such as performing *yagnas* and observing only certain religious festivals and occasions, the common practices by the Madrassis (and non-Madrassis) of smoking ganja (marijuana), consuming alcohol during and after *Ramayana satsangs*, and even consuming meat on *Diwali* day were also abjured. Interestingly enough, the Madrassis practised their own refinement of the caste system, with those engaged in *hog-puja* (religious ritual involving the sacrifice of a pig) relegated to the lowest position. Many Madrassis refused to attend such pujas, deeming them 'dirty and low.'[6] However, some other Madrassi practices, notably those not directly contingent on Sanskritic Hinduism such as *Kali* worship, and some funerary and wedding rituals were not totally expunged.

The Bhakti form of worship, prevalent in the Ganges basin during the period of recruitment for indenture, and hence, widely subscribed to by Hindus in Trinidad, posed a formidable challenge to sanskritisation. The excision of the intermediary between the devotee and God – the hallmark of Bhakti – promoted the awareness that priests were not necessary for the acquisition of spiritual merit and that anyone, not just Brahmins (and including women), could perform the necessary rituals. This would eventually contribute to a decrease in the ritual monopoly and social importance of the Brahmins some of whom, it must be said, responded by adopting several features of the Bhakti form of worship.

In addition, while Brahmins were still the principal holders of the proverbial trump card in ritual performance and knowledge of

Sanskrit mantras, their jealously guarded monopoly even in this vital area was increasingly challenged. The Arya Samaj, the reformist Hindu sect formed in India in 1875 and existent in Trinidad since around 1910, initiated the translation of Sanskrit mantras into both Hindi and English, making them more accessible to the wider population. Those who considered the sound of the Sanskrit words integral to these chants questioned whether any translation was appropriate, but some of the mystery was obviously lost.

Persons aspiring to improve their personal ritual and, in effect, social status adopted what can be termed as *personal sanskritisation*. This involved the adoption, in varying degrees, of various elements of a sanskritised lifestyle such as vegetarianism, teetotalism, and becoming particular about the performance of such religious activities as regularly reciting from the holy texts, attending and participating in religious discourses, and joining religious groups. This usually led to the individual rising in the esteem of his relatives, friends and community. Sometimes, however, especially if the individual hailed from a very low caste, he might become an object of ridicule. Though tinged with satire, the issue of personal sanskritisation was quite realistically examined in Seepersad Naipaul's *Adventures of Gurudeva and Other Stories* (Naipaul 1976). In his aspirations at priesthood, Naipaul's protagonist, a non-Brahmin, became a vegetarian and teetotaller, learnt to read and write Hindi, constructed a temple in his yard, chanted from the religious texts and conducted pujas daily, gave religious lectures, and began wearing only dhotis and kurtas, the traditional garb of pundits. It was not uncommon for a non-Brahmin, especially those who functioned as priests of their respective castes, to officiate at the smaller scale *satsangs* and readings of the holy texts. Such individuals however, in preparation for the role of priest, would engage in temporary sanskritisation, abstaining from meat eating and other vices for several days, and would also meticulously dress the part. Many shared the view that pundits then could be 'any capable person, not just Brahmins.'[7] The larger scale *yagnas* and weddings however, were still the exclusive domain of the Brahmin priest, though they had to share the space (but not the ritual status) with non-Brahmin pundits with regard to performing pujas.

Possibly the most blatant, though singular, example of the challenge to Brahminic supremacy was the initiation in 1943 of a non-Brahmin woman, Deokie Devi, as a pundit. A notice in the *Trinidad Guardian* on January 31, 1945, together with her picture, read:

> First Sanatan Woman Pundit in Trinidad, Shrimattee Deokie Devi, 22 year old daughter of pundit Ramlalak of Couva, will appear in public for the first time on February 25 to perform the ceremony of the Sri Satnarine Katha at the San Fernando Hindu Temple. Pundit Shrimattee Devi is trained in Hindu Vedic Philosophy, Hindi and Sanskrit and comes from a family of four pundits. She is the granddaughter of the late Hindu priest, Lal Beharry of India.

Although the first formal initiation and recognition of a woman as a priest, this isolated incident simply echoed the common presence of female saintly figures (*sadhuians*) and healers in Hinduism. Such individuals also had to subscribe to the previously noticed elements of a sanskritised lifestyle (in addition to abstinence from sexual activity) and through these means acquired a certain aura of holiness and evoked an appropriate level of community respect. The ascension of non-Brahmins to the status of ritual and social leaders was substantially facilitated by the egalitarianism of Bhakti worship. Some contribution to this development, though, came from the fact that many Hindu socio-religious (often non-Brahminic) organisations emerged during this period, and also from the absence of any authoritative body or formal structure to pronounce on religious claims or pretensions.

During this period the qualities and requisites of leaders, both spiritual and lay, were being redefined. While among the general Hindu population Brahmins (priests and non-priests) continued to receive respect and adulation, newer factors were added to the customary, largely ritually and hereditarily ascribed list of prerequisites of Hindu leadership. These included the level of English education, personal and family financial status, personal credibility and appeal, and the individual's potential as a credible representative or spokesman of the Hindu community in the eyes of the wider society. In addition, an understanding of the philosophical aspect of Hinduism rather than just ritualism and personal reputation based on one's own religious competence and on other factors such as if, and how many times the individual had visited India, all acted as hierarchical markers among Brahmins. Pundits who had acquired an English education and had a working knowledge of the non-Hindu community tended to look down upon others as ignorant and unschooled. For example, Pundit Capildeo, grandfather of V.S. Naipaul, refused to perform a wedding ceremony with another pundit citing his reason as: 'I don't want him to say that he did a wedding ceremony with me, for he is an illiterate man' (DeVerteuil 1981, 132).

While in India the process of sanskritisation has normally been initiated by the lower groups, in the diaspora it has proven to be two-dimensional, initiated variously by both the lower and higher groups. According to Clem Seecharan, in Guyana the Brahmin caste, in response to the threat of conversion, admitted those of the lowest castes (who had traditionally belonged to cults and sects with distinctive gods and rites) to the mainstream of Hinduism, *Sanatan Dharma* (Seecharan 1997, 41). In Trinidad, this move was also discernible, albeit with great variation, and more so during the latter part of the 1940s. While some reported that certain Brahmins absolutely refused to perform Sanatanist rituals at the homes of *chamars* and other low caste individuals, most agreed to do them out of fear also of losing control of their flock to the non-Brahmin pundits. They would, however, refuse to take part in the ritual feast associated with the event.[8] This attitude on the part of the Brahmins echoed the nature of competitive politics within the Hindu community, and the 'love-hate relationship' existing between the Brahmins and the lower castes. The Brahmins needed the numbers of the Hindu masses to support their dominant position, and in return, the lower groups gained a higher level of recognition and respect from having a Brahmin perform at their functions. The Brahmins, however, were careful to limit the boundaries of their participation, so that their relative status would not be compromised.

During this period, Hindu rituals and festivals were also undergoing change. While not a new phenomenon, non-Brahmin pundits were also increasingly taking advantage of the economic and educational opportunities to enhance their social and ritual status. Frequent notices in the local press such as that of one Pundit

Seusankar Seunarine, Secretary of the Sanatan Dharma Pratinidhi Sabha, going abroad to study medicine, published in the *Trinidad Guardian* on January 3, 1945, provided evidence of this development. There was a steady notable rise in the quantum and scale of rituals and celebrations performed at a community level such as *Ramleela, Krishnaleela, Ramnaumi, Krishna Janam Ashthami,* and *Shiv Ratri*.[9] This was facilitated by a marked increase in the appearance of temples in almost every major area where Hindus lived. Activities organised by groups usually reflected an awareness of the perceived need to revive, reform and promote Hinduism in a manner which would impart a greater degree of visibility and acceptability of both the religion and its adherents.

The rise of temple-based worship at this time was also observed in Guyana. Dale Bisnauth, in his study on Indians in Guyana, tried to explain collective worship in *mandirs* as an influence of Christian modes of worship on Hinduism (Bisnauth 2000, 142). However, group temple worship has been an integral part of traditional worship in South India. It became more noticeable in Trinidad during this period owing to remarkable growth in the construction of temples. The durability of the material being used (stone, clay, bricks, wood), the addition of the *kutiya* alongside the traditional temples, and the temple's increasing use for the purposes of preaching and politicking provided additional indicators of changes in Hindu society. According to Carolyn Prorok, 'changes in temple form reveal changes specifically associated with the Hindu population...changes which indicate processes of Sanskritisation and Westernisation' (Prorok 1988, 74–75). Temples also served as the preferred meeting places where issues relating to the Hindu community, many times in relation to their social mobility as a group, were discussed, debated and sometimes resolved. Thus, they functioned as both the basis and markers of the increase in Hindu organisational development during this period.

The inclusion of non-Hindu elements and observances, while all reflecting Hinduism's accommodative and assimilative nature, exemplify attempts – though very possibly not deliberate – at incorporation into the wider society. During the period of indenture, the La Divina Pastora deity was adopted into the Hindu pantheon as *Sipari Mai* (Mother of Siparia). This was facilitated through the Goddess-worship aspect of Hinduism and the prominence placed on spiritual-curative aids. Since then, Hindus continued to journey to Siparia to make offerings to the statue, which was quite similar in appearance to some *murtis* of female Hindu deities. The deity was worshipped in the church in a recognisably Hindu manner. The primary purpose of visits to *Sipari Mai* was to secure relief from illnesses, and to pray for offspring. Many Hindus often conducted the first ritual shaving of a child's hair at that location and symbolically offered the shaved hair to *Sipari Mai*. The inclusion of La Divina Pastora into the Hindu pantheon also instigated the observance of Good Friday as an auspicious day. All Saint's Day was also incorporated into the rituals pertaining to the dead. On that day, many Hindus cleaned the graves of their dead, decorated them with flowers, and lit candles on the graves in the evening.

The religious texts, primarily the *Ramayana* and the *Bhagvad Purana*, assisted in the dissemination of knowledge about the Great Gods, and in the spread of a common culture throughout the country. Through the medium of the stories of the Puranas, certain basic theological ideas of Sanskritic Hinduism were able to reach ordinary folk. These texts also filtered out many, usually questionable, and in the quest for social mobility, often undesirable elements of the local folk tradition, such as animal sacrifice and the associated deities. The promotion of essentially sanskritic ideals in areas such as family life, social organisation and politics using the actions of the characters in these epics as the model, further prompted the Hindu population to aspire towards such values and behaviour, and to relinquish those that did not conform. The advent of Indian films in Trinidad brought the texts and gods to life through films. Such films included *Sita Swayamvar* (*Sita's Selection of a Husband*), *Gopal Krishna* (*The Cowherd Krishna*), and *Mahasati Anasuya* (*The Great Sati Anasuya*), thereby deepening aspirations for the sanskritic culture exalted in these films.

Any examination of mobility within Hindu society demands some insight into the existent (or non-existent) dynamics of caste within the specific geographical, historical and cultural context. Much work has been done on the caste system within the diaspora, and it has been established that, rather than a full-blown transplantation, there was more of an attenuation and reworking of the traditional system, resulting in emphasis on the basic and very diluted gradation of the four main varnas (caste groupings).[10] The various restrictions encountered in the attempt at adjusting and reconstructing an Indian social system in an overseas setting saw, among many other modifications, the almost total dissolution of the concerns, restrictions and boundaries of the numerous jatis or sub-groups within the four major varnas (Brahmin, Kshatriya, Vaishya, and Sudra). The system of power relations encountered in Trinidad proved to be at variance with the traditional caste system, itself a system of power relations based on very clearly defined occupational categories permeated by the notion of ritual purity and pollution. In these circumstances, the recreation of the traditional caste system was virtually impossible. Thus, rather than a fixed caste system, what emerged by the end of the nineteenth century can more aptly be described as a very modified and fluid ideology or sentiment of caste, becoming even more diluted and modified through constant interaction with divergent systems, lifestyles, values and beliefs.

In the discourse on the traditional Hindu caste system, one point has provided notable contention, namely the authenticity and validity of the claim to Brahminism in Trinidad. The seeds of this controversy were sown largely during the indenture system itself. In-depth research done on the origins of the Fiji Indians recruited from the same catchment areas which supplied indentured labourers to Trinidad, and based on the immigration certificates of all the indentured immigrants, has shown that the percentage of indentured immigrants recorded as Brahmins (3.7 per cent) was relatively low in proportion to the percentage of Brahmins recorded in Uttar Pradesh at that time – 10.1 per cent in 1891, 9.9 per cent in 1901, and 9.9 per cent in 1911 (Lal 1983, 70). Since the same general system of recruitment applied for all the countries to which Indians were indentured, these figures would have generally reflected the Trinidad situation. During the 1879–80 and the 1889–90 recruiting seasons, the number of indentureds to Trinidad recorded as Brahmins was 5.6 per cent and 1.04 per cent respectively (Weller 1968, 133–34). The fear of losing caste from crossing the *kala pani* (literally, 'black waters' but also generally referred to the sea) and the social and ritual supremacy of the Brahmin caste in India can account for their reluctance to migrate. This proportionately smaller number of Brahmin immigrants seems to support the view held in some circles that non-Brahmin individuals later assumed the title and status of Brahmin. Further support for this theory of passing is based on the almost desperate need of the Indian immigrants to fill the gap of ritual specialists in their attempts at the reconstruction of community which predisposed them to welcoming anyone with knowledge of the sacred mantras and religious rites and rituals. In addition, the benefits from passing as Brahmins and the fact that such claims could be neither absolutely confirmed nor nullified seem to add further momentum to this argument. By the 1920s rivalry among pundits and other leaders was another factor underscoring the desire for the status of Brahmin.

On the other hand, one can also speculate that the gravity of the deed, coupled with an intrinsic fear of God might have deterred the desire to falsely assume the role of a Brahmin, who was perceived as being the closest to God ritually, and in the case of pundits, the link between man and God. Contributing to the contentiousness of the issue is the possibility that genuine members of the Brahmin caste may have denied their Brahminism in the initial stage of their indenture and reclaimed their original caste later on. Such a strategy was employed either because they were fleeing the 1857 revolt and its consequences (especially as members of the higher castes were considered ringleaders in the uprisings), or due to the notion held by officials that Brahmins would be troublesome on the estates and were not effective enough as labourers.[11] Though never a resolved issue, Brahmins were a very real dimension of Indian society, and it can certainly be argued that Brahmins were indentured to Trinidad; the question is how much? Who? And how 'genuine' were they?

Hinging on the issues of both social mobility and Brahminism, is the origin of the surname 'Maharaj.' Ship records and emigration certificates show that none of the indentured immigrants bore this name, but interestingly enough, returnees to India in the later period of indenture and Trinidad Indians who journeyed to India for brief visits are recorded as having 'Maharaj' as a surname. The names of those indentured immigrants claiming to be of the Brahmin caste included Ramsaock, Gopaul, Jankie, Mahadaie, Gosain, Surjodin, Rama Nand, Bachawnie, Hemraj, Jogeshur, and in all instances, only a first name was recorded.[12] The term 'Maharaj' literally means great king or ruler and was used in Indian society as *a term of respect and honour* for Brahmins, and as an equivalent of 'your majesty,' 'liege' and 'highness.' It would appear the title or surname 'Maharaj' was possibly conveniently assumed by Brahmins to cement and further exalt their religious and social authority, and by non-Brahmins also in an attempt at personal sanskritisation.

The issue of naming also provides an interesting dimension to the process of sanskritisation. A number of the interviewees reported that, until the 1920s, caste was a major deciding factor in the assigning of names to individuals. The Brahmins reserved special names for members of their caste, and gave 'lower caste names'[13] (such as naming persons according to the day of the week on which they were born) to the non-Brahmin population. By the 1930s many were opting for names with such prefixes as *Ram*, and *Jag* (a variation of *yagna*), and for the names of the gods and deities such as *Krishna, Sita, Latchman*. The tendency for children to assume the first name of the father as their surname[14] made it more possible for persons, and eventually their families, to acquire a ritually higher name. The varying, seemingly contradictory combinations of both Hindu and non-Hindu (given) names also revealed the interplay between the retention of Hinduness and the desire for acceptance within the larger society. Such combinations included non-Hindu and Hindu, Hindu and non-Hindu, non-Hindu and secret Hindu name, Hindu and secret Hindu name.

Family and Community Negotiation

Within Hinduism, the institution of the family and the roles of its members have been greatly defined by religion, with the ideals based, to a large extent, on ritual and textual prescription. Thus, when faced with contextual accommodation in Trinidad and the increasing influence of secularisation, westernisation, modernisation and individualism, conflict was inevitable. While researchers such as Klass and Niehoff have classified the Indian family in Trinidad as an excellent example of cultural survival,[15] others like Tikasingh (1973), Malik (1971) and Vertovec (1992) view it as a basic unit of structural, ideological and cultural change. As Patricia Mohammed noted:

> There had been much discussion on the persistence or recreation of the Indian family in Trinidad – possibly too much by those outside of the group itself. This has confused the issue of how a family system actually emerged out of the confines and constraints of indentured labour and redefined itself against, and in relation to, a new culture in which different family forms existed (Mohammed 2002, 217).

Mandelbaum's classification of the family as 'the fundamental multipurpose organization for many of the principal life functions of the individual and of society' (Mandelbaum 1972, 33) foreshadows the view that the institution of the family, in terms of both its structure and its values, has always been one of the most prominent indicators and conductors of social change among Indians. By the late 1920s, with the gradual leavening of the age and sex ratio, a stable though not rigidly standard pattern of family life was being established. Characteristic of this pattern was a subscribing, in some cases more pronounced than in others, to the traditional features of the Indian family. Such features included the interplay between patrifocality and matrifocality, authority based on age and sex, focus on the family as a group rather than on the individual, and the ideal of deference to elders.

In both practice and the ideal, the extended family structure prevailed among Hindus during this period. This notion of extended however, should be tempered with the fact that it involved a number of compositional variations at the different stages of the cycle of the Indian family structure (Mandelbaum 1972, 95–96). At strategic points, there would be the breaking away of a specific sub-group which would then proceed to form the nucleus (nuclear family) of another imminent extended system. In a period where male siblings usually earned their livelihood by working on family occupied (owned, rented or leased) land, the common situation was one where the sub-unit would set up household either adjacent to or on the same property of the original unit, or would even choose to stay at the same house while setting up separate kitchens. While factors such as Western education, non-agricultural occupations and the geographical location of such occupations would influence the rate, extent and nature of this breaking away, there would almost always be strong ideological and emotional ties with the original extended system.

Within the new nuclear situation the principal male figure, previously subordinated by the grand patriarch and elder siblings, was then upgraded to the position of head of the household. The wife assumed the position of female head of the household, which included the domestic, ritual, and, to varying extents, the economic spheres. While this transition to the nuclear family structure did allow for the mobility of the primary members, the physical proximity to and the deep-seated sense of filial relations still permitted the head of the whole group to wield a considerable level of authority and influence in major issues affecting the family unit. The death of the patriarch inevitably led to the weakening of the ideal of fraternal relations and often set the stage for the materialisation of formerly subtle, internal conflicts, often rooted in inheritance struggles. One fallout was the subdivision of landholdings and other property according to traditional prescriptions. This promoted greater autonomy for the resultant sub-divisions, since the cohesive powers of neither parent figure nor common property was at work.

Transformations in the ideal, values and relationships surrounding the Hindu family accompanied the changes in its structure. Within the traditional system, sibling status was based primarily on age and sex. During this period, this basis was slowly being put to task by the acquisition of English education and non-agricultural or urban jobs. Through these avenues, younger males were able to, though not demonstrably, break the monopoly of age as the determining factor of sibling hierarchy. According to oral sources,

> ...people began to look down on agriculture as a lowly form of occupation, and the people who had these 'white collar' and clerical jobs, they were looked upon as people with very high status.[16]

This disarrangement, however, was only acknowledged on occasions of active, verbal conflict. The emergence of a sense of individualism in a tradition whose major institutions atrophied the needs and desires of the individual in favour of collective well-being was also partly due to secularisation, the acquisition of English education and the increasing infiltration of Western thinking. Thus, younger males began opting for the more glorified, even though lower-paying, non-agricultural jobs instead of those traditionally engaged in by their families such as agriculture, craftsmanship and labouring.

In areas of domestic life usually dominated by the family as a unit, such as the selection of a marriage partner, individuals were slowly (though often with heavy repercussions) beginning to assert themselves. Nevertheless, arranged marriages remained the prevalent practice and this allowed the family to function as the strongest propagating agent of caste sensibilities. The higher castes, Brahmin and Kshatriyas, tended to be rather strict about marrying within their castes. However, even in their case, marriage to a girl from the Vaishya caste was not uncommon. Quite apparently, such marriages acted as an avenue to mobility within the Hindu community, for it was the norm for the young bride to give up many of her lower caste practices. Mixed caste marriages could result in reverse situations though. According to one interviewee,

> Divali day my father-in-law used to want cascadoo and *Dhallpuri* [type of unleavened flat bread with a filling of ground split peas] to eat....When I gone there and see they doing that, I say well what kind ah madness is this...? I had to cook it for him.[17]

Here, the bride was obviously married into a lower caste and had little choice but to conform.

On the other hand, another female Brahmin interviewee articulated the deep apprehension of the ritual burden that the marriage of a Brahmin individual into a non-Brahmin family could have on the latter. During the initial arrangements of her marriage to a non-Brahmin man (initiated by her father), the father of the prospective bridegroom responded:

> *Beti tunee Brahmin baate, ham na maange Brahman ki betee aaw hamaar ghar mein, jhutha bartan dhowey...hamaar u paap baa hamke.* [Child, you are a *brahmin*. I don't want a brahmin girl come in my house and wash dirty dishes....That is a sin on us].[18]

He then clasped his hands in supplication and, insisting that he, an *ahir*, would never be able to atone for such a sin, begged off the offer. Generally however, persons tended to marry within their own castes, or as it was popularly called 'nation,' aware that marriage to someone from either a lower or higher caste could lead to problems both in the religious and social spheres. According to one female Brahmin interviewee, 'I get to dislike the boy when I find out that they kill a hog at the birth of every child.'[19] There were, however, cases of marriages by choice, or rather elopements, which transcended caste boundaries.

The ideal of husband-wife relations was based on loyalty and support of each spouse to the other, and sanctioned by the most popular religious text the *Ramayana*, wherein both the hero Rama, and his wife Sita observed monogamy. Though monogamy was held as the ideal among Trinidad Hindus, there were digressions on the part of both spouses. These digressions, viewed against the ideal, impacted directly on the status of the individual within both the family and the larger community. The most glaring aspect of this was the discrepancy in attitude towards males and females. With a mixture of pious castigation, grudging admiration and sometimes not so secret approval and understanding, the social standing of the adulterous male remained relatively intact. This was especially where it was suspected that the wife was barren. It may even be said that extra-marital relationships were covertly expected of the more prominent men in the community. In the case of those whose status was based on ritual purity such as the Brahmins and the pundits, there was a more pronounced effect. This involved a combination of largely private ridicule, a decline in the individual's viability as a religious leader and yet, paradoxically, the continued faithful following of his disciples.[20] Women, on the other hand, still viewed as the receptacles of the ancestral seed, the sustainers of the lineage, the foundation of family life and honor, and through whose fidelity male sexual prowess was measured were heavily reprimanded, ridiculed, beaten, and even ostracised by immediate family members and, often, the community as well. As a female interviewee now in her sixties explained:

> If as soon as he [husband] leave to go with a next woman I take up with a man, they [society] will say she was just waiting for this man to leave to take up somebody. Then they wouldn't think anything good about me...but whatever a man do was well done.[21]

The status of Hindu women during this period was highly conditioned by the desire to control female sexuality through child marriages, glorifying female reproductive powers, and preferring sons over daughters. The prevailing attitude was further marked by a lack of sympathy for widows and for widow remarriage, and by glorifying women whose husbands were alive, considering them a source of prosperity and assigning to them exclusively certain rituals and rites. The selective shaping of religious texts and doctrines aided this mood. Verses from the *Ramayana* cemented both the ritually and socially inferior position of women, for example:

> *Sahaj apaavanee naaree patin sevat gati lahai.*

> A woman is impure by her very birth; but she attains a happy state (hereafter) by serving her lord (husband).[22]

The strong perception of menstruation as unclean and not compatible with spirituality also contributed to the inferior position of women on the ritual scale. Menstruating women were forbidden from entering any consecrated space, from having any kind of contact with religious paraphernalia, from cooking for Brahmins, and indeed, possessed an innate feeling of impurity.[23] Western notions concerning this issue would not influence Hindu thought for a very long time to come. However, local factors did serve to uplift the value of women. These comprised the highly prized position of Indian women during the indenture and immediate post-indenture period when they were in scarce supply, and their continued status as co- or sometimes sole breadwinners of the family. Within the essentially patriarchal values and ideology that characterised Hinduism during this period, 'women invariably negotiate[d] within their domestic spaces for changes which will improve the conditions of their lives and that of their families' (Mohammed 2002, 13–14).

By the 1940s it was both imminent and evident that secularisation was beginning to influence, and in some cases, even decrease the importance of traditional sanskritisation. Factors such as literacy, education, occupation, the acquisition of wealth and in some cases power, began to either work with or displace some of the traditional sanskritic values and virtues as a formula for status, authority and power. This was most evident in the ceaseless, though almost always subtle battle for authority between the two highest Hindu castes in Trinidad, the Brahmins and the Kshatriyas. The increasing influence of secularisation allowed the Kshatriya and even lower caste groups in possession of material wealth – especially land – to pose a serious threat to Brahmin supremacy, which was still based primarily upon their ritual purity and knowledge of the sacred rites and verses. Non-Brahmin wealthy or English-educated and hence respectable individuals were increasingly called upon to settle small disputes and to act as moneylenders. The subtly strained relationship between the Brahmin and the Kshatriya figures of authority was echoed in the most popular Hindu religious text of the time, the *Ramayana*, where the hero and incarnation of God, Rama, is a Kshatriya, and not a Brahmin – a point that local Kshatriyas were always eager to make. The Brahmins themselves seemed predisposed to accommodating economic realignments. Thus wealthy and influential non-Brahmins were accorded preferential treatment, which many times led to what may be termed sanskritisation by association. Many low caste wealthy individuals sought to increase their social standing through this method. However, most Brahmins shared the opinion that 'while he [the non-Brahmin] may gain a little more respect because of the money, that feeling of being lower will always be there; on both sides.'[24]

Traditionally, factors of respectability among Hindus included caste affiliation, economic status based primarily on land ownership, and adherence to ritually and socially ascribed morals, values and duties. This notion of respectability was manifested in almost all aspects of life: manner of dress, interaction with and deference to seniors, interaction with members of the opposite sex, ritual and religious activities, and general behaviour. Increasing contact with Western elements resulted in slow but steady alterations in both the factors and manifestations of respectability. Although women continued to be careful about bodily exposure, and to wear the *orhani* (thin, almost transparent veil; possibly the most definitive marker of female respectability) certain Western styles of dress (such as the whole dress, shirt and trousers for men, and both male and female underwear) were slowly being adopted. Many sought the more material markers of higher social status such as motorcars, better housing structures, facilities and amenities. One interviewee claimed that her father insisted on purchasing a car even though he could not drive and though there were no roads in his immediate area; thus he had to keep it at someone else's house and hire a driver.[25]

The introduction of Hindi films into Trinidad in the year 1935 added another dimension to the process of sanskritisation; the perpetuation of modern India as an ideal. Through this medium, individuals began aspiring to what was being projected as Indian culture in terms of dress, names, music, dance, language (standard Hindi), song, and even some rites and rituals. Narsaloo Ramaya, a pioneer of Indian music in Trinidad, articulated the impact of Hindi films as one where 'Indian people became more conscious of their Indianness, their Indian identity and their culture and their music.'[26] However, what was being projected was an admixture of both traditional Indian and Western cultures; a Bombay view of Indian society at that time. While overtly promoting the propagation of Indian culture, these films were inadvertently permitting a more rapid and somehow more justifiable (since it was done in India) infusion of elements of Western lifestyle into the local Hindu community. Thus, by emulating these models, the local population was, in effect, assimilating elements of both cultures. Hindi films also reinforced the standards of family relations, social interaction and important life cycle rituals such as marriage ceremonies and death rites. In this respect, what the advent of Hindi films in Trinidad did was to establish within the Hindu community a sense of affirmation and rejuvenation of both Hinduism and Indian culture by providing a more tangible though tempered form of the culture and lifestyle which the community had constantly striven to emulate since the days of indenture.

While the process of sanskritisation was being pursued, the context of the wider non-Hindu society stimulated a reverse, de-sanskritisation, the paramount factors of which were conversion and biracial marriages. Many converts found themselves virtually ostracised, emotionally and sometimes physically, from both their immediate kin and their community. Added to this were their feelings of alienation, religious and cultural superiority and, sometimes, a deep-seated sense of betrayal on their part. Although the degree of the ostracism sometimes eventually subsided, there was never a total acceptance of the individual, unless Hinduism was reclaimed.

The issue of biracial marriages was an extremely sensitive one. Indeed, the surest way to get ostracised for life (*kujat*) by both one's kin and community was to marry someone of African descent. The initial reaction was predominantly one of strong, unforgiving disapproval and non-acceptance. In areas such as Felicity, Barrackpore and Bejucal, where the villages were almost exclusively Indian, the accompanying ostracism was indeed a life sentence. Yet the fact that in some areas such as Pasea, Sangre Grande and Plum Mitan (on account of possibly the greater degree of contact and the geographical location), there were some cases of this type of union suggests that, even in this most tabooed area, considerations of ritual purity and social status could be overlooked.

The reaction to inter-marriages with non-Africans, was more complicated. A substantial portion of the higher castes (Brahmin and Kshatriyas) did not view such unions as desirable and considered them a contamination of their ritual status. However, many of the lower castes did not seem to mind too much, especially if the person was of European descent. Perhaps this reflected the situation whereby the European, on account of his prominent position in society, his skin colour, and physical features, was more likely to be accepted and may even have been deemed a medium of social mobility while someone of African descent was relegated, in the Hindu scheme of things, to the very bottom of the largely ritually ascribed social ladder. All the same, according to popular opinion, despite certain fixed boundaries, relations with the few non-Indians living in predominantly Indian villages were quite cordial.

Internal Organisation and Social Mobility

While *Indian* organisations (in the Western sense) such as the East Indian National Congress (EINC) or the East Indian National

Association (EINA) have been highlighted by the studies on Indians in Trinidad, the Hindu community possessed their own system of organisational structure and function, which became increasingly active during the period under discussion. Though not as noticeable to the wider society as the EINC or EINA, Hindu organisations such as the Sanatan Dharma Board of Control (SDBC) and Sanatan Dharma Association (SDA) were already serving as representatives of the Hindu population. This was evident in the rallying of the pundits throughout the island into a national panchayat in response to the flogging to death of an Indian during the strikes of November and December 1919 (DeVerteuil 1989, 138). As Kelvin Singh has explained, the Hindu priest was viewed as 'extremely important in giving the mass of the Indians psychological protection in a society basically hostile to them, racially, culturally, economically...' (Singh 1974, 41). Anthony DeVerteuil also recognised that pundits 'helped to form gradually and imperceptibly, a politicized opinion among the Hindu community in Trinidad' (DeVerteuil 1989, 138). Such deductions aptly, though not exclusively, situated pundits and Brahmins at the core of Hindu socio-religious organisation.

During the 1920s, there emerged a number of organised Sanatanist groups usually labelled as Hindu Sabha throughout Trinidad. By 1928, there were various attempts at integrating these organisations and the larger Hindu community into a more united body. According to an article in the *East Indian Weekly* on May 28, 1928, these included the formation of a Trinidad Hindu Mahasabha whose aims and objectives were 'the political, social, moral, educational and religious advancement, and the uniting and consolidating of the Hindu community of the island...' whereby 'the views of the entire Hindu community can be expressed...,' and wherein 'every Hindu shall be eligible to membership whether he is a Sanatanist, Arya Samajist, Kabir Panth, Seonarayani....'

The article confirmed that there was also an All Trinidad Hindu Conference geared towards 'unifying Hindu Sabhas throughout the country.' By the 1920s however, the increasing adoption of the classically-based and communally shared Sanatan Dharma by most of the smaller sub-sects of Trinidad Hinduism left the Arya Samaj as the only potential adversary to Sanatanist, and hence, Brahminic religious authority (Vertovec 1992, 112). Formally established in 1934, but existent in Trinidad and Tobago since around 1910, the Arya Samaj posed a most direct and formidable challenge to one of the major structural and ideological pillars of Hinduism at that time, caste ideology. This organisation espoused a paradoxical admixture of Western organisational forms and procedures, and selective, often reinterpreted Vedic ideology aimed towards Sanatanists and their existent religious belief systems. Its negation of the idea of caste by birth provided the platform from which many of the extremely low castes could achieve both religious and social mobility. Its followers, leaders and priesthood (some of whom had failed to win acceptance by orthodox Brahmins) comprised mainly non-Brahmins. Younger persons, with some degree of formal English education, usually of the middle class, were prominent in the group.

According to the *East Indian Weekly*, the Samaj organised a series of lectures on topics such as 'On the Sublimity of the Vedas,' 'Vedic Culture and Mother Language,' and 'Human Ideals.' These appeared to focus on philosophy rather than ritual. The Samaj also criticised child marriages and the suppression of women. This, together with many attractive Western elements such as the wearing of Western garments at religious congregations, sitting at a table on chairs rather than on the floor, and a structured discourse also added to the Samaj's appeal. In addition, many converts to Christianity who had previously occupied the position of almost an outcaste were readmitted into Hinduism through the Samaj, thereby re-establishing and sometimes increasing their social standing. This was done through a ritual known as *Shuddhi*, a rite that also enabled non-Hindus to join the Vedic religion. The practice of allotting Hindu names to converts can be considered another aspect of sanskritisation within the Samaj.

The Samaj challenged the foundation of the existing Sanatanist system of power relations, the Guru-Chela (preceptor-disciple) system, which had as its basis the precedence of personal loyalties over communal or principle-based loyalties, and which ensured Brahmin socio-religious and political authority regardless of personal and public behaviour. This system was regarded by the Samaj as the root of factional conflict and as greatly responsible for the Hindu society's lack of mobilisation, solidarity and consequently, social mobility as a group in the wider society. The Samaj's attempts at adherence to democratic, constitutionally regulated organisational forms and procedures provided a possible avenue out of the stranglehold of the priestly caste and towards social and religious uplift, both for individuals and for the group as a whole.

The derisive attitude of the Samaj towards Trinidad Sanatanist Hinduism went as far as labelling it *'gobar* Hinduism.'[27] Stung by those attacks, the Sanatanists embarked on their own drive towards mobilisation of their followers. As reported in the *Port-of-Spain Gazette* on April 10, 1938, Sanatanist pundits and supporters organised themselves, so that by April 1938 more than 21 local Sanatan Dharma Sabhas had been established. Community meetings and lectures were regularly held, and Sanatanist scholars from India were invited to Trinidad, the most notable of whom, Parsu-Ram Sharma, assisted in further organising the Sanatanists under the SDBC. The existing SDA was reorganised and incorporated in 1932.[28] In the drive for Hindu social mobility and visibility, the Hindu community eventually rejected the input of Christian Indians, which was previously welcomed, or at the least tolerated. The President of the SDA, Sarran Teelucksingh, a Christian, was replaced in 1938 by a pundit. As reported in the November 6, 1938 *Port-of-Spain Gazette*, one Pundit Tiwary explained:

> Mr Teelucksingh, Mr A.C. Singh and other Christian friends were not to be blamed because certain pundits always begged them to be in the Association. These pundits were responsible for the state of affairs.

The 1930s entailed a great deal of organisational activity among Hindus. The SDBC made strong proposals to the government for the allocation of ecclesiastical grants to the Hindu community. The legal recognition of Hindu marriages, the language issue in relation to adult franchise, and divorce, formed the core of debate among Hindu organisations. In addition, the drive towards Indian independence, the collection of funds for the Bengal famine and the lobbying for the construction of Hindu and Indian denominational schools all led to collective action among Hindu organisations otherwise wrought with strife and conflict. Both the efforts and successes enhanced the pride and sense of visibility among the Hindu population. This was especially the case with the opening of the Hindu-Muslim school in 1930. According to the *Port-of-Spain Gazette* on April 22, 1937, the East Indian Advisory Board, chaired by the Protector of Immigrants, was formed in 1937 for the purpose of advising 'government on all matters relating to East Indians in the colony.' Of a total of ten members, at least three were Hindus. In 1938, there was an amalgamation of the two major organisations, the SDBC and the SDA. Attempts at co-operation were even made by the Sanatanists and Arya Samajists.

Such attempts at co-operation notwithstanding, during this period Hindu leadership was defined by factionalism and a general lack of solidarity and unanimity, which was quite often reflected in, and even obstructed the pursuit of many official matters pertaining to Hindu social mobility. Almost 20 years after the introduction of the Hindu Marriage issue into the Legislative Council, the Hon. T.M. Kelshall, a member of the appointed committee, while reflecting both his and the wider society's misunderstanding of Hindu organisational function and structure, concluded that one problem was 'the question of priests. Every sect of priest objected to every other sect of priest.'[29] As reported in the *Trinidad Guardian* on February 22, 1945, the Governor, Sir Clifford Bede stated that if 'the Hindu bodies were more closely united they would become eligible for capitation Grant.'

Within the Hindu community however, this issue of factionalism elicited seemingly contradictory attitudes. While in the eyes of the wider society and on the administrative level factionalism did prove a problem, many Hindus, entrenched in the Guru-Chela system and not bothered about religious diversity, were not too concerned. When verbal or physical altercations did erupt, it was more of a reaction to condemnations of aspects of their religion and religious practice, than due to any innate bond with a certain organisation. Pundit Lutchmie Persad, an eyewitness of altercations between the Arya Samaj and Sanatanists explained that 'the Arya Samaj will say that Rama is not God; Krishna is not God. Argument will start... fight...real fight.'[30] The newness of and uniformity inherent in essentially Western forms of organisation, in reality, could not cater to the diversity of Hinduism's ideology, practice and structure. This was noticeable in the ongoing lack of unanimity, despite the official resolutions of many issues. In essence then, one can surmise that conflict was, in a sense, an outside imposition; a result of trying to impose a framework which made sense to the wider society but which could not fully accommodate the divergences of Hindu systems and structures.

The institution of marriage emerged on a national level as possibly the most contentious of Hindu issues in the form of the Marriage Bill, highlighting, yet again, the conflict between Hindu and Western ideologies, the Hindu attempt at being accepted as equally valid members of the Trinidadian society, and the reluctance of the Brahmins to endanger their stronghold on their followers. This issue was taken up from as early as 1923, at the seventh meeting of the Ordinary Session of the Legislative Council. Conflict was many and multifaceted. His Christianity notwithstanding, the Hon. Sarran Teelucksingh attempted an explanation of the situation:

> The problem is rendered difficult because of differences of opinion among the Indians themselves....The point of divergence lies in the appointment of marriage officers. Most of the Pundits feel that if Marriage officers are appointed they would be eliminated. The point is small but sharp, and the difficulty is obvious (*The Observer* 1942, 6).

The problem was, however, more deeply ensconced in the conflict of religions, ideologies and cultures. The following article in the *Trinidad Guardian* on March 6, 1945, entitled 'Pundit Opposes Hindu Marriage Bill' touched on almost all the major Hindu grievances with this proposed Bill:

> There is nothing in the religious Hindu Dharma Shastra where marriage registration is necessary, nor is any mention made of divorce. If the Government has seen it necessary to register the Hindu Marriage for the protection and interest of the parties concerned, then why not include divorce? Neither registration nor divorce is in accordance with the religious Hindu Dharma Shastra's teaching, and if one side of it is included – registration, the binding – then divorce, the unbinding should follow. A standing age limit is not mentioned in the Religious Book mentioned. The age limit of

16 years to be passed will be debarring Hindus of a very sacred part of marriage (*Kanya Danum* or the *Sacred Gift*).

Thus, in addition to the disagreement about marriage officers, several other concerns variously related to religion were raised within the Hindu community. The registration of marriages, a civil ceremony, was far removed from the sacred nature of the Hindu ceremony and rituals. As far as the Hindu community was concerned, once their ceremony had been performed, and hence, sanctioned by their Gods and other major characters of the religious texts, no further validation was needed. Many aspects of the ceremony such as the *Kanya Daan* (gift of a virgin) were being undermined by the conditions of the proposed Marriage Bill. In keeping with the Western notion of a virgin as someone who had not had sexual intercourse, the suggested age of sixteen for marriage seemed reasonable. However, since according to the Hindu interpretation, *kanya* meant not literally a virgin but, rather, but a (female) child who had not yet started menstruating, the age of 16 directly contradicted the innate significance of this ritual. In addition, the actual ritual involved the child sitting on the lap of her father, which ought not to be done if the girl was no longer a *kanya*. According to a popular *nauni*,

> ...they use to marrid them before they period, some of them...they call them *kanya*...but nowadays they don't marrid them so because they big...so them is not *kanya*, so they don't put them on they lap.[31]

Connected to the issue of the legalisation of Hindu marriages, was the illegitimacy of persons born of such unions. Within the boundaries of the Hindu community, neither was viewed as an issue since their traditional marriage ceremony was all the validation needed for both the union and offspring. However the need to ensure inheritance rights was a key push factor in that direction, since, in addition to lengthy and expensive court procedures, there were many cases of property being escheated to the state upon the death of the owner. The Hon. T.M. Kelshall voiced this concern:

> Is Government aware that (a) children born out of Hindu wedlock are branded as 'illegitimates' in the Colony, thereby leaving the stigma

of immorality on their parents and (b) that they are dispossessed of their rights of inheritance of their parent's estate?[32]

The removal of the stigma of illegitimacy would also serve to enhance the status of the Hindu community in the wider society.

The issue of divorce also generated conflict, which was fuelled by the multiplicity of Hindu texts and textual interpretations. As Mr C.W.W. Greenidge, the Acting Solicitor General argued:

> There is no unanimity on the point. Some pundits declare it does not exist, but other pundits quite as authoritative maintain that their sacred book, the *Vedas*, do permit divorce on the grounds of sterility and adultery (*Hansard* 1931, 658).

He later quoted C.B. Mathura as saying that 'the learned Manu had written that a man might marry 50 times but a woman only once' (*Hansard* 1931, 780). Numerous letters were received by Indian Members of Parliament from their constituents on the issue. In one such letter to the member for Caroni, Mr S. Teelucksingh, one Ramnarin Pundit argued that 'in accordance with the teachings of the Vedas a man can put away his wife on the grounds of adultery and a pundit can marry him again' (*Hansard* 1931, 762). On the other hand, 31 pundits attached their signatures to a statement that 'there is no divorce in the Hindu Religion' (*Hansard* 1931, 760–61). Hindu women could not be divorced (with the hope of remarriage) since a bride must be a virgin at the time of marriage.

In Hindu religious law, marriage was deemed indissoluble, except in cases of sterility and the non-consummation of the marriage. But the Divorce Bill published in 1931 had as its major underlying principle the dissolution of marriage solely on the grounds of adultery. Within the Hindu community, adultery evoked considerable ambiguity; the overriding concern was for the larger family and community unit and hence, adultery hardly ever resulted in the dissolution of marriage. In addition to the debate over whether or not divorce was permitted in Hinduism, another point of contention resided in the absence of any reference to divorce in the Hindu Marriage Act. Yet, it was argued that since the State was making provision for the lawful binding (Marriage Bill), it must also make the unbinding accessible.

It can be argued that Hindu men saw divorce as a threat to the level of control exercised over their women, providing the latter with an avenue of escape from abusive or undesirable situations. It also threatened the male dominance of property ownership, since, in the advent of divorce, the wife would have undeniable access to part of the husband's property. In addition, it raised questions about what should happen to the gifts given during the marriage ceremony (dowry), especially the more valuable ones such as sums of money, property, land or animals.

In the end there was a practical yet reluctant and gradual acceptance of both the Marriage and Divorce Bills. Yet, while the Hindu population saw the move as necessary in their upward social mobility, they did not hold it as in any way more legitimising than their own ceremony. This attitude was evident in a report in the *Port of Spain Gazette* on March 28, 1930 which stated that

> Hindus who seem to be the chief opponents to the measure, appear to realize the necessity for what they term 'notification' (as distinguished from what the state calls 'registration') of all marriages.

The acquisition of education in both Hindi and English was another major agent of social mobility within the Hindu community and on a wider level. In 1921, only 12.6 per cent of the Indian population was classified as being able to read. In 1931, this number rose to 22.8 per cent, and in 1946, to 40.2 per cent (Ramesar 1994, 114). The 1946 census classified as illiterate (either able to read only or unable to read and write English) 50.6 per cent of Indians. In the same year, just over 25 per cent of pupils attending both primary and intermediate schools were Hindus.[33] Despite the economic and social constraints, suspicions, fears and taboos, the desire for both individual and communal mobility resulted in the increasing gravitation towards the acquisition of education in both English and Hindi.

The desire to educate Hindus in both Hindi and Hindu ideology and culture led to the rise of numerous Hindi schools and *pathshalas* in almost every Hindu residential area. These *pathshalas*, according to the caste background of the teachers, variously influenced the specific community's attitude towards Brahminic supremacy and the caste system. That is to say, if the teacher was a Brahmin there was a greater possibility that Brahminic ritual superiority would be invoked. The situation would, not unexpectedly, be reversed in the case of non-Brahmin teachers. From as early as 1928, meetings were held to discuss the inclusion of Hindi and Urdu into the Western school curriculum.[34] In order to sensitise the Hindu community on the issue, public lectures on the importance of education were held. According to the *East Indian Weekly* of August 31, 1929, one wealthy merchant even began distributing Hindi primers free of charge to the population. In addition to the localised *pathshalas* and Hindu schools, this period saw the emergence of the first few formalised Hindu schools with a curriculum mirroring that of the wider educational system. The forerunner in this development was the much prized Hindu-Muslim school established in Chaguanas in 1930, which though identified in the popular mind with the Arya Samaj, was rather a collective effort on the part of non-Christian Indians.

The increasing gravitation towards Western education provided Hindus with another, though quite complicated, agent of mobility – that of conversion. Since the 1868 contact with Presbyterian proselytising efforts (Seesaran 2002, 73), conversion has been a persistent concern among Trinidad Hindus. It has been argued that the major motive for religious conversion before the establishment of Hindu schools in the 1950s was socio-economic mobility (Seesaran 2002; Ramesar 1994). The issue, however, transcends this deceptively obvious explanation to include a more complex range of factors on the sides of both the Canadian Mission (CM) and the Hindu community. Firstly, one has to consider the nature and agenda of the activities of the CM among Indians in Trinidad. One can argue that under the shroud of education, the CM embarked on very vigorous attempts at communicating their 'light and knowledge' to a 'lamentably degenerate and base' group of people who retained but a 'feeble sense of moral obligation.'[35] The techniques employed were formulated and administered in such an astute manner that they were both indiscernible by the members of the Hindu community and possibly misinterpreted by several scholars as a natural, practical dimension of the CM's efforts at educating and socialising Indians in Trinidad.

Possibly the most skilful tactic was the incorporation of Indian forms of organisation and worship into their efforts, thus packaging the fundamentally Christian values, beliefs and principles in a veneer of Hinduism. Some of these techniques included the naming of Presbyterian churches, such as *Dharm ka Suraj* (the splendour of truth) and *Jagat ka Prakash* (light of the world), in Hindi so that they conveyed Christian messages in Hindi words (Samaroo 1975, 8). In some cases, the meeting of the Presbyterian minister and elders was re-christened 'the panchayat' (Samaroo 1975, 8). Hindi terminology was also extended to aspects of the Christian service. For example, prayer meetings were renamed *Yisu Katha*, (literally, the story of Christ, but also imbibing all of the religious connotations of a Hindu *katha* which, among Trinidadian Hindus, often refers to the reading of Hindu scriptures within the context of a puja). The consecrated bread distributed at Christian communions was duly named *jewan ki roti* (bread of life) (Samaroo 1975, 12). Another method was the sale of Christian literature in Hindi. These included the Bible, bhajans (Hindu religious songs) with Christian messages, a critique of the *Valmiki Ramayana*, and Hindi editions of the Church periodical *The Trinidad Presbyterian* (Samaroo 1975, 9–10). Drawing on the deep-seated emotional bonds held by Trinidadian Indians towards India, the CM also brought missionaries, pastors and other helpers from India (Samaroo 1975, 10).

The foregoing techniques operated within the context of the highly assimilative and accommodating nature of Hinduism. Thus, unsuspecting Hindus quite comfortably recognised Christ as a divine representation and even accorded him a place in their pantheon of Hindu gods and goddesses. This tolerance was largely responsible for the lack of any Hindu offensive towards the CM. Thus, unlike the Muslims, Hindus seemed to brook the CM's preaching and opening of schools, and at times even came to the rescue of Presbyterian preachers in moments of difficulty (Samaroo 1975, 21). It can be argued that this attitude on the part of Hindus accomplished almost one half of the CM's project. The other half, however, namely the renunciation of Hinduism, proved considerably more trying for the

Table I: Presbyterian Proselytisation among Indians in Trinidad

YEAR	INDIAN POPULATION	INDIAN PRESBYTERIANS	COMMUNICANTS	SCHOOL ENROLMENT
1911	112,790	7,000	1,295	11,275
1925	125,238	9,439	1,848	17,461
1930	133,277	10,000	2,066	18,359
1942	150,000	11,456	2,500	25,000
1951	216,500	12,000	3,000	30,000
1955	259,875	20,000	4,000	32,000
1959	263,000	20,000	5,000	35,000

Source: Brinsley Samaroo, 'Missionary Methods and Local Responses: The Canadian Presbyterians and the East Indians in the Caribbean,' Appendix I.

Mission. Table I indicates the low level of success at Presbyterian proselytising among Indians in Trinidad. By 1942, despite the fairly enthusiastic response (16.7 per cent) to the CM's educating efforts, just 7.6 per cent of Indians were Presbyterians, with a mere 1.7 per cent as communicants.

Thus, it can be deduced that the rather passive attitude of Hindus towards the proselytising activities of the CM was hardly indicative of apprehensions about the capacity of their own religious persuasion, since such an attitude would have yielded a higher degree of conversion. The Hindu propensity for tolerance and diversity of other faiths did not stretch as far as non-resentment to the denigration of their religious beliefs and practices. In other words, Hindus were prepared to receive Christianity conditionally, as long as it did not impinge on their religious and personal life. If one were to add another spin to the situation, it could be argued that, for the Hindus, rather than being the patronised, they were the ones according a space to Christianity within the framework of their own extensive compendium of beliefs and practices. The idea of the superiority of Christianity was either not considered or was deemed just mere wishful conjecture on the part of the CM. Thus, when eventually faced with the uncompromising insistence by the CM ministers to denounce Hinduism, most Hindus would have unhesitatingly refused, since the thought was most probably never even entertained.

The proselytising tactics employed by the CM were substantially complemented by its academic efforts. Although oral sources claim that there was no formal pressure at the CM schools to convert, the hidden curriculum suggested otherwise. The school atmosphere was infused with Christian values, behaviour and religious principles. Extra attention was paid to students who showed academic promise. In such cases, teachers often visited the parents of these students to reiterate the importance of not stifling the child's academic potential. This quite often resulted in the child being placed in the care of the missionaries or in one of the residential Presbyterian secondary schools; both of which often resulted in a renunciation of Hinduism.[36] Indeed, in a 1928 publication, the Mission reiterated the primacy of its evangelical aspirations over its academic agenda, stating that 'the primary motive in establishing schools is evangelism...' and that residential schools 'provide a special opportunity for doing so.'[37] As Trinidad historian Brinsley Samaroo noted:

> ...well into the 1950s preference [for jobs] was given to Presbyterians in the schools (primary and secondary) administered by the missionaries; and non-Presbyterians in the Training College for Teachers were the exception than the rule (Samaroo 1975, 26).

Thus, Hindus were faced with having to choose between their religion and socio-economic mobility. This dimension of conversion, however, confronted mainly those who were seeking secondary education and eventual entry into the professions, especially teaching. The acquisition of education in English greatly enhanced the possibility of getting out of the cycle of agriculture-based occupations. In addition to the ability to read and write English, the other more secondary aspects of education in the CM such as etiquette, manners and general comportment further prepared individuals for non-agriculture related jobs. In other words, the CM seemed to promise the individual a holistic preparation for the journey out of agriculture. Thus, one was frequently faced with the choice between conversion and the cane fields in the quest for personal social mobility since, until the 1950s, Indian opportunity for education was dominated by the Canadian Presbyterian Mission. With the establishment of Hindu primary schools this first phase of conversion came almost to a halt.

On a wider scale, the large portion of the Hindu population's ignorance of the English language served both as a hindrance to assimilation into the wider society and imposed the stigma of illiteracy on the group. The communication gap proved a nuisance in both personal and official interaction. For example, according to a report in the *Port-of-Spain Gazette* of October 15, 1939, one Sookha, an old man,

> ...went to the Warden's Office to apply for Old Age Pension and up to then had not succeeded. He further stated that the man who looked after it spoke in English and most of the Indians could not understand him and experienced great difficulty.

These issues were brought to the fore in the debate and Indian protests over the inclusion of the Language Test (ability to read and understand the English language) as a deciding factor of Adult Franchise. In a Minority report to the Report of the Franchise Committee in 1944, the Secretary of State argued:

> To deprive those who can read and appreciate Oriental literature of the vote because they cannot understand the English language when spoken, and at the same time to grant illiterate persons the vote merely because they can understand the English language when spoken would seem to be most unfair.[38]

The removal of the language test in 1945, and the subsequent granting of franchise to all added to the visibility of the Hindu community as a whole.

The emphasis on organisation had profound impact on the existing condition and structure of local Hinduism. Formal organisation now allowed for a wider networking, and hence, the opportunity for mass consultations among pundits and leaders and for more standardised decisions. Large-scale *yagnas* were now being arranged and advertised through the press. Amidst the prevalent factionalism within the Hindu community during the 1930s and 1940s, each sub-group resorted to varying degrees of borrowing from the other in order to increase their viability and status both within and beyond the boundaries of the Hindu community. Thus, while the Samajists promoted several essentially Western and Christian forms, many Sanatanists began adopting some of these forms, such as daytime weddings, Sunday Services, and Western clothing.

The traditional Hindu panchayat system also demonstrated evidence of social mobility and change. Internally, being a member of the panchayat meant occupying the highest social position in the village; one accorded possibly the greatest degree of respect and authority. Judgements of the panchayat could have direct bearing on the status of both individuals and entire families in the village. The most outstanding evidence of this was the application of the state of *kujat* (outcaste) which involved the barring of the offender(s) from any kind of social interaction with fellow villagers; with the duration of the ban dependent on the gravity of the offence. Such offences included intra-village, inter-religious, or worst of all, interracial marriages; and the time period could range from a few months, to a few years, to life.[39]

Until the early 1920s the composition of the panchayat was based on a flexible combination of caste, age, moral uprightness, scriptural and religious knowledge and a sound sense of judgement. By the late 1930s, however, factors such English education and economic status were added to, and sometimes even superseded, the more traditional determinants. In addition to the presence of wealthy non-Brahmins, the age restriction was being broken with the infiltration of some comparably younger members on the basis of their level of English education. However, the one enduring prerequisite for members was good character. As with most tradition-based systems and institutions, the authority of the panchayat remained unquestioned as long as the traditional order which sanctioned its role remained intact and its rulings could be enforced. Thus, from the 1950s, the increasing awareness and adoption of the alternative (State Law), resulting from the increasing entry of individuals into the wider society, generated a gradual reduction of the authority of the panchayat's decisions, since individuals could now override unfavourable decisions, and appeal to a much higher order.

Conclusion

It is quite evident therefore that the Hindu community in Trinidad possessed its own unique systems and values, neither exclusively Indian, nor exclusively Trinidadian, but which rather, was a checkered combination of both. Along this perspective, the proposed theory of selective sanskritisation works to best elucidate social mobility within this religious group. It is clear that in this period the defining characteristics of Hinduism such as it being a way of life (rather than a religion in the Western sense), the inextricable interaction of the religious and the secular, the diversity and flexibility of the tradition, and the precedence of group dynamics over individualism were at work in almost all spheres of Hindu life. This led to unavoidable conflict when faced with, more often than not, opposing Western and secular values, institutions and procedures.

While factors such as caste, level of subscription to the dominant sanskritic culture, landownership, economic position, and the guru-chela and panchayat systems of power relations were still the major determinants of social rank and mobility, they were being increasingly tempered by the gradual infiltration of Western elements such as education, urbanisation, and secularisation. This of course was most evident among those individuals or groups, usually the higher class/castes, engaged in a conscious drive for social mobility. The process of natural filtration and the desire to emulate the socially higher groups gradually guided this interplay into the lives of the larger Hindu community. However, the diversity of both the Hindu religion and the local Hindu population generated great variation in the degree, rate and adopted factors of this interplay of cultures, lifestyles, and structures. In the seemingly contradictory attempts at both becoming Trinidadian within the framework of Hinduism, and retaining the desired level of Hinduness in the interaction with the wider society resides the crux of the concept of selective sanskritisation.

CHAPTER TWO
The Ramayana *Tradition*

Perhaps the most celebrated product of the Trinidadian Hindu community, V.S. Naipaul, described the *Ramayana* as something that 'lived among us' and as 'something I had already known' (Naipaul 2002, 12). Working along such assumptions, this chapter seeks to demonstrate that the *Ramayana* tradition has always been an intrinsic aspect of the Trinidad Hindu society, and has functioned as both agent and mirror of developments and transformation therein. The chapter also argues for a uniquely Trinidadian recension of the *Ramayana*. According to Romila Thapar:

> variants [of the *Ramayana*] point to the richness of a narrative which has been appropriated by a vast number of people in diverse ways.... Investigating these would involve investigating authorship, audience, location and purpose (Thapar 2001, vii).

In other words, since this proposed version would have been conditioned by the Hindu experience in Trinidad, an examination of the former would, in effect, divulge related dimensions of the latter. This inevitably bears upon the idea of the *Ramayana* as mirror and metaphor of social change among Hindus in Trinidad.

Socio-historical Context

In Trinidad, the Hindu experience has been greatly conditioned by the changing social milieu. During the indenture period, the restrictions of the system, the constant uphill struggle to eke out a living, the extremely strong emotional connection to India as the Motherland, and the pervasiveness of the Bhakti form of worship, left neither time, energy nor inclination for formal religious reconstruction. By the end of indenture the Hindu community, though characterised simultaneously by a substantial degree of homogenisation and an equally notable level of transience and variation, still displayed a predominantly unchallenging approach to religious matters. The ensuing 40 years proved to be quite dynamic for the Hindu community in almost all spheres of life, including the realm of religion. The tangible and visual aspects of religion were variously affected by the intriguing interplay between the traditional and the modern, the religious and the secular, and the retention and transformation that pervaded this period. However, the more deep-seated affective dimensions of the relationship of the Hindu community to its religion remained largely unaffected. Thus, the attitude of unquestioning sanctity and reverence surrounding most religious beliefs, practices and, by extension, texts, persisted until the late 1960s.

During the late 1940s and the 1950s, large scale attempts at community organisation, culminating in the construction of a large number of Hindu schools, infused the community with a substantial level of socio-religious empowerment and the promise of additional enhancement. The Sanatan Dharma Maha Sabha, though never totally free of structural and personnel problems, seemed finally to provide the type of organisational form capable of representing the Hindu community. The 1960s, however, was characterised by less emphasis of the more public Hindu forms and practices such as temple and school construction, and organised, publicly observed religious events. The political transformation of that decade (independence, the assumption of political power by the People's National Movement (PNM), and the perceived anti-Indian attitude of both the party and its leader) worked to curb the attempts at publicisation evident in the 1950s. This, in turn, resulted in the religion being more driven internally, focusing instead on its preservation and propagation from the inside. In addition, intensified internal organisation problems and the increasing preoccupation with social advancement created a somewhat ambivalent, sometimes conflicting attitude towards matters of religious import. This increased the susceptibility of the Hindu population to evangelical groups (Haraksingh 1985, 165–66). Anthropologist Barton Schwartz identified both a 'pervasive languor' and an 'infrequent and selective commitment to Sanatanist beliefs and practices' by both priests and the layman.[1] Selective commitment, facilitated by the multiplicity in Hindu practice and trends of thought, more readily captures the general religious ethos of this decade and could quite probably account for much of the seemingly conflicting attitudes. While complicating the torturous drive towards socio-religious standardisation, the availability of options was largely responsible for the survival of many folk traditions and practices, and for arresting Brahminic aspirations of unmitigated, unchallenged authority over the Hindu population.

Owing to a combination of potent factors, the 1970s saw a further decline in 'religious participation and commitment' (Vertovec 1992, 125). The death of Bhadase Sagan Maraj, President General of the major Hindu socio-religious organisation, the SDMS, evoked a spate of controversies within the organisation. During this period a significant number of smaller socio-religious organisations were variously affiliated to the SDMS, and on this basis one can argue that the general dysfunction within the umbrella group extended to the sub-units. Finally, this socio-religious turmoil served to sustain the incursion of Christian proselytisers. In his study of Hindu institutions in Trinidad, Joseph Nevadomsky attested also to a considerable level of ritual laxity and an increasing shift away from religious sentiments during this period (Nevadomsky 1980, 39–53). However, rather than a shift away from religious sentiments, a transformation, greatly influenced by prevailing trends in the wider society, can more aptly describe the Hindu socio-religious ethos of this period. The aforementioned factors of the period 1950–75 stimulated a discernible erosion of the fervent and uncritical adherence to Hindu religious prescriptions, practices and principles, which not unexpectedly, was extended to the textual sphere.

For Trinidad Hinduism, the period since 1975 has been one shaped by social, political and economic ascendance and stability. The academic advancement of Hindus evoked a marked level of philosophical and spiritual probing into religious dictates and practices; rituals and devotion-oriented practices and beliefs would no longer suffice. There was also a discernible rejuvenation of the organisational and communal aspects of Hinduism, and a rise in the number of sub sects within the religion, which collectively served to further diversify and promote the religion in the public sphere.

As discussed in the previous chapter, Hindu socio-religious mobility before the 1950s involved a marked degree of standardisation of socio-religious practices. From the 1950s, the increasing foray of the Hindu community into the wider society enhanced efforts at standardising the many trends and threads of what had evolved into Trinidadian Hinduism. According to reports in the *Trinidad Guardian* on January 25, 1950, the issue of government grants to Hindu primary schools in the 1930s and the possibility of a Hindu representative on the Education Board were other such instances. The 1970s socio-religious revitalisation (Vertovec 1992, 162) that attempted to curb the high level of conversion and general religious decadence of the previous decade saw the most marked acceleration of such efforts at standardisation. During the first half of the twentieth century aspirations within the Hindu community towards ritual purity, inherent in Brahminic culture and practice, provided the impetus for standardisation. However, the requirements, attitudes and systems of the wider, non-Hindu society constituted the major underlying factors of standardisation since the 1970s. From the persistent multiplicity of Hindu socio-religious organisations, and the great degree of heterogeneity that continued to define Hindu practices, philosophy and notions in Trinidad, it was evident that the diversity of Hinduism continued to be a potent force. Within this framework, the *Ramayana* tradition in Trinidad unfolded, expanded and engaged the Hindu community, therein directing and mirroring the process of Hindu socio-religious change in Trinidad.

The *Ramcharitmanas* in Trinidad

A major dimension of the local *Ramayana* tradition is the written or textual aspect. Although the *Ramayana* tradition comprises several hundred written and oral varying interpretations, this study focuses on the *Ramcharitmanas*, the recension brought to Trinidad by indentured Indians. Composed by the saint-poet Tulsidas around 1574, it has been central to the literary, cultural and religious heritage of India (Lutgendorf 1991) and almost every other country of the Indian diaspora. Original neither in terms of plot nor theme, the *Ramcharitmanas* is rather an interpretation of the Valmiki myth of Rama, with influences and borrowings from other prominent texts of sixteenth-century India, such as the *Adhyatma Ramayana* (*The Spiritual Version of the Ramayana*) and the *Bhagvadpurana*, and dramas based on the Rama story such as the *Mahanataka* (*The Great Drama*) and the *Prasanna Raghava* (*The Delightful Descendant of the Solar Race*) (Bulcke 1980, 62). In fact, the author Tulsidas readily admitted that his version is a retelling, that Valmiki was the original composer of the story, and that the story has been part of the oral tradition for many centuries.[2]

Although the chief aim of the author was the exposition of the pathway of devotion to God (Bulcke 1980, 59), the Rama myth gradually evolved into a narrative that permeates not just the religious but, in keeping with the popular notion of Hinduism as a way of life, almost all spheres of Hindu and Indian life. This was due to factors such as the popularity of the Rama story, the universal appeal from the sixteenth century onwards of the concept of Bhakti, and the social, religious, cultural, political and emotional ethos (in northern India) of the time of composition (Bahadur 1976, 1–10). The poetic genius of Tulsidas, which was derived 'not from ostentation but by simplicity' (Bahadur 1976, 4) comprised a gripping narrative, simple language, a skilfully chosen and crafted network of character, plot, themes, setting and symbolism, augmented the text's more aesthetic appeal.

Popularity of the *Ramcharitmanas*

Since the beginning of the Indian presence in Trinidad, the *Ramcharitmanas* has occupied the unchallenged position of *Dharmashastra* par excellence in all facets of Trinidad Hinduism, providing 'the major framework of the theological edifice of Hindu migrants' (Haraksingh 1984, 19). So pervasive is this version that many refer to the author as the Father of Caribbean Hinduism. During the indenture period, the vast majority (between 1876 and 1879 over ninety percent) of the indentured immigrants originated from the Uttar Pradesh and Bihar regions (Brereton 1981, 103), which was by then deeply immersed in the Bhakti tradition and hence permeated by Tulsidas's encapsulation of it. This can account for the *Ramcharitmanas* quickly becoming a religious, social, cultural and emotional anchor for the early indentureds amidst an alien and often hostile environment. It is not improbable that the South Indian immigrants (the principal component of the remaining ten per cent) and their descendents would have had, up to the early post-indenture period, their separate recension of the *Ramayana*. This, however, together with most aspects of South Indian tradition, would eventually be subsumed by the increasing dominance of the North Indian Hindu tradition; especially if it contradicted the latter's major precepts and beliefs.

The well-known and familiar story of the *Ramcharitmanas* with its human interest and its largely ethical nature attract a larger audience than the *Bhagvadgita's* pure philosophy and revelation (Bahadur 1976, 3). Verses from the *Ramcharitmanas* can be set and sung to music, adding considerably to its appeal. The story is dramatic and loosely knit, and the narrative propels it in such a manner that both despite and due to the lack of active sermonising, the philosophy hits home. The author's conception of Bhakti possesses 'deep appeal' (Bulcke 1980, 60) especially to a community entrenched in this (Bhakti) tradition. It has also been suggested that the text's seemingly equilibrial and harmonious presentation of the potentially paradoxical relationship between the social world and the transcendent other, simultaneously situating it within a social context and offering the possibility of spiritual gratification, lies at the core of its enduring appeal (Lutgendorf 1991, 340–41). Relatedly, E.J. Babineau locates the text's appeal in both its underlying message of the ultimate compatibility of 'social duty' and 'love of God' (Babineau 1979, 189), and in the poet's 'special aptitude for acclaiming renovation without destroying tradition, for promoting change without sacrificing continuity' (Babineau 1979, 192).

The specifically diasporic appeal of the *Ramcharitmanas* was based on a number of factors. Its focus on the Bhakti tradition served as a link to the emotional and cultural ethos of the motherland. Its treatment of the exile theme provided immense solace and emotional support, 'a balm for troubled minds' (Bahadur 1976, 11) to the immigrants who, considering their indenture as a type of exile, identified with the trials and tribulations in the text, while upholding

Rama's dignity and endurance as an ideal worthy of emulation in their own situation. The idea of exile and return that runs deep in the text provided yet another point of identification and solace, since many, especially in the earlier phases of indenture, nurtured the hope of one day returning to the Motherland. So intense is the diasporic appeal of the *Ramcharitmanas*, and so ingrained is the perceived analogy between Rama's exile in the *Ramayana* and the experience of Indian indenture, that Vijay Mishra, studying the Indian experience in Fiji, aptly titled his study 'Rama's Banishment' (Mishra 1979).

The uncomplicated nature of the story, along with a clearly established dichotomy between good and evil rendered it an appropriate authority in the attempts of the Trinidad Hindu community at reconstruction and reconsolidation. Stories from the *Ramayana* impacted on the Hindu, and sometimes non-Hindu perceptions of the new environment to the extent that the significant unknown other, or potentially threatening agents, such as white colonial oppressors and Trinidadians of African descent, were referred to as Ravan (the villain of the story). In his study entitled *The Development of the East Indian Community in British Guiana, 1920–1950*, Clem Seecharan confirmed that this was also the case in British Guiana where stories from the *Ramayana* greatly influenced Hindu perceptions of the new environment, and where President Burnham acquired the title of Ravan on account of his overtly anti-Indian policies. The *Ramcharitmanas*' focus on interpersonal relationships provided both positive and negative models for the reconstruction of both family and community networks. The following, an interview published in the *Trinidad Guardian* October 14, 1990, is but one of numerous responses that support this function of the text:

> *Ramayana* projects the highest values of righteous conduct that pertains to family life. There are portraits of the love between brothers, the duties of a wife, the relationship between father and son and the responsibilities of a king towards his subjects among other things.

Since many aspects of caste interaction in India could not obtain overseas (Vertovec 1992, 34), the *Ramcharitmanas*' propensity for non-casteist interpretation (though this depended on who was doing the interpretation) proved extremely applicable to the Hindu community in Trinidad. In addition, the large number of non-Brahmin textual exponents increasingly engaged this non-casteist dimension of the text.

Dimensions of the Ramayana *Tradition in Trinidad*

Ramleela

The Ramayana tradition in Trinidad comprises many dimensions. The most longstanding of these is undoubtedly the *Ramleela* (depiction of the Rama story in dramatic form), the first performance of which was staged in 1888 in Dow Village, California, in Central Trinidad. Public notices of later productions began to appear as early as 1898 in the *Indian Koh-I-Noor Gazette*. The vagaries of time, space and society notwithstanding, the following analysis of the *Ramleela* in India has significant bearing on the local situation:

> The whole thing is as much a religious ceremony as a dramatic performance, as well as having a significant role in the transmission of faith in Rama among the illiterate masses (Brockington 1981, 171).

Although modern, technological, economic and educational advancements led, over time, to changes in the drama's form, physical setting, grandeur and scale, the actual content remained relatively standard. Considering the drama's more than one hundred year old existence in Trinidad and the relative autonomy of each production, one can speculate that such attempts at standardisation – deliberate or not – reflected the general attitude and emphasis within the larger Hindu community. In an article in the *Sunday Express* March 2, 1986, *Ramleela* actor Buchoon Singh confirmed that the *Ramleela* committee of Dow Village comprised solely village members, Hindu and non-Hindu, from as early as 1908. Fifty years later, in 1958, this trend was still evident in the information given by a leader of the Debe Ramleela Committee. He reiterated Niehoff's observation that 'every village you go to is planning to have their own [*Ramleela* celebration]' (Niehoff 1960, 125). However, according to newspaper notices during the 1920s and the 1930s and other sources, there was, amidst the autonomy, a great degree of standardisation with respects to the content of the drama. By the 1980s such homogenisation in the *Ramleela* exemplified concerted attempts at standardisation of Trinidad Hinduism as a whole. Thus, the standardisation of the *Ramayana* story in the *Ramleela* mirrored social practice and transformation in social and religious thought, thereby underpinning the notion of *Ramayana* as a metaphor of Hindu society.

Indeed, the dramatic form of the *Ramleela* served as a very effective means of incorporating uniquely Trinidadian issues and elements into the *Ramayana* tradition. The most popular motif for this has been the depiction of Ravan. Whether it was the white colonial oppressors, the Africans, the negative impact of Western elements, or any other more palpable threatening agents such as drugs, violence or criminal activity, the actual physical representation[3] of the evil Ravan constantly reflected the concerns of the Indo-Trinidadian society. One observer at a performance during the late 1990s recalled noticing a Nike emblem on the effigy's earrings and was told that this signified the negative influences of the 'Americanisation' of Trinidad society.[4]

One can thus notice a trend of 'Ravanisation' of potentially threatening and negative elements, which increasingly extended out of the boundaries of the *Ramleela* performances into the wider society. Social, religious and political leaders all made use of this motif to effectively drive home their arguments. This persisted despite continuous objections by a prominent Hindu leader. In an article in the *Trinidad Guardian* on August 18, 2001, he argues that the local portrayal of Ravan as a dark man was a 'false, malicious and anti-Hindu interpretation' geared towards 'the attempt to introduce racist interpretations of Ravan into *Ramleela*.' Another suggested that the earlier association of Africans and Ravan reflected an extension of the attempt to 'Ravanize' colonialism.[5] He proposed that, since the white colonial rulers were also associated with Ravan, this relation was not a 'racial thing' but, rather, stemmed from the political and economic juxtaposing of Africans and Indians. One can safely surmise that these seemingly concerted efforts at purging the Ravan motif of any racial undertones demonstrated the active though sometimes superficial attempts at denying and negating such undertones, which were a feature of public life in the 1990s.

Another related issue is why the colour black was such an integral feature of the Ravan figure and the entire demon army since the earliest *Ramleela* productions. Considering the socio-economic, socio-religious and ethnic tension that have characterised the relationship between persons of African and Indian descent in Trinidad, the tongue-in-cheek association of the demon king with the Indian perception of Afro-Trinidadians cannot always be written off as fortuitous. The licentiousness, lack of thrift, excessiveness and lasciviousness assigned to Afro-Trinidadians by Indians were all (coincidentally) prominent characteristics of Ravan. This, together with the ridicule and contempt that characterised the general attitude of Africans towards Indians, can account for this practice throughout the first half of the twentieth century. From the 1950s, the essentially 'non Hindu-friendly' policies of the ruling People's National Movement generated presentations of the Ravan figure as an indirect expression of dissatisfaction of Hindus at the treatment meted out to them by those in authority – namely the Afro-Trinidadian political elite. One can see in the Ravan figure, then, a somewhat easy categorisation of the power relations of the land; and in this specific context, a metaphor of the perceived abuse of authority and power by the African-dominated leadership. However, the colour black also carried additional negative connotations and associations. Within the traditional Hindu caste system, skin colour was always a defining if not deciding factor. In addition, the colour black was always associated with elements of black magic, evil spirits and other malevolent entities. The latter can also account for the ambiguity that has surrounded the goddess Kali (assigned the colour black) and Kali worship in Trinidad.[6]

From the 1980s, however, there was an increasing move to reclaim the figure of Ravan. The heightened ethnic consciousness of the late 1980s, together with the increased emphasis on the exploration and application of textual matter to either supplement or usurp traditional practices and attitudes, can explain the attempt to reclaim Ravan, not just as an Indian (as opposed to his African consignations), but as the Brahmin that the *Ramayana* story and

Hindu mythology proclaim him to be. In addition, the more analytical, holistic and philosophical approach to Hinduism has led to several relatively new interpretations of Ravan and his function. In the reclamation of his Brahminism, Ravan is seen as akin to the tragic hero of such literary works as *Hamlet* and *Macbeth* where the protagonist ascends to great intellectual, political and authoritative heights but succumbs to a flaw of character and loses everything. In this retelling of Ravan as a Brahmin, he is seen as an unconquered warrior, versed in the scriptures, who possessed the grace and awe of the Gods and ruled in glory over the prosperous city of Lanka. Like all such characters, what makes Ravan the quintessential tragic hero is the fact that he acknowledges his mistake (his arrogance in his superhuman powers as a warrior and his unbridled lust leading to his abduction of Sita), but a little too late, since in the scene almost immediately following his epiphany of sorts, he is killed in battle.

In keeping with the Hindu view of one's life and the world as preordained – a sort of proto-play directed by the Divine – Ravan's actions were increasingly viewed (though not justified) as his designated role in the divine *leela* (divine play). Thus, it was suggested that one should consider his character as the necessary personification of all that one should not do. This detracted from the negative sentiments heaped unto the persona himself, especially with the highlighting of his Brahminism by Brahmin priests and leaders. Thus, the ritual purity and behaviour expected from those belonging to the Brahmin caste was not marred by Ravan's actions, since he was acting in accordance with Divine mandate. By extension, the fluidity and ambiguity of the notions of good and bad are further compounded by the Hindu view of reconciliation of opposites:

> Ultimately, there is no good or bad. God did not create evil as a force distinct from good....From the pinnacle of consciousness one sees the harmony of life....This releases the human concepts of right and wrong, good and bad....Evil is often looked upon as a force against God. But the Hindu knows that all forces are god's forces, even the waywardness of *adharma* (Subramuniyaswami 1993, 139–43).

All of the aforementioned echoed the transformations in Hinduism wherein a more holistic, intellectual, proactive approach fuelled by social, religious, ethnic, political and economic ascendancy was gradually adopted since the 1980s. The working of contemporary issues into the oral commentary that accompanied the performance further supplemented the local flavour of the tradition. Verbal comparisons were made between Ravan and any threats to the stability of the society; the destruction of Ravan was paralleled to the need to purge society, both in an Indo-Trinidadian and wider sense, of such destabilising elements. Such interpretations of Ravan also found root within the daily interaction of, not just Hindu, but Indian family and community life. A man accused of spiriting away another's wife earned himself the title of Ravan. In addition, persistent errant behaviour such as a propensity for getting involved in disputes or fights, excessive alcohol consumption and lasciviousness, and even extreme gluttony often earned an Indian individual either the title of Ravan or at least the epithet *Rakshas*, signifying a devil or clansman of Ravan.

Social changes were also evident in the *Ramleela*. Before the 1960s the drama was performed solely by men who undertook various preparatory acts such as a three-month fasting period (intended to purify both body and mind). Throughout the performance of the *Ramleela* the major actors lived together in *kutiyas* (temples or sheds provided by a supportive villager). These arrangements arrested the advent of women actors before the 1960s. The absence of women in the *Ramleela* was compounded by the socio-cultural constraints that relegated the woman largely to the home, the censorious attitude among Hindus towards female public performances and female performers, and the ritual impurity assigned to menstruation. During the 1960s however, female performers began their incursion into the *Ramleela* arena. At first, their roles were minuscule and largely restricted to communal scenes where the entire audience could be integrated into the performance (such as when Bharat went into the forest with an entourage to meet his brother Rama, Rama's return to Ayodhya and even Rama and Sita's wedding). By the 1970s though, females were portraying major characters in many of the productions. The still widely held stigma of impurity associated with menstruation saw a predominance of pre-pubertal girls, rather than adult women, performing such parts. By the 1990s, attitudes to this issue echoed the wider attempts at navigating between the dictates of religious doctrine and traditional practices, and the more rational and analytical approach to religious matters tempered with the increasing infiltration of Western and secular considerations. The major female roles were commonly portrayed by women (indeed it would seem out of place now to witness a man portraying female roles) with astute calculation and navigation of the menstrual cycle being a major deciding factor in the choice of these female actors.[7]

The varying perceptions of and the dilution of caste boundaries in Trinidad were also visible in the *Ramleela*. With relatively little time, effort and inclination for caste considerations, *Ramleela* productions during the latter half of the nineteenth century were not strictly bound to caste distinctions. By the 1930s, however, there emerged a tendency for the major characters to be portrayed only by members of the Brahmin caste in many of the productions. This was due to the fervent efforts by members of the Brahmin caste to establish themselves as the socio-religious leaders of the Hindu community. This development can be deemed contradictory in several ways. Firstly, most of the principal characters in the *Ramayana*, including Rama himself, belonged to the Kshatriya caste. Secondly, within the sanskritic tradition, public performance was generally deemed a low unbrahminic activity. What then accounted for the Brahmin foray into a field that carried the danger of tainting ritual purity? One can surmise that the considerably diluted concerns and the substantial ambiguity that surrounded the caste issue in Trinidad, and the conviction in Rama's divinity stimulated this attitude. Also, the almost consuming desire on the part of Trinidad Brahmins to establish themselves at the top of the socio-religious ladder, presented the *Ramleela* in its social and religious capacities as a prime method of cementing Brahminic socio-religious authority. The discipline involved in preparation for the production such as the Hindu mode of fasting, the associated rituals, and the portrayal of the role of God and his close relations also seemed to the Brahmins as belonging to their domain. This preference for Brahmin actors echoed the contentious yet undeniable prominence of Brahminic sensibilities in the ritual realm of Trinidad Hinduism.[8] However, there was always a simultaneous consistent disregard of caste in the choice of actors in a large number of the productions. A marked overall decline in adherence to the religious strictures was apparent in the determinedly more lax attitude by both performers and audience to the issues of meat-eating during the performance period, the inclusion of women performers, and the consecration and level of sanctity assigned to the performance grounds.

Derek Walcott referred to the *Ramleela* performance in the village of Felicity in Trinidad as both a metaphor of history and a vital aspect of the Indian attempt at community reconstruction within the diasporic context (Walcott 1993). He asserted that 'the performance was like a dialect, a branch of its original language, an abridgement of it, but not a distortion or even a reduction of its epic scale' (Ibid. 1993, 6). This conclusion overtly supports the argument for a local version of the *Ramayana*; one which has retained the basic thread of the story, relevance and reverence of the Rama myth; but which, like a dialect, has sprung out of and thereby mirrors the very history of the society. His conception of the drama as operating on faith rather than on the regular mechanics of the dramatic form echoes the intense affective and emotional appeal that this tradition has exercised over Hindus in Trinidad:

> They were not amateurs but believers....They believed in what they were playing, in the sacredness of the text, the validity of India, while I, out of the writer's habit, searched for some sense of elegy, of loss, even of degenerative mimicry...I was polluting the afternoon with doubt and with patronage of admiration (Walcott 1993, 4).

The fact that they were engaging in producing the *leela* or story of God would naturally invoke a most fervent desire for excellence in their performances. Indeed, the emotional and spiritual rush experienced by the actors portraying the role of Ram (God) was something of an epiphany, since, instead of the actor perceiving himself as 'a reality entering an illusion,' he is 'an illusion that finally enters reality,'[9] a mere human who assumes divine proportions.

The Arts

In addition to the *Ramleela*, the *Ramayana* tradition comprises numerous other pervasive and enduring dimensions. The advent of Hindi films in Trinidad in the 1930s was accompanied by the depiction of the *Ramayana* in the form of visual recordings. Since then, and especially until the late 1970s, various films based on the *Ramayana* (and other religious texts) each with their own variations and interpretations, were shown in public cinemas. However, with the increasing ownership in television sets and video recorders during the 1970s the films were largely relegated to the shelves of the local video shops, or shown on local television on special Hindu days. The other significant development in terms of visual renditions of the *Ramayana*, was Ramanand Sagar's television serial of the late 1980s.[10] Even though its visual impact was not as strong as the previous cinema presentations, a great portion of the Hindu population, placing religious and cultural import and significance on it, organised their daily routine around the showing times. There were also several versions of the *Ramayana* aimed at children, including abridged prose narratives and comic books, which have been in circulation from the 1970s. During the 1990s, attempts were made by a local publishing company to present events of the *Ramayana* in the form of colouring books and storybooks for younger children; *Ramayana*-related crossword puzzles and word sleuths were also formulated.

Scenes and tales from the *Ramayana* were also depicted in dance and dance-dramas by both visiting and local companies. In an article in the *Sunday Guardian* October 25, 1992, the Shankar Kala Kendra's totally local production of a *Ramayana* ballet, was praised as 'one of the most detailed versions of the Ramayana ever staged in Trinidad...an eye opener in that it added authentic touches to hazy areas of that great Hindu scriptural text.' The National Council for Indian Culture facilitated several productions and ballets of the *Ramayana* at its annual Divali celebrations at the *Divali Nagar* site[11] without a charge for admission, rationalising, in the *Sunday Guardian* on October 14, 1990, that a fee just cannot 'be levied on those to whom the immortal words of *Ramayan* have given everlasting sustenance.' In addition to such formal stage productions, the more informal *Sarwan Kumar* dance-drama[12] was embedded in the story of the *Ramayana*. As with most aspects of the popular tradition in Hinduism, elements of daily life – especially such social ills as alcoholism, domestic violence and drug abuse – were readily infused into the presentations. Presented primarily in English, the dialogue and related anecdotes actively connected the story to contemporary life, inevitably lending a Trinidadian feel to the whole production.

Various art forms also constituted a part of the local *Ramayana* tradition. Scenes from the *Ramayana* were depicted on murals in public and private temples and at various socio-religious events. *Murtis* (image of a deity) and paintings of varying sizes of the major characters reflected the varying stages of artistic development. The sanctity that enshrouds the *Ramayana* tradition was evident even here too. As one *murti* maker explained, in the *Sunday Guardian* on October 14, 1990, 'the making of the *murti* of *Shri Ram* is in itself a worship, a *Sadhana* [worship].' Other handiwork reflecting motifs and scenes from the *Ramayana* included pottery and clay wind chimes.

Trinidadian writers, especially but not exclusively Indo-Trinidadians, contributed yet another dimension to the *Ramayana* tradition by working into their novels and short stories various aspects, functions and images of the *Ramayana*. The novel *A House For Mr Biswas* (Naipaul 1969) is permeated by the ever-imposing Hanuman house,[13] Biswas chants 'Rama' as the Greenvale house falls apart, and the character of Seth is referred to as a *'rakshas'* (demon). In Seepersad Naipaul's *The Adventures of Gurudeva* (Naipaul 1976), the main character's attempts at becoming a teetotaller includes chanting 'hari ram,' writing the name 'Ram' on his temple wall, and reading verses from the *Ramayana*. In her novel *Butterfly in the Wind* (Persaud 1990), Lakshmi Persaud emphasises the role that the interpretation of the *Ramayana* plays in the formation of morals and values, and refers, in her later novel, to the notion that brides should be like 'Rama's Sita.' (Persaud 1993). Harold Sonny Ladoo (Ladoo 1974) makes ample reference to the entire abduction image involving Rama, Sita and Ravan. Local poetry also mirrored the Rama myth. The most popular contexts included the indentureship theme, Divali, the symbolic return from exile, and the fight against threatening forces. Derek Walcott utilised the Rama myth in poems such as 'Exile' (1969) and 'The Saddhu of Couva' (1979). One local aspiring poet attempted to echo Trinidad's political turmoil within this aspect of the *Ramayana* tradition in the following lines published in the *Sunday Guardian* October 14, 1990:

When leaders ram-a
Jay,
And auction empty
Promises –
For the price of ballots;
Are euphoria,
And deflowered hopes
The ka-ram (harvest)
We reap
Once more...?
He Ram!

The names of individuals added another very interesting aspect to the local *Ramayana* tradition. The names of many of the characters in the epic such as *Ram, Sita, Lakshman, Dashratha* and *Hanuman* were extremely popular among Trinidad Hindus. Understandably enough, most individuals refrained from naming their children after the villains, such as *Kaikeyi* (*Rama*'s stepmother, who was responsible for his banishment), Ravan or Manthara (the maidservant who instigated *Kaikeyi* to have *Rama* banished). One interviewee recalled having known a young classmate with the name *Kaikeyi* who, whenever she displayed any errant behaviour, was told that she was just living up to her name.[14]

The evolution of the element of music in the *Ramayana* tradition mirrored the development of the aesthetic dimension of the Hindu experience in Trinidad. The general austerity and poverty that characterised ordinary life in the first half of the twentieth century left little means or inclination for what would then have been deemed frivolous initiatives in the area of music. Until the 1930s, the very few singing groups focusing on the imitation of Indian musical styles such as *ghazals, thumries, bhajans*[15] had no bearing on the textual tradition, since the metre of such compositions did not concur with that of the verses of the *Ramcharitmanas*. Instead, these groups concentrated on reproducing the music emerging from the Indian sub-continent and on composing their own items along these musical styles. Since the earliest period of indenture, the *Ramcharitmanas* had its own repertoire of traditional tunes, whose appeal was based on a kind of semi-forlorn melodiousness that seemed to both echo and provide solace for the community's straitened conditions of existence. The sole form of musical accompaniment during the indenture and very early post-indenture period was the use of several small cymbals (*jhals*) to accompany a particular mode of *Ramayana* recitation. This style, inevitably called *jhal Ramayana*, was characterised by a very vigorous tune and rhythm. Prominent also in both Mauritius (Burton 1961, 130) and Fiji, this style demanded a certain degree of skill and specialisation, and so prevented it evolving into a widespread mode of presentation. Also, the inherent vigourousness and din detracted considerably from the overall religiosity of the event and was not appropriate to some occasions such as pujas and death ceremonies.

By the 1930s, a new group of singers such as Youseff Khan, Haniff Mohammed and K.B. Singh began showing a more active interest in the development of Indian music in Trinidad,[16] and this had an impact on the rendition of *Ramayana* verses. Since the text was, in any case, written as lyrical verse, it was not difficult to apply music to the recitation. However, the reluctance to depart from traditional practices and systems, especially with regard to religious matters, prevented this newly emergent style from being considered the norm. The majority of *Ramayana*-singing groups and individuals continued until the 1960s to follow what was termed *sadharan Ramayana* (verses sung without musical accompaniment).

The advent of Hindi films in Trinidad in 1935 had a substantial impact on the Hindu textual realm, helping eventually to increase both the degree and range of musical accompaniment in *Ramayana* singing. With the advent of the *Ramcharitmanas* as the major text at the *yagna* forum in the late 1960s, musical accompaniment became the norm with both the formal and popular aspects of the *Ramayana* tradition. At first there was a small array of musical instruments including the harmonium, dholak, *majeera, dhantaal*, violin and mandolin. By the 1970s the norm at *Ramayana yagnas* would be the *Vyas* sitting on the *singhaasan*, and a small group of accompanying musicians sitting on the floor – the latter labeled '*Bhuyaa Saaj*' (literally, musical group on the ground). According to the *East Indian Weekly*, February 23, 1929, audio-recordings of verses from the *Ramcharitmanas* done in India were available to the local population since at least the early 1920s. However, during the 1970s the first local (vinyl) recordings of *Ramayana* verses sung to musical accompaniment were produced.

This set the stage for a steady flow of local renditions on cassettes, and added to the local flavour of the tradition by rendering verses of the *Ramayana* in what is locally known as the classical singing style. Again, it proved most difficult to lure older Hindus to this new style, many of whom argued that the advent of music in the textual sphere diminished the amount of actual reading from the text, the level of religiosity, and overall quality of the proceedings.[17] Many even scathingly referred to pundits who relied heavily on music in their renditions as mere songsters.

By the 1980s, there was an increasing working of the tunes of popular Hindi film songs to fit the verses of the *Ramcharitmanas*, and also a reworking of the traditional tunes to cater to new musical preferences. By the 1990s, music in the textual realm was being further transformed as many pundits and other presenters of the texts acquired formal musical training. This eventually led to a mélange of the elements of formal Indian music such as *taals* and ragas, of film songs and, of course, the traditional tunes. Several pundits situated this shift in the 'need to appeal to the younger ones; make it more lively, make it more meaningful, make it more dramatic.'[18] The intrinsic affinity of Hindus for music, and the normative position that music occupied in local culture led to music becoming an essential ingredient in discourses on the *Ramcharitmanas*. So intrinsic had music become to the *Ramayana* tradition that almost all of the more popular pundits and Ramayanists were accompanied by their own group of singers, trained musicians with Indian and Western musical instruments and modern sound systems. One such pundit explained this development as 'pundits were moving with technology also. People wanted to hear good sound reproduction, good acoustics...all these things help in the music.'[19] Music, thus, had become a key component of the motivational and presentation tactics of the major expounders. The following sentiment was quite popular among textual expounders:

> Our discourse must be balanced in terms of the story of the *Ramayana* itself, the philosophical content in terms of the application to everyday life, in terms of the balance of the singing and the volume of speech. All of these things have to come together to make a perfect blend.[20]

The various types of Indian folk songs in Trinidad such as *biraha*, *jhoomar*, *chowtaal* and bhajans comprised another salient aspect of the musical dimension of the local *Ramayana* tradition. While most carried religious connotations, those that were not restricted to solely religious settings, but formed a vital part of wedding celebrations and other more secular forums, sometimes de-emphasised the religious to highlight the more contextually suitable aspects. Such verses included:

> *Raam ji ke bagiya, Sita ke phoolwaari, Latchiman devar rakhwaari.*
> In Ram's flower garden Sita is the flower and Lakshman is the watchman.[21] (*biraha*)

Also,

> *Raamji ke shobha dekh Siyaji ke man lobhaa,*
> *Jhaak jharokha laagee nandani Janak ki.*
> The moment Sita saw Raam in Janakpur she fell in love.[22] (Local classical)

Thus, locally composed verses, while conferring the sanctity of the *Ramayana* unto the occasion yet not directly invoking the religious dimension, somehow facilitated the early inclusion of the *Ramayana* into settings where alcohol, ganja, meat-eating and hip-swaying devices were not uncommon. This inadvertently paved the way for the much later controversy surrounding the use of religious lyrics in secular forums such as chutney singing and other cultural events.

By the late 1980s, the emergence of what is termed chutney music out of the confines of the home and immediate community into the public non-Hindu eye led to a contentious interplay between the religious and textual elements of this art form, and its increasing status as essentially secular entertainment. The most troublesome point was embedded in the issue of 'wining' (in Trinidad, this term refers to the sexually suggestive gyration of the hip) and the general sensuous (some say lewd) dancing that chutney music seems to evoke, juxtaposed with references to the *Ramayana* and other religious literature in the lyrics. Since this interplay of the religious and the secular has always been an integral aspect of local Indian folk music, one can surmise that the points of contention resided in contemporary socio-religious issues. These included concern about the public perception of Hindus, the increasing trend toward standardisation, and the conscious or subconscious attempt to emulate the decidedly more clear-cut dichotomy between the sacred and the secular evident in the major Christian religions in Trinidad. An overtly subtle move to institute more orthodox (one can surmise Brahminic) beliefs and systems into a traditionally diverse Hindu community also marked this conflict. Interestingly enough, while almost everyone will verbally disapprove of sensuous dancing to religious lyrics, many – most probably intoxicated by the rhythmic beat of the music and alcohol, and not too concerned then with separating the sacred from the 'profane' – will participate in such activities. Though arguable, this type of duplicity is not unexpected when viewed within the context of the pervasive, fluid and diverse nature of Hinduism.

Other very popular folksongs which have continuously borrowed from the *Ramayana* are the vigorous *chowtaal* and the *ulaaraa*, most commonly sung during the *Phagwa* season. Traditional songs such as the following dominated *Phagwa* celebrations throughout the country:

> *Holi khele Raghubeeraa Awadh mein, holi khele Raghubeeraa.*
> *Raamaa ke haath dholak bal sohe, lachman haath majeeraa...ohhh latchman haath majeeraa....*
> Raghubeer (Raam) is playing *Holi* in the city of Awadh.
> Rama is playing the *dholak* (hand-drum), and Lakshman is playing the *majeeraa*. *(Ulaaraa)*

Another example:

> *Siya Raam Lashan douu joree ho khelat horee. Mahaaveer daphlaat lagaawai, Angad dholak joree. Khelat phaagu mahaa madhure sur, aru khelat hai sab goree, ho khelat horee.*
> Sita, Raam and Lakshman are all playing *holi* together. Mahaveer (Hanuman) is playing the tom-tom, and Angad is playing the hand-drum. All the men and women are playing *holi* in a very pleasant atmosphere.

The *Phagwa* festival was another forum for the intermingling of the sacred and the secular. In fact, until the sanskritising efforts of the SDMS from the 1970s, alcohol, bhang and ganja were readily consumed during *Phagwa* festivities by both singers and the other male celebrants. The earliest attempts at weeding out intoxicants from this festival proved extremely difficult. In fact, the first public *Phagwa* celebration at Aranjuez Savannah in 1968 was marred by alcohol-related misdemeanours. Substantial success in this undertaking was achieved only during the 1980s in the context of rejuvenated efforts at purging Hinduism of elements that threatened to stigmatise both the religion and its adherents. The *chowtaal* and *ulaaraa* musical styles dominated *Phagwa* festivities until the mid-1990s when the very controversial *pitchkaaree* made its appearance, embodying an attempt at situating Hindu elements more readily within the Trinidad context.

Life Cycle Rituals

The *Ramayana* also encompassed the major life cycle rituals of birth, marriage and death which comprised the major socio-religious events in the lives of most Hindus. Changes in the rituals mirrored the evolution of the socio-religious aspect of Trinidad Hinduism and, by extension, changes in the attitude towards the *Ramayana*. Until the 1970s, a vital aspect of the sixth and twelfth day birth rituals (*chhati* and *barahi* respectively) was the celebratory singing of songs by women to the vigorous beating of the dholak, bottle and spoon, *lota* and spoon or coin, and *majeera*. Many of those songs depicted the birth and childhood of Rama and his brothers. A typical example is the following:

> *Are Brahma diye bardaan raja ghar beta bhaiyaa....*
> *Kowsilya ghar Rama, Sumitra ghar Latchiman...,*
> *Aur Kaikeyi Ghar Bharat Bhuwala, Raja ghar....*
> God gave you a blessing, a gift of this child....
> In Kowsilya's home, Rama; in Sumitra's home, Lakshman,
> And in Kaikeyi's home Bharat was born....[23]

The celebrations almost always entailed the consumption of alcohol and meat, in which the singers themselves often participated. This suggests that, from the very earliest stages of Trinidad Hinduism there was a very blurred line between the religious and the secular, between the sacred and the profane, between the prescribed orthodoxy and popular folk culture. By the 1970s, the increasing preference for having babies delivered in the hospital rather than at home resulted in a rapid decline in the performance of this life cycle ritual and consequently, this aspect of the *Ramayana* tradition. This was due to the discordance between hospital births and modern post-partum care for both child and mother, and the traditional practices that surrounded home births. By the 1990s, the sixth and twelfth day ceremonies were sporadically observed, but the focus of the celebration was now more on presenting gifts to the newborn. The live singing that facilitated the infusion of the *Ramayana* was replaced by the plethora of readily available pre-recorded chutney and Hindi film music.

The *Ramayana*'s impact on the Hindu wedding ceremony has been more substantial, enduring and diverse. While there was no direct reading of the text, the formal and informal discourse during the ceremony entailed elaborate descriptions of the marriage of Rama and Sita, emphasising the divine couple as a role model for the newlyweds. Within this context, verses from the *Ramcharitmanas* were recited. The actual wedding vows did not originate in the *Ramayana*, but from the *Dharma Sastras*, and were compiled into the *Vivaah Padathi* or 'Wedding Texts.'[24] However, it was not uncommon for the officiating priest, with the intent of augmenting the vows' cogency, to verbally situate the vows within the context of Rama and Sita's wedding in the *Ramayana*. While there may not have been much variation in the choice of verses at wedding ceremonies, there was a reworking of the points of emphasis, especially with regard to spousal relations. Before the 1970s, the prominence of some verses suggesting divine ascriptions to the persona and office of the husband and stressing total wifely dedication to the husband echoed the predominant character of Hindu husband-wife relations during that period. A good example is the following:

> *Binu sram naari param gati lahaee. Pati vrata dharma chhaari chhal gahaee.*
> Those wives who without guile take a vow of fidelity towards their husbands, attain with the greatest ease the eternal gift of salvation.

And,

> *Saasu sasur gur sevaa karehoo, pati rukh lakhi aayasu anusarehoo.*
> Serve the parents of your husband and other elders and do the bidding of your lord according to his pleasure.[25]

By the 1980s, reliance on such verses was disappearing in the face of a new-found emphasis on the importance of mutual understanding and co-operation between wife and husband. The timing and degree of such transformations simultaneously depended on and reflected the extent and nature of the social, economic and religious transformation occurring both within the Hindu community and the wider society.

However, what really cemented the *Ramayana*'s impact on the Hindu wedding ceremony was the fact that, despite the transformations generated by time, place and circumstance, the core rituals and their basic format corresponded significantly to those contained in the *Ramcharitmanas*. The emphasis placed on operating within the prescribed auspicious times, the ceremonious but celebratory reception and departure of the bridegroom's party, the application of *sindoor*, circumambulation of the ritual fire, the tying together of the bride's and groom's garments, the tying and untying of the sacred thread around the couple's wrists as protection against evil forces, along with the general décor, festivities and forms of entertainment were just some of the points of similarity.[26] The singing of wedding songs such '*Siya dale ram gale jai mala*' (Sita has placed the marriage garland around Rama's neck),[27] which depicted parallel scenes of Rama and Sita's wedding added another enduring dimension to the *Ramayana*'s prominence in this ceremony.

In light of the role of the *Ramayana* in the wedding ceremony, the variety in Hindu wedding types provided an interesting paradox. If the *Ramayana* was such an influential factor in this ceremony, what then accounted for the flourishing of other marriage styles? One can point to prevailing socio-economic trends and conditions. During the earliest indenture period, the 'sit down' relationship where the couple quite frequently just started living together was a common form of union. This was on account of the disparity in the male-female ratio and the uncertainty and general instability of that period. In addition, the high level of both male and female infidelity during this period would have deterred any active inclusion of the *Ramayana* into marriage rituals, since the *Ramayana* promoted essentially monogamous behaviour. The emergence of Indian villages from the 1880s onwards stimulated a focus on community and family reconstitution, and led to the reconstruction of fragments of the traditional Hindu wedding ceremony. This facilitated the *Ramayana's* entrenchment in the Hindu psyche and its incursion into the ceremony and ideology of marriage. Eventually, the ceremony depicted in the *Ramayana* became the prime model. This was a result of the intense socio-religious activity of the first three decades after the end of indenture, the markedly higher level of stability in conjugal relationships which was then achieved, and the wide subscription to the ideal of monogamy as advocated in the *Ramayana*.

The Arya Samaj in the 1930s introduced the 'table wedding' ceremony which was shorn of many of the rituals of the traditional Hindu ceremony. Of course, it was not only in marriage ceremonies that the Arya Samaj abjured rituals. The table wedding[28] also proved popular in cases of pregnancy before marriage. By the 1980s, the increasing intrusion of Western values as well as the exploration of the diversity of Hindu practice led to numerous innovations in the traditional ceremony. Since each of the varied ceremonies contained some shade of at least a few of the major defining rituals associated with Hindu marriage, it was almost impossible to either identify the right way or to denounce any one as not valid. This was compounded by the fact that the signing of the marriage register was the most socially and lawfully binding element of the ceremony and, as some argued, had usurped the authority of the rituals. However, the overall application of the *Ramayana* as the major doctrine in terms of family life, social relations and its emphasis on commitment, love and monogamy within marriage – all held as ideals within both the Hindu and non-Hindu society – best accounts for the dominance of the wedding ceremony that was depicted in the text. In this respect, other texts such as the *Bhagvadpurana*, the Vedas and other Puranas, which all recognise polygamy, were at variance with the social norms of both the Hindu and non-Hindu Trinidad society.

The *Ramayana*'s presence in death ceremonies and rituals changed over time. Until the late 1960s, pertinent verses from the *Ramcharitmanas* were sung in a suitably forlorn tone during the procession to the cemetery or, significantly less frequent, to the cremation site. This was eventually overtaken by pre-recorded verses from the *Ramcharitmanas* played at first within the confines of the hearse, and by the 1980s, amplified for public acknowledgement of the procession. This transformation was evoked by factors such as the legalisation of Hindu cremations, and the opening of cremation sites situated away from the villages thus making the walking procession almost impossible, along with the substantial rise in vehicle-ownership and the use of heavy Western-style coffins. One specific cassette recorded by Pundit Nirmal Maharaj retained its popularity in this realm. In addition, the continuous prominence of the chant *Ram naam satya hai* (In the name of Rama lies truth) attests to the sanctity and importance that surrounded the persona of Rama and the *Ramayana* tradition in death rituals.

For about 10 to 14 days following the death of an individual, recitations from the *Ramayana* were conducted at the home of the departed by popular ramayanists. These nightly *satsangs* served as an immense source of comfort and solace for the bereaved family. *Kathas* dealing with the death of major and minor characters in the text were especially, though not exclusively, focused upon. In addition to the *Ramayana*, the *Garud Purana* (which details the prescribed death rituals, their importance for the deceased and the trials of the soul in the hereafter), and relevant sections of the *Bhagvadgita* were also read during these *satsangs*. The incentive for this extended period of chanting was the belief that reciting the name of God on behalf of the dead assisted the soul in the journey to the hereafter.

The *Ramayana Yagna*

As a primary forum of socio-religious discourse throughout the post-indenture period of the Hindu presence in Trinidad, and therefore in constant intercourse with the social, religious and economic climate, the *Ramayana Yagna* was a major indicator of currents of socio-religious change. As a founder of a local Hindu group explained in the *Sunday Guardian*, October 14, 1990:

> The *Ramayana Yagna* effects a great continuity in tradition. In establishing itself in the local landscape, it has invited the creativity of the tradition with a view to establish continuity...invite a Hindu western audience, and vie for acceptability beyond the frontiers of the Hindu fold.

This comment accurately brings to bear the dialectic of change and continuity, and the flexible and accommodative tendencies that are intrinsic features of Hinduism. It also echoes the ineluctable nature of Hindu socio-religious transformation within the multicultural context of Trinidad and Tobago.

Both the frequency and the changing physical setting of the *yagna* echoed the socio-economic position of Hindus. The depressed economic conditions of the 1950s were evident in the sparse setting of the *yagna* which comprised a makeshift bamboo tent; fruits, flowers, leaves and branches as decoration, and the audience seated on the floor. Relative poverty also accounted for the fact that up to the 1960s most *yagnas* were community organised undertakings, aptly called the *Panchoutie Yagna* or *Bhagwat*. Several newspaper reports and advertisements revealed this activity. A good early illustration is the following, which appeared in *The Observer* in 1943: 'Hindoos of Cedros held a Panchowtee Bhagwat at the Sewalla on June 20, and prayers were said for peace with victory.' Before the 1970s only few families could manage the expense involved in staging a *yagna* on their own. However, the oil boom of the 1970s would change the situation and result in a dramatic rise in the number and types of individually sponsored *yagnas*, with some persons promising to host these events annually for three and sometimes five consecutive years (Vertovec 1992, 164–74).

Transformation in *yagna* types also provided clear evidence of the evolving intellectual and religious trends in the local Hindu population. While the traditional *Bhagwat* and *Ramayana Yagnas* sufficiently catered to the largely Bhakti orientation of Hinduism up to the 1980s, both the economic amelioration of the 1970s, and the 1980s' stirrings of religious reform substantially augmented the *yagna* spectrum. The means and the incentive to observe a greater number of Hindu religious occasions on a larger, more public scale were now available. Thus, religious observances such as *Ram Naumi*,

Krishna Janam Ashthami, *Nau Ratam*, and *Shiv Ratri* provided additional occasions for formal discourses from texts such as the *Ramcharitmanas, Bhagvatpurana, Bhagvadgita, Devi Purana* and *Shiv Purana*.

In its various functions also, the *yagna* echoed attitudes and socio-religious trends within the Hindu community. That it was always a major socio-religious event is not in doubt. Until the 1950s, it provided the chief occasion for communal cohesion and, especially for females, a socially sanctioned forum for interaction outside the boundaries of the family home and kinship unit. By the 1970s, the *yagna*, now more visible yet not in any way more understood by the wider society, extended and intensified its socialising function, and became an important vehicle for formulating a response to Christian proselytising efforts. In addition, the decline in the institution of arranged marriages by the 1980s saw the *yagna* functioning as a major socially sanctioned, albeit not in an overt manner, forum for male-female interaction and potential matchmaking. The strong trends of revitalisation that dominated the last 15 years of the twentieth century expanded the scope of the *yagna*. From a forum confined to imparting religious solace and moral codes to Hindus, the *yagna* began to function as an active institution for the exploration of major issues affecting all dimensions of Hindu life in Trinidad, both within the community and in relation to the wider society.

Questioning and Doctrine

Notwithstanding the overall mood of uncritical acceptance that seemed to define the attitude of Hindus towards their religion up to the 1980s, the *Ramcharitmanas* has always generated a tradition of questioning. The fact that the text is structured along several levels of dialogue contributes significantly to this tradition of questioning. Paradoxically, with the increasing formalisation of the overall structure of *satsangs* and the steady infiltration of more intellectual trends and approaches, there has been, since the 1970s, a notable decline in this tradition of questioning during the *satsang* session. One can speculate that the influence of the Christian structure of religious service (where the congregation was primarily a receptacle for the proceedings conducted and directed by one figure of religious authority) contributed to the decline of this convention of questioning. However, while the desire to have the usually pre-planned sessions proceed uninterruptedly continued to discourage questioning during sessions conducted by younger individuals, questions were still sometimes entertained after the discourses, but more so in sessions conducted by older individuals whose style was rooted in the 1950s and 1960s. By the 1990s, the nature of such questions reflected the society's attempts (or dilemma) at reconciling religion with their own contemporary, considerably Western and modern values and beliefs. And sometimes other motives were at work. As a noted ramayanist ruefully commented:

> ...long ago when you ask question it used to be valid, now when we ask question it is to either test the man ability; they want to humiliate him or they want to make a joke out of him.[29]

The use of ganja and bhang during textual discourses and other socio-religious events quite vividly exemplified the interplay of both the sacred and the secular, and the elements of the Little and Great Traditions. Though seemingly paradoxical to the high level of reverence allotted to the religious realm, it was common, until the 1950s, for the main readers to each 'take one pull' of the ganja in cigarette form since, in the words of one interviewee, 'it opens your intellect and helps you to remember, and it keeps your voice in tune.'[30] He was quick to add that this was never done with the intention of 'getting a high or anything like that.' Yet this selfsame 'high' was the major reason for the consumption of bhang; as a reader explained: 'bhang is a thing whatever mood it catch you in, it keep you right there until it wear off.'[31] Of course, its association with the god Shiva provided the perfect justification for its consumption in a religious setting since 'this is a Mahadeo *Prasad.*'[32] By the 1980s, the increasing dissemination of the values of the more orthodox Hindus led to such intense criticism of these practices that even the smoking of cigarettes, let alone ganja and bhang consumption, was considered taboo, or at the least disrespectful, at textual discourses and other religious observances. However, the religious undertones of bhang still seemed to justify its consumption (though rare and secretly) at *Shiva Ratri* and other events where the very vigorous *chowtaal* was sung.

The Ramayana *Tradition as Doctrine*

The validity of the *Ramcharitmanas* as a social doctrine is evident in the great influence which the ethics, morals and values of the text has had on Hindus in Trinidad. That the story has a historical base makes the author's instruction more effective, for people can feel that whatever is taught was actually once practised by persons and is not mere precept. These codes of conduct are presented through concrete, convincing characters in crisis situations, rendering them more easily digestible than abstract philosophical and moral expression. As reported in the *East Indian Weekly* on January 5, 1929, Pundit Jaimini during his visit to Trinidad in 1929 explained that Mahatma Gandhi himself used the *Ramayana* as a teaching tool:

> Mahatmaji in this lecture, took *Ramayana* as his text and explained the ideals of Vedic civilization from the life of the Holy *Ramayana*. He explained how unparalleled and unique was the attachment of Lakshman towards Rama, sacrifice of Gharat [sic], fidelity of Sita towards her husband and devotion of Hanuman which no history in the world could ever portray adequately. His allegories and anecdotes magnetized the hearts of the audience, literate as well as illiterate, Hindus and other religionists, old and young, men and women.

The major characters are faced with situations which parallel the challenges of everyday life, and they all face real temptations. When they fall from grace, the opportunity is provided to revaluate the boundaries of ethical behaviour. Among Hindus in Trinidad, the nature of revaluation was determined by changing attitudes towards social institutions and codes of conduct, arising from their continuous encounter with non-Hindu influences. The increasing visibility of individuals and groups advocating a more pragmatic approach to religion also led to new textual interpretations and shifts. In this light, the *Ramcharitmanas* can be deemed 'the excellent reorientation and adaptation to new needs of an older moral and spiritual code in an age when theocracy is passing into a secular society' (Khan 1965, 10). In its role as socialising agent within the framework of a multicultural society, the *Ramayana* has succeeded in traversing the boundaries of religion in several ways. From the earliest days of the *Ramleela*, many Muslims played key roles in both the organisation of and actual performance of the production. Some even participated in formal recitation of verses from the text.[33] Many non-Hindus also attended *Ramayana yagnas* and *satsangs*.

Ramayana and Hindu Family Life

Hindu family life in Trinidad has been greatly influenced by the values prevalent in the *Ramcharitmanas*. The text highlights various forms of interpersonal relationships, outlines acceptable tenets of behaviour and provides role models for almost all categories: Rama is the ideal husband and son; Sita is the ideal wife, daughter and daughter-in-law; Bharat and Lakshman are the ideal brothers; Hanuman and Sugriva are the ideal friends. Since the daily recital of the *Ramcharitmanas* on the plantation barracks, the text continued to refresh the strong Indian tradition of family life. This was evident in remarks of interviewees in the *Sunday Guardian* October 14, 1990, such as '*Ramayana* projected the highest values of righteous conduct that pertain to family lives,' and 'some of the major influences the *Ramayana* has had on my life have been in the areas of family life, the exercise of authority, and my relationship with less privileged persons.' However, since the 1970s, major changes within the East Indian family in terms of its structure, function and ideology prompted recastings of the text.

The transformation of the Hindu family structure from an extended to an increasingly nuclear one mandated a grudging de-emphasis of the structure and values of the traditional extended family during textual discourses. Though the extended family was still held up as the ideal, the lived reality, characterised by increasing disagreements among in-laws, arguments over inheritance rights, and the changing dynamics of husband-wife relations, increasingly persuaded reciters of the text to tone down the emphasis on this ideal. The decline of the extended family arrangement usually meant that immediate family members no longer lived close to each other and this often diluted the intensity of emotional bonds. This led to attempts, during textual and verbal discourse, at working the values and ideals of the extended family system into the nuclear system. Thus, while Rama's dedication to his father and the love that existed among the four brothers were still accentuated, situations such as the four brothers living together with their respective families in the same home, and Sita's unwavering dedication to her in-laws were either reconsidered or downplayed. Consequently, instead of focusing on Sita's unquestioning obedience to her in-laws, as would have been done before the 1970s,[34] now mutual respect, love and admiration were emphasised as the defining and desirable traits of that particular relationship. This was reinforced by verses such as:

> *Main puni putrabadhoo priya paaee. Roop raasi guna seel suhaaee.*
> *Nayan putari kari preeti bardhaaee. Raakheu praan Jaanakihi laaee.*
> Again I have found in her a beloved daughter-in-law, who is amiable and accomplished, and beauty personified. I have treated her as the very apple of my eye and loved her ever more; nay, my very life is centred in Janaki [Sita].[35]

However, even by the 1960s this attitude was still more of the ideal than the reality since many daughters-in-law continued to experience misery at the hands of diabolical and controlling mothers-in-law.

The presentation of sibling relations during textual discourses was also adjusted to conform to the changes within the family structure among Trinidad Hindus. The role and status of the eldest son/brother in the family deserves special attention. The following verse, spoken to Lakshmana, Rama's younger brother, echoed the pre-1970s position of the eldest brother as second only to the parents/father in terms of the level of respect he received, his inheritance rights and his family related responsibilities:

> *Tumha kahu ban sab bhaati supaasoo. Sang pitu maatu Raamu Siya jaasu.*
> You will be happy in every way in the forest since you will have with you your father and mother in Rama and Sita.[36]

The transformation in family structure created a situation wherein the eldest brother still managed to retain a sense of authority, but in a much diluted form, and invoked mainly in moments of extreme family crisis and for religious rites and rituals. The foregoing verse's presentation of the elder sister-in-law as mother to the younger brother-in-law touched upon a very provocative issue within the traditional Indian family setting where these two individuals sometimes shared an erotically charged 'joking' relationship that, according to popular opinion, occasionally developed into full sexual activity. One can argue that the studied oblivion and the light critical jest with which the issue was treated by immediate family members and the community respectively can partly be situated in the tradition of *niyoga* in India where a man was allowed to marry his brother's widow. One wonders then if Tulsidas, in order to negate such relationships, deliberately imbued Sita and Lakshmana's relationship with maternal overtones.

During the 1970s, the increasing primacy of the sense of individualism over kinship relations further detracted from a wholesale acceptance of the *Ramcharitmanas'* traditional presentation of family relations. By the late 1980s, family relationships, excluding perhaps those involving parents, were becoming increasingly reciprocal in nature, especially in terms of the level of respect and interaction. In this setting, even the *Ramcharitmanas'* presentation of parent-child relations was becoming increasingly problematic. The idea of unchallenging obedience and loyalty to parental dictates emphasised in verses such as the following was met with ambiguity, though usually unvoiced and tinged with guilt:

> *Mor tumhaar param purushaarthu. Swaarathu sujasu dharamu paramaarthu.*
> For us two brothers, you as well as myself, the highest achievement of our human life, nay, our material gain, our glory, our virtue and our highest spiritual gain consist in this that both of us should obey our father's command.[37]

Despite the increasing subscription to a more nuclear family structure and ideologies, the strong sense of filial obligation inherent in traditional Indian society frequently generated remorseful feelings of inadequacy among offspring with regard to taking care of infirm parents.

Women in the *Ramayana*

The *Ramayana* has always had an undeniable impact on the position and role of women in both the family and the society at large. The essentially patriarchal family system that developed during the early post-indenture period held Sita – chaste, submissive, faithful and loyal to her husband – as the highest ideal of womanhood. In addition, several incidents in the *Ramayana* highlight the 'inherently inferior and potentially dangerous and wicked nature of women,'[38] while some verses refer to women in the same breath as animals and untouchables.[39] Verses such as the following also served to cement the notion of women as morally, intellectually, spiritually, physically and socially inferior to men:

> *Mahaabrishti chali phooti kiaaree, jimi sutantra bhae bigarahi naaree.*
> The embankments of the fields have been breached by rains just as women get spoiled by freedom.[40]
> *Sahaj apaavani naaree patinsevat subh gati lahai.*
> A woman is impure by her very birth; but she attains a happy state (hereafter) by serving her lord (husband).[41]

The character of Sita and the general *Ramayana* ideology were also used to discourage transformations in the traditional concept of the Hindu woman. This was duly reflected in Seepersad Naipaul's article in the *East Indian Weekly* November 24, 1928, entitled 'Dangerous Feminine Evolution' in which he condemned the growing affinity of Indian women for Western fashion:

> The advent of bobism in the Trinidad world? What of the inglorious styles...and their garments? Cannot these atrocities be helped... to clip the hair to enhance the beauty is a wasteful and ridiculous excess.

He further supported his position with the following quote from the *Ramcharitmanas*:

> *Chalat kupanth veda maga chhanday. Kapat kalewara kali-mali bhanday.*
> Treading the path of unrighteousness they have forsaken the doctrines of the Vedas; deceit being their food in Kaliyug.

Although exceptions did occur, such perceptions of women persisted until the socio-economic transformations of the 1970s. Since then, and especially since the 1980s, a number of issues have demanded constant reconsideration of both the *Ramcharitmanas*' and some of the reciters' projections of women. Such issues included the changing concept of the ideal Indian wife and woman; the increasing sense of individualism among Hindu women; the changing role of women in rites, rituals and religion; the rapidly increasing numbers of women in almost all occupational fields; and the shifts in priority. The following excerpt from the *Trinidad Guardian* on November 10, 1996, which analyses Sita as an individual in her own right who challenges her husband for not wanting her to accompany him to the forest, confronts and chastises her abductor Ravan, holds herself in very high esteem, and marries only he who proves worthy of her, provided an apt example of such reinterpretations:

> The woman of the '90s must emulate Tulsidas' Lakshmi by standing on her own, if necessary, to make a positive statement of her own self worth by not following the crowd, by not giving in to circumstances but constantly striving to be true to her self, her Devihood.

The ideal of Sita's womanly virtues was increasingly put to task, with Rama's treatment of Sita, in spite of her constancy, as the major point of argument. This point will be examined more fully in the following chapter. In fact, it is quite interesting to note that while Sita was idealised for her womanly and wifely virtues, in the local Hindu tradition this figure never attained the prominence of the other more aggressive, independent female deities such as Lakshmi, Durga and Kali. Until the early twentieth century, the extremely active role of women in the reconstitution of the Indian community and their status as valuable property could have accounted for their preference of the more action-oriented, distinctive and even combative representations of womanhood, instead of one who complied with all of her husband's wishes and was, in effect, defined by him. It can be argued that, since the 1980s, this tendency was reinforced with the advent of the 'independent and modern' Hindu woman. Even during the period between the 1930s and the 1970s which was dominated by patriarchal values, the figure of Sita never attained the status and popularity of the more independent female deities.

Conclusion

The foregoing examination of the *Ramayana* tradition in Trinidad has yielded a number of salient points. The multiplicity of its manifestations, together with the fact that all are variously influenced by the social, cultural, political, and religious dimensions of the dynamic Trinidad Hindu experience endorse the argument of a uniquely Trinidadian *Ramayana* tradition. In addition to the textual aspect of the tradition, the rich oral tradition that has both surrounded and fed upon the Hindu experience proves an equally valid and pregnant metaphor that has been extensively imbued with the operatives of change and continuity, tradition and modernity, accommodation and rejection. The varying levels of manifestation of the tradition in almost all spheres of life evince the pervasive nature of this tradition, and by extension, Hinduism as a religion. The constant attempts at striking the right balance between reworking various aspects of the tradition to meet the demands of social change, while retaining its fundamental literary, affective and religious essence is a most outstanding indication of the nature of the socio-cultural dilemmas that have plagued Hindu society from early indenture.

The endurance and dissemination of the *Ramayana* tradition within Trinidad's multicultural society through the periods of indenture, community reconstruction, conflict and affirmation echoed the dynamism and flexibility that have enabled the tradition to flourish globally throughout the Indian diaspora. Judging by the endurance and function of the more longstanding *Ramayana* traditions in India, Asia and other countries of the Indian diaspora, one can surmise that the last 165 years have been a period essentially of establishment of the *Ramayana* tradition. During this time it has emerged as an integral dimension of Trinidadian Hindu life, but one which is still substantially influenced by the values, cultural nuances and systems of the Indian subcontinent. The stage is now fully set, in the twenty-first century, to explore whether the *Ramayana* tradition in Trinidad – immersed in the country's swirl of socio-economic, sociocultural and political transformation – will, like the attempts of the Southhall Black Sisters in Britain, engage in a higher level of 'Trinidadianization' and shed even more of its exclusively Hindu application. Conversely, nostalgia for the traditional that is continuously fed by Hinduism's propensity for continuity amidst the change could work to deter the weaning away of the tradition from its ancestral homeland, India. Either way, the *Ramayana* tradition in Trinidad will undoubtedly continue to act as both mirror and metaphor of the Hindu experience in Trinidad. The following chapter provides a detailed examination of the most prominent aspect of the *Ramayana* tradition in Trinidad – the textual dimension.

CHAPTER THREE
The Hindu Textual Tradition

The dialogue between the body of Hindu religious texts and the historical, social and cultural contexts of Hindu existence in this and other regions of the Indian diaspora can be described as dynamic, intricate and multi-dimensional; in other words, a most apt metaphor of the Hindu experience in Trinidad and Tobago. Within the framework of this study, the Hindu textual tradition is conceived of as a collection of the texts, the contexts in which they are situated and, associated accoutrements. This concept of text transcends the definition of 'a written or printed work' (Pearsall 1999, 1483) to include related aspects of the oral tradition and popular practice that have direct, intimate bearing on the status and function of Hindu religious texts in Trinidad and Tobago. In Trinidad and the wider Hindu contexts, the oral dimension possesses the ability to enhance, elucidate and sometimes even challenge the written dimension. This, ultimately, facilitates a more profound insight into the mechanics, not only of the textual realm, but also of the society in which it is located.

Socio-Historical Context

As with any other situation of migration, the historical context of the Indian diaspora in Trinidad (especially during the indenture and early post-indenture periods) includes two streams. The first reverts to the ancestral homeland, India, and the second involves an examination of the developments in the present homeland, Trinidad. A mental image of the immigrant with '*jahaji bandal*' (the few belongings, usually wrapped in cloth, which some of the immigrants took with them onto the ships) on his head and *Ramayana* in hand situates Hindu religious texts within imaginings of the earliest indenture experience. Though derived from the mythology that surrounds the indenture experience, this image bespeaks both the earliest mode of transposition of the text into Trinidad, and how deeply ensconced it was in the psyche of the Hindu migrants. The transmigration and subsequent recreation of the Hindu textual tradition form an integral aspect of what has been termed the *'bidesia'* tradition. Coined as early as 1838 when migration from the Bhojpuri region to the Caribbean began (Tinker, 53–54) this term was used to refer to the migrants by their loved ones whom they had left behind. It has since been extended to the new folk culture that emerged out of this migration in both the homeland as well as in the destinations of the migrants. This *bidesia* folk culture, mainly an oral tradition, is represented in many cultural forms such as theatre, song, dance, painting and literature (Tewari 2003, 12). In India, the *bidesia* tradition developed within the emotional turmoil and sense of longing caused by the departure of the immigrants. Thus, the various cultural forms revolve around the process of displacement of the Bhojpuri migrants, the memory of the immigrants held by those they left behind, and the pain of separation.

The oral folk traditions that comprise the *bidesia* culture were a fundamental component of the cultural baggage of the immigrants, which provided them with a great degree of solace in the destination countries. Throughout the period under study, the *bidesia* idea has been important in attempts by descendants of the immigrants at reconstructing the history of their ancestors. Hindu religious texts, in their capacity as Hindu literature that has been subject to constant reinterpretation, and which has evolved into an entire socio-religious and socio-cultural tradition conditioned by the experiences of the Indian immigrants and their descendants, can be situated within this *bidesia* tradition. The fact that both Hindu religious texts and the *bidesia* idea serve as metaphors for the cultural traditions of the Indian diaspora and the changes therein, further endorses this association.

Textual Navigation

The Hindu textual tradition in Trinidad can be described as very fluid and broad based, variously recognising almost all of the major Hindu texts such as the *Vedas*, the *Smritis*, the *Puranas*, the *Upanishads*, the *Brahmanas*, and the epics as sacred literature. What emerged, however – and reflective of the larger Hindu condition – was a situation where the dictates of time, place, circumstance, and propensity promoted the supremacy of some texts over others. In Trinidad, the *Ramcharitmanas*, the *Bhagvadpurana*, and the *Bhagvadgita* variously shared this position of textual supremacy. While the others, especially the *Puranas*, were an integral aspect of religious discourses and other religious intercourse, they served largely to reinforce or extrapolate the arguments, state of affairs and directives of these principal texts. However, there were occasional discourses and *yagnas* based on these secondary texts, usually related to specific religious observances or festivals such as *Shiva Ratri*[1] (*Shiva Purana*) and *Nau Ratam*[2] (*Devi Purana*).

It is possible to identify two dimensions to the textual sphere: the formal – namely the *yagna* forum, and the popular – namely *satsangs*. From the earliest post indenture attempts at community reconstruction until the 1950s, the *Bhagvadpurana* was the primary text of focus at *yagnas*, which were popularly referred to as '*Bhagwats*.'[3] Three major factors accounted for the supremacy of the *Bhagvadpurana* during this period. Firstly, the language of the text, Sanskrit, with its status as language of the Gods, allowed the *Bhagvadpurana* to elicit a higher level of reverence than those texts not composed in the Sanskrit language. Secondly, the socio-religious supremacy of the *Bhagvadpurana* in the formal sphere served Brahmin aspirations at socio-religious authority, since the knowledge of Sanskrit was held almost exclusively by Brahmins. Thirdly, it was held that this text encapsulates what is referred to as a 'complete incarnation' of the Divine (as opposed to the *Ramcharitmanas*' 'partial incarnation').[4] This substantially enhanced the *Bhagvadpurana*'s level of sanctity. As a Brahmin pundit with 57 years of experience in conducting *yagnas* explained:

> They [the Hindu community] consider that [the *Bhagvadpurana*] the highest in our texts as you get the complete incarnation [*poorna avatar*] of Shri Krishna; the avatar of Shri Rama is partial...so they used to have a higher adoration, respect for the *Bhagvad*. Anybody could read the *Ramayana* at home, any family. But the *Bhagvadpurana*

was solely to graduates only who was up to certain standards in the Brahmin family. They used to call him the *Vyas*. They adore him and know him as God himself.[5]

This status quo was maintained until the 1970s (Vertovec 1992, 165–66), when the *Ramcharitmanas* (and hence, *Ramayana yagnas*) began eclipsing the *Bhagvatpurana*. By the 1960s, the rise of English as the primary mode of communication among Hindus increasingly relegated the Hindi language to the more intimate, domestic and religious spheres of life. Simultaneously, the marked decline in the knowledge of Sanskrit, together with an increase in the popularity of Hindi bhajans and other religious literature served to endorse Hindi as a quasi-religious language, a category previously reserved for Sanskrit. The musical tracks from Hindi films also had substantial bearing on this transformation. This, together with the unchallenged popularity of the *Ramcharitmanas* among ordinary Hindus, and the fact that, by the 1950s, that text was being referred to as the '*Pancham Veda*' or 'Fifth Veda' accounted for its ultimate ascendancy over the *Bhagvadpurana* in the formal dimension of the textual sphere of Trinidad Hinduism.

While the *Ramcharitmanas* retained its position of textual supremacy, increasing trends towards a more philosophical, intellectual, spiritual and analytical approach towards religion had, by 1990, created a growing space for the highly philosophical and spiritual *Bhagvadgita* in the formal aspect of the Hindu textual tradition. As a respected pundit explained:

> There is a great need to teach people the philosophy of the *Gita*. We are coming into a more intellectual class of people. Hinduism has taken a major swing. Hindus are more educated now so you have to be able to express Hinduism as an intellectual religion...which it is. It cannot only remain at the level of Bhakti again in Trinidad and Tobago. It cannot only remain at the level of stories, *itihas*. It cannot only remain at the level of rites and rituals and pujas. It is to be lifted to the level where people understand that Hinduism is about living life; it is a living religion.[6]

The textual tradition that developed with respect to the *Ramayana* in Trinidad (and to a more or less similar extent in India) can be understood within the framework of several equally active notions:

that of 'text as encyclopedia,' 'text without boundaries' and 'text as living document.' Text as encyclopedia hinges on the following widely held opinion:

> Every aspect of society is represented in it [the *Ramcharitmanas*]; and every aspect of human nature in daily living could be identified in this textbook...it is the encyclopedia for humanity.[7]

Or, as one pundit very poetically puts it, 'from womb to tomb, that *Ramayana* has everything.'[8]

Indeed, from providing emotional solace to Indians in indenture, to forming part of the 1990s political dialogue of the country, the *Ramcharitmanas* was applied to almost every aspect of the Trinidad Hindu experience. Its capacity to cut across the restrictions of time, space and circumstance and accommodate almost any issue – due largely to its malleability to multiple meanings and interpretations – resided at the core of its function as encyclopedia. The religious texts are imbued with the capacity to provide a plausible answer for all the problems encountered in everyday life. This, of course, served to heighten the power of both text and religion, and to tighten the relationship between the sacred and the secular.

The notion of text without boundaries points to the intertextuality of the tradition; that is to say, the constant use of material from other sources to substantiate events and arguments of the text. This is further substantiated by the cross referencing which almost all of the later texts themselves display, and the fact that the value-systems, scope of plots, philosophy, and characterisation which they contain show remarkable similarities. This correspondence is related to the supposed skill of the Brahmin authors of these texts, namely, to achieve the harmony and reconciliation that characterise the Great Tradition in Hinduism. Attesting to both the notions of the *Ramayana* as encyclopedia and that of intertextuality, Haraksingh saw the *Ramayana* as:

> ...allowing reciter and moralist, and the audience as a whole, a wide field in which to practice the art of embellishment....The story was often spun out from the central core to accommodate the various recensions of Puranic literature, to embrace allusions and references over a wide area, and to make a connection with common experience in field and village (Haraksingh 1998, 10–11).

In Trinidad, cross referencing between the *Ramcharitmanas* and other written versions of the Rama story reflected changes in the intellectual and social development of the Hindu community, and the changing demands that they placed on religion. Notwithstanding the *Ramcharitmanas'* popularity, oral interpolations from and references to other versions of the Rama story, such as *Adhyatma Ramayana (The Spiritual Ramayana), Ananda Ramayana (The Pleasant/ Delightful Ramayana), Bhusundi Ramayana (Bhusundi's Ramayana), Ravidas Ramayana (Ravidas' Ramayana)*, and especially, the *Valmiki Ramayana* (the first written version) was an integral aspect of the local *Ramayana* tradition. A bi-modal approach was usually employed by expounders. This involved either acknowledging that reference was being made to another version or, consciously or subconsciously working borrowed material into the story of the *Ramcharitmanas*, oftentimes creating the impression that the orally interpolated material was contained in the latter. Until the 1950s, however, the *Valmiki Ramayana* was the version that was most consistently used for cross referencing. Based on the fact that the author of the *Ramcharitmanas*, Tulsidas, admitted in the text to his work being a modified reproduction of the Valmiki version, local exponents of the *Ramayana* made very innovative attempts at either promoting the supremacy of the *Ramcharitmanas* over its parent text, or establishing their commensurability by such claims as Tulsidas was indeed Valmiki reincarnate. Until the late 1960s, due to the uncritical and highly reverential attitudes to the text, to the Bhakti-orientation of Trinidad Hinduism, and to the general inability of the lay audience itself to read the text, cross-referencing between these two versions of the *Ramayana* was fairly unproblematic for the expounders. The audience generally accepted what was presented to them as the actual story of the *Ramcharitmanas*. The fact that, in general allusions, the *Ramcharitmanas* was referred to as 'the *Ramayana*' cemented this perception. It is also quite safe to assume that, barring the pundits, other readers and religious enthusiasts, the majority of the population may not have been aware of the existence of other versions of the Rama story. Thus, similar to the situation in North India, few could describe how Tulsidas' version of the Rama story differed from Valmiki's (Lutgendorf 1991, 12).

In addition to various versions of the *Ramayana*, there were also a number of different editions of the *Ramcharitmanas*. As with the oral and wider *Ramayana* tradition, the inherent problem in the variety of editions was the common practice by the editors to alter the text (through additions, omissions, variations and emphasis) usually with some socio-religious or socio-political agenda in mind. Of course, unless one had other editions with which comparisons could be made, there was almost no way of differentiating between Tulsidas's words and those of an editor. Sometimes, however, the editor himself acknowledged his personal input into the text. One can label such editions as 'retellings of a retelling' that further reified the *Ramayana*'s function as a metaphor of history and society, but in this case of India where the editions were produced.

By the late 1970s, the changing face of Hinduism and the increasing appearance of other versions mandated a reconsidering of the approach to the many variations of the Rama story. It was, by then, general knowledge that the *Ramcharitmanas* was but one of numerous versions of the former, and also that the *Valmiki Ramayana* was the first written version. Realising that the various versions of the Rama story could no longer be ignored, textual exponents began including elements of the latter in their discourses. However, aspects that posed any possibility of a threat to the supremacy and major prescriptions of the *Ramcharitmanas* were either omitted or reworked. This attitude was evident in explanations such as the following:

> We need to be careful when making that kind of reference because many episodes that are present in *Valmiki Ramayana* are not in Tulsi's *Ramayana*, and some in Tulsi that are not present in Valmiki, certain details. We need to be careful not to confuse our people as to what really happened. Both are correct. It's just that Tulsi has written the details as he perceived. He has chosen the facets of life of Shri Ram that meant greatest to him.[9]

Apart from versions of the Rama story, other texts were involved in this practice of intertextuality. The recurrence of the same characters and similar events in different texts was the major source of this interconnectedness. For example, Hanuman who appeared in the *Ramayana* as Rama's dutiful servant was also present in the *Mahabharata* as the brother of Bhima, one of the major characters in the epic. Rama's willingness to waive his rights to kingship (in the *Ramayana*) was contrasted to the war resulting from the desire for political supremacy in the *Mahabharata*, and supplemented by verses from the *Bhagvadgita* on the notion of duty. The growing demand for more intellectual, philosophical and rational approaches to and analyses of religion to supplement and sometimes even subsume the previous focus on faith and devotion, was a primary underlying motive for this practice of intertextuality, especially since the late 1980s. The ability to draw references across the range of texts substantially enhanced the expounder's degree of competence and knowledge. This, in turn, augmented his appeal as a figure of religious authority. According to one very popular pundit and interpreter of Hindu religious texts:

> ...wherever I go to read I always do cross comparisons between all the *Ramayanas*. I also try to trace the *Ramayana* back into the *Bhagvadgita* because I feel that in preaching Hinduism and in teaching the *Ramayana*, we must now lift the intellectual ability of the individual by now introducing *slokas* [verses] of the *Gita* into the *Ramayana*, with reference to the *Ramayana*.[10]

The need to cater to the Hindu society's growing demand for intellectual, philosophical and logical approaches to and analyses of religion to supplement and sometimes even subsume the previous focus on devotion and blind faith was a primary underlying motive for this practice of intertextuality, especially since the late 1980s. Popular opinion also supported that this practice often enhanced the perceived level of the reader's competence and knowledge of the range of Hindu scriptures and hence, substantially validated his discourses.

Inadvertently, the rise of a marked number of sub-sects during the 1990s generated diverse attitudes to the issue of cross-referencing and intertextuality. A leading figure of the Society Working for the Advancement of Hindu Aspirations (SWAHA) for instance, saw what he referred to as cobwebbing of the scriptures as more applicable and beneficial to Trinidad Hinduism. Arguing that the multiplicity of texts was potentially confusing, he proposed the retention of the *Ramayana* as a doctrine on behaviour, the *Bhagavadgita* as a source of philosophy, and the *Bhagvadpurana* to support both.[11] Incorporated in Trinidad and Tobago in 1993, SWAHA is embedded in the *Shankaraacharya* tradition in India, which is an extremely orthodox thread of Sanatan Dharma based on the Advaita Vedanta (the sixth branch of Indian philosophy). Another organisation, the Chinmaya Mission, initiated in Trinidad by Swami Chinmayananda during the 1960s but revived and formally established in 1997 by one Brahmachari Prem Chaitanya, has as its focus metaphysics or Vedanta. While admittedly using the *Ramcharitmanas* to promote Vedantic philosophy, and supporting Rama's divine status and the 'encyclopedic' character of the text (slipping in that 'Tulsidas intended it also'), the Mission proposed that focus on the *Bhagavadgita* and the *Upanishads* would better meet the requirements of the new intellectual and philosophical approach to Hinduism. In fact one of the major objectives of this organisation is the revival of these texts in Trinidad and Tobago.[12]

Members of the Satya Sai Baba Organization in Trinidad (rejuvenated in 1983) adhere to the teachings of non-discrimination, love, peace and social service promoted by their guru in India, Satya Sai Baba. They claim to hold the *Ramayana* and all other religious texts in the same reverence as the 'orthodox' Hindus, and work the teachings of the texts into their discourses 'on Baba's advice' explaining that 'Baba is the same said Rama...he says that devotees must go out and propagate the Ramayana.'[13] The Brahma Kumari Raja Yoga Center was founded in Trinidad in 1975 during the visit of one Sister Hemlata, a senior member of the organisation in India. With their focus on matters such as the mind, spirit, consciousness, soul and energies, and their interpretation of 'God is light,' followers of this organisation view Rama as just a deity 'parallel to Christ, Buddha and Mohammed.'[14] They consequently 'look at the spiritual aspect and meaning of the *Ramayana*' instead of the 'physical [literal] meaning' and use such examples in their discourses.[15] It is evident that each of these organisations was engaged, in one way or the other, in manipulating Hindu religious texts to meet their respective objectives and orientations. That each acknowledged the primacy, if not divinity, of the *Ramcharitmanas* among Trinidad Hindus evinced both the text's status and the recognition of the benefits to be had from the text's popularity and its socio-religious application. Thus, even though in theory this text may not have been as applicable to their specific orientations, the *Ramcharitmanas'* widespread and deep-seated appeal mandated its inclusion or reworking into the ideologies of almost any religious organisation that hoped to gain a substantial Hindu following in Trinidad. It can be surmised that an absolute denying of the socio-religious validity of the *Ramcharitmanas* was not an option for Trinidad Hinduism.

Physicality

The physical aspects of the texts reflected Hindu socio-religious transformation. Of utmost importance here was the format and language of the texts. Until the 1940s, these texts were available mainly in the Hindi (Devanagiri) script, with very few editions in Sanskrit or the other Indian language spoken in Trinidad, namely Tamil. There were various Hindi publications and editions of the *Ramcharitmanas*, of which the *Shri Goswami Tulsidaskrit Ramayana* edited by Pundit Jwala Prasad was the most widely available.[16] The typical format of a *Ramayana* in Hindi script included verses, each followed by prose renditions. These verses are of six major types: the *chowpai* (four line verse), the *doha* (a couplet), the *chhand* (six line verse), the *sortha* (another type of couplet), the *shloka* (two or four line verse), and the *stuti* (two or four line prayer) – each of which has its own metre and singing style. Other *Ramayana* texts, done in either purely Hindi prose or poetry were also available, but these did not match the popularity of the combined verse/prose compositions.

The introduction of the English language into textual discourses added another dimension to the physicality of the text. While English translations of the *Ramayana* (with or without Hindi accompaniment) appeared as early as the 1940s in Trinidad,[17] it was not until the 1970s that their presence in the field of textual presentation became noticeable. This was due to the population's overall lack of literacy in English, and to the absolute disassociation of English from Hindu religious matters. By the late 1970s, both the textual sphere and the wider Hindu community had fully adopted English as their primary mode of communication. By the 1980s, this facilitated the appearance of texts with English translations in both popular and formal settings, but more so with readers under the age of forty. The most popular format of this type included the Hindi verses followed by corresponding Hindi prose renditions, and accompanied by English translations of the Hindi prose (which, essentially, was a retelling of the Hindi verse). By the 1990s, however, there were versions in which the Hindi prose renditions were omitted. The resulting format of Hindi verses followed by English prose translation was a possible reflection of the status of Hindi in Trinidad as a language that was formally taught and learnt, and where the skills of reading and writing were more readily acquired than those of speaking and understanding. According to established importers of Hindu religious texts, the most popular publications of texts with English translations were those from Gita Press and Motilal Banarsidas Publishers of India.[18]

This interplay between English and Hindi in the textual sphere generated new concerns. Foremost was the insistence of persons generally over 50 years of age that textual presentation should be done in Hindi, the language to which they assigned greater sanctity, affection and cogency. This both prolonged the transitional process and demanded the inclusion of varying levels and forms of the Hindi element. Secondly, due to differences in the syntax and semantics of the languages, the level of correspondence of English translations and explanations of the Hindi script was sometimes problematic. Thus, several readers admitted that some of the nuances of the Hindi language were inevitably lost or manipulated during translation. Nevertheless, since the 1980s, the increased focus on the formal and detailed education of pundits in Hindi, Sanskrit and English, together with a holistic and multidisciplinary approach to textual interpretation, assisted in more fully capturing and extending the Hindi nuances into the English language.

In addition to texts with English translations, there were some that contained renditions in Hindi in the Devanagari script, with transliterations of the Hindi into the Latin script. The fact that the few versions where the Hindi script was totally absent were not at all popular at formal discourses attested to the paradox of the population's ignorance of Hindi and their hesitance to relinquish all ties with it. Also, due to phonological divergences between Hindi and English, the transliteration of the Hindi script into the Latin script often led to faulty diction, with the potential sometimes to alter the entire meaning of a line. While the affective appeal diminished somewhat, the introduction of English into the textual sphere assisted in stemming the constant complaints of the young people of not understanding what the pundit was saying, and in curbing the wave of conversion to Christian evangelical persuasions begun in the 1960s. It also facilitated the presentation of textual matter and Hinduism as a whole in a manner that was more easily understood and easily applicable to the daily lives of individuals. This echoes Indian historian Romila Thapar's view on the impact of the act of translation on narrative:

> ...translation changes the cultural role of the narrative, for it introduces into the play, the culture and world view of the society using the language of the translation and of its ideologies (Thapar 2000, 15).

Not surprising then, a pervasive sense of nostalgia for the 'long time days and ways' continued to evoke scathing ridicule from the older individuals, textual interpreters and otherwise, towards what they label as 'copybook pundits.'[19]

Although during the indenture and early post-indenture period the most popular type of text was the bound work, there were also some loose-leaf versions. They contributed to the sanctification of such paraphernalia associated with the text as the red cloth in which it is wrapped and the wooden frame used to keep the leaves in a position conducive to reading. More than with the *Ramayana*, this loose-leaf form, until the 1980s, was very popular with the *Bhagvadpurana* and many of the other *Puranas* especially at formal readings. The fact that they were physically different from the usually bound books, and had to be separated leaf by leaf during reading without, however, disrupting the flow of the rendition, served to distinguish them from the other 'ordinary' books. That this loose-leaf type of text was part of ancient Indian tradition also contributed to its veneration.

Another physical aspect of the texts that adds considerably to the level of veneration is the presence of illustrations of major characters and scenes, usually on the first few pages of the text. In terms of texture, format and general appearance, these pages were substantially different from the rest of the text, but quite similar to the popular pictures and posters of Hindu deities. Echoing the religious primacy of such illustrations and images in Hinduism, these glossy, highly colourful, often bordered depictions would, until the 1980s, almost always evoke physical displays of obeisance, especially if accompanied by invocatory mantras and rituals. In addition, several of these illustrations in the text were almost exact replicas of some of the popular representations, the most prominent of which is a very regal, enduring depiction of Rama as king, his wife Sita, his brother Lakshmana, with his servant Hanuman sitting in supplication at his feet. By 1990, it was still very much the norm at *satsangs* and *yagnas* to open the text to the page with such illustrations and conduct a number of venerating and invocatory rituals, usually just before the discourse. These included the offering of a seat, flowers, water, food, clothing, incense, money, and the performance of *aarti* (moving consecrated flame circularly around the text). Sometimes, however, the *aarti* was also performed at the end of the discourse.

Making an Icon of the Text

Hindu religious texts function as religious and social doctrine and as the storehouses which canon-formation in the Indian religious traditions draws upon (Dalmia et al. 2001, 4). However, rather than being solely contingent on what is in the text (content), the appeal of a Hindu religious text is also deeply ensconced in what *it is*. From his examination of textual authority in the *Bhagvadpurana*, Martin Christof deduced that religious texts are not necessarily sacred. However, where there is sanctity, this is

> ...discernible in its careful preservation; in the care over its transmission; the dignity of its contents; the way it is recited or used in ritual or healing; and very often by the fact that it is written down in the first place (Chirstof 2001, 62–63).

Thus, notwithstanding the value of the content, the status of cultural icon could be assigned to the text based on the aura surrounding the idea of the text itself. That the *Ramcharitmanas*, *Bhagvadpurana*, *Bhagvadgita*, and other religious texts were assigned a level of sanctity both based on and indicative of their status as custodian and wellspring of the story and teachings of God in Trinidad Hinduism is indisputable. There were, however, several appurtenances of the textual realm which, by association, were infused with the sanctity that surrounded the major Hindu religious texts, and simultaneously contributed to the texts' function as cultural icons. Since the earliest post-indenture years, the wrapping of the religious texts (apart from performing the practical function of protecting them from damage and holding the loose leaves together) acquired definite religious undertones, both in Trinidad and in other countries of the Indian diaspora including South Africa and Mauritius. Specified colours were used for the wrapping: red for the *Ramcharitmanas*, yellow for the *Bhagvadgita* and the *Bhagvadpurana*, and blue for the *Shiva Purana*.

The local Hindu community's perception and treatment of the cloth wrapping simultaneously influenced and mirrored the level of reverence assigned to the texts, and by extension, the Hindu community's changing attitude towards religion in general. Reasons such as 'it is not an ordinary book'[20] and 'supposed to have it wrapped'[21] echoed the pre-1970s' more unchallenging approach to religious matters. Later, the increasing perception of the need to infuse more philosophy and rationality into what could be loosely termed 'modern' Trinidad Hinduism was reflected in the following reasons:

> Red is the colour of life, the colour of strength. Colour scheme in Hinduism is important and all carry special meaning. In Hinduism we surround ourselves with symbolism to remind us that God is around us.[22]

Also,

> there is no great significance. In earlier times red cotton was readily available to the pundits through cloth offerings made to Hanuman. There is no great sanctity in the cloth itself.[23]

The *rehal* or wooden bookstand used either at home or at discourses for the practical function of keeping the text in a position best conducive to reading was, until the 1980s, still not treated as just another bookstand, but was accorded some sense of respect, if not reverence. Until the 1980s also, religious texts were almost always kept at the family shrine or in the less common 'puja room.' This added to the sanctity of the cloth and the *rehal*. The actual way in which the texts were kept in the shrine – wrapped in the cloth, either placed on the open *rehal*, or with the closed *rehal* on top of the wrapped text – created an air of distinction and divine mysteriousness around them. By the 1980s, the increasing modernisation with regards to the structure of houses, the equipping of homes with libraries and bookshelves, and the significantly lower level of reverence assigned to the more available English translated texts, while probably not affecting the overall reverence of what the texts represent, led to a decline in the level of sanctity assigned to these accoutrements of Hindu religious texts.

The reverence surrounding religious texts and discourses was also reflected in the physically elevated position assumed by both text and reader at *yagnas*. The text's position on the substantially elevated *singhasan* (literally, throne, but in the *yagna* setting it refers to the consecrated, elevated area upon which the pundit conducts the readings), deriving from traditional, scriptural and ritual sanction, remained unaffected by the incursion of modern trappings. Until the 1970s, it was the norm at *satsangs* for everyone – readers and audience – to sit on the floor. Hence, although the idea that the text should not be situated in a physically lower position than either audience or reader (which for the latter would have been quite inconvenient) was embedded in the psyche of Hindus, it was not much of an issue. This preoccupation arose with the appearance of chairs and benches at *satsangs* during the 1970s. By the late 1980s, however, a diminishing concern – even among the older persons – with the physical situation of the text was noticeable. The appearance of chairs and benches, coupled with the changing lifestyles and standards of the members of the Hindu community, and the overall more practical approach to English translated texts collectively accounted for this transformation. However, reflective of the paradoxes that seem to characterise Hinduism, there was a predominant unsettling feeling at actually having the text at close proximity to one's feet that seemed to cut across the boundaries of age, level of education or variation in approaches to the text. The emphasis on religious texts, and books in general, as repositories of knowledge, and the popularly held notion (until the 1980s) that 'Saraswatee (the Goddess of knowledge) was in the book' served to enhance the sanctity of Hindu texts, and by extension, deepen the reluctance to touch religious texts (and other books) with one's feet.

The obeisance shown by bowing with clasped hands in the direction of the text was yet another form of textual veneration. This is very pronounced in Sikhism, where the text known as the *Guru Granth Sahib* occupies the role of Guru or teacher. At *yagnas*, one can argue that this veneration was aimed, not exclusively at the text, but at the entire consecrated area. In that physically cordoned off area, the rituals were performed, the *singhasan* with text and reader was situated, the display of images of the various deities was located, and the *shrotas* (those persons taking an active part in the performance of the rituals) who would have ritually purified themselves by appropriate undertakings such as various forms of abstinence, were seated – all of which enhanced the sanctity of that area. Removing one's footwear and the covering of their heads by females were also acts of veneration. At *satsangs*, however, while this bowing of the head may have been directed to the small, sometimes informally consecrated area, the decline in the spiritual aura in several types and settings of *satsangs* by 1990 saw this form of obeisance being observed primarily by older persons. Personal convictions about this religious aura, however, also influenced responses.

Adding significantly to the level of reverence allotted to religious texts were the rituals used in their propitiation, which were similar to those accorded to a deity. These rituals, also an integral dimension of *Ramayana satsangs* in Fiji (Wilson 1979, 89), suggested a condensed version of the puja. In addition, several special bhajans, mantras and invocations, glorifying the presiding text, were sung at both *satsangs* and *yagnas*. The two major compositions included the *Ramayana Aarti* and the *Ramayan Sumiran*. The *Ramayana Aarti* is a song in praise of the benefits obtained from reciting the *Ramayana*, which is sung while the *aarti* is being performed. This ritual, in effect, substantially enhanced the level of veneration of the text. This *aarti* song also confirms that the deities themselves indulged in the recital of the *Ramayana* story. The *Ramayana Sumiran* comprises verses from the invocatory section of the *Ramcharitmanas,* which invoke the graces and blessings of the major deities with respect to the reading of the text.

Almost all of the other major Hindu religious texts were venerated in a similar manner, each with its specific *aarti* song and invocatory verses that lauded either the text or the deity around whom the text is spun. Also, verses taken from the texts themselves, such as the following from the *Ramcharitmanas,* were used for further exaltation:

> *Ramcharitmanas muni Bhavan. Biracheu Shambhu suhaavan paavan.*
> *Tribidh dosh dukh daarid daavan. Kali kuchaali kuli kalush nasaavan.*
> The holy and beautiful *Ramcharitmanas* is the delight of sages; it was conceived by Lord Shiva. It puts down the three kinds of error, sorrow and indigence and uproots all evil practices and impurities of the Kali age.[24]

The veneration of texts was connected with attitudes towards the caste and gender of the readers. While the popular dimension of the *Ramayana* tradition was not greatly underscored by caste considerations, the *yagna* – the formal sphere of textual presentation – was the exclusive domain of Brahmin pundits until the 1970s. However, the 1980s witnessed a substantial growth in the number of non-Brahmins officiating at *yagnas.* The widespread practice of non-Brahmin *Ramayana* readers officiating at the less formal and informal *satsangs,* since the very earliest days of indenture, eventually extended itself into the *yagna* forum with the entrance of the *Ramcharitmanas* into that domain. The increasing leniency towards caste considerations in ritual and religious matters, and the conscious and unconscious drive to rework Hinduism to include the values and nuances of the society and changing times also accounted for this transformation. This was met with mixed and interesting reaction from both the Brahmin and non-Brahmin population. Non-Brahmin religious aspirants and pundits focused on the seemingly anti-caste incidents from the *Ramcharitmanas* and other religious texts to validate their equal right to textual presentation. Many were quite emphatic in denouncing Brahminic attempts at retaining their pretensions to exclusivity in this sphere. Some even referred to the association of caste with the division of labour to argue their point of view, as in the following remark: 'People who preach caste don't practice it.

All pundits' sons are not pundits, but they are doing other people's occupations, due to the 'almighty dollar.'²⁵

Within the Brahmin fold, there were two discernible attitudes towards this issue. Some, obviously considering the indisputable reality of the presence of non-Brahmins in the ritual and textual sphere, and concerned with popular appeal offered views (sometimes grudgingly) such as 'many non-Brahmins are already pundits so you have to accept them, once they fulfil the role properly.'²⁶ However, the more orthodox Brahmins, especially those affiliated with the Sanatan Dharma Maha Sabha vehemently opposed this practice:

> It is not right for everybody to be reading the texts. Your duty must be of a high standard spiritually. You must be born into a certain caste to read the texts. And that caste that you born in, those are the ideas and standards that you have to live; like the Brahmins are meant to do that. Ramayanists could read if you want something home but not on the *singhasan*. That is only for people who come from the Brahmin lineage. But they all mix it up now.²⁷

From as early as the 1920s, there were female *Ramayana* readers in Trinidad. One such young woman who was admired by her fellow villagers for her '...beautiful chanting of the *Ramayana* and other Hindu scriptures...' even caught the attention of the Presbyterian missionaries. She was eventually converted to Presbyterianism (Samaroo 2002). The reaction towards female *Ramayana* readers was ambivalent. The intrinsic love and affinity for the *Ramayana* among ordinary people served to suppress outright condemnation of female readers. However, the patriarchal norms and attitudes of the pre-1970s period, enhanced by the many ritual prescriptions that served to socially subjugate women, restricted textual presentation by women both in terms of frequency and scope. Both the idea and the reality of female presence on the sacred *singhasan* evoked interesting responses which reflected the varying trends of thought within Trinidad Hinduism. The prevalent attitude of the priesthood, both Brahmin and non-Brahmin, was one of grudging resignation to women 'preaching Hinduism' and even reading the *Ramayana*, but only in informal settings, and definitely not on the *singhasan* at *yagnas*. Their arguments were largely founded upon scriptural prescriptions, and the impurities associated with the menstrual cycle. This, however, was tempered with the reality of female socio-economic and intellectual advancement, and the enhanced religious position and role of women especially within many of the rapidly increasing Hindu groups. Attempts to simultaneously retain male and Brahminic monopoly in this sphere, and to accommodate the mindset of the contemporary Hindu woman and society at large, elicited responses such as the following to the issue:

> When we look at our scriptural texts we are hard-pressed to find evidence of women holding priestly positions. Women have been assigned a very honourable position, a very high position in that they are the *Devi*, the very Goddess in our homes....It is not to say that women are debarred from elevating themselves spiritually.[28]

It is evident that Hindu women were able either to break out of or to work around the bonds of scriptural and traditional prescriptions in almost all other aspects of their lives. However, notwithstanding the more liberal approach to women of some new Hindu organisations such as the Hindu Prachar Kendra and the Trinidad Academy of Hinduism, popular opinion, until the 1990s, revealed reservations towards (though not as deep-seated or as endemic) or outright unacceptance of women acting as ritual and textual specialists. Unacceptance was more marked especially in the *yagna* setting. This echoed both a characteristic reluctance in the religious sphere to effect such a monumental transformation and the still prevailing though often denied patriarchal tendencies of the Hindu community. Nevertheless, the 1990s witnessed the first yagnas conducted by females, organised by the Hindu Prachar Kendra.

The major argument against female involvement in certain rituals and formal textual interpretation was the impurity assigned to menstruation. Indeed, one wonders, given the sometimes erratic nature of the cycle, how feasible it was to schedule the discourses around this period of impurity. One can surmise that the earlier pundit Deokie Devi, given the fastidious adherence to this taboo at that time, would have had to resort to having another pundit perform her religious duties, or, have them rescheduled. Interestingly enough, sometimes a terse yet pregnant excuse of 'I not fit to read today' would convey all.[29] Female readers, since the 1980s however, displayed a relatively more lax attitude to this issue. While most continued to abstain from readings during their menstrual period, some admitted to having participated in the reading, but refraining from physically touching the text. This usually occurred when the individual was at odds with the stigma of impurity allotted to menstruation, or, paradoxically, out of sheer embarrassment of having to discuss such a personal matter with the usually elderly and respected male leader of the group. A few, justifying their pragmatic approach to the issue with the notion that the menstrual cycle is 'God's work,' participated in all aspects of the discourse.

The issue of meat eating also revealed the attitudes towards Hindu religious texts. This was an aspect that seemed to be distinct to the diasporic situation, since in India, even in the popular tradition, there was a strict adherence to the dietary restrictions of a ritual specialist. In Trinidad, this issue was embedded in the fact that most of the popular *Ramayana* readers, far from living an ascetic life or from being fully dedicated to religious and spiritual matters (as is the norm in India), treated this skill as just one of several other dimensions of their life. They continued to operate as spouse, parent, child, breadwinner, and to engage in activities related to those roles. However, since the time of readings was generally prearranged, it was fairly simple to negotiate between one's diet and religious activities. Problems arose, however, when readings were required in conjunction with unscheduled observances, such as those related to the death of an individual. In the pre-1960s period, considering that, primarily due to economic constraints, meat was a special food reserved for weekends or special occasions, the dilemma rarely presented itself.[30] When the situation did arise, the norm would be for the readers whose services were sought to refer the family of the deceased to another reader, or if absolutely no substitute could be found, to take a bath before engaging in the reading.[31] It was however, not unusual for the chief reader in a group or a prominent solo reader to have given up the consumption of meat altogether. This abstinence persisted through the 1980s, indicating the high level of reverence still assigned to the text. Paradoxically, while not the norm, it was not uncommon for the musicians to attend the impromptu death-related *Ramayana satsangs* in spite of having recently consumed both meat and alcohol. Most of these venerating practices are universal to the *Ramayana* traditions in many parts of North India (Lutgendorf 1991, 178–84) and the Indian diaspora.

'De-ritualising' of the Text

Since the 1970s, the process of secularisation served to divorce Hindu religious texts from some of their magic, mystery and general iconic appeal. This, however, was not so much a secularisation of the texts themselves, but referred more so to both the diversity in the setting in which they were increasingly being situated along with changes in their physical attributes. Throughout the pre-1970s period, Hindu religious texts enjoyed a relatively high level of deification. Since then they have gradually moved out of the boundaries of the *satsang* and the *yagna* into the multi-dimensional world of the media. This was collectively due to the prominence of English translations of Hindu religious texts by the late 1970s, the multiplicity in versions, publications, sizes, colours, print and general appearance (generated in part by the increase in importers and retailers of Indian goods), together with a notably more liberal attitude towards a mixing of the sacred and the secular. By the 1990s then, the text was as commonplace (as any other textbook) on a bookshelf in a shop or family library as in the family shrine. Television productions of the *Ramayana*, *Mahabharata* and other Hindu epics, along with the multitude of websites on Hindu religious texts further pushed the latter out of the boundaries of the sacred into the secular sphere. The traditional, large, cloth-wrapped version, however, still managed to elicit quite a substantial level of reverence.

The mode of invitation to textual discourses, especially to *yagnas*, also revealed the influences of modernisation on Trinidad Hinduism. Until the late 1960s, an oral invitation accompanied by the ritual handing over of a few grains of yellow rice by a person specially appointed by the host (usually the village *nau* or *nauni*) was the primary mode of invitation.[32] During the 1970s, the traditional *nau/ nauni* began taking a few printed flyers along; these were, however, secondary to the traditional elements of the invitation. By the 1980s, however, this traditional method gave way to the increasing use of printed invitations in the form of flyers indiscriminately strewn out of passing vehicles, equipped with loudspeakers blaring out either a pre-recorded or live invitation to the *yagna*, and interspersed with suitable music. While this form of invitation both reflected and met the evolving requirements and tastes of the Hindu population, it failed to capture the affectivity and sanctity that enshrouded the personal invitation, and more so, the giving of the yellow rice as a symbol of invitation. Interpretations of the significance of this practice included:

> Rice is sacred in Hinduism, so too the colour yellow. It is an invitation for you to attend an event with a religious component. It emphasizes the religious aspect of it.[33]

Also, 'the rice helped to remember the invitation. To give rice is to give life. It is the symbol of giving food, giving grains; it is the preservation of life.'[34]

It is to be surmised that it was more difficult to ignore a traditional invitation than one denuded of its ritual elements. Interestingly enough, by the 1990s, the yellow rice had made a reappearance stuck onto invitation cards to *yagnas* and to weddings. The fact that rice was always an integral part of Hindu pujas, where it was blessed and given to the host by the pundit as a symbol of prosperity, underscored its reappearance. The various degrees and constructs of rejuvenation that seemed to be facing the Hindu community by the 1990s, together with some kind of latent nostalgia partly accounted for the increasingly apparent tendency to revive certain traditional religious practices that had been disappearing since the 1970s. The physical appearance and format of invitation cards and flyers also reflected transformations within the Hindu community. It must be noted that the ability of most of the more modern forms of invitation to capture both the sanctity and inherently Hindu issues surrounding the event was quite circumscribed.

Since the earliest attempts at reconstruction of community, the Hindu community has held the text of the *Ramayana* as a primary sanctioning element in religious and social matters. Thus, despite the pre-1970s dominance of the *Bhagvatpurana* in the formal *yagna* setting, among Hindus the *Ramayana* functioned in a similar manner as the Bible among Christians and the Quran among Muslims with respect to the taking of oaths. This occurred quite frequently at panchayat mediations in the village and even in the domestic sphere during more serious family disputes that occasioned the act of swearing. Before the 1950s, the *Ramayana* (and very rarely the *Hanuman Chalisa*) shared this sanctioning function with water (imbued with the holiness ascribed to the water of the Ganges River in India) and the *lota,* the brass vessel containing the water. The eventual transplantation of this practice of swearing by the 'Ganges water' to swearing on the *lota* alone was explained by statements such as '...when they hold the *lota* it means that they swear by Ganga. Ganga does not only mean water, Ganga also means purity.'[35]

In 1986, the *Bhagvadgita* was used at the swearing in of the first Hindu Minister of Parliament. The association with oath taking further enhanced the perception of Hindu religious texts – in this case, the *Bhagvadgita* – as the 'Hindu Bible.' Ironically enough, the *Bhagvadgita* never performed such a sanctioning role within the Hindu community. Many reasons have been proffered on the eclipsing of the *Ramayana* by the *Bhagvadgita* in this sphere. Firstly, the *Bhagvadgita* is physically a much smaller text than the *Ramayana,* and hence, was much more convenient for the purposes of official oath taking. Secondly, the installation of the *Bhagvadgita* in India itself as the 'official text' of Hindus could have influenced this decision in Trinidad. Thirdly, since the late 1980s there was a somewhat intense focus on the *Bhagvadgita* by several of the more recent sub-sects of Hinduism, and even by the traditional propagators of Sanatan Dharma. Fourthly, this text's accentuation of philosophical ideas that could be applied to and understood by the wider non-Hindu population, de-emphasising the rituals for which Hinduism had been the butt of widespread ridicule, could have led to the perception that it was better suited for official functions. This 'legalisation' of a religious text also contributed to its de-ritualisation. The normal taboos associated with the physical handling of the texts such as meat eating and menstruation could not be observed in such contexts. Also, while perceived of as a holy text, it would most probably be stored on a bookshelf, devoid of its venerating accoutrements and practices.

'Christianising' of the Text

The Indian community's extended and intricate contact with Christian elements has impacted significantly on almost all aspects of life. Due to deep-seated ideological and operational differences, various conflicts comprised a fundamental aspect of this relationship, especially in the sphere of religion. These were most evident in the textual realm. The term 'holy' is defined as '...dedicated to god or a religious purpose; or, morally and spiritually excellent and to be revered' (Pearsall 1999, 678). Though in essence quite applicable to Hinduism, Western and Semitic perceptions and interpretations of both the notion of holy and of religion had inevitably been (mis) placed in relation to Hindu texts. This erroneous conception was further cemented by the notion of the *Ramayana*, and sometimes, the *Bhagvadgita*, (held both by Hindus and non-Hindus) as being the 'Hindu Bible' from as early as the 1930s and possibly even before. That Trinidadian Hindus themselves promoted such an analogy echoed several religious trends within the community. In a report in the *Port-of-Spain Gazette* April 8, 1937, a 'Hindoo hermit' was said to have 'learned about his religion from the Hindoo Bible, the *Ramayan* and truly believes it.'

That Hindu religious texts have always been considered sacred is unarguable. Before contact with Christian elements, however, this sacredness was defined, measured and manifested in a totally Hindu sense of the word. So that, this notion of the *Ramayana* as the 'Hindu Bible,' rather than a new assignment enhancing the prestige of the text, just added a further gloss of sacredness as the Bible to a text that had been established, centuries before, as a religious and social authority. The implausibility of such a parallel was based on several factors and on innate differences between the Semitic and Indian traditions. Firstly, it reflected the general absorptive capacity of the religion (Hinduism), especially operative when faced with potent opposing forces. Secondly, there is the debatable idea that Hindus in Trinidad might have been, subliminally, considerably Christianised in terms of both their systems and values. Lending credence to this notion were the Hindu observance of 'Sunday services,' the relegating of Hindu weddings and other religious observances to the weekend in order to conform to an essentially Christian-oriented calendar, and the perception of the *Dharmachaarya*[36] as the 'Hindu Archbishop,' all of which echoed Christian systems and principles. Thirdly, such infiltration of Christian ideas could be seen as a response to the criticism heaped unto Hindu social and religious beliefs and practices by non-Hindu members of the larger population. In his examination of Hinduism in Fiji, John Kelly identified two additional possible effects of this influence of Christianity on Hinduism. Firstly, the dialogic influence of the Christian missions and schools had a notable impact on the institutions of the Arya Samaj movement, which eventually filtered into the larger Hindu community. Secondly, it was also quite possible that the structural pressure generated by the Christian Holy Book led to the Hindu need to somehow formally establish a 'Holy Book of truth and punishment powers' (Kelly 2001, 329–51). Both these factors were also evident in Trinidad Hinduism during the 1930s and the 1940s. The close association in Trinidad between Presbyterianism and Indians also accounted for the inevitability of such pressures and influences.

An examination of Hindu texts and their divergences from the Christian notion of holy text would be incomplete without some insight into the perception of 'the Word' in India. Firstly, scripture in India is not necessarily written. While there is verbal material in highly crystallised form (quite specific and even written), this operates alongside other manifestations of the scriptures that are '...dynamic and open-ended rather than bounded and reified.'[37] Secondly, primacy is placed upon the experiential factor so that '...a holy verbal event is first and foremost an oral or aural experience, the holiness of holy words not being a function of their intelligibility.'[38] Thirdly,

> ...sanctity often appears to be inversely related to comprehensibility: Hindus have affirmed that the holiness of the Word is intrinsic, and that one participates in, not by understanding, but by hearing and reciting it.[39]

This is demonstrated in the emphasis placed on the recitation of verses from religious texts as well as mantras since, according to Hindu thought, active recitation of – rather than just listening to the praises and word of God – is considered a major pathway to salvation. This notion would inevitably enhance the practice of textual veneration. In his study of scripture in India, Thomas B. Coburn further elaborated on the central dynamics of the Hindu treatment of the Word:

> The dynamic revolves around the tension between (1) the desire to preserve and recite, and not necessarily to understand, a verbally fixed (usually oral) text, and (2) the desire to understand, both for oneself and for others, religious ideas that are presented in verbal form.[40]

In the Semitic tradition, the expression 'Word of God' can be understood on three levels, each of which can also be applied to the Hindu textual tradition. Firstly, there is the Word of God 'as an originating event: it is the very act of God's speaking by which God communicates with humans' (Muslim-Christian Research Group 1989, 16). The *Bhagvadgita*, wherein Krishna revealed his divine form and expounds his (God's) treatise on Dharma (duty and proper conduct) echoes this first interpretation of 'the Word.' One can thus argue that the seemingly global drive to promote the *Bhagvadgita* as the major Hindu doctrine was embedded in this analogy. Secondly, there is the Word of God 'as an occurrence: this is the advent of the Word of God through the mediation of history and prophetic witness' (Ibid. 1989, 6). In Hinduism, it is claimed that the teachings of the Vedas were imparted to the saints and sages through divine insight, and that the story of the *Ramayana* was 'revealed' to its original author, Valmiki, in a similar process. Thirdly, there is the Word of God 'as scripture' (Ibid. 1989, 16) which, in itself, extends to the Hindu tradition. The fact that analogies can be therein identified suggests that the fundamental difference between both traditions must have been situated more in tradition and selective projection (rather than in such attempts at objective analysis) namely, the Hindu focus on the dynamic experiential and affective connotations of 'the Word' as opposed to the Semitic tradition's emphasis on 'the Word' as 'sanctified law' since it is viewed as the (revealed) words of God. This would, consequently, lay the foundation for the divergences in the respective traditions' perceptions of Holy Text.

This oral dimension of 'the Word' within the Hindu textual tradition in Trinidad entailed two aspects: the first directly relating to the textual material, and the other, detailing the various time-resistant forms such as songs, dance, poetry, drama, and allegory. Within the general illiteracy that characterised the early post-indenture period, religious scripture, especially the *Ramayana*, abiding by the smriti tradition (developed, expounded by men, and preserved and transmitted through memory), both fed on and reinforced an intimate connection with orality. Long-standing tradition bearers and pundits, until the 1950s, both significantly depended upon and exulted in their ability to memorise and recite verses and, sometimes, entire passages from the texts. The opportunity to show off one's expertise in the area would be readily seized at *yagnas*, *satsangs*, pujas, and weddings, by both laymen and pundits alike. Rather than a conscious attempt at memorising the verses, such 'recitation' could better be characterised as '...slow, systematic, storytelling recitation, interspersed with prose explanations, elaborations, and homely illustrations of spiritual points.' This kind of systematic recitation and exposition is known as *katha* (Lutgendorf 1991, 115).

In addition, Tulsidas' constant reinforcing of the active, performative, oral dimension of the *Ramcharitmanas* as a *katha* or a 'telling,' and his encouragement to listeners to become future tellers of the *katha*, thereby continuing the chain of transmission, partially accounted for and enhanced the oral dimension of the written word. This was apparent in verses such as the following:

> *Man kaamnaa siddhi nar paavaa. Je yaha katha kapat taji gaavaa.*
> *Kahahi sunahi anumodan karahee. Te gopad iva bhavnidhi tarahee.*
> Men who sing this story in a guileless spirit attain the object of their soul's desire. Nay, they who tell it, listen to it, and even approve of its recitation cross the ocean of mundane existence as they would a cow's hoof print.[41]

That entire discourses were sometimes swayed by memory-based (sometimes heated) arguments, added considerably to the interpretive capacity of the textual tradition. Since the late 1960s, this committing to memory of verses from the holy scriptures occurred in a comparably limited capacity. The Hindu society's own emphasis of the written over the oral relegated memorising to more of an ideal – and that too, primarily among the older pundits and *Ramayana* readers, rather than an element of practical reality. One can surmise then that, based on the paradox of the fundamental divergences between the Hindu and Christian concepts of 'holy text' and the prominence of the transference of the Christian conception unto the Hindu conception, the *Ramayana* (and later on, the *Bhagvadgita*) more aptly emerged as a sort of quasi Bible rather than a 'Hindu Bible.' That is to say, these texts, while seemingly functioning in a manner parallel to the Bible, possessed their own distinctly Hindu operational dictates and aspects from which, as long as they were situated in the Hindu realm, they could not of course be fully divested.

Text and Purpose

The actual occasions for presentation of religious texts have provided some level of elucidation on what the Hindu community held as important enough to warrant association with the divine, and also on some aspects of its evolving social and religious lifestyle. They also mirrored the changing boundaries and relationship between the sacred and the secular. Since the earliest days of indenture, *satsangs* were an important aspect of both the religious and social life of Hindus. These weekly or fortnightly readings hosted in rotational fashion among different families persisted in the villages during the early post-indenture period. The Presbyterian missionary K.G. Grant testified to the popularity of such *satsangs*, noting that '...snatches or *slokas* from this great epic (the *Ramayana*) are often heard in song, accompanied by cymbals and drums, when the days work is over...' (Grant 1923, 71). By the 1930s, the substantial rise in the number of temples and *kutiyas* (Prorok 1988) provided another setting for such communal readings, both as an extension of the existent weekly or fortnightly system, and by hosting the very popular monthly communal 'full moon *katha*' (puja performed on the full moon day of each month). Such readings also formed an integral part of the annual 'ritual complex' (Vertovec 1992, 115) of pujas extending from Friday through Sunday, and performed in almost every Hindu household. That the puja held on Saturday was dedicated to Hanuman, a major character in the *Ramayana*, also accounted for the inclusion of readings from that text on the Saturday night.

The death of an individual also occasioned readings and chanting from the texts. Popular and pertinent verses from the *Ramcharitmanas* were chanted by members of the funerary procession on the way to the cemetery, and readings were conducted by laymen for between ten to 14 days afterwards, and at the six month or one-year death anniversary. These all provided a measure of spiritual and emotional solace for the bereaved family. Also, reference to, or sometimes, entire discourses from the *Garud Purana* (Hindu text pertaining to death) had always been an integral aspect of such death-related readings. Since the 1980s, pertinent verses from the *Bhagvadgita* were also worked into this context. Finally, the fulfillment of promises made in the quid-pro-quo style characteristic of divine-human relations especially regarding events such as a fruitful agricultural season, a child's outstanding academic achievement, recovery from a serious illness, and travel overseas occasioned both *satsangs* and, less frequently, *yagnas*.

By the 1970s, economic advancement and the increasing influence of non-Hindu ideas both increased the frequency and altered the spectrum of occasions for textual discourses. Added to pujas, promises and death, the emphasis on birthdays, wedding anniversaries and personal achievements and successes variably provided increasing forums for *satsangs* and *yagnas*. Individuals were also more economically equipped to simply fulfill a desire to host both *satsangs* and *yagnas*; the latter unavoidably leading to a simultaneous decline of the *panchoutie yagna*. Reflecting Hinduism's infusion of the religious into practically all other dimensions of life, textual discourses, in this sense, trod on the heels of the Hindu community's social, economic and political ascension and expansion – both within the community and in relation to the wider society.[42]

Dissemination

The methods of transfer of knowledge of the texts, especially of the *Ramayana*, have been considerably conditioned by the socio-economic conditions of the Hindu community. Before the 1970s, the *pathshala*, usually located in the village *kutiyas* or temples and the principal avenue for the dissemination of Hindi and scriptural knowledge, contributed enormously to both the formal and popular aspects of the textual sphere. Newspaper sources since the late 1920s provided ample evidence of the presence of such institutions in areas occupied by Indians. The popular situation was one where both Brahmin and non-Brahmin young boys and girls were tutored indiscriminately by village elders, a sadhu or (time permitting), a pundit in Hindi. This followed a very structured system that commenced with the Hindi alphabet and culminated in the reading of the texts such as the various *chalisas* and the *Ramcharitmanas*. At that point the cleavage between the formal and popular traditions took root. While the non-Brahmins continued using the *kutiya* as a base and forum for their weekly or bi-weekly discourses, the Brahmins usually enhanced this knowledge with further formal education on rites, rituals, texts, philosophy and the trade of *punditai* (Hindu priesthood) under the astute guidance of their fathers (themselves usually pundits) and gurus.[43]

In terms of operation, function and physical setting, the *pathshala* paralleled the *baithkas* in Mauritius, which formed the nucleus of religious life during the indenture and early post-indenture periods (Boodhoo 1999, 84–87). Conversely, in the Mauritius Hindu tradition, many persons took to learning Hindi in order to be able to read the *Ramayana*. According to an article by Dr L.P. Ramyead in the *Sunday Guardian* on October 14, 1990, there, the popularity of the *Ramcharitmanas* created

> ...a new class concept as distinct from the caste concept...a class of Ramayanis...who had become sanskritised....They were graduates not of London or Delhi, but graduated as it were of the University of Tulsidas, much looked to for their Ramayana learning, regardless of their status in other matters.

The *Ramayana* was in fact the basis of non-formal education in Mauritius, so much so that the slogan '*Ram gatti dehu sumati*' (the path of Ram leads to wisdom) became the motto of all Hindi schools (Boodhoo 1999, 26). The *Port-of-Spain Gazette* on March 20, 1938 confirms that in the 1938 celebrations of the birth of Rama *(Rama Naumi)* the Sanatan Dharma Board of Control (in Trinidad) organised competitions in *Ramayana* chanting, and *Ramayana*-related poetry, bhajan singing, dialogues and essay writing, which further evinced the prominent status of the *Ramayana* and religion in the Hindu notion of education.

The establishment of Hindu primary and secondary schools by the Sanatan Dharma Maha Sabha and other Hindu organisations from the 1950s fulfilled the need to include religion and the *Ramayana* into the formal education system. Amidst the infusion of Hinduism into the daily school life at all SDMS schools, the primary schools' *Baal Vikaas* festival (a festival/competition showcasing children's skills and knowledge in various aspects of Hindu culture) initiated in 1986, added to the *Ramayana* tradition with both its *Ramayana* studies quiz and its *Ramayana* singing competition. This novel introduction of a dimension of the *Ramayana* tradition into the Hindu primary school system proved quite effective in creating an early awareness of and affinity for the tradition in the younger members of the Hindu and sometimes, non-Hindu community. Also, by the 1970s, the rise of Indian cultural and educational institutions in Trinidad provided more formal avenues for learning Hindi, a prerequisite of textual interpretation.

Textual Presentation

Knowledge of the social, physical, emotional, economic and even political disposition of the respective audience is a crucial component in the presentation of the religious texts. Such insight is compulsory both in the formal and popular spheres with regard to such matters as style, focus, topic, context, language and level of reverence. Consequently, the focus of textual interpretation and presentation is a definite indicator of socio-religious change in Trinidad Hinduism. During the first half of the twentieth century, Hindu attitude toward religion was marked by an overall unchallenging and almost fatalistic acceptance of religious texts, authority figures and prescriptions. The rare instances of serious interrogation of matters pertaining to religion would almost certainly be quelled and satisfied by textual quotation or a reference to time-honored traditions, or by the actions and teachings of religious figures. All of the aforementioned factors influenced the style and content of textual presentation.

Until the 1980s there was a marked emphasis on the narrative content of texts, that '...meant everything to our elderly mothers and fathers.'⁴⁴ Despite the popular, though questionable view of the earlier narrative style being just story-telling, this traditional approach functioned as a vehicle for both moral and spiritual teachings, and emotional and psychological solace. According to an elderly pundit who still adhered to this style,

> ...you follow the story. Yet every line is a lesson, so it is not a story then....You used to give a little *itihas* (story), you used to make a little parable, a joke...you have to be an experienced person to fit in all of that.⁴⁵

Indeed, verses such as '*Raam te adhika Raam kar daasaa* (Greater than Rama is Rama's servant)'⁴⁶ cemented the supremacy of the Bhakti approach to text and religion as a whole. Philip Lutgendorf identified this as a major factor in the rise and prominence of Hanuman worship in India also (Lutgendorf 1997, 311). This deity's inextricable connection to the *Ramayana* is also evident in Guadeloupe, where the *Ramayana* tradition (and Brahmanic Hinduism) is largely subsumed by elements of the Little Tradition namely, worship of the Mother Goddess in folk manifestations. Hanuman's primary function as guardian of the temple of the goddess Kali is reminiscent of his role as 'captain and standard-bearer of Rama's army...' (Singaravelou 1976, 45).

From the 1950s, social, economic and religious transformations generated a gradual amelioration in the status of Hindus, and consequently, created a need for more than just the story and devotional aspects of the text. Hence, by the late 1970s, there was a gradual yet accelerated move away from the predominantly narrative mode to one that simultaneously and variously reflected the rise of Hindu philosophical probings, a decline in subscription to superstitions, taboos and certain traditional practices, and an overall more practical and analytical approach to religion. In addition, the spate of conversion which plagued the Hindu community during the late 1960s and 1970s served as a catalyst for what was described by Klass as a period of 'revitalisation' in Trinidad Hinduism (Klass 1991). One pundit had the following to say of the issue:

> Then due to conversion we saw the need to let people know what the Ramayana means, how they relate it to their everyday life....Now there is need to explain what is being done. People, especially the youths, need reason.[47]

Thus, by the 1990s, the traditional narrative style was being either infused with or sometimes superseded by a focus on the philosophy inherent in the text, and connected to contemporary social operatives and issues. Interpretations such as the following published in the *Savera Magazine* on June 9, 1996 emerged:

> Looking at the *Ramayana* from a broad philosophical perspective, we see that the city of Ayodhya represents the human body. The manifestation of Sri Ram in Ayodhya represents the *Atma* trapped in the body. The story of Sri Ram represents the unfolding of the *Atma*, amidst all the trials and tribulations, disappointments and frustrations of life.

The presentation skills of expounders of the texts have always impacted on the appeal and popularity of Hindu religious texts (though not necessarily on the level of reverence allotted to this aspect of Trinidad Hinduism). In as much as they were contingent upon the contemporary conditions, preferences and needs of the Hindu community, such techniques varied throughout the twentieth century. Even during the pre-1960s' extremely reverential attitude towards religious matters which left little need for conscious efforts at making the proceedings appealing, many factors were taken into account by those expounding the texts. One popular pundit who had conducted *yagnas* from 1945 confirmed his application of certain tactics.

> You look at the people...the type of people (in the village), their temperament, their taste, their ways and habits. I read to suit your village....If I go to Port-of-Spain, the people have a different understanding, so I need to suit them now....Things that I know will be too difficult for you, I wouldn't apply it right away, will do it gradually....That is where you as a pundit have to study human psychology for at least three years, how to deal with people when you meet them; the method of approach.[48]

Popular Ramayana readers also attested to this importance of analyzing the audience: 'As a reader, the moment you sit down you must assess that crowd, and if you can't do that then don't sit down there, you will make a fool of yourself.'[49] This particular reader's strategy also involved singling out the most socially or intellectually prominent individual in the audience and procuring his approval on what was being presented, either verbally or by the use of eye contact. Lutgendorf analysed such techniques as both reflective of 'the interactive milieu essential to good performance in the Indian context and...a reminder of the archaic sense of *katha* as "conversation."' (Lutgendorf 1991, 189).

While almost all dimensions of the textual tradition in Trinidad succumbed to considerable variation, elements of the earlier approach were still noticeable, albeit with varying degrees of modification, augmentation or dissipation. Indeed, one can safely say that, since the 1980s, textual interpretation and presentation evolved into an institution that variously borrowed from the schools of art, science and psychology. The community was studied beforehand, goals were set, and this largely determined the choice of content (which was prepared in advance in great detail). This was accompanied by an assessment of the nature and composition of the audience (with age and the perceived intellectual level being the major underlying factors). This consequently determined how the content was pitched, the level of language used and the balance or bias between the narrative and philosophical modes. Generally, and quite reflective of the earlier period, a congregation predominated by persons over 50 years of age entailed an emphasis on the story of the *Ramayana* with simple references to mundane occurrences and minimal emphasis on the philosophical and potentially contentious aspects of the content. References were made to the more popular verses of the text with which members of the audience were able to identify. Verses from the text were sung in the more traditional melody reminiscent of earlier decades, and evoking memories of the solace gained from these verses in the early days of toil and hardship. One pundit acknowledged that he '...may not be able to meet the criteria of the old time pundits that make them happy, but [has] learnt to deal with it in a different way.'[50]

A predominance of younger individuals in the gathering consequently mandated an inversion of the foregoing. The commonality of mixed audiences, moreover, demanded an admixture of the narrative and the thematic as the most popular contemporary approach to textual presentation. One pundit who frequently officiated at *yagnas* identified four types of audiences: those who want to sing, those who want to hear the story, those who want Bhakti (devotion) and those who want *gyaan* (knowledge). His discourses were thus formulated to accommodate all four types. A typical session comprised bhajan singing, a period of narrative, an emphasis on love and devotion to God, and a bit of related *Bhagvadgita* philosophy, all expertly tied together at the end of the discourse. In this resulting more holistic approach '...dramatics, body language, speech, everything is compacted in that so you cater to the entire congregation.'[51]

Textual (Re)Interpretations

The impression of interpolations and (re)interpretations has dogged Hindu religious literature from the very earliest times since they sanction, respectively, the inclusion of new elements and the manipulation of the existing material. Both have served, in some way, to promote and exalt political, social, personal, cultural and even economic purposes within the specific temporal and spatial ambit. In the form of a narrative – either fictional or claiming historicity – such interpolations and (re)interpretations address themselves to a historical moment and, consequently, are significant to the understanding of the past. While they may not authenticate the story, retellings can reveal perspectives of a time and society. The changes manifested can provide us with a view of historical change, and the differing perspectives of contesting interpretations can also provide evidence for historical constructions (Thapar 2000, 1–2). Accordingly, in Trinidad Hinduism, the *Ramcharitmanas* endured – albeit with a continuous stream of variations and alterations that mirrored the demands of society in a continuous state of transition. The fact that these variations were not incorporated into the written text rendered the text more susceptible to varying interpretations and deviations at possibly every discourse.

Such cross-referencing, interpolations and reinterpretation of the *Ramayana* story, along with the Hindu population's increasing application of analytical and intellectual thought in the approach to religious phenomena and ideas, collectively served to draw attention to some of the 'chinks in the armor'[52] of the story of the *Ramcharitmanas*. These occur especially in the more ambiguous situations where complex decisions are made, and where multiple choices for resolution present themselves. The equivocality of both the situations and the choices contribute to the susceptibility of the *Ramcharitmanas* to varying explanations and interpretations. This is further facilitated by the poetic license inherent in the verse form of the text. Given the presentation of Rama as both Divinity incarnate and '*Maryada Purushottam*' (the Most Excellent of Men), several of these issues are embedded in the tension between both presentations. Before the 1970s, most of these issues were resolved by the more correspondent social norms and the unquestionable power of the figure of God/Rama to subsume any and everything else. Predictably, both Hinduism's penchant for interlacing the sacred and the secular, and Trinidad Hinduism's ever-increasing consideration of the practical and contemporary (often non-Hindu) systems and values were vividly echoed in the more popular explanations of these sticky points. Not in any way unreflective of the Trinidad situation, Lutgendorf cited the following as some of the major tactics employed in dealing with such 'cracks in the mirror' of the *Ramcharitmanas*: highlighting of the specific context of place, time, situation and character; playing upon multiple meanings and interpretations of both situations and words; evoking elaborate etymologies; ignoring the problem verses and focusing instead on the more inspiring ones (Lutgendorf 1991, 397–400).

Possibly the major issue that occupied the attention of Trinidad Hindus was Rama's treatment and ultimate banishment of his wife Sita. While great care was exercised not to question Rama's characteristic impeccable judgment and just actions, the apparent injustice inflicted upon that epitome of wifely devotion increasingly mandated interpretations that catered to the social, intellectual and cultural dictates of both time and place. Thus, the dominant explanation that Rama's status as a king duty-bound to his subjects took precedence over his role as a husband seemed to provide the most acceptable resolution of the issue. In what may be termed a direct reflection of patriarchal attitudes, this issue, especially before the 1980s, was either downplayed, sidestepped or even ignored, with emphasis being placed instead on Sita's unwavering wifely devotion 'like a Gibraltar Rock' to her husband.[53] In addition, Rama's deliberate display of human fallibility, and the strategic highlighting of verses attesting to the fickle nature of women (though never directly aimed at Sita) were enough to steer the audience away from any deep reservations on his actions.

Poetic licence was capitalised upon, sometimes to the extreme, leading to explanations of Sita's banishment in her asking to return to the forest alone,[54] or in her promise to the sages of the forest that she would return,[55] with the point of ambiguity being the length of her sojourn. By the 1990s, many interpreters also chose to focus on her retribution at the end of the epic (where she refused to return to her husband despite his ardent requests, but opted instead to descend into the earth with her mother), highlighting her preserved dignity both amidst and in spite of the adversities she encountered. Tied to the issue of Sita's banishment was the fact that she was pregnant at that time. While the text does give evidence that Rama was aware of the pregnancy, it was almost the norm to claim that he was not; the social and moral stigma attached to deserting a pregnant wife cut across time in its severity. Thus, having God/hero desert his wife for the 'greater good' is one thing, but doing so while she was pregnant would not have been as easily digested in a society that placed considerable emphasis on the sanctity of family life and considered their offspring as their riches. Many, even those in positions of socio-religious authority, expressed their 'personal difficulty' in reconciling Rama's banishment of his wife. However, the conflict inherent in attempting to reconcile religion and absolute objectivity aborted the few concerted attempts at treating the issue objectively. One pundit claiming such aspirations was promptly cautioned by a 'senior learned person in the field' that 'if you continue like this people will discredit Rama...you are giving them too much of a new concept of Sita which they would not be able to accept.'[56]

Rama's killing of the monkey king Vali while supposedly hidden behind a tree – a serious transgression of the Aryan code of warfare – was another point of contention in the *Ramcharitmanas*. This issue evoked several attempts at vindication which collectively drew upon practicality, logic, contemporary values, systems, and trends of thought, major Hindu principles and the potentially elusive distinction between the Divine and the human standings of the major character of the text. Hinging on the stipulation of Rama's banishment that he could not enter any city, the metaphoric facet of poetry was invoked to argue that 'behind the tree' really meant 'in the forest.'[57] The law of incarnation was invoked to explain that Vali, in his previous life, had been divinely blessed with the ability to draw half the strength of any adversary who faced him, so Rama had to attack while concealed. The law of karma provided another explanation which proposed that Vali was the hunter who shot the previous divine incarnation, Krishna, and now his death at Rama's hand was an inevitable 'reaping of what he sowed' in his previous birth.[58] Yet another explanation, now drawing on the divinity of Rama, asserted that had he come face to face with Rama, Vali, recognising Rama's divinity, would have submitted himself in devotion to the Lord. Rama, in turn, would have been compelled to forgive Vali his atrocities, thereby breaking his promise to the latter's offended brother to destroy him. Finally, an overriding suggestion was that this, and the other points of conflict, could be effectively subsumed by the larger issues of the text: Rama was duty bound to rid the society of such menaces and Vali, in any event, attained moksha (liberation) by being slain by Rama.[59]

Yet another issue that evoked substantial argument was that of Dashratha – Rama's father – having three wives. While the major, not illogical justification suggested that he did so in order to produce an heir, the issue was constantly alluded to, especially in attempts by males to justify their having more than one wives. However, the fact that Rama (the real hero and Divine figure) was faithful to his wife throughout her sustained banishment, and refused to remarry even for political purposes continued to overshadow his father's (Dashratha's) polygamy. It was not uncommon, however, to find otherwise versed expounders of the text claiming varying degrees of obscurity on the incidents in seeming attempts at keeping Rama's title of '*Maryada Purushottam*' or the Most Excellent of Men free of any blemish. The ultimate justification for most of these points, however, was that Rama was just a vehicle for the greater good of mankind. Also, in keeping with the whole idea of the '*leela*' (God's play), he was acting in accordance with what had been preordained; this was his role in the *leela*, and such shortcomings were deliberate demonstrations of human fallibility.

Conclusion

That the prominent Hindu religious texts in Trinidad, especially the *Ramcharitmanas*, have had a time-honoured and intimate relationship with the local Hindu society and history is undeniable. From the earliest days of indenture until the present time, the vicissitudes of the Hindu experience drew upon the authoritative and affective functions of this text in its continuous search for solutions and solace. It is evident that Hindu religious texts had undergone substantial change in terms of how they were perceived, their form and their function. Many of the issues and processes such as iconising, de-ritualising, and Christianising that affected these changes could, to varying extents, be located in the Hindu community's increasing interaction with the wider society. This reflected the perpetual tension between the change and continuity evident in almost every aspect of Hinduism.

The occasions for textual readings, the attitude towards the associated paraphernalia, and the treatment of related issues collectively evinced the symbiotic relationship between change in the textual sphere and wider socio-religious transformation. This intimate social and textual interflow, inherent in the concept of text as encyclopaedia and the practice of intertextuality, in turn, underscored the proposed status of Hindu religious texts, especially the *Ramcharitmanas*, as cultural icons. The fact that this status of icon was generated largely by the socio-religious aura that developed around the texts themselves (rather than just by their content) validated this ascription. It can be surmised, therefore, that the Hindu textual tradition, based on its function, its transformation, and the attitude that it has elicited from the Hindu community, provided a most applicable metaphor of the Hindu experience in Trinidad and Tobago.

CHAPTER FOUR
Socio-Religious Change, 1945–90: The Private Domain

Political and Economic Context

The period 1945–90 was characterised by tremendous economic and political change which, in turn, served to shape the extent and nature of Hindu socio-religious transformation in Trinidad. The first half of the period (1945–62) saw an overall growth in the country's economy, facilitated largely by an upswing in the oil industry. Given Trinidad's heavy dependence on oil for export earnings and government revenues, oil was rightly regarded as 'the prime mover in the economy' (Brereton 1981, 216). The sugar industry, however, also contributed substantially to the country's economy and employment. This was largely as a result of the stabilisation of the market and the preferential prices generated in the wake of the Commonwealth Sugar Agreement of 1951. The development of a significant manufacturing sector, stimulated largely by the Aid to Pioneer Industries Ordinance and the Income Tax (In Aid of Industry) Ordinance in 1950, also contributed to the strengthening of the economy (Brereton 1981, 218). Throughout the late 1950s and into the early 1970s, the Government promulgated a series of five-year plans which essentially favoured industrialisation over agriculture. This served to further distance rural Indians from the party in power. However, poor Blacks were also disenchanted, and the stark conditions and social disparities of the period fuelled political and social upheaval, which were to climax in the Black Power Movement of 1970.

The increase in crude oil prices by OPEC (of which Trinidad was not a member) in 1973, together with important off-shore oil discoveries, paved the way for windfall gains in the oil revenues of Trinidad and Tobago, and for a subsequent boom in the economy during the 1970s and early 1980s. Some Indians were also to profit from this economic windfall, achieving a substantial degree of economic prosperity and social mobility. Nevertheless, a combination of factors simultaneously hastened the collapse of agriculture, and hence, worsened conditions for other Indians. The over reliance on oil revenues was cruelly exposed when a steep drop in international oil prices, together with a decline in Trinidad's oil production in the 1980s, ushered in harsh economic conditions. By 1990, the country was still struggling to emerge from an economic abyss; a situation that impacted upon every section of the society.[1]

Socio-economic developments in Trinidad were significantly influenced by the Second World War. At the same time, the government used the war as a convenient and plausible excuse for suppressing potentially troublesome political and union activities (Brereton 1981, 189). Subsequently, the end of the war saw further developments in both the economic and labour situations. The displacement of thousands of workers formerly employed on the U.S. bases in Trinidad, the ensuing rapid inflation and prevailing low wages generated widespread dissatisfaction and increased labour activity and unrest. However, due to a combination of factors, the labour movement lost impetus after 1950. The advent of universal Adult Suffrage in 1945 heightened the organisation of political groups, and simultaneously paved the way for the dominance of middle class politics. In addition, constitutional change in 1950 for the first time gave elected members a clear majority in the Legislative Council and further transformed the face of politics in Trinidad and Tobago. The elections of that same year, however, provided stark evidence of the fragmentation of Trinidad politics. Further constitutional change in 1956 opened up the possibility of party government, if a single party gained a clear majority of the elected seats.

Against this backdrop, the People's National Movement, led by Dr Eric Williams, emerged to dominate Trinidad and Tobago politics until the 1980s. Williams, however, refused to be party to any deal with the leading Hindu politicians, especially the leader of the People's Democratic Party, Bhadase Sagan Maraj. He portrayed the PDP as a reactionary, communal Hindu organisation and consistently attacked that party and its sibling organisation, the Sanatan Dharma Maha Sabha. This won him some support from Indian Muslims and Indian Christians, and succeeded in isolating the PDP to the rural Hindu districts. On a more profound level, however, the PNM's anti-PDP and anti-Hindu tactics '...helped to heighten racial fears and to institutionalize patterns of voting and political mobilization along racial lines' (Brereton 1981, 237). Stung by the results of the 1958 Federal Elections in which, in Trinidad and Tobago, the PDP won six seats to the PNM's four, Williams bitterly and publicly denounced what he saw as that party's appeal to race and religion in its campaign. In a speech that seemed to reflect the black middle class' longstanding fear of the possibility of an Indian appropriation of political power, Williams went on to castigate the Indian population as a '...recalcitrant and hostile minority of the West Indian nation masquerading as 'the Indian nation' and prostituting the name of India for its selfish and reactionary political ends' (*Trinidad Guardian* April 2, 1958). The campaign for the 1961 general elections was characterised by violence, a state of emergency and hysterical speeches. It evolved into more of a struggle between two ethnic groups for political power than a campaign on issues and policies. Thus, while the PNM was victorious, it was a country deeply divided along ethnic lines which it took to Independence in 1962.

Within this context, the Hindu community proceeded on its efforts at transforming and establishing itself in terms of both its internal operations and its relation with the national community. This entailed substantial navigation, assimilation, excision and accretion, often seasoned with a diametric pull between the community's intrinsically Hindu systems and values and the sometimes dissonant systems and values of the wider Trinidad society. The crux of the challenge of Hindu socio-religious development and change during this period resided in the establishment of a balance between retaining the essence of Hinduness in the more private settings, while simultaneously yielding to the often contradictory requirements of integration into the wider Trinidadian society.

Socio-Religious Change
Village, Caste and Class

Within the Hindu population a deep sense of nostalgia for the 'long time feeling of community' seemed to resonate among interviewees of 40 years of age or over. This common sentiment can be located in reminiscences of village life characterised by deep emotional relations, not dissimilar to those shared among members of an extended family. This was rooted in several factors. These included socio-economic interdependence, traditional systems, communally observed socio-religious events and festivals, and a high level of loyalty, mutual respect and trust. The persistence of the feeling of community despite the social and sometimes residential segregation based on caste sensibilities within villages[2] reinforced the depth of this notion. Such sentiments were evident in responses such as the following:

> Long ago people lived like family. You could go by any neighbour and ask for anything. Then there was a lot more respect. A neighbour could pull up on anybody's child. Now it is no longer so.[3]

Numerous accounts of villagers liberally chastising each other's children suggested the extension of elements and attitudes of the more intimate sphere of the family to interaction within the village. The high degree of mutual respect, varyingly based on age, socio-economic and socio-religious status, was especially apparent in the extension of Hindu kinship sentiments and titles to fellow villagers. Thus, persons belonging to one's parents' age group and social circle were accordingly addressed as '*kaakaa*' (father's brother), '*kaakee*' (father's brother's wife), '*mowsee*' (mother's sister), '*mowsaa*' (mother's sister's husband). The spouse of one's contemporary, depending on the age of the latter, was a '*bhowjee*' (elder brother's wife) or a '*barkaa*' (elder brother-in-law). Even persons marginally older were often accorded the respect of either '*bhai*' (elder brother) or '*didi*' (big sister).

Such titles, however, extended beyond their literal meanings to encapsulate what can be termed a cultural element; in other words, these titles were resonant of the customs, institutions and beliefs of the Hindu community. This was underscored by the disinclination on the part of Indians to assign such titles to non-Indians, even close friends and longstanding neighbours. Such individuals were instead often fondly referred to in English as 'uncle' or 'auntie.' Though possibly more subconscious than deliberate, such reservations reflected the tendency to guard the more intimate aspects of Hindu religion and culture. In addition, the precise nature of the titles, along with the specific emotions and the behavioural ascriptions that accompanied each term, could not be transferred unto individuals who did not exist within the cultural ambit in which such terms were located. For example, the term *'chhotki'* (younger brother's wife) connoted a severely restricted and impersonal relationship, including the prohibition of any kind of physical contact between the elder brother and the wife of his younger brother. The full impact of such connotations could not be invoked with non-Hindu individuals. In addition, many of these terms carried a ritual element, which also could not be transferred out of the Hindu context. This ritual element refers to the rituals that sometimes initiated and thus sanctified such relationships, and also to the socio-religious practices that were often the exclusive duty of the particular individual given his station in life. For example, in Hindu life cycle ceremonies certain rituals could only be performed by specific individuals. The restricted relationship between the eldest brother-in-law *(barkha)* and his sister-in-law *(chhotki)* was reinforced by the ritual in which the eldest brother-in-law placed a pink woolen garland around the neck of his brother's bride *(taag paat ceremony)*. This initiated his status of father figure to the young bride, together of course with the implication of an asexual relationship.

It can be argued that until the 1970s the feeling of community, in its spatial as well as social sense, among Trinidad Hindus was more discernible at the level of the village. This was rooted in the almost self-sufficient, self-contained nature of most predominantly Hindu villages. This was largely due to the overriding dependence of Hindus on agriculture, the substantially low level of formal education among Hindus, the endurance of traditional systems and values, and the relatively modest – though not negligible – influences of the wider Trinidadian society.[4] Until the 1960s, the predominance of traditional social institutions such as the panchayat, *bhaiyachaarya*, (a co-operative brotherhood in building homes and cultivating crops), *kujat* (state of outcaste) and *praja* (traditional Indian patron-client relationship), and caste sentiments also tightened the sense of village.[5] It is the experience of the majority of persons over the age of 40 that '...people lived in close harmony and assisted each other in cutting and beating rice, and to build houses. This led to a greater feeling of community.'[6] The de-emphasis of the individual in favour of the collective body, rooted in the secondary position of the individual to the family unit, was also a contributing factor. The presence of village councils, various youth groups and socio-cultural organisations formally catering to the need for interaction at the village level further enhanced the strong sense of village. The centrality of communally observed socio-religious events such as pujas and *yagnas* for the welfare of the village, and *satsangs*, also ritually sanctioned and reinforced such village feelings.

Sporadically observed events such as *yagnas* and *Ramleelas* did generate interaction among various villages. Marriage, however, was the most frequent of such occasions since, until the 1970s, the search for prospective marriage partners was cast, ideally, outside of the village. The socio-economic and emotional ties to ancestral lands, and the persistence of traditional Indian structures and values surrounding Hindu family life created a situation where male members of the family usually continued residing in their ancestral villages. This generated a high degree of consanguinity within villages which, in turn, prohibited marriages within villages. Also, the kinship sentiment of the *jahaji bhai* relations (relationships established aboard the Indian immigrant ships and usually sustained during and after the indenture period) albeit fictive, continued to exist among the descendents of the indentured immigrants, though in increasingly diluted degrees. Thus, along with the actual event of the wedding, affinal bonds generated by such unions greatly enhanced inter-village interaction and relations, and the gradual crystallisation of Hindu group sentiments.

Notwithstanding the high levels of loyalty and respect that permeated village life, there was another side to this situation. Although most of the persons interviewed shared varying levels of nostalgia for the past, shades of romanticising were discernible. This could not obscure the fact that matters such as adultery, the stealing or destruction of food crops and livestock, and disputes over property boundaries were an intrinsic part of village life. In addition, the pervasiveness of the notion of *neemakharam* (disloyalty and ungratefulness) further suggested the occurrence of internal conflict.

Developments during the 1970s diluted or dismantled several elements and provided the catalyst for a gradual overall transformation of this traditional concept of the village. The increased prospects of socio-economic advancement and the increasing degree of formal education among Hindus diverted both physical and emotional energies away from the village towards the fulfilment of individualistic goals. The displacement of agriculture as a nucleus of Hindu communal interaction, along with the simultaneous and sometimes resultant dissolution of many of the traditional social systems further eroded physical and emotional ties to the village. Thus, systems such as the *bhaiyachaarya* and the *praja* declined in their economic function; consequently, so did the related social norms and values. Other systems such as the panchayat and *daheja* (the system wherein members of a village assist each other at weddings) which both thrived on and promoted the village as the nucleus of Hindu life, respectively succumbed to the legal system and socio-economic norms of the wider Trinidadian society. From the 1970s, the growing participation in the social and recreational life of the larger Trinidadian community gradually curtailed interaction among younger persons from within the village. One can even argue that the village was fast becoming primarily a place of repose at the end of the day's work.

The increasing infiltration of Western values and systems generated mutations even in the more intimate aspects of community relations. Thus by the late 1980s, the traditional terms of address were overridingly subsumed by their English equivalents which, of course, failed to capture the affective connotations of the traditional terms. The rise of the nuclear family form and the accompanying shift in kinship relations saw a near demise of the extension of kinship sentiments to the village, and the increasing adoption of what was referred to in more than one interview as a 'keeping to yourself' attitude.[7] By the 1990s the overriding situation was one wherein collective assistance at wedding and *yagna* preparations and in times of distress or grief still persisted, but where the overall sense of village was 'not as strong as before.'[8] It was clear that the village was no longer the nucleus of social and economic interaction.

It can be argued that, until the 1970s, emphasis on the village somewhat worked at odds with the creation of a Hindu communal feeling; that is to say, as a distinct, united religious grouping in Trinidad as a whole. Although there were attempts at Hindu mobilisation on a national level, these occurred sporadically and were usually associated with issues that challenged the Hindu population as a religious or ethnic group within the wider society. Such issues included the question of Adult Franchise, the Marriage and Divorce Bills, the Cremation Bill, and education. Although the emergence of the SDMS during the 1950s generated the largest and most enduring period of Hindu communal sensibilities, it failed to detract from the village's status as the centre of Hindu activity and existence during that period.

However, the decline of the village as the nucleus of activity during the 1970s, notwithstanding the primary focus on socio-economic advancement, created a void; the need for socio-religious interaction continued to run deep. The revitalisation of Trinidad Hinduism during the 1980s (Klass 1991) further emphasised this need. Thus, during the 1980s, Hindu group feelings, which were previously entrenched in the village, were channelled into two spheres: the non-village temple and socio-religious organisations. Although the village temple continued to function as the centre of collective worship for many religious festivals and observances, the previous deep sense of allegiance to the temple in one's own village was gradually diluted. This was largely on account of the decline of the village as the nucleus of life among Hindus. In addition, the increasing search for religious guidance (that offered more than just the performance of rituals and discourses from the texts), namely gurus or preceptors, was increasingly cast outside of the village. This led to the evolution of the non-village temple which was defined by its allegiance to either a religious figure or organisation, rather than, as before, to its location.

During this period also, there was a simultaneous increase in the appeal of Hindu sects and organisations such as the Divine Life Society, the Bharatiya Vidya Sansthaan, the Satya Sai Organization and the Hindu Prachar Kendra as centres of Hindu socio-religious activity and Hindu group sensibilities. Yet, even this shift did not evoke Hindu communal feelings in the sense of a single unified group. This was largely due to the diversity in beliefs, focus and leadership that underscored the multiplicity of Hindu organisations, and which was sanctioned by the larger Hindu religio-structural principle of unity in diversity. Was there then a Hindu community at a national level? Although the centre of focus shifted from the village to organisations and temples, a duality persisted. In other words, on one level the sense of a national Hindu community was discernible when the group was challenged as a religious community, and even then too diversity was evident. On the other hand, diversity and individual and organisation-based loyalties characterised the very notion of Hindu communal interaction.

The fluidity of the period 1945–90 provided a most interesting context for caste and class dynamics within Trinidadian Hinduism. During the 1940s, notions of caste were still very evident within the Hindu community, albeit with a persistent stream of opposition from non-Brahminic individuals and groups. The often-conflicting information from oral and written sources evinced the protean and complex nature of the subject during the 1960s. Klass described the situation as a '...complex one, exhibiting different facets in different contexts, and inviting different – but equally valid – conclusions given different kinds of questions' (Klass 1991, 45). Among the studies conducted in different Indian communities in Trinidad during the 1950s and 1960s, Arthur Niehoff concluded that caste was 'functionally a matter of little concern' among Hindus of the Oropuche Lagoon area (Niehoff 1967, 162). Barton Schwartz proposed that the major elements of the caste system were missing and as such, caste did not exist in the southern village of 'Boodram' (Schwartz 1967, 141). Colin Clarke, however, concluded that caste did not seem 'to have been especially eroded in the industrial, multiracial, and multi-religious environment of San Fernando' (Clarke 1967, 196). However, it is clear that there were two principal areas wherein caste considerations were visible and persistently dominant until the 1970s; these were the priesthood and marriage. By the 1940s, it was generally preferred that ritual specialists (pundits) should be of Brahmin stock. The following captures the most common rationale of such an attitude:

> I would prefer a Brahmin pundit because he is from a high nation [caste]. They come from a home where they are religious. They don't mix with all different kinds of things. They are a high nation. It is better to have a godfather [spiritual preceptor] or pundit like that.[9]

Appealing to the population's reverence of religious accoutrements, a popular Brahmin priest gave the following interpretation of the issue:

> You should do your duty. Just like you doing puja and they tell you to put a *tulsi* leaf in the *prasad*, you would not take a black sage leaf or a pepper leaf to put in there.[10]

Using practical allusions such as '...you want to have a dog to protect your house; no pot-hound, but shepherd or doberman,'[11] the case for Brahmin supremacy was further driven into the largely devotion-oriented psyche of the pre-1970s Hindu population. Brahmin priests also sought to actively confirm their ritual supremacy during textual discourses by ignoring or de-emphasising those verses that 'would affect their status.'[12] Verses such as the following, in support of the idea of caste were, in turn, emphasised:

> *Poojiya bipra seel guna heenaa. Sudra na guna gana gyaan prabeenaa.*
> A Brahmin must be respected though lacking in amiability and virtue; not so a Sudra, though possessing a host of virtues and rich in knowledge.[13]

When non-Brahmins with priestly aspirations either embarked upon projects of personal sanskritisation or functioned openly as non-Brahmin pundits, their non-Brahmin status was either a moot issue or the catalyst for intense criticism of Brahminism. While Brahminic control of the priesthood was resented by non-Brahmin pundits, this was most often aired in the more private domains of the home, or in intimate cliques and among their personal following (chelas).[14] Although there were active attempts at confronting and opposing Brahmin authority, these almost always deferred to the latter's ritual, and often, economic superiority. During the 1950s and 1960s, however, an increase in the influx of swamis and other religious figures from India, many of whom denounced the ideology of caste, generated a more active counteraction of Brahmin aspirations at monopolising the priesthood. The following excerpt, published in *The Observor* on June 1947, from an address delivered by a visiting Indian author and lecturer, Mr Chaman Lal, to the local Hindu community gives an idea of the tone and basis of such arguments:

> The caste system among the Indian people is based on 'karma' and not 'birth'.....No one should consider himself superior through the accident of birth, as that would be entirely a wrong notion.

Between 1950 and 1955, the village of Felicity was visited by three swamis from India, one of whom, Swami Purnananda, stayed for two years. During this period he travelled throughout Trinidad '...spreading the knowledge of pujas and *sandhya* previously held by pundits. He also spoke against the caste system saying that all should be treated with equality.'[15] Organisations and groups emerging from the visits of such individuals also espoused anti-caste sentiments. The establishment of the Trinidad Academy of Hinduism by a group of largely non-Brahmin pundits who were refused official recognition as Hindu priests by the SDMS was possibly the most visible challenge to Brahmin religious supremacy.

During the 1980s, caste considerations in the priesthood were further reduced. This was due to the erosion of caste considerations in other areas. Influences from the wider society, especially the claims of the individual over those of the group, hastened this development. Increasingly more individuals began to speak out about Brahmin pretensions. According to an article in the *Express* on August 22, 1975, a major concern was that Brahmins continued to '...forcefully extract financial worth from the harijans while enjoying their confidence....' It was also argued, in a similar article in the *Express* on August 13, 1981, that Brahmin efforts at defending Brahminism exposed '...an inherent tendency that is characteristic of all Brahmins in not tolerating any form of opposition – whether they teach half-truths or even total nonsense.' Verses such as the following from the *Ramacharitmanas* contesting the hierarchical dictates of the caste system, were often invoked in these arguments:

> *Jaati paati kul dharma baraaee....Binu jal baarid dekhiya jaisaa.*
> Despite caste, kinship, lineage, piety...a man lacking in Devotion is of no more worth than a cloud without water.[16]

An increasing number of individuals began to express the view that pundits 'don't have to be Brahmins.' As one person said, 'I would not mind a non-Brahmin pundit doing my puja. He must be a learned person with good character, who can guide by example and precept.'[17]

However, despite the proliferating support for a non-Brahmin priesthood, the preference for Brahmin ritual specialists was still the norm, even by the 1990s. This echoed the deep-seated affinity for tradition and custom, and a wariness of deviating from the 'correct way' with regard to religious matters. However, the post-1960s rapid dissolution of the already attenuated sensibilities of caste mandated a change in (at least the exhibition of) this attitude. Emphasis on the ritual superiority of Brahmins was increasingly replaced by arguments surrounding the original purpose (of the caste system) of 'allotting responsibilities and roles in society.' This was often accompanied by grudging acknowledgement of the '...many atrocities that have been committed because of people's own interpretation of the caste system.'[18]

Non-Brahminic rites and rituals have been an integral part of Trinidad Hinduism since the period of indenture. By the 1950s, however, the notion that such practices challenged Brahminic hegemony and culture was already firmly established. Yet, despite the mass socio-religious mobilisation led by the obviously Brahmin-dominated SDMS during the 1950s, the practice of many non-Brahminic rites and rituals persisted. According to oral sources, until the 1970s a communal *Kali puja*, involving the sacrifice of a goat, was performed annually in many villages for the safety and protection of the village and villagers. At the level of the family, *Dee pujas*, often involving the sacrifice of a rooster, were performed at agricultural plots to ensure a safe and fruitful season, at the very first stage of constructing new homes, and as a yearly ritual to ensure the safety of one's family and personal property.[19] One interviewee even admitted to performing a *Dee puja* with a rooster to prevent her goats from mysteriously 'dying out.'[20] In addition, members of the *chamar* 'caste' performed annual pujas to the goddess Parmeshwari, which often involved the sacrifice of a pig. Although this ritual was exceedingly repulsive to almost all other Hindu individuals and groups, it was of prime significance to its participants since it was commenced with the birth or marriage of a son in the family. It was believed that failure to perform the ritual annually would result in some grave calamity, even death, befalling the son or the entire family. However, what the SDMS failed to accomplish was soundly realised by the widespread socio-economic aspirations and, possibly as a result of the latter, the general religious languor of the 1970s. These factors worked in unison. The increased emphasis placed on socio-economic advancement led to a de-emphasis of many religious practices and observances, especially those that could possibly add to the still widely though covertly held perception of Hindus as a superstitious or idolatrous group. In addition, the deep-seated ambiguity emerging from the lack of effective leadership and group mobilisation, especially after the death of Bhadase Sagan Maraj, contributed significantly to this languor and religious indifference.

Thus, from the mid-1970s, there was a rapid decline in the frequency of those elements of the Little Tradition that involved the sacrificing of any life form, both at the communal and individual levels. In the case of the more popularly performed *Dee puja*, the sacrifice of the rooster was omitted and symbolically replaced by crackers and butter as the main offering. A growing distaste for animal sacrifices, along with the widespread belief that the defective performance of this type of ritual is dangerous or, as put by one interviewee, 'from the time you do something wrong in *Kali puja*, is trouble for you' hastened this decline.[21] In fact in several villages, perhaps to make the observance doubly sure, Brahmin pundits were engaged to put a formal end to the performance of *Kali pujas*. This involved a process of delicate navigation between getting the job done right and not offending the Brahminic sensibilities of the pundit. The first phase of the procedure involved the performance of the necessary rites, quite similar to those of a normal puja, by the pundit. The second phase, involving the sacrifice of a goat, commenced only after the Brahmin pundit's departure from the site. However, instead of being distributed for consumption, the carcass was buried in its entirety, all to ensure that no calamity would befall the participants or the village.[22]

While no cases of Brahmins actually performing rituals involving life sacrifices have been unearthed, several Brahmins and non-Brahmins have claimed that members of the Brahmin caste performed the *Dee puja*, but without the sacrifice of an animal. The proliferation of this modification by the 1990s reflected the perpetual struggle between adhering to ancestral rituals yet refraining from those that may bring bad comment. However, despite the decline in such practices on the individual level, there emerged, during the 1970s, a number of 'modern Kali temples' (Guinee 1970, 4) in Trinidad, several of which performed animal sacrifices. Crucial to this development was the influence of Guyanese practitioners of Kali worship (McNeal 2003, 224). In his study of Kali worship in Trinidad, Keith McNeal identified the contact of a group of Indo-Trinidadians with one Jamsie Naidoo, a Guyanese pujari (priest for Kali worship), as the beginning of a '...series of exchange relationships that precipitated the emergence of modern temple-based Kali worship in Trinidad' (McNeal 2003, 237). He located as markers of this Guyanese influence the use of the *tappu* drum at weekly puja services at temples dedicated specifically to Kali, and the use of the local English Creole during 'spiritual consultations;' all intrinsic aspects of what he termed as 'modern Kali worship' in Trinidad (McNeal 2003, 237–38).

One can speculate that the languor that pervaded mainstream Trinidad Hinduism could have instigated and facilitated the rise of such temples. Also, parallel to its role in the rise of *yagnas*, the 1970s oil boom substantially enhanced the economic means for the construction of these temples and the increase in the sometimes costly *Kali pujas* and other closely related forms of Shakti worship. It is also quite probable that the adage 'strength in numbers' would have been at work among proponents of Kali worship who capitalised on the aforementioned conditions, and attempted to mobilise and validate themselves as an aspect of Trinidad's socio-religious spectrum. In addition to mobilising the practitioners of and believers in this mode of worship, the Kali temples also increasingly appealed to persons who were not previously proponents of Kali worship.[23] Some of this was due to the failure of medicine to cure many ailments, as well as dissatisfaction with the high cost of medical services. By the 1990s, Hindus and non-Hindus of various socio-economic and professional brackets were visiting these temples in hope of relief from physical ailments, reprieve from an inexplicable period of bad luck, or to deflect strange happenings which seemed to extend beyond the realm of the scientific and the logical.

At the level of the village, the temple provided the most noticeable area in which the intimate aspects of Hinduism could be observed. During this period, Hindu temples in Trinidad evolved from the simple *kutiya*-type structure (a hall extending away from the traditional temples) to a multi-functional socio-religious and cultural centre. In her study of Hindu temples in Trinidad, anthropologist Carolyn Prorok explained that the:

> ...form and function of Hindu temples reflect the dialectic of being a Hindu Indian in Trinidad and being a Trinidad Hindu.... Hindu temple building, Hindu ethnic identity, and Hindu political organization are interwoven experiences, each given definition by the other, each bound together by symbolic action, and yielding a specifically Hindu experience in time and space (Prorok 1988, 3).

Thus, the processes of westernisation, sanskritisation and other changes affecting the Hindu community were indicated in the transformation of the temple. In this light, the transformation of the *kutiya* can be seen as the most significant element in the development of the temple since 1945. Until the 1960s, the observance of almost all religious festivals and events were conducted in the home. The temple functioned primarily as the formal house of the Gods and as a village community centre where panchayats, village council meetings, lectures, discussions, Hindi language and music classes were held. The use of temples during the mid-1940s general elections, and the SDMS's deliberate concentration during the 1950s on restoration and construction of temples illustrate the close relationship between religion and politics in Hinduism. The fact that it was not unusual for persons to donate land for the purpose of building temples, or to make an outright grant of the land upon which a temple was already erected, reflected both the level of reverence and importance assigned to temples, as well as Hindu socio-religious mobilisation instigated by the SDMS. This readiness to donate land for temples was evident even during the early twentieth century.[24]

Following the socio-religious languor and the general neglect of the temple and temple-based activities during the 1960s and 1970s, the later drive towards revitalisation generated a significant transformation in the function of the temple. The economic boom of the 1970s led to the rise of family or communally organised *yagnas* and pujas at temples, and the revitalisation of Hinduism saw an increasing number of festivals and religious occasions being communally observed in that setting. During the 1980s, a number of temples became the venue for free medical clinics, run mainly by Hindu doctors and nurses.[25] By the mid-1980s, due substantially to the work of the Bharatiya Vidya Sansthaan, temples were functioning as not only the formal Hindu house of worship but also as a cultural centre where Hindi, Indian music, dance, singing, yoga and Hindu philosophy were taught. Temples also continued to function paradoxically as the symbol and vehicle of both factionalism and a pan-Hindu identity within the context of Trinidad society. In the former sense, the founding or organising bodies of many temples often perpetuated the factionalism within Trinidad Hinduism either by affiliating themselves to one of the larger Hindu socio-religious groups, or by striving to maintain their independence, which sometimes resulted in the evolution of yet another sub-group. Clearly, temples provided the physical and emotional space for Hindu mobilisation and advancement as a socio-religious community. Thus, by 1990, Hindu temples were an important link between the individual and his immediate community, between immediate community and larger Hindu society, and – through their function as a forum for politicking and Hindu mobilisation – between the Hindu community and the national society.

Language

Language change among Trinidadian Hindus has exposed many of the internal developments of the community. Until the 1950s, the use of Bhojpuri dominated the more intimate settings of the home, village and workplace. However, elements of the English language had already begun filtering into those settings. This was facilitated by the efforts of the Canadian Mission schools, as well as by the Hindu population's increasing interaction with the English-speaking population. By 1945, the local English dialect could already be found in Hindu homes and in immediate community interaction, to the extent that a sort of bilingualism of multiple orientation (two languages interacting and spoken in varying blends) characterised the linguistic situation. This included the following situations: where persons spoke and understood both languages, with varying degrees of competence in English; where English was understood but not spoken (usually by older persons); where Bhojpuri was understood but infrequently spoken (as was the case with young children).

By the 1970s, following two decades of slow metamorphosis, there was an almost total appropriation of Bhojpuri by English as the primary mode of communication. Giving momentum to this transformation was the marked increase in formal education in English through the establishment of SDMS and Arya Samaj primary schools. It is interestingly ironic that the efforts of the Hindu community in the form of Hindu schools contributed to the demise of the Hindi language. The move away from agriculture-based occupations to occupational areas that were more integrated into the wider English-speaking society also hastened language transformation. By the 1970s then, the use of Hindi and Bhojpuri was restricted to particular contexts, and this was to steadily decrease throughout the ensuing two decades. The nature of the interplay between Bhojpuri and English can be best illustrated in the following examples. By the late 1960s, the often bilingual dialogue between the elder and younger members of a single household, with the older persons speaking primarily in Bhojpuri and the younger persons in English, led to a fluid intermingling of both languages. Thus, expressions such as the following captured the nature of such 'code mixing and switching' (Bhatia, 1988): '*Aawo hyah haali*' (*come *here quickly*), with the '*hyah*' being the 'Bhojpurisation' of the English word '*here*'; '*faitam kar*' (*fight*) with the '*faitam*' being a 'Bhojpurisation' of the English '*fight*' and the '*kar*' functioning as the imperative. Needless to say, such developments in language were most evident in the popular cultural expressions. Local lyrical compositions such as '*nana chale aage aage, nani going behind*' or, '*chal hamaare ghar mein chalo na Suraajee I really want to see gyul, how much yuh love me,*' were especially revealing of this synthesis. [26]

In her study of the Bhojpuri language in Trinidad, Peggy Mohan proposes that one can classify a language as dying when

> ...its ethnic community begins to use it for less and less of its in-group communication, as more 'serious' work is left for a 'more modern' language, and when the community itself ceases to use it as a native language (Mohan 1996, 2).

Along the lines of such analysis it can be surmised that, by the 1980s, the metamorphosis, indeed the 'death' of Bhojpuri, was almost complete. By the beginning of that decade, the dialect was spoken primarily among persons over 50 years of age and that too in rapidly decreasing contexts and frequency. Such contexts included socio-religious settings, in discussion relating to private and intimate matters, and in jocular conversation (especially when laced with sexual innuendos) not intended for the younger family members or other inquisitive ears. Among the younger population, the situation was a proverbial turning of the tables, where the presence of Bhojpuri, as with English during the first half of the twentieth century, was reduced to just words or phrases worked into otherwise English conversations. The 1990s further reduced even this use.

The situation with Hindi, though following along similar lines as its dialect, Bhojpuri, was much more contrived in the sense that it has never really been the first language as such at any time, and also since attempts at its preservation were much more deliberate. In fact, it can be argued that it was more of a second language kept alive for specific purposes, but primarily because it was the language of the major Hindu religious texts. This was reinforced by the introduction of Hindi language films in Trinidad in 1935, the ever present desire to connect with the Motherland, and the constant flow of religious figures and scholars from India. These factors collectively account for the propagation of Hindi by village and private *pathshalas* from the early twentieth century. Hindi was also a major dimension of the cultural revitalisation of the 1980s. The awareness of the tenuous status of Hindi generated a conscious attempt to revive the language through a significantly increasing number of formal classes in Hindi, allied with instruction in Indian music and Hinduism. The more analytical approach to religion generated growing interest in learning to read the religious texts, to recite and understand the many mantras and bhajans, and to revive and participate in many of the waning cultural forms instead of, as before, leaving such activities primarily up to the pundits and other religious figures. Since recitals from the religious texts and the singing of bhajans were often done through English transliterations, the dissonance between the Hindi and English rules of linguistics and pronunciation led to considerable confusion and misconstruction. The first step in addressing the problem, therefore, was the learning of the language.

This emphasis on Hindi extended to the more official spheres of Hindu interaction. In an article in the *Trinidad Guardian* September 28, 1985, the Secretary General of the SDMS criticised the Government's Draft Education Plan, claiming that '...the word 'Hindi' had been 'blacked out,' but was still visible on close inspection,' adding that the SDMS was '...promised this subject in the Education Plan.' In addition, Hindi's status as a standard language as opposed to Bhojpuri's dialect status, seemed to better dovetail with the Hindu community's attempts at social mobility within the context of the wider society. However, the contrived nature of both its status and preservation was evident in the annual Teachers' Examination, the results of which echoed problems which usually arise when learning a second language.[27] As Administration Reports repeatedly specified, there was '...a tendency to neglect the Hindi Grammar, but nearly all could read and translate well.'[28] It was also proposed that

> ...better attention to Grammar is necessary if this subject is to be continued on the Course. The spelling of even simple words...was inexcusably bad, for which reason, but for the examiner's leniency, others might have failed.[29]

Yet, by the 1980s, Hindi had been established as 'the informal second language of the Hindus,' despite the fact that it was infrequently spoken and that a relatively small number of people could claim to be literate in it.[30] By the late 1970s, more formal institutions such as the Bharatiya Vidya Sansthaan began conducting Hindi classes in a considerably more structured format than the by then almost extinct *pathshalas*. Such institutions increased considerably during the next decade. As confirmed in reports in the *Trinidad Guardian* on March 6, 1987, the preservation of the language was further fortified by the rejuvenation of other cultural forms such as song, dance and drama, along with the organisation of workshops and a Hindi conference in 1987. The establishment of the Hindi Nidhi Foundation during the 1980s, with the preservation and promotion of Hindi as its primary purpose, served to 'institutionalise' the language (in ideology, if not in reality) thereby augmenting its status. It should be noted that parallel developments in the Arabic and Urdu languages occurred simultaneously within the Trinidad Muslim community (Kassim 1999, 59–102).

One scholar has sought to explain that the evident diametric pull between the efforts at retention and the gradual decline of the Indian languages reflected a situation where '...the fear of losing language was bound up with a fear of a loss of identity, but the retention of the original language was also a disability to advancement in the new society' (Mohammed 2002, 78). It can be argued, however, that any 'disability to advancement in the new society' would be situated more in the Hindu population's inability to speak the English language rather than in their retention of the 'original language,' Bhojpuri. Furthermore, as was evident in numerous dimensions of Trinidad Hinduism, the display of the 'original language' within the context of the wider society rather than the actual 'retention' would more probably have been the deterrent to advancement.

In every language there are words and expressions which, in addition to their literal and connotative aspects, possess another dimension that can only be fully articulated by a consideration of the social and emotional contexts within which they are used. This can provide substantial insights into the affective realm, namely attitudes and feelings of the community, which may otherwise be either misinterpreted or overlooked if one were to consider just the cognitive aspects of such words. In Trinidad, there are many Hindi and Bhojpuri words which have endured but were transformed with regards to their emotive content, thereby both capturing the Hindu community's most intimate attitudes towards certain issues, and reflecting the often contradictory nature of Hindu socio-religious change. The most common words in this context include *jutha, sharam, neemakharam, madinga, graha,* coolie, and *jhanjat.*

The changing attitude towards 'eating someone's *jutha*' (partaking of food which has been either contaminated by another person's saliva or just partaken of by another) can be seen as a direct indicator of the locus of the caste-based idea of ritual purity and pollution. While the concern of contracting some sort of physical infection or disease was a constant factor, there was a more deep-seated, often inchoate fear of pollution that transcended the physical. This was conveyed in remarks such as '...it just not good to eat any and anybody *jutha.*'[31] The concern with physical and spiritual contamination was palpable in explanations such as '...it is like acquiring another person's fault through this type of contact...plus your own.'[32] Until the 1970s, there was, within the Hindu community, a strong distaste for partaking of such *jutha* food, save for within the immediate household. While there was, since then, a marked decline in the power of this taboo, many people of all ages continued to observe this restriction.

The term '*neemakharam*' also carried deep emotive content. In the most literal sense, it means to be ungrateful to the (person whose) salt one has eaten. The idea of 'biting the hand that feeds you' is central to the most popularly given description of *neemakharam* as '...when you eat and drink with somebody and you betray them.'[33] However, in order to fully grasp the magnitude of this offence, one has to consider the possible origins of such a notion. It may have been rooted in the *praja* relationship within Indian society, and which was, to an extent, reconstructed within the Indian diaspora. The crux of this relationship was the strong sense of loyalty on the part of the dependent towards the patron. As the Indian community sought to reconstitute itself, this notion was gradually transferred to other parallel relationships. Thus, until the 1980s, large-scale sugar cane or cocoa farmers, in their capacity as employers and moneylenders who could rescue persons from dire financial straits, and as holders of large plots of land who could sublet parcels to the less fortunate, were in positions to pronounce the stigma of *neemakharam* unto those individuals who were previously indebted to them and who afterwards exhibited some form of ingratitude. Individuals who accommodated near or distant relatives in their homes, other individuals who may have assisted fellow villagers in times of need, and of course, politicians and other leaders who may have met some form of individual or communal need could also brand those individuals who had received their favours as *neemakharam*. With the decline of the traditional patron-client type of social institutions, the term lost quite a substantial degree of its significance. During the 1970s, the increasing gravitation towards more formal sources for economic and social assistance such as banks, unions and other organisations further reduced the connotative weight of the word.

The Family

In his examination of marriage and the family among Indians in the Caribbean, Indian sociologist, Kailas Nath Sharma identified the period between 1951 and 1983 as one of destabilisation (Sharma n.d.). Indeed, destabilisation in the sense of a steady erosion or transformation of traditional structures and values characterised the Hindu family between 1945 and 1990. The structure and values of the extended family which have been examined in Chapter One persisted well into the 1960s. From the early 1970s however, there was a persistent shift away from the traditional extended family structure to the nuclear system. This was largely due to the rise in formal education among Hindus, the resultant diversity in occupation and the increasing adoption of non-Indian notions and attitudes. The move away from agriculture and the locus of the village, generated in large part by the economic prospects of the immediate post-oil boom years, also contributed to this shift. This, however, was a gradual process with the young married couple continuing to live within the extended family until they could establish their own home. Sharma, thus, described this as a transitional stage when the extended family was becoming '...a kind of waiting-room in the family cycle, facilitating the young married couple...' (Sharma n.d., 54).

Even more gradual than the change in the family structure was the transformation in values and ideology. The emergent nuclear family form took with it discernible strands of the patriarchal values, hierarchy, and deep-seated filial bonds characteristic of the extended system. By the 1980s, however, it was evident that even these dimensions of family could not escape the impact of the larger socio-economic transformations. For both the parents and the young married couple the nuclear family form increased in its appeal. For the newly married couple (and especially the young bride) this shift provided the kind of autonomy, privacy and direct control over their lives that would have been severely restricted within the extended family system. Though often only grudgingly conceded, an increasing number of parents advocated the nuclear system as the most practical way of avoiding family conflicts, especially between the mother-in-law and daughter-in-law, or among the sub-units that were generated by the marriage of the male members of the family.

By the mid-1980s, both the increase in the number of women working outside the home, and the more assertive attitude of Hindu women to their academic and professional lives, created a gradual blurring of the boundaries of the traditional male-female roles within the nuclear family form. No longer supported by members of the extended family, the couple had to devise methods of managing the home and their own family. Men assisted more and more in taking care of the children and in performing some household chores. The size of the family was also markedly transformed. Economic and practical considerations, reshaped by rising educational levels of women and the growing awareness of family planning, led to a substantial reduction in the family size. Most individuals preferred to have between two to four children. The widely held notion of children being one's 'riches' was subsumed by rapidly changing notions of both child care and the role of parents. Thus, the parents' capacity to properly clothe, feed, educate and otherwise provide for the child became the primary determinant in the size of the family. In addition, with the move away from agriculture, the perceived economic advantage of having a large number of children was dissipated.

Until the 1960s, authority in the joint family was based on seniority and sex. The oldest male was usually the figure of authority, and the female members of the family were usually under the control of the eldest female, oftentimes the spouse of the male in authority (Klass 1961, 131). During the 1970s however, the level of education and, consequently, socio-economic status of individuals became major determining factors of authority within the family. It was not uncommon for a younger brother with tertiary level education to be commanding either the same or an even greater level of authority than the elder, less educated brother. Thus, throughout the 1980s, authority within the Hindu family was based on an interesting amalgam of age, education, and socio-economic status. The varying levels of schooling and the shift away from agriculture resulted also in marked socio-economic independence of siblings. In that situation, the father wielded a substantially diluted type of authority among his adult children. That is to say, the ideology of the father's authority still persisted but, in reality, adult sons and daughters were increasingly assuming control of their own lives. Thus, the final decision on such issues as marriage and occupation now resided with the young adult rather than with the parents. By the 1980s, parents were in a sort of pseudo-authoritative role where the young adults skilfully navigated the dimension of asking to tactfully informing parents of their decisions. The parents on the other hand, aware of the futility of any strong opposition, usually opted to work with the offspring's decision, often just voicing any objections and concerns.

Until as late as the 1970s, Hindu parent-child relationships were characterised by a high level of respect, duty, obedience, and even fear on the part of the child. Many described the situation as one where the child was seen and not heard. During the 1970s, however, the increase in formal education and the shift away from both agriculture and the extended family generated a transformation, not in the ideology itself, but in the stringency of those attitudes. Whereas primacy was previously placed on the family's economic situation, the focus was steadily shifting to the education and occupational enhancement of one's offspring. This had a two-fold effect. On the one hand, parents seemed to develop a more approachable demeanor, still expecting obedience, respect and the sense of duty, but not necessarily deference located in fear. On the other hand, there developed within the child a deep sense of gratitude for the sacrifices made by his parents. This, together with the still strongly ingrained sense of respect, loyalty and obedience, served substantially to inhibit children from either disappointing their parents or leaving their expectations unfulfilled.

From 1945 until around the 1960s, the lives of Hindu women were heavily influenced by socio-religious prescriptions which

> ...drew heavily upon sexual imagery transmitted through myths, cultural symbols, artifacts, religious rituals and festivals, which expressed ideas about what constituted male and female characteristics and behaviour (Mohammed 2002, 136).

Thus, although it was not uncommon for the wealthier or more urban-based Hindu families to consent to their daughters either going abroad to study or to engage in occupations outside of the immediate community, even they shared the general consensus of the woman's place being in the home, as daughter, wife and mother. Yet, Hindu women had always been able, amicably and astutely, to navigate patriarchal restrictions while aspiring (though not always successfully) to some sense of self and personal fulfilment. One should remember though, that during this period even such aspirations were subconsciously defined to a great extent by traditional codes and values, and textual prescriptions. Hence, the character of Sita in the *Ramcharitmanas*, who demonstrated unwavering loyalty, support and devotion to her husband, was emphasised as the model for Hindu wives. It should not be much of a surprise, then, that according to oral sources, the acquisition of a moneyed and socially affluent husband who would ensure a secure and promising life for the woman, her offspring, and maybe even her relatives, could be identified as the highest aspiration of most Hindu women before the 1960s.

However, for the majority of Hindus, the idea of the woman's place being in the home was more socio-religious idealism than lived reality. Under indenture, Indian women were working women. After indenture, women continued to work alongside their husbands, families and friends on sugar and cocoa estates and on private garden plots.[34] However, by the 1960s, the growing number of Hindu women opting for non-agricultural jobs was treated with a mixture of scorn, disapproval, resignation, and superficial admiration. This gravitation to non-agricultural jobs was due to the increase in primary and, to a lesser extent, secondary education among Hindu women, with the increasing assimilation of non-Indian ideas, values and lifestyles enhancing this move. Since Indian women were working outside of the physical space of the home and immediate community from the period of indenture, one can surmise that the point of irritation, since the 1960s, resided in the alien nature of the occupations rather than in the actual idea of working. Also, the physical and social settings of many of the later occupations were often at variance with the established norms of the Indian community. In addition, the absence of any male relatives to protect the virtue of the women (and by extension, of the family) in such settings further aggravated the point. However, according to oral sources, the unsupervised interaction between Hindu women and men of African descent was probably the most deep-seated concern.

Such points of aggravation, in turn, created the foundation of what would eventually become, by the late 1970s, a hotly debated issue within the Hindu community: the 'traditional Hindu woman' versus 'the modern woman' – dichotomy or compatibility? Although the persistence of varying degrees of the traditional idealistic prescriptions for the Hindu woman could be noticed, there was nevertheless a growing awareness (albeit sometimes grudgingly) of the need to redefine the role and position of the Hindu woman. The Hindu woman's physical and ideological exodus out of the confines of the parameters of the home and immediate community into the wider Trinidadian society was accelerated during the 1980s. This was on account of the harsh economic conditions of the post oil-boom period, socio-economic aspirations, and the substantially high levels of academic achievement (of women). According to Vertovec's survey of the Penal Rock Road village, in 1960 40 per cent of the employed women worked in agriculture, 43 per cent in manual labour, and 15 per cent in non-manual jobs. By 1980, the figures had shifted to four per cent, 18 percent and 76 per cent respectively (Vertovec 1992, 148). The most popular occupations among working women included clerical and sales related work, service work and certain professional and technical areas (Vertovec 1992, 150). However, certain occupations such as waitressing and working on the U.S. base were often regarded with suspicion. Both oral sources and literary works on the Indian community confirmed this attitude. For example, in Seepersad Naipaul's *The Adventures of Gurudeva*, the protagonist's love interest, Daisy, is a young Indian woman who works on the American base. She is totally westernised in dress, speech and general comportment, openly flaunts her liaisons with American sailors, and manages to divert Gurudeva's affections away from his wife and unto herself (Naipaul 1976).

The acknowledgement, if not acceptance, of the changing position and function of Hindu women by the major socio-religious organisations was evident in the number of activities focusing on women, organised during the religious ferment of the 1980s. In 1985, the women's arm of the SDMS held a *Sangha Shakti Sammelan* (Hindu Women's Conference). During that same year, the NCIC staged the first ever Women's Singing Competition, which was to become a very popular annual event. In 1986, the Caribbean Hindu Centre and the Hindu Swayamsevak Sangh jointly organised an awards distribution ceremony in commemoration of the United Nation's 'Decade of the Woman' (1975–85). It should be noted that, notwithstanding the intent, the sporadic and arguably superficial nature of and approach to most of these events deterred them from having any substantial impact on the role and position of Hindu women in Trinidad.

Quite predictably, changes in the role of women evoked varied responses reflecting the specific fears, concerns and transformations within the Hindu community. The more traditional yet socially aware, in an attempt probably to defend the traditional role of Hindu women, and by extension Hinduism itself, expressed concerns such as the following:

> There are social norms which our women folk must not cross...but some women do and then society degenerates....Women cannot do certain things that the opposite gender can do, you cannot go certain places that the opposite gender can go because you are the female

> species; you are the hunted one by the male. The Hindu woman is not a passive woman....She has invented the ideal leadership role: she leads her husband, her family and her community from behind. She is the leader in every community. But to go up to the microphone and make speeches and so on, she leaves that to the others...shaking hands, she leaves that to the others...this is the culture of the Hindu woman.[35]

Several explanations can be proffered for the exclusion of handshaking from 'the culture of the Hindu woman.' The social interaction and 'assertiveness' that the gesture suggests, especially with members of the opposite sex, contradict the not uncommonly held notion that the Hindu woman should 'lead from behind.' The physical contact of this essentially non-Hindu gesture both reinforces the contradiction and seems to bring the 'hunted' in closer proximity to the 'hunter.'[36]

As reported in the *Trinidad Guardian* on April 17, 1987, the main speaker at the launching of the Caribbean Hindu Conference in 1987, described the position of Hindu women as '...still spiritually and socially consigned to an inferior status...' notwithstanding considerable advances in several areas. Most interviewees for this study agreed that Hindu women were striking a good balance between their customary and newer roles. However, the concern for the preservation of family and religious life remained paramount, as in the following comments:

> Hindu women are very nicely marrying both traditions and keeping the dharma alive. But the problems occur when the family is under stress – poverty, woman seeking independence from male control.[37]

> Now Hindu women are going out of the homes. There can be temptations and there is potential for disruption in the family life; family may suffer. If they can manage a balance between both, then it can work.[38]

Thus, it seems that by the 1990s, the concern resided in whether the Hindu woman could function as effectively in both roles, without detracting from her roles as mother, wife and primary preserver of Hindu religious and cultural traditions, rather than in whether she should be in the home or a working woman. One wonders, though, if concern for the welfare of the family was totally free of a hidden agenda, namely, the preservation of male control. Also, the fear of women being more susceptible to committing adultery persisted. However, more than in just the succumbing to temptation, the fear seemed to be rooted in the uncertainty about how 'the new Hindu woman' would react to the shortcomings of her spouse.

Marriage and Divorce

Connected to the changes in attitudes towards women's work were transformations in the realm of marriage and divorce. Despite the changing socio-economic milieu, the notion of Hindu marriage as a sacred, socio-religious bonding of individuals and families remained strong, as did its function as a primary cohesive and socialising agent within the Hindu community. However, the wedding ceremony itself underwent substantial change. This was largely due to an interesting amalgam of influences from the wider society, and paradoxical attempts at standardising Hindu socio-religious practice in the midst of a mushrooming of various sects and groups. Hence, by 1990, many aspects of the Hindu marriage ceremony exhibited traits both departing from and consistent with those of the 1940s. All, inevitably, reflected the socio-religious and socio-economic conditions of the Hindu community.

While in the customary Sanatanist ceremony there was an overall attempt at retaining the fundamental rituals, the sequence, duration, method, and associated material reflected a substantial degree of variation. The duration of the entire ceremony, depending on the context, the officiating priest and the wishes of the parties, was shortened from about three hours to time frames ranging between one and three hours, with condensing rather than omission being the general rule of thumb. In the case of the 'table wedding,' factors such as prenuptial pregnancy, poverty or just the personal desire (not insignificantly influenced by modern and Western influences) to have a simple ceremony led to the omission of some of the otherwise major rituals such as the symbolic giving away of the bride and the ritual circumambulation of the sacred fire. Of course, any variation from customary practice generated lively and sometimes not so congenial disputes about the correct way, with some pundits and laymen supporting the unabridged ceremony (while oftentimes covertly grimacing at its length). Others, due either to discomfiture at having to sit through a long ceremony or to a somewhat flippant attitude towards the many rituals, opted for varying shortcuts. It should be noted though that some of the major rituals such as the application of *sindoor*, the bride and groom switching seats after the *sindoor* ritual, and the *kicharee* ceremony have been retained. This persistence of the more fundamental rituals in the Hindu wedding ceremony, despite some cosmetic changes, echoed the nature of the transformation that was taking place during this period in the wider Hindu realm wherein the major underlying beliefs and ideologies persisted despite changes in some of the more peripheral aspects. The wedding ceremony of the Arya Samajists drew on their distinct (from Sanatanist Hinduism) religious tenets, based on Vedic rather than Puranic prescriptions. It was usually an hour-long ceremony with some of its rituals analogous to and others at variance with those of the Sanatanist ceremony.

In addition to the foregoing patterns of Hindu marriage ceremonies, the *baithana* (literally 'a sit down,' but in this context a common law relationship) arrangement has always been present among Trinidadian Hindus. This was usually a result of parental disapproval of the relationship. Due to the kinship sentiments that enshrouded the village, the marriage of individuals belonging to the same village was generally frowned upon, since they were deemed 'brother and sister' (Klass 1961, 116). Thus, such relationships were deemed pseudo-incestuous. One wonders, though, how strong the incest taboo was since, according to oral sources, sexual relationships between first or distant cousins were not unheard of among Hindus. Socio-economic considerations, religious differences and caste sentiments provided other grounds of parental disapproval (Klass 1961, 116–17). *Baithana* relationships also occurred when one or both parties were previously married or had children from a previous union. Also, sometimes, economic constraints just did not permit the luxury of a formal ceremony.

Oftentimes, however, conjugal unions would be consecrated with a puja which included several of the major aspects of the Hindu marriage ceremony, such as the ceremonial application of *sindoor*, the exchanging of *malas* (flower garlands) and the performing of the consecratory *havan*. Thus, if one were to assess such unions in totally Hindu terms, attempting to deny their validity would prove quite problematic. Compounding the matter further was the fact that, except for the legal implications and concerns of not being legally married, persons in common-law unions did not consider themselves any less married than their more formally and legally wedded counterparts; and the community often took the same view. In addition, the absence of a formal ceremony or even of the consecratory puja did not detract from the notion of a lifetime commitment to the union that underscored the formal marriage ceremony. In other words, the fundamental ideology of the Hindu marriage was equally strong in this type of union, notwithstanding the absence of elaborate rituals.

Can one then deduce that, unlike in the non-Hindu notions where the ceremony validates and sanctifies the ideology, within Hinduism the ideology takes precedence? This can offer a probable explanation for the variety in the forms of marriage ceremonies within Hinduism wherein the exchanging of garlands, the application of *sindoor* and the circumambulation of an open flame can each, on its own, consecrate a Hindu marriage. Therein resides a major point of divergence between the Hindu and non-Hindu concepts of common-law unions. However, concern with the legal implications served, eventually, to persuade parties of these unions to register their marriage under the Marriage Act of Trinidad and Tobago.

Probably the most significant marker of the changing attitudes towards the Hindu wedding was the clandestine consumption of meat, which was usually kept in the boots of cars. Until the 1970s, the Hindu wedding ceremony as a whole was treated as highly sacred by the couple, their immediate family members and the larger attending community. Hence, while fasting (abstinence from meat, alcohol and sometimes sex for varying periods of time as a purifying ritual) was not mandatory for guests, meat was not served at Hindu weddings. It was considered defiling to both the occasion and the physical place which the family had purified by fasting for at least three weeks, and had further consecrated by the rituals that sometimes began one week before the actual wedding day.[39] But the economic upswing of the 1970s generated several changes, which were to have a direct impact on the overall attitude towards this life cycle ritual. Firstly, the substantial increase in the number of persons owning cars facilitated a relatively easy transplantation of the aura of a 'lime' (essentially having a good time with a group of friends) onto the Hindu wedding, especially for the *baraat* (the groom's wedding procession), and more so in cases where long journeys were involved. This usually included a series of stops to have a drink and snacks on the way to the wedding venue. It should be noted that there was an overall greater hesitation to indulge in this kind of behaviour if the ceremony was being held at a temple. The perpetual paradox that seemed to classify Hinduism's transformation during this period was quite visible in the fact that persons who consumed either alcohol or meat, except the absolutely drunk, would assiduously refrain from getting too close to the immediate area of the ceremony, well aware of their polluted condition.

Alcohol, however, has always enjoyed the status of an unannounced yet fully acknowledged 'backdoor' guest at Hindu weddings. Alcoholic drinks were often served to select persons, usually family members, close friends and important guests, at the hindquarters or inside the house, even while the ceremony was in progress. Sometimes, there was a wait for the pundit to leave before alcohol was served, or served overtly. In addition, alcohol was almost always a part of the Friday and Saturday night pre-wedding festivities. The attitude of pundits and other religious leaders to the presence of alcohol at wedding ceremonies varied. While some pundits strongly denounced the practice, others feigned ignorance or issued a mild, semi-jocular reprimand.[40] This relatively tolerant attitude to the issue has several explanations. Since the 1970s, pundits increasingly followed other occupations in addition to *punditai*. These occupations often entailed socialising in non-religious settings where alcohol was served and where persons consumed it socially. It can be argued that this somewhat diluted the religious restrictions surrounding the consumption of alcohol, or rather, the pundits' attitudes towards these restrictions. In addition, the post 1970s intensification of the social dimension of many Hindu religious events (weddings, birth celebrations, death) could have also contributed to this more lax attitude towards the consumption of alcohol at Hindu weddings. One can discern a blurring of the sacred and secular even in this aspect of the Hindu wedding ceremony.

Both the suggestion of the use of similar intoxicants in the religious scriptures and the association of the intoxicant *bhang* with the God Shiva have been used to rebut arguments against the consumption of alcohol at weddings, but mainly by the more enthusiastic consumers. Many have tried to argue that since alcohol is made essentially from the sugar cane plant, it is not a meat-based product and cannot therefore be a polluting agent. It can also be argued that the increasing number of pundits coming from non-Brahmin families which may not have been immersed in a tradition of *punditai*, and where the consumption of alcohol by other family members may have been or still was a reality (especially in the case of extended families) had somehow further diluted the sense of taboo surrounding this issue. Finally, the decline of this taboo can also be situated in the perceived futility in attempting to divest the festivities of this element.

The transformation that occurred with the traditional forms of entertainment at Hindu weddings provided even more insights into the dynamism of this Hindu socio-cultural event. Until the 1970s, the major forms of entertainment at the *bhatwaan* (festivities on the night before the wedding ceremony) were so-called local Indian classical singing, the singing of Hindi film songs (usually by a small group of persons with just a few musical instruments), the singing of traditional folk, wedding-related songs by women, and dance-dramas based on stories from the Hindu epics.[41] During the 1970s, the growth in the number of Indian music bands, locally called 'orchestras,' and the general economic upswing led to the increased preference for such orchestras at the 'farewell.' These orchestras often comprised less than ten members with just the basic musical instruments – harmonium, dholak, *dhantaal, majeera*, and sometimes, mandolin and accordion – rendering Hindi film songs and local Indian classical compositions. There were however a number of larger bands that boasted a more elaborate array of musical instruments. The rise in popularity of this form of entertainment contributed to the demise of the more stylised dance-dramas and, during the 1980s, folk singing by women. However, the local classical singing form retained a great degree of popularity. Yet, while the traditional style continued to be appreciated, it was simultaneously modified by the more modern styles, instruments, forms and themes of both Indian and Western music.

During this period, intermarriage across caste and race continued to be one of the most sensitive issues within the Hindu community. In terms of caste exogamy, the attitudes and situation detailed in chapter one persisted until around the 1960s, when arranged marriages, and hence caste considerations, began to rapidly yield to 'love marriages' and the influence of non-Hindu attitudes and practices. Thus, by the 1980s, the situation existed where caste considerations in marriage were discernible almost solely within the Brahmin caste. Morton Klass came to a similar conclusion during his re-examination of the village of 'Amity' in 1985 (Klass 1991, 60–61). The compulsion of Brahmins to preserve their perceived level of ritual purity could not, however, totally elude the factors that led to the erosion of caste considerations among the laymen. Thus, whether consciously or subconsciously (since many would deny personal caste considerations), there was an evident tendency to caste endogamy among Brahmins.[42] Even with love marriages among Brahmins and there was a kind of subconscious system at work where the person would ensure, as far as possible, that the prospective spouse was of Brahmin stock before initiating a substantial relationship. Yet, common were the accounts of individuals not being permitted to marry the person of their choice because he or she 'was not a Maharaj.'[43] However, according to oral sources, the marriage of a high-caste male to a female of a lower caste was more easily (though not readily) accepted than that of a female from a high-caste family to a male from a lower caste family. Since according to the principles of the Hindu caste system the children assume the caste of the father, the marriage of a high-caste woman to a man of lower caste entailed a decline in the socio-religious standing of the offspring of the union. Also, in this situation, the woman had to adopt elements of a lifestyle many of which would have, before marriage, been deemed defiling, low-caste behaviour, or even taboos. It must be noted though, that there was also a considerable degree of contextual social, economic and communal variance with regards to such caste considerations.

With the decline of caste considerations, there seemed to have been a simultaneous, though not related, increase in the number of biracial marriages. According to oral sources, the majority of these unions involved Hindus who had converted to Christianity, especially to the Evangelical persuasion. However, there was a gradual increase in this tendency among practising Hindus, though the numbers involved classify it as more of a remote exception than the norm. Several factors collectively accounted for this breaking of what was once held as possibly the biggest taboo within the Hindu community. Firstly, the greater level of interaction with the wider society since the 1970s had gradually diluted many of the negative perceptions of the other races, especially of the Afro-Trinidadians. This set the foundation for responses based more on personal experiences and conviction, rather than on collective, sometimes invented, generalisations. Secondly, the decline in the influence of parental, familial and socio-religious sanctions, generated by the rise of individualism and non-traditional occupations, curtailed the constant reinforcement of the traditional attitude towards this issue. 'The attempt to hit out at one's own culture and religion, due maybe to a bad experience...,' and the widely held notion that the '...African male knows that the Hindu woman is a good homemaker, mother, wife, peaceful, committed to family life, values...'[44] were two popular postulations on the issue. Sociologist Patricia Mohammed suggested that this '...interbreeding and intermingling between the races, especially between Indian women and African men, was a ripe source of disaffection between Indians and the other races' (Mohammed 2002, 83). This both echoed and evoked the persistent, quite possibly politically motivated conjectures of the Indian fear of 'douglarisation' and the designs of men of African descent on Indian women.

As anomalous as it was, the reality of biracial marriages evoked various reactions, characteristic of the discord inherent in the Hindu community's encounter with non-Hindu systems and attitudes. As detailed in Chapter One, the dominant attitude towards this issue was one of strong disapproval. Indeed, strains of the pre-1960s punishment for this practice, *kujat* (outcaste), were visible in the varying levels of alienation of the individual by both family and community members, even until the late 1980s. In situations of Hindu women marrying men of African descent, it was quite common for the Hindu father to cut all ties with his daughter for many years, or even for life.[45] Since intermarriage with men of African descent usually resulted in the parents having to 'hang their heads in shame' and 'face the comments of the community,'[46] this disassociation from the individual functioned as a public declaration of the parents' disapproval, thereby tempering the community's scorn with some sense of sympathy for the helpless parent of an errant offspring.

That religion was most frequently resorted to as the basis of their rationale demonstrated just how fundamentally disturbing an issue it was. This was evident in comments such as 'God meant each race to marry with each race. Our religion clearly dictates who we should marry. Yet we can co-exist with no "anti-feeling."'[47] As indicated in the following argument, religious texts were also invoked for this purpose; as in the following comment:

> In the *Bhagdvadgita*, it is said that when there is a mixture of caste and religion, there will be a breakdown in society. Intermarriage thus, equals the destruction of a society and the pure races.[48]

Such marriages were generally preconceived as failures since they '...destroy family tradition and later on there will be problems.'[49] There was also the more emotional preoccupation with '...it does not look good...it feels funny to see an Indian and negro together.'[50] That there was such an emphasis on a holistic approach to the nullification of unions between Hindus and persons of African descent illustrated the high level of distaste which the issue continued to evoke among members of the Hindu population.

Until as late as the 1970s, this attitude was also evident in the more mundane sphere. Interaction between the races was minimal and largely superficial, more often than not generated by necessity rather than desire. In ethnically mixed communities and villages, especially where Indians were the overwhelming majority, an inherent ambiguity characterised the issue. Popular opinion confirmed harmonious and amicable co-existence. There were even instances where elder individuals of African descent were on village panchayats.[51] However, situations that entailed the transgressing of other more intimate boundaries evoked a different response. Thus, although it was common practice to invite non-Indian members of the immediate community to Hindu socio-religious functions, special utensils (except when leaves were used) were provided for guests of African descent, who were also seated separately. They were also, as far as possible, not hosted inside of the house. While many '...wouldn't want them in their place because they eat pork and beef...,'[52] suspicion, based largely on the stereotyped perceptions of the African, underscored the maintenance of such distance. This was echoed in statements such as 'Creole is a thing, from the time you give them one thing, they take two. They are anxious to get close to Indians. They want to have a power over them.'[53] The more emotional and probably more polite sentiment that '...you know, you just don't put the Hindu and Creole to eat together; you separate them...'[54] was also commonly proffered.

By the 1980s, Hindu socio-economic aspirations added another dimension to the issue. While the foregoing factors still applied, though in an increasingly diluted form, non-Indian colleagues were often invited to home-based Hindu socio-religious functions. This, however, was often marked by an overly hospitable attitude of the host, not necessarily shared by other members of the family, especially if the guests included his seniors at the workplace. In such situations there was, sometimes, a reversal of the traditional reaction (though not necessarily the attitude) whereby such African guests were allowed certain privileges not extended to other guests. These included dining inside the house, being served on plates rather than on leaves, and having access to indoor toilet facilities. One can interpret this as a reflection of the still prevalent discomfort on the part of many Hindu individuals with extending what was perceived as the more retrograde aspects of Hindu religion and culture to the public gaze. This, of course, was compounded by the growing desire for acceptance by both one's non-Indian colleagues and friends, and the wider society.

The less stringent attitude towards unions between Indians and Whites outlined in chapter one persisted during this period. In fact, by the 1980s, except for among some Brahmin and Kshatriya families who still held caste and race endogamy as the ideal, there were three dominant responses to the situation. Many, especially parents, resigned themselves to the individual's choice of spouse, though not without varying degrees of displeasure. In such instances, the parents usually sought comfort in the knowledge that the prospective spouse was not of African descent. Secondly, some, usually the peers or young relatives of the individual, did not have a problem in accepting the union. This, however, was usually accompanied by tongue-in-cheek or overt teasing of the Hindu individual about his or her choice of spouse, usually revolving around the differences in the white spouse's social, cultural and even physical disposition. Finally, there were those who viewed such unions as moving a rung up the socio-economic ladder since the prospective white husband was almost always of a substantially higher economic standing than his Hindu bride. This attitude was intensified during the migration of Indians to North America in the late 1980s. Then, such unions were sanctioned with the promise of a better life for the Hindu spouse. In addition, the frequent (often expected) sponsoring of members of the Hindu spouse's immediate family for residential visas to Canada and the United States substantially erased the agitation among relatives about the union.

Transformations in both the attitude towards and the frequency of separation and divorce reflected various issues which engaged the Hindu community since the late 1940s. From the early twentieth century until well into the 1970s, religious prescription and the belief in reincarnation rendered separation or divorce the very last resort in cases of marital discord. Formal divorce, a largely Western institution, with its complicated and relatively costly proceedings, was usually employed by the estranged wife faced with the financial and emotional responsibility of taking care of the children as a very last resort in acquiring financial assistance from her husband. Until as late as the 1980s, the initiation of divorce proceedings by men was quite rare, and usually at the relentless behest of the women with whom they were involved in long-term relationships, subsequent to separation from their wives. Interestingly enough, the application of *sindoor* was almost always a prerogative of the first wife, oftentimes even in the case of official second marriages, a reiteration of the tension between the Hindu and non-Hindu ideologies.

Much more popular than divorce, yet not the norm, was the phenomenon of separation; the duration, nature and outcome of which were quite varied. Until the 1970s, separation almost always occurred because of either excessive physical abuse or adultery. The wife would leave the conjugal home, either with or without the children, to stay with immediate or distant relatives for an indefinite period of time. Almost without fail, the husband, due largely to the disruption of the workings of the household, embarked upon a series of visits to his wife which often involved a lot of cajoling and promises to address the point of contention. Although the duration and intensity of this period of enticement varied, it almost always resulted in the wife returning to the conjugal home. This was collectively due to concern for the welfare of the offspring of the union and the prominence of the idea of the indissolubility of Hindu marriages. This cycle of beatings, leaving and returning was depicted in Seepersad Naipaul's *The Adventures of Gurudeva*. In that illustration, the protagonist's wife, Ratni, repeatedly returns to an extremely abusive relationship even though there was no offspring to consider (Naipaul 1976).

In addition, the social and religious disfavour with which separation was met, and the possible financial inconvenience and disapproval of the immediate community which could be imposed upon her relatives provided further stimulus for the woman to return to her spouse. Her return, however, was not necessarily an indication of a genuine improvement of the situation. In fact, in many instances the cycle of leaving and returning was so recurrent that the situation was trivialised as a normal thing. However, a deeper reflection points to the futility and frustrating ineluctability of the situation, especially for the woman whose life and fate were socially, religiously and economically bound to that of her husband and the matrimonial home. In her study of rural Indian women in Trinidad, Shaheeda Hosein proposed that Indian, and by extension, Hindu women were fully cognizant of their importance within the family, and thus more frequently opted to create and negotiate their own space and establish a new balance of power (in their favour) within the family instead of resorting to separation (Hosein 2002, 276–81). Such negotiations, however, were still often considerably defined, or at least influenced, by both the dominant patriarchal socio-religious systems and ideologies and by the particular woman's perception of her place and role in both the family and community.

However, with the increasing economic independence of Hindu women, there developed, by the 1980s, a significantly lower level of tolerance for the previously much endured physical and emotional abuse, acute indolence, philandering and adultery, and one-sided rules and prescriptions at the hands of not just a few husbands. In addition, the focusing of the Hindu woman's time and energy outside of the family seemed to place a lot of tension, both real and conveniently contrived, on family life. This was enhanced by the disintegration of the extended family system and its inherent support. Adultery on the part of the woman became both a growing fear and reality. Also, the Western concept of marriage as more of a union of two individuals grounded largely in social and emotional considerations, as opposed to the Hindu concept of it as an indissoluble union of two souls and their respective kin that extends to the afterlife, seemed both more appealing and compliant with the increasing interaction with the wider society. The foregoing factors can account for the gradual but discernible increase (though still low in comparison to other non-Hindu segments of the society) in the number of divorces within the Hindu community by the 1990s.

Land and Money

The Hindu relationship with land has been a longstanding and intimate one, infused with religious, social, economic and political connotation, and which, by extension, was indicative of varying levels of transformation within the Hindu community. One can safely propose that this intricate bond was largely on account of the fact that in nineteenth century India, agriculture, and hence land, was at the core of both the daily subsistence of most of the peasant population, and the wider Indian economy. This attitude was transported to the Caribbean where, in the context of the sugar plantation, it was propagated if not strengthened. In her analysis of the Indian contribution to the formation of Trinidad's peasant class, Brereton described this affinity to the land as the Indians' '...special love for the land' (Brereton 1985, 27). By the 1940s, this relationship with the land had intensified. By then the Hindu community had succeeded in its attempts at community reconstruction, with its major socio-religious and economic systems operating more along the lines of those in India than those of the wider Trinidadian society. Agriculture continued to be the primary field of occupation. In addition, save for those belonging to the richer middle class, the desire to infiltrate into the workings of the wider society was not yet very pervasive in the general Hindu community.

One can understand then – if not appreciate – the emotions that accompanied the ownership of land, since it represented for the Indians a sense of belonging and affinity, and served as the major marker of material wealth. Until the 1980s, the practice of passing the land on to one's offspring as opposed to selling it, with the inherent notion of somehow keeping alive the legacy of the family, was strictly observed. In addition to this socio-emotional dimension, land has always occupied a prominent position in the religious life of Hindus. In almost all pujas, after the initial worship of Lord Ganesh, the Remover of Obstacles, obeisance is paid to *Dharti Mata* (Mother Earth) and her life-giving and sustaining force. In addition, the major Hindu doctrines of karma and reincarnation also support the earth's deification as mother (since it was possible that a dead relative could be reincarnated as a tree, thereby making the earth his or her mother). The question of whether the deification of the land evolved on account of its acute practical importance, or if both these aspects evolved autonomously yet not in an unrelated manner, remains, like many religion-related issues, largely unresolved.

The socio-economic and political implications of land ownership are more clear cut. Simply put, the more land one owned, the greater one's economic, social and political power. Hence, until the 1970s, one can propose that land was a major power factor in the internal sociopolitical workings of the Hindu community (Singh 1987, 33–60). By the 1980s, however, the large-scale exodus out of agriculture-based jobs generated a profound overall transformation in the Hindu attitude towards land. No longer the major source of livelihood, the many plots of land left idle were viewed more in the light of a saleable commodity.[55] In addition, since many were leaving ancestral villages for the more urban areas, the cash that could be acquired from selling the land seemed more in compliance with the new shift in focus and lifestyle. Also, the large-scale migration of Indians from Trinidad to North America in the 1980s led to a marked increase in the sale of family lands. However, a deep affinity to land still persisted among a large portion of the Hindu community, some of whom, even in economically trying times, preferred to keep the land in a state of disuse instead of selling it.[56]

While the acquisition of wealth has not been more outstanding a preoccupation among Hindus than any other group in Trinidad, the nature of the Indian attitude towards earning and saving money has always intrigued the wider population. This has led to the Indian attitude towards money acquiring what can be loosely termed as 'legendary' undertones. What has been perceived by the wider population as frequent accounts of self-deprivation with respects to diet, clothing, entertainment, education and various other basic amenities can be read differently. Examination of the nature of this so called deprivation suggests a measuring of the Indian lifestyle and standard of living with those of the wider society. While this is certainly not misplaced when considering Indians within the larger Trinidad context, such an approach runs the risk of overlooking the internal mechanics of the Indian community. Although it is unarguable that the Indian community was faced with social and economic adversities, a lot of what has been termed deprivation can be situated in the difference between what was given precedence in the Indian community and in the wider society. For example, the popular idea of the Indian 'banding his belly' can be read as simply a difference in his standard diet to that of other members of the wider population. Thus, the importance given to augmenting the family's savings account should be considered more as an ingrained value in the Indian community rather than as the root of deprivation.

Until the late 1970s rise in conspicuous consumption, savings were jealously guarded, both in the banks and at home. Only the purchase of items promising potential profit such as land, cars, tractors and other agricultural implements, the building of homes, and the education of children were considered important enough to create some sort of dent in these assiduously accumulated sums.[57] The female genius was definitely evident in the fact that the majority of the female interviewees themselves, along with their mothers and grandmothers, had some sort of personal savings stashed away in mattresses, buried under the *chulha* stand, or hidden in the grass roof of the house. Inevitably, this money was used for the benefit of the entire family in the purchase of much needed clothes, small indulgences for the children, and for the woman's sparse personal entertainment, usually in the from of excursions, weddings and not infrequently, alcohol.[58] Substantial portions were also used to purchase jewellery. This echoed the traditional Indian notion of jewellery as a lucrative and mobile financial investment. According to oral sources, until as late as the 1970s, almost every rural-based Hindu family was involved in some activity, usually an integral part of their lifestyle that either generated additional income or reduced the family's expenditure. The most common of such activities included cultivating a vegetable garden, rearing cows which provided milk for both the family and for sale, rearing poultry and eggs for sale and consumption, and the preparation of essential products such as coconut oil, curry and rice at home.[59] The accepted practice of simply taking whatever vegetables you needed from fellow villagers' gardens (but only in small portions sufficient for the family meal), along with the equally common practice of sharing one's harvest with relatives and immediate neighbours also provided a valuable, cost-free supply of food items.

Until the 1960s, the attitude of Hindus towards formal banking systems was one of mistrust. The fear of being cheated was largely fuelled by their inability to read and write the English language, and hence fully comprehend the paperwork that was often involved in banking procedures. This fear, along with the secrecy and possessiveness with which Indians treated their savings, also deterred them from seeking assistance on the matter from individuals literate in English, especially from non-Indians. The placing of their life's earnings in the hands of a stranger, thereby rendering it very much out of their immediate control and reach, was too much of an antithesis to the intimacy and privacy which usually surrounded the Indian treatment of money. Even the prospect of gaining interest on their cash sums was unable to lure most Indians to such banking systems.

This mistrust was also enhanced by the perception that banks were primarily concerned with manipulating their clients into procuring loans. For Hindus, however, loans were perceived as a most undesirable practice that incurred the unnecessary loss of money. The extreme reluctance to procure loans can be situated in the fear of the consequences of being indebted to another. This can be traced back to the atrocities endured by the Indian population at the hands of moneylenders and others in positions to provide assistance to those in financial difficulty. In addition, the prominent practice of living within one's means, which placed little importance on whatever was not considered essential, also contributed to this attitude. The 1960s, however, saw a gradual relaxing of this Hindu response to loans, though not necessarily in their intrinsic attitude. The increasing infiltration of the social and economic workings of the wider society into the Hindu community, along with the growing desire for social mobility and better standards of living began rendering loans as a viable option. However, even then loans were procured only as a very last option and in the most urgent situations such as the purchasing of land and other farming equipment, and for weddings. So ingrained was this suspicion of loans that even matters such as the construction of homes and higher education, let alone the more trivial items such as furniture and even cars, would only much later be deemed important enough to warrant the procuring of loans.

Very much in accordance with the Hindu tendency to eventually deify that which is important, money, by the 1940s, was already one of the many items present at the family shrine. In cognizance of the goddess Lakshmi as the giver of wealth, it was a common practice to place a small portion of one's wages near to the Goddess' image, and to keep 'blessed' money in one's purse, taking care not to spend it so that '*dhan barhaawelaa*' (the money will increase).[60] The use of money in pujas as one of the major elements of offerings to the deities also enhanced its religious undertones. Money was also a primary offering in almost all of the major Hindu life cycle rituals (birth, marriage, death). It was also a most common gift item on the occasions of births and marriages where it was imbued with the socio-religious aura of the respective contexts. Until the 1970s, money was the most commonly gifted item to a newborn baby at the sixth and twelfth day birth rituals, with the understanding that such sums would be used in purchasing items for the child. Then, the performance of the birth rituals inevitably ritualised the gift of sums of money. Since then, the Western practice of gifting purchased items became the norm. However, rather than displacing money as a major gift item, other gifts served to somehow further push the former into the realm of tradition and ritual. The fact that the money was given at the first glimpse of the newborn, often after ceremonially encircling the child with it, also added to the ritual dimension of this practice.

At Hindu weddings money was used as an offering at both the pre and post-marriage rituals (such as the *maticor, lawa,* burying of the *kangan*) and during the marriage ceremony itself. Similar to the birth rituals, sums of money, referred to as *neotaa*, given to the parents of the bride and groom also accompanied the other purchased gifts. In addition, the *kicharee* (literally a dish of rice and peas cooked together, but in this context the entire ceremony surrounding the consumption of the dish) ritual of the ceremony further invoked money's function as a ritual gift. During this ritual, the groom and four of his relatives were seated in or near to the ceremonial canopy and were each given a portion of the rice dish. The bride's relatives, followed by members of the audience, then proceeded to gift sums of money to each of them. The objective of the ritual was for the groom and his party to amass as much money as possible before agreeing to consume the dish placed before them. Since refusal to partake of the dish could suggest a financial limitation, and consequently be considered an insult to the bride's party, the groom usually began eating when he noted a decline or cessation in the frequency of the gifting. This was also often instigated at the semi-jocular behest of his new in-laws, or by sometimes serious arrangements made prior to the ceremony. Yet, quite often, the amount of money received by the groom during the *kicharee* ritual was often a bone of contention later on in the marriage, between both the couple and their families.

A most outstanding documentation of this ritual can be found in V.S. Naipaul's *The Mystic Masseur* (Naipaul 1964, 43–46). Locating the *kicharee* in the earlier practice of dowry can explain much of the attitude surrounding the ritual. That the money collected during the ritual was invested with the name of the ritual, *kicharee*, also added to its ritual dimension. A similar gifting of money occurred when the marriage party returned to the groom's house. Again, the money itself acquired the name of the ritual, '*muh dekhaai*' (the seeing of the face), to mean the gift given when seeing the bride for the first time.

By the late 1970s, however, the changing socio-economic and occupational structure of the Hindu community, and the associated changes in values, attitudes and points of emphasis significantly altered this attitude towards money. The frugality that characterised the attitude of the previous decades was increasingly displaced by the contagious desire for a higher standard of living. It can be argued that the economic windfall of the early 1970s, by rendering the acquisition of money a realisable goal, also contributed to the more liberal attitude towards spending. Vertovec analyses the 1970s and 1980s with the marked increase in conspicuous consumption among Hindus as

> ...a period of 'en' less money' when a man could work in the fields for a few hours in the morning, eat well and relax in comfort at home all day, and drink excessively in the rumshop all night (Vertovec 1992, 145).

Although the eventual economic depression of the 1980s curbed the level of spending, the more liberal attitude towards the spending of money persisted. However, even the copious spending of the 1970s was not at the expense of personal savings. Drawing from oral sources, one can surmise that the liberal attitude was situated more in the increased access to money than in any sort of decline in the importance given to thrift.

Attitudes Towards India

By the 1940s, the relationship between India and the Hindu community in Trinidad could be described as one based on socio-religious, emotional and ancestral affinity. The almost desperate need by Trinidad Hindus to sustain connections – along with some sort of self-validation – with the country in which their religion, culture, values and systems originated can account for this affinity. In addition, due to the derisive attitude of the larger society to their religious and cultural systems and practices, there was the general perception among Hindus that attempts to situate Hinduism within the context of the wider Trinidadian society would prove impractical and futile. This reverberated in the fact that the middle class Hindus and other Indians, amidst acute efforts at assimilation into the wider society, expended as much effort in creating and sustaining socio-religious links with India, though now almost totally void of any desire to reclaim India as home. Although most such attempts were indeed initiated by the persons belonging to the middle class, the larger Hindu population responded in a more intensely sentimental manner to issues relating, in one way or the other, to India.

This was evident in the emotionally charged concern with the events surrounding India's independence, which was both fuelled by and reflected in the event's extensive coverage in the major national newspapers and Indian publications in Trinidad. Articles such as 'Mr Bose Vanishes' in the *Hindu Maha Sabha* (1941, 2), 'Gandhi Talks With Wavell' in the *Trinidad Guardian* on April 10, 1946, and 'Hindus Want Federation for India' in the *Trinidad Guardian* on April 16, 1946 often read or related to the then highly illiterate (in English) Hindu population, were the primary topic of discussion at village council meetings, *satsangs* and informal *baithaks*. The large sums of money collected for victims of famines in India (Kirpalani et al. 1945) evinced not just an abstract idea, but a real manifestation of this deep-seated concern. Mahatma Gandhi proved to be as celebrated and revered a personality in Trinidad as he was in India. According to reports in the *Trinidad Guardian* on October 2, 1946, the celebration of his birthday in the form of a motorcade '...from Princes Town to Penal to Siparia to Fyzabad,' and cultural programmes in districts such as Princes Town, Carapichaima, Arima, San Fernando and Waterloo bore evidence of this. Gandhi's assassination evoked island-wide prayer and memorial services by all the major religious denominations, the closing of Indian businesses and offices, and flags at half mast, which collectively reflected 'the profound feeling that seemed to settle over Trinidad' (*The Observor* 1948, 7:3). The unveiling of a statue of Gandhi in 1952 in the country's second major town, San Fernando, also suggested the acceptance of his status as hero.

The visits of Indian holy men and scholars such as Dr D.P. Pandia in 1941, Dr Kunzru in 1945 (leading to the establishment of the not surprisingly named India Club), and Pundit Satya Charran Shastri in 1946 reinforced the affinity with the Motherland by appealing largely to social, religious and cultural sentiments. This trend continued during the 1950s and 1960s with the arrival of Professor H.S. Adesh, Swami Chinmayananda, Swami Purnananda and Swami Satchidananda. Hindi films, along with the frequent visits of famous Indian cultural artistes in the fields of song, dance, drama and music served to refresh both the forms themselves in Trinidad and cultural links with India.

It was evident, however, that this emotional connection was not reciprocated by Indians of the Motherland. In the political realm, the attitude was one of almost patronising acknowledgement of the sentiments of Indians in the Caribbean for India. According to the 1948 report on Constitutional Reforms in Trinidad, the Government of India always asked '...to be informed beforehand and be given opportunity to comment on any important legislation on Constitutional changes affecting the fortunes of Indians in the Colonies,' and that Nehru did not '...fall far behind his countrymen in his interest in the fortunes of Indians overseas.'[61] However, this Indian interest in the affairs of Indians in Trinidad would remain largely at the level of written correspondence. In addition, it was underscored by a constant reminder that the country of birth, rather than India, was the homeland of the descendants of indentureds. This was clear in the following proposal of Prime Minister Jawaharlal Nehru:

> Indians domiciled there sometime or other have to choose....We have told them that they are perfectly free to choose. We are interested culturally and otherwise, and if they continue to be our citizens we are politically interested (*The Indian*, July 1952).

There was, though, a constant urge by Indian nationals that Indians in Trinidad should always be aware of their responsibility and links with the Motherland. Pundit Satya Charan Sastri, in his address at a local celebration of India's first anniversary of Independence, suggested that

> ...our countrymen in this colony should remember that every son and daughter bears some responsibility to Mother India in that they are expected to interpret her culture at this end. I hope they will not disappoint us and will rise to fulfil this mission (*The Observor* 1948, 7:9).

The support of even the Indian missionaries in Trinidad of this type of 'selective association' was evident in Swami Chinmayanada's Independence Day message reported on the following day in the *Trinidad Guardian* on August 31, 1967:

> They (Indians and non-Indians) must consider themselves as the children of Trinidad and Tobago....One word to my Indian brethren – wherever you are, in whatever conditions you remain – your spiritual home is India; and you must impart its universal message to all others around.

By the 1970s, however, the scope and depth of the emotional ties with India were being further curtailed by the socio-religious laxity of the period. The focus on socio-economic amelioration and the increasing penetration of the values and systems of the larger society into the Hindu community further accelerated this development. Thus, by the 1980s, despite the sustained varied interaction with India, what existed was a substantially diluted, idealisation and idolisation of the ancestral homeland, but with many still nursing a deep-seated, somewhat romantic desire to visit the country before they die. This desire could, to an extent, be situated in the popularity of pilgrimages in Trinidad Hinduism, thereby rendering a trip to India the ultimate pilgrimage. Although there was a unanimous recognition of Trinidad as the official homeland, situations that juxtaposed this ancestral pull with patriotism (such as cricket and international beauty pageants) and the posing of the question of whether one was Indian or Trinidadian revealed a much debated ambiguity in loyalties. This generated constant, sometimes exaggerated attempts at reaffirming Hindu patriotism and loyalty to Trinidad and Tobago. A most popular argument is reflected in the following observation extracted from an article in the *Express* April 20, 1987:

> ...the special bond which Hindus have with India has never compromised their loyalty to Trinidad and Tobago or inhibited their commitment and contribution to the development of this country.... In years past and even more recent times, this tie has been unfairly singled out and unjustifiably used to question our patriotism.

Is it questionable, then, whether diasporic communities can ever totally extricate themselves from their ancestral homelands, or indeed, if they will ever really want to. The validity and regeneration inherent in sustaining ties with the source of one's religion, culture, beliefs and practices seem to be indispensable in the sustenance of diasporic cultures. This is especially so in the context of a multicultural society.

Conclusion

The nature and degree of change that affected the more intimate aspects of Hindu life evince both Hinduism's propensity for adjustment and the inevitability of such change within the context of a multicultural society. That the elements of westernisation, modernisation and secularisation were allowed to penetrate gradually and to be accommodated into the spheres of family life, religious practice and belief, and intra-community dynamics (despite their often conflicting orientations) challenges the popular but misconceived notion of the Hindu community as backward and static. However, the simultaneous retention of the most fundamental concepts, systems and values, though often in varyingly mutated forms, exemplifies the tendency of diasporic communities to cling to their reconstructions, since they seem to provide the major source of identity and stability in an otherwise often ambiguous and tenuous situation. In the Trinidadian context, this diametric pull between change and continuity is situated largely in the tension between being Hindu while belonging to a national community.

It is evident that the period 1945–90 involved a high degree of transformation in the intimate spheres of Hindu family, religious and communal life. Such transformations were almost always related to the community's state of transience between the retention of the traditional and the adoption of the modern. At the personal level, transformation in the areas of occupation, education, economics and some religious practices revealed the changing attitudes and values among Hindus. No longer comfortable with restricting themselves to the limitations and vagaries of predominantly agriculture-based livelihoods, many Hindus chose to rework the foregoing areas to increase their opportunities at the socio-economic amelioration both within the Hindu community, and with respect to the wider society. Yet, judging from the substantial degree of retention of the more fundamental socio-religious principles and values, especially until the mid-1970s, it was clear that the process of selection was at work. That is to say, in order to enjoy the best of both worlds Hindus seemed to be regulating the nature, extent and locus of transformation in the more intimate aspects of their lives. This was evident in the paradox and ambiguity that characterised many issues.

At the level of family life, the gradual replacement of the structure and values of the extended family system by those of the nuclear system further signalled the increasing precedence placed on socio-economic amelioration, since persons were willing to rework this most private dimension of their life. Yet, the constant lamenting, by the 1990s, of the eventual loss of some of the traditions associated with Hinduism reiterates the complex nature of the dialogue. Transformations in structures and attitudes at the communal level also succumbing to the impact of Western and modern influences indicated the collective or, one can suggest, the 'official' acknowledgement by Hindus of the need to at least consider the prescriptions of the larger Trinidadian society. In order for Hindu religious and social practice and belief to obtain within the larger Trinidadian society, the need for omissions and accretions was recognised.

CHAPTER FIVE
Socio-Religious Change, 1945–90: The Public Domain

In addition to transformations in the more intimate aspects of Hindu life discussed in the previous chapter, there was considerable ferment in the public domain. Most of these issues, though operating within the Hindu community, were in some way related to the desire for public recognition and acceptance as both equal citizens of Trinidad and Tobago, and as Hindus. A loose distinction between the periods 1945–70 and 1970–90 is evident throughout. This is because the early 1970s was a watershed of sorts for the Hindu community. During that time almost all aspects of Hindu life were heavily affected by the conditions of the wider society. In addition, during the 1970s, those who had had the benefit of schooling in the Hindu elementary schools were, in numbers and competence, in a position to invoke the promise inherent in the words of the National Anthem that '...here every creed and race finds an equal place....' Thus, while until the 1970s Hindu socio-religious activity was rooted largely in internal communal sensibilities, an increasingly deliberate drive toward what can be termed a 'nationalisation' of the religion was initiated during that decade. Such shifts were of two types. The first comprised efforts that were deliberately engineered for the purpose of enhancing the visibility and acceptance of the religion as a valid aspect of Trinidad society. The second included those movements that can be read as the natural result of the religion's location in the dynamic, multicultural context of Trinidad and Tobago. Echoing Hinduism's propensity for blending the sacred and the secular, aspects of religion were evident in almost all dimensions of activity, either influencing or reflecting transformations in attitude, systems, and values. Such transformations collectively defined what has been termed the 'Hindu revitalisation' of the 1970s and early 1980s.[1]

Political scientist, John La Guerre has argued that the Black Power disturbances of 1970, while failing to attract the support of Hindus,[2] nevertheless served to '...re-ignite Indian consciousness and to galvanise them into the recreation and the revitalisation of Indian culture' (La Guerre 1995, 274). As he said:

> Negritude in short, was the spark that re-ignited East Indian consciousness. The East Indian response comes perilously close to mimicry. The Kurta and pyjama, the readings of the Bhagwat Gita, the retreat into Islam and Hinduism, the appeals for purity and the calls for more holidays – these constitute the euphoria of the movement. It was a plunge into the depths of the 'irrational' which the 'Black Power Movement' in its day took and which today the movements for East Indian regeneration seems it too must take (La Guerre 1985, 177).

This analysis, however, fails to acknowledge the internal mechanics of the Hindu community, and the various levels and degrees of transformation and ferment that were occurring simultaneously with the Black Power Movement which functioned as more of a catalyst for regeneration than the Black Power Movement ever could. The impact of the Black Power Movement on the Hindu community, rather, could be more aptly described as one, but not the only, significant stimulus for the traversing of elements of the religion (Hinduism) into the wider national space. The issues of ethnic and African cultural identity that were evoked in the Movement served to quicken the pace of the bid for Hindu socio-religious visibility, which was already astir within the Hindu community by the 1970s.

Hindu Leadership

The debate on Hindu leadership in the period 1945–90 revealed a great deal in terms of the changing demands and focus of the Hindu community. Highlighting its distinction from the Western construct, Haraksingh described Indian leadership during indenture as '...the art of inducing people to act or refrain from acting in a particular way...leadership may be viewed as a permanent state or as a temporary response to some problem or danger' (Haraksingh 1976, 11.3:18). He also identified three types of leaders within the traditional Indian domain: the natural leader, the leader by virtue of command, and the leader who depended on force. While there was considerable transformation, by the mid-twentieth century the major underlying principles of this idea of Hindu leadership were still evident. Until the 1960s, the predominance of tradition and religion-based systems and values demanded little, save for scriptural and ritual knowledge, and sometimes an eminent socio-economic status from Hindu socio-religious leaders. While formal education in English did add to one's social standing, it could not yet usurp more traditional factors. In fact, the mere sight of a dhoti and kurta unfailingly elicited a high level of respect from members of the community, both for the individual and for the station invoked by that mode of dress,[3] especially if the person was aged or indigent.

From the 1970s, however, this construct of Hindu leadership began to elicit mixed reactions, especially over the qualities and functions of the pundit. Pundits were commonly criticised for not being '...trained or equipped enough to deal with changes in society...,'[4] and for '...wanting their egos honoured.'[5] By the 1980s, the general preoccupation with socio-economic amelioration, along with visible changes in the way the pundits conducted rituals often elicited stinging criticism, especially of their perceived avarice. Some of this censure even came from fellow pundits, as in the following statement:

> Many are business pundits. They don't care how they teach the people or what they put out as long as the dollars coming. The older pundits were more serious regarding religion.[6]

The emerging ideal of Hindu leadership, then, was one that gave primacy to the community and how effectively the leader could serve his flock. This was evident in statements such as the following:

> A leader must possess good character, be open-minded, have vision for your people, earn the people's trust (by the way you live, not forced), be articulate and consistent, and have knowledge of the scriptures.[7]

However, this could not replace the awareness that '...they [pundits] did yeoman service to keep Hinduism alive even though they started with a disadvantage, so we should respect them.'[8]

The increasingly critical approach to *punditai* indicated transformation within the Hindu community on several levels. The growing move away from unquestioning loyalty to pundits and gurus, from obedience to their dictates, and from turning a blind eye to their transgressions reflected a more discerning approach to religion apparent since the 1980s. Perhaps some of the criticism was rooted in factional disputes, a feature characteristic of the Hindu community from as early as the 1920s. However, by the 1980s, other issues were significantly augmenting both the scope and depth of such criticism. These included the growth of secondary and tertiary education among Hindus and the perceived need by socio-religious organisations and leaders to rework aspects of religion to mirror transformations within the society. No longer was the community satisfied with leaders whose credentials rested largely on their lineage, their knowledge of the sacred mantras, and on their aura of pseudo-divine mysticism. Instead, the onus now resided heavily on the pundits to prove themselves capable and worthy of the title of leaders of the Hindu community.

Leadership in the socio-political arena remained quite reminiscent of the Indian patron-client relationship, where loyalties were anchored to a socially and economically distinguished persona who provided some form of assistance or amenity to either an individual or group. This was demonstrated in the relationship that existed between Bhadase Sagan Maraj (commonly referred to as Bhadase) and the members of both the SDMS and the larger Hindu Sanatanist community. Morton Klass confirmed such sentiments in his examination of the village of 'Amity' during the late 1950s (Klass 1961, 221–29). In the years immediately after Bhadase's death, the SDMS was reduced to an almost non-functional muddle of confusion and strife devoid of any sound sense of direction; this clearly showed Bhadase's overriding role in the organisation.

The distinguishing characteristic of Hindu socio-political leadership was, however, its inextricable connection to religion. Notwithstanding its prominence in the history of Trinidad Hinduism, this relationship between religion and politics in Trinidad was enhanced by the fact that a substantial section of the socially and economically elevated individuals either belonged to or were descendants of the Brahmin caste, who capitalised on their socio-religious status. Whether due to circumstance or coincidence, almost all of the Hindu leaders who represented the community on the national level until the 1990s were of Brahmin stock. A survey conducted in 1965 showed that Brahmins dominated the political life of Indians, with eleven out of fourteen political leaders claiming Brahmin origin (Malik 1971, 47). Mitra Sinanan, a third generation descendant of Brahmin stock and born into a wealthy business family, '...used his professional services to help the cause of labour' (Basdeo 1984, 14) in the latter half of the 1930s. Adrian Cola Rienzi of Brahmin parentage, emerged as a key figure '...to spearhead the drive for the unionisation of workers and the establishment of a national working class movement' (Singh 1985, 53). Both Rienzi and Sinanan were converts to Christianity, yet their Brahmin lineage was consistently invoked to elicit the support of the Hindu community. Rudranath and Simbhoonath Capildeo both belonged to a Brahmin family with a reputation based on elevated socio-economic status and a history of priesthood (DeVerteuil 1989, 127–45). Bhadase Sagan Maraj, in his station as wealthy Brahmin, could '...draw on the resources of two influential Hindu elites – the one religious-traditional, the other secular-modern – in his bid for political power' (Singh 1985, 54). Basdeo Panday, the first Hindu Prime Minister of Trinidad and Tobago, is also of Brahmin stock. Until the 1970s, there was little need to actively flaunt their Brahminism as a claim to socio-political authority. There was a silent underlying acknowledgement, both by the Brahmin leaders and the larger Hindu community, that the former had a prerogative to leadership and were more suitable for that role. However, by the 1970s (as was the case with pundits), the notion of Hindu political leadership was also being reworked. Accordingly, during the elections of 1976, Brahminism was not much help in either restoring credibility to the Brahmin-led (Gosine 1986, 163) Democratic Labour Party or in securing votes for its members.

The large-scale social transformation initiated in the 1970s led to an eventual subordination of religion-based considerations by such universal prerequisites as dedication to a cause, education, charisma, proficiency and good articulation. Although caste ceased to play any noteworthy role in national politics, religion was still a major determinant of leadership within the Hindu community. This was borne out in the interviews conducted. Most of the Hindus interviewed, though quite often very critical of Hindu leaders, would not divert their loyalties, and of course their votes, elsewhere. Thus, by the 1990s, Basdeo Panday somehow seemed to assume the mantle of Hindu political ascension that had been left largely inert since the 1970s. If Bhadase Sagan Maraj was the proverbial Rama who fought to release his community from the *rakshasas* (demons) of social, economic, religious and political depression while in *vanvaas*, (exile) then Basdeo Panday can be viewed as the Rama bearing promises of transporting the Hindu community, now out of the state of *vanvaas*, to that utopian state of *Ram Rajya* where Hindus would be second to none in the society.

Since the period of indenture, Hindu leadership, in ideology if not in practice, was largely directed by Hindu religious texts, especially by the *Ramcharitmanas*. This text revolves around polity, administration, diplomacy and war. The benefits of good government and democracy are exemplified in the *Rama Rajya* (the reign of Rama; an utopian state) while the contrary is shown under the rule of Ravan. This political dimension has always played an important role in both the reconstruction and sustenance of Hindu life in Trinidad. While the obvious difference in time, place, social and political contexts did not allow for the application of the political systems and codes in the *Ramayana* in Trinidad, the principles of good government and leadership outlined in the text were very interestingly worked into the local situation. Rama's embodiment of the perfect leader was constantly alluded to in the community's search for and affirmation of its own figures of authority. The principles of *Ramrajya* – peace, justice and reverence of socio-religious authority – were presented and seemingly accepted as the ideal among local Hindus. Conversely, the text's anti-hero, Ravan, illustrated the epitome of corrupt leadership.

Before the 1940s, when Hindus were accused of being essentially apolitical, *Ramayana* politics was apparent only within the Hindu community, influencing matters such as panchayat constitution and decisions, and the selection of immediate community leaders.

However, there were sporadic instances when *Ramayana* politics was extended beyond the boundaries of the Hindu community. For example, in an article in the *Port-of-Spain Gazette* October 1, 1939, reporting that local Indians 'unanimously passed a resolution of loyalty to the British Raj,' the political situation in the *Ramayana* was analogised to the World War, as follows:

> The love of the Mother of Bharata [Kaikeyi] was that of Hitlerism. She was rebuked by her son because it was based on deceit; so the righteous sons of Germany are saying (or will someday say) to Hitler: we do not thank you for the throne of Poland (and other countries). Britain, like unto Latchmana is being told (and will be told) to do their [sic] duty by assisting France, for therein lies the support of righteousness....

In the panchayat's function as mediator and judge in social problems of almost every nature, the *Ramayana* provided a source of reference, guide and confirmation in decision making, and also a source of divine yet human role models for both community and family life. Usha Devi Shukla confirmed the profuse quoting of verses of the *Ramcharitmanas* in the panchayat's attempts at solving community problems among Hindus in South Africa (*Sunday Guardian*, October 14, 1990). Thus, for example, the very troublesome but socially sanctioned issue of oral promises would be supported by reference to Rama's renouncing of kingship to fulfil his father's promise, and by quoting verses such as the following:

> *Ragukul reeti sadaa chali aayee, praan jaayee baru vachana na jayee.*
> It has always been the rule that one's plighted word must be redeemed even at the cost of one's life.[9]

Conflict among siblings over issues of inheritance frequently evoked references to the relationship between Rama and his brothers and how they dealt with succession. Marital discord almost always occasioned a lauding of Rama and Sita's ideal relationship, with an intrinsically patriarchal focus on Sita's unwavering dedication to her husband, even in the face of substantial odds.

Until the 1980s, there was minimal allusion to the *Ramcharitmanas* in the national politics of the country. However, the steadily increasing Hindu presence in the political arena since the 1980s, culminating in the election of a Hindu Prime Minister and a government comprising a significant percentage of Indians, imparted national significance and ramifications to *Ramayana* politics. The entrance of Hindus into the politics of the country, along with the vibrant rejuvenation of Hinduism since the 1980s, paved the way for the working of the political idiom of the *Ramayana* into the country's political dialogue.

Both national and community figures and leaders (pundits, gurus, counsellors and socio-religious leaders) began highlighting and reworking ideas in the *Ramayana* such as *Ramrajya*, Rama's ideal portrayal of kingship, leadership, loyalty, nature and functions of ministers, political harmony, selflessness, cooperation, and the primacy of the state and subjects in their bid to influence their audience. The merits of both Rama and his rule were often attributed to leader and party respectively, while opposing parties were inadvertently Ravanised. Comparisons between the ideals of *Ramrajya* and the local political situation were common at both *yagnas* and *satsangs*, as well as at rumshops. That both young and old, whether at *yagna* or rumshop, regardless of the varying levels of formal education, related to and analysed current affairs within the framework of the *Ramayana* highlights the pervasiveness of the *Ramayana* text and tradition. Such discussions were frequently instigated by pertinent verses such as the following:

> *Daihik daivik bhowtik taapaa. Raam raaj nahi kaahuhi vyaapaa.*
> *Sab nar karahee paraspar preeti. Chalahi swadharma nirat shruti neeti.*
> In the whole of Shri Raam's dominion there was none who suffered from affliction of any kind....All men loved one another; each followed one's prescribed duty, conformably to the precepts of the Vedas.[10]

The permeable lines between the sacred and the secular, together with Hinduism's pervasiveness in all dimensions of life, led to an increasing use of *yagnas* and *satsangs* as political platforms. Hopeful political aspirants capitalised on the religious atmosphere of these gatherings to gain the support of the Hindu audience, and usually correlated their own political ideologies to that of the *Ramayana*. Not surprisingly, the mixing of the sacred and the secular in that particular framework generated considerable conflict. The fact that this debate emerged during the earliest Hindu attempts at socio-religious organisation echoed the complexity of the issue. This was apparent in an address by T.R. Mahabirsingh of the *Trinidad Hindu Mahasabha*, reported in the *East Indian Weekly* on May 26, 1928:

> We do not wish to be steeped in politics but it is so entwined with the welfare of mankind that it is well nigh impossible to eliminate it. We hope however to confine ourselves to such politics as is conducive to the maintenance of our religious rights as conceded to us by Her Majesty Queen Victoria, the Good.

The idea of Hinduism as a way of life renders dichotomy between the sacred and the secular virtually impossible and sometimes, even undesirable. Thus, Hindu politics and religion (in this case the *yagna* and *satsang* settings), barring any compromising of the auspiciousness of the events, can have a positive, symbiotic relationship, where each enhances the other, especially within the context of the wider Trinidad society. On the other hand, however, it was argued that puja and politics should not co-exist since:

> ...there is no theological or scriptural basis for the politicising of, or political interference in the religious traditions and practices...there is no provision for secular leaders (which politicians are) officiating in any capacity in religious ceremonies....The act of speech making by politicians and other secular personalities in pujas and *yagnas* therefore runs counter to tradition. Furthermore the making of partisan political speeches not only destroys the sanctity of the ceremonies but also is in opposition to the spirit, intent and purpose of *yagnas*/pujas (Persad 2002, 3).

From the late 1980s, textual reinterpretation for political purposes was increasingly noticeable. This was partly stimulated by the fight against proselytisation and the rise of a number of Hindu socio-religious organisations, each attempting to present their own interpretation of Hinduism. The leader of one such group claimed that such interpretations could be seen as 'widening the scope of the *Ramayana*,' and as necessary in meeting the needs of society.[11] On the other hand, a prominent pundit contended that while persons of other religious denominations accepted their texts literally only Hindus, in an attempt 'to appear to be intellectual,'[12] engaged in textual interpretation. He argued that too many interpretations could lead to confusion. However, textual (re)interpretation has always been an intrinsic aspect of Hinduism, and owing to the multiplicity in Hindu traditions, texts, philosophy, sub-sects and socio-religious figures, there was always a tussle to establish which or whose interpretation should be preferred.

Hindu Organisational Function

Since the 1940s, Hindu organisational function has proven to be most dynamic and multi-layered, simultaneously engendering and reflecting various facets of change in Trinidad. The most prominent issues emerging from this ferment included inter-organisation conflict followed by attempts at unity, the formation of a number of new sects, the role of such sects in the national politics of the country, and the revitalisation of many public socio-religious and cultural events. Amidst the high level of conflict and diversity, by 1945 the larger more formally structured Hindu organisations had been recognised as representatives of the Hindu population on a national level. This was reflected in the decisive roles of such organisations as the Sanatan Dharma Board of Control, the Sanatan Dharma Association, and the Arya Samaj in the formulation of the Hindu Marriage Bill of 1945, and in taking the Hindu position on such issues as divorce, education and adult franchise. Without doubt, the most significant development during this period was the merging of the SDBC and the SDA into the SDMS in 1952.

The aims and objectives of the SDMS, outlined at its inception in 1952, reflected a vision of holistic social and religious amelioration of the Hindu community with special emphasis on education, religious liberties, establishing some sort of structure to Trinidad Hinduism, and enhancing the status of the religion in the colony.[13] These objectives were underscored by the implementation of a Hindu primary school system, the partial funding of numerous temples throughout Trinidad, and by a high level of mobilisation and socio-religious enthusiasm. The SDMS seemed, finally, to provide the kind of structured, large-scale, unified representation promised for decades by previous socio-religious bodies, but difficult to achieve for reasons which were evident in the following report of Indian scholar, Dr Parasuram Sharma:

> ...it would be impossible to unite and advance the Hindus in Trinidad through any of the existing local Hindu organisations. Nearly all these organisations were the monopoly of one or a few individuals, and they were all very jealous of each other. Their mutual jealousy far surpassed their desire for Hindu unity and advancement. Each of these individuals regarded his organisation as his pet baby and could not tolerate any interference by any other person, not even suggestions for improvement (*Hindu Maha Sabha* 1940, vol.1).

Several issues are apparent in this analysis. The jealous monopoly of 'one or a few individuals' echoed inherently Hindu systems of power relations (guru-chela, *praja, jajmani*) which, until the 1970s, were functioning in Trinidad. Regarding an organisation as one's 'pet baby' and being closed to any kind of 'interference' reflected the unchallenged authority that characterised Hindu power relations. In addition, the idea of unity in diversity which allows for the relative autonomy of individuals and groups under the umbrella of Hinduism was the underlying principle of Hindu organisational function. Thus, attempts at collapsing the numerous Hindu groups into organisational unity in the Western sense would have been challenging the major foundational principles of traditional Hindu group dynamics. Hence, the crux of the difficulty resided, not in advancing the Hindus in Trinidad through any of the existing local Hindu organisations, but in attempting to do so through one singular body.

It was not surprising, therefore, that less than a decade after its inception, cracks in the structural, ideological and functional framework of the SDMS were evident. According to a report in the *Trinidad Guardian* June 16, 1960, the Annual General Meeting of 1960 was brought to an abrupt halt due to a '...heated debate on the executive committee's annual report, and carping criticisms levelled against the executive.' The argument centred around the executive's failure to produce the constitutionally required audited financial report, a default which, according to some members, had been occurring for a number of years. The meeting ended with more than 75 per cent of those present declining to vote on matters at hand. Notwithstanding the apparent cracks in the organisation, one can speculate that procedures such as audits and written reports, and even the structure of the meetings were incompatible with traditional Hindu notions of organisation. Until the 1970s, Hindu socio-political and religious leaders were accustomed to virtually unchallenged authority. It is not difficult then to envisage such leaders not assigning much import or even refusing to abide by such procedures and forms, viewing them as challenges to their authority, or even questioning their word and worth. This was especially the case of the SDMS and its leader, Bhadase Sagan Maraj, who both founded the organisation and channelled substantial sums of his personal money into it. Honorary Secretary of the Democratic Labour Party, F.E. Brassington, described Bhadase's preoccupation with regaining control of the DLP which he lost to Dr Rudranath Capildeo in 1960 as one that 'consumed him and distorted his objectivity' (Brassington n.d., 168).

By 1966, the internal strife had reached the courts in a dispute over the organisation's leadership. This forced the Sanatan Dharma Pundit's Parishad to appeal '...to the three factions of the Maha Sabha of Trinidad and Tobago to form one body and withdraw the dispute' (*Trinidad Guardian*, February 3, 1966). However, the three factions, led by Pundit Lutchmie Narine Panday, Bhadase Sagan Maraj and Jang Bahadoorsingh respectively, were asking the court to declare, among other things, who were the 'proper officers of the association.' A report in the *Trinidad Guardian* April 21, 1966 confirms that at a meeting called to discuss the issue, a move was instigated to unseat the *Dharmaacharya* of the SDMS, Pundit Jankie Persad Sharma. During the court proceedings, the plaintiffs (Lutchmie Narine Panday, Dhanraj Mahabir and Sieudath Laloo Hingoo) belonging to one faction of the SDMS, were seeking '...an injunction to restrain the defendants from exercising any of the duties such officers may be called upon to perform' (*Trinidad Guardian*, October 19, 1966). The defendants (Bhadase Sagan Maraj, Harry Persad Beharry, Jang Bahadoorsingh and Ram Surat Singh) belonged to the other two factions of the organisation. Despite repeated claims that the disputants were working out their divisions, strains of discontent and conflict persisted within the organisation, and were to deepen immediately after the death of Bhadase Sagan Maraj in 1971.

At the core of the strife was the formulation of a new constitution which sought to remove '...the sweeping powers given to the president general...' and which was designed for the '...total involvement of all Hindus...and the decentralisation of power' (*Trinidad Guardian*, May 22, 1972). Officers were to be elected by the full executive instead of, as previously, by the president. In addition, it was proposed that the president be elected annually but not hold power for more than three consecutive years. This increasing agitation for the decentralisation of power within the executive mirrored, in addition to the apparent lack of efficiency, the community's increasing gravitation away from the traditional dictates of unchallenging loyalties to leadership towards the more democratic forms of the wider society. As reported in the *Trinidad Guardian* on March 11, 1972, a prominent Hindu social worker cited the reason for the SDMS's disintegration as '...due mainly to the fact that prior to the death of the President, Mr Bhadase Sagan Maraj, no effort was made to organise the members.' This was again a possible indication of the incongruence between the Hindu mode of organisation and that of the wider society. Within the Hindu framework, there was no pressing need to organise the members, since, rather than organisation, loyalty and obedience to the leader were the primary underlying principles.

With the infighting apparently not dissipating, members of the Pundits' Parishad of the SDMS decided in 1972 that

> ...in view of the failure of the Executive of the Maha Sabha to carry on, the Pundits should consider taking their rightful position to safeguard and protect the religion by organising themselves to run the affairs of the Maha Sabha with the help of all Hindus in the country (*Trinidad Guardian*, July 6, 1985).

Simultaneously,

> ...a group of young Hindus and some of their elders teamed up to draft what they describe as a 'master plan' to knock away the dead weight at the top of the SDMS, and lift the 20 year old body out of the educational and spiritual doldrums (*Trinidad Guardian*, April 3, 1972).

Such infighting characterised the workings of the SDMS through the 1980s. For example, the *Trinidad Guardian*, May 25, 1972 reported that some pundits within the SDMS were opposed to the power of the central executive to appoint an 'Archbishop.' In 1981, a meeting was designed to oust the Secretary General Satnarine Maharaj from the SDMS because of his political affiliation with the PNM during the 1981 general elections campaign (*Trinidad Guardian*, November 24, 1981). Such internal dissension sometimes resulted in the creation of vigilante committees within the SDMS. While some of these committees eventually broke away from the SDMS to form new socio-religious groups, many were eventually subsumed by the overarching structure and policies of the organisation.

In its initial stage, the popularity of the SDMS was situated largely in its development of the Hindu pimary school system, and the partial funding of temples. The decline in both these activities during the 1960s served to gradually stem the euphoric support received by the SDMS from the Hindu community. This, together with the internal strife which we have noted, led to a marked decline in the credibility and popular appeal of the SDMS throughout the 1970s and 1980s. Many localised committees, bristling at the decline in the contribution of the SDMS to the maintenance and activities of the temples, disassociated themselves from the parent organisation. Some, like the members of the Hindu Temple at Gittens Street in Tacarigua, even went as far as filing injunctions against members of the SDMS from 'trespassing and entering' the temples (*Express*, June 27, 1984). According to both oral and written sources, the SDMS forced their way into many temples constructed and operated by the villagers themselves. An executive member of the Couva Temple, seeking a similar injunction to prevent the SDMS from trespassing provided the following description of the SDMS appropriation of the temple:

> The temple doors were always open. Then, [electric] fans and a tape [recorder] started appearing. A lock was put on the door, but that was smashed and those 'men' put their own lock, and then applied [to the State?] for registration of the temple [as a branch of the SDMS] (*Express*, August 18, 1974).

Since the police refused to intervene, stating that it was a 'private matter,' legal injunction was sought since '...the Couva Temple wanted to remain independent of the Maha Sabha [in order to] keep away from politics' (*Express*, August 18, 1974). Numerous articles appearing in the press bore evidence of the widespread disillusionment. One such letter to the editor in the *Trinidad Guardian* February 25, 1981 claimed that the 'Maha Sabha speaks only for Brahmins...' and stressed that 90 per cent of its executive was Brahmin (ten per cent of the Hindu population), while ten per cent of its executive was non-Brahmin (90 per cent of the Hindu population). The letter further argued that when in possession of 450 branches, and providing money, labour and schools, the SDMS could then have spoken for the population, but with only 75 branches, and dominated by Brahmins at the executive level, its authority was no longer valid.

The high degree of internal strife and resultant public disillusionment with the organisation created the ideal conditions and space for the emergence of a number of new socio-religious groups. Interestingly enough, quite a number of these organisations were either founded or influenced by missionaries and scholars from India. Such organisations included the Gandhi Seva Sangh in 1952 (*Trinidad Guardian*, March 21, 1952), the Divine Life Society in 1966 (*Hindu Times* 1966), the Vishwa Hindu Parishad of Trinidad and Tobago in 1966 (*Trinidad Guardian*, July 23, 1966), the Bharatiya Vidya Sansthaan in 1966, and the Brahma Kumari Raja Yoga centre in 1976.[14] Notwithstanding the constant bickering described as backbiting and 'crab in barrel syndrome'[15] that persisted, there were concerted efforts at establishing some level of consensus and harmony among these organisations. By then the idea of unity (in the sense of being presented as a single whole) was no longer coveted, since it could have entailed the compromise of the objectives, methodology and tenets of individual organisations. An article in the *Trinidad Guardian* on January 17, 1967, entitled 'Hindus make a bid to unite' reported on a meeting of delegates from the DLS, APS, VHP, KPA, SDMS and Sieunarine Dharam Sabha wherein a '...Constitution for the formation of a United Hindu Organisation was unanimously approved.' This proposed body was classified as '...strictly a religious and cultural organisation with a primary objective to consolidate, strengthen and unite all Hindu organisations and not replace them.' The ultimate goal was '...to develop Hinduism in order to move forward with other religious and cultural organisations in making a

greater contribution to the progress of this cosmopolitan society...'
(*Trinidad Guardian*, January 17, 1967).

The following excerpt from a speech delivered by the President of the DLS on his organisation's tenth anniversary celebrations echoed the general attitude:

> There can be no doubt that we are on the threshold of a new era — an era that demands a revolutionised approach to our Hindu method of organisation and community development. If we are to take a rightful place in this cosmopolitan community, the attitude towards our responsibilities and duties must necessarily be extended (*Sanatan Dharma News*, September 29, 1972).

The emphasis on taking one's rightful place in this cosmopolitan community reflected what was to become a major preoccupation among Hindu organisations in Trinidad from the 1980s. This became the primary push factor in the incorporation of non-Hindu principles and practices into, not just Hindu group mechanics, but almost all aspects of Trinidad Hinduism. By the 1990s, this contributed to the decline of many fundamental aspects of Hindu organisational structure and function which were seen as limiting the scope and degree of situating Hinduism within the wider cosmopolitan society. The inherent ideology, however, was a lot more enduring. By the late 1980s, it was evident from the nature and focus of the emerging organisations that the emphasis was on reworking and procuring for Trinidad Hinduism acknowledgement (by both the State and the wider society) as the religion of 24.9 per cent of the population.[16] Thus, organisations such as the Hindi Nidhi, the National Council for Indian Culture, the National Council of Hindu Organisations, the Hindu Seva Sangh, and the Hindu Prachar Kendra began aspiring for large scale national observances and events.

Such a change can be viewed as natural and necessary within the context of an increasingly dynamic and thriving community and society. A leader of one organisation viewed this as:

> ...a natural growth in Hinduism to cater to time. New forms of expression emerge to validate finding new things and dealing with changes. Before all our effort went into preserving, which was unhealthy. In Hindu tradition, creation, preservation and destruction pervade all processes. Change may not be as visible; stability is more

> visible. Unconsciously change is happening, but consciously we emphasise preserving.[17]

However, as Vertovec noted in the early 1980s, '...the fairly recent multiplying of national Hindu organisations has not benefited the cause of the religion in Trinidad, since they often tend to engage in much criticism of one another' (Vertovec 1992, 91). Indeed, this rise of organisations unaffiliated to the SDMS, and quite often in contradiction to the latter's methods and attitudes, intensified the dissension that had defined internal Hindu politics. Senior members of many such organisations attested to varying degrees of hostility from the SDMS, especially from the Secretary General, during the 1980s. It would not be erroneous to surmise that the perceived threat to its status as the primary representative of the Hindu community was the underlying factor in the attitude of the SDMS towards other Hindu and Indian organisations. Until 1990, however, the desire for such unity was stagnated at the ideological stage. Fundamental differences in terms of focus, methodology, objectives, and of course, leadership, were at the core of this dissonance.

Publicisation

The nature and degree of organisational activity during this period was most evident in the socio-religious and cultural ferment of the time. Encouraged by the educational prospects provided by the SDMS's education system, a heightened awareness and distaste of the sense of alienation from the wider society, and the religious ferment, Trinidad Hinduism was empowered with confidence to assert itself on a national level. The growing appetite for transporting elements of its religion and culture out of the communal and into the national sphere heightened considerably during the 1960s. This attitude reached the Legislative Assembly where, immediately following independence, an elected member for a constituency with a large Hindu electorate argued that

> ...Hindus have always been an integral part of our nation. This Government has no right, by its neglect, to relegate the Hindus of this country and the children of these Hindus to the lowest possible class, and to be the pariahs in our social structure. What is being

done to keep these children when they grow up to be the hewers of wood and the drawers of water, as the forefathers have been before them.[18]

This was most evident in the struggle for the declaration of the Hindu festival of Divali as a national holiday. According to an article in the *Trinidad Guardian* on January 8, 1966, entitled 'Hindus Ready To March For Their Own Holiday,' the Member for Caroni South, Surendranath Capildeo, received a petition from the Dow Village Hindu Youth Organisation to press for the granting '...of at least one public holiday in honour of the second largest religious group in the country.' If not, they would be prepared to hold marches and public meetings throughout Trinidad to agitate for the holiday. Their efforts proved successful when Divali day was declared a public holiday in 1968.

Not unexpectedly, the political life of the country provided a major forum for the unfolding of these developments, which during the 1960s, often seemed to be characterised by self-serving, biased concessions. Though nursing intense feelings of alienation from the ruling People's National Movement, the Hindu community was not ignorant of the need to gain favour with the Government. This was evident in such instances as the following reported in the *Trinidad Guardian*, November 18, 1966 where, at a ceremony at the Debe Hindu Temple, executives of the Pundits Parishad and the SDMS

> ...prayed for the welfare of the new Government...paid tribute to the Government and offered special prayers that goodwill will prevail in the minds of the rulers so that everything that was good for the country would be achieved.

The Government, possibly patronising, but definitely aware that the Hindu community could no longer be dealt with as an invisible entity, seemed to reciprocate. This was evident in events such as an islandwide Indian singing competition sponsored by the National Council of Indian Music and Drama '...as part of the PNM's tenth anniversary celebrations' (*Trinidad Guardian*, January 4, 1966). This apparently more receptive attitude was also evident among several of the other religious denominations. According to a report in the *Trinidad Guardian*, February 17, 1967, a Government senator, the special guest at the seventh anniversary observation of the Vishwa Hindu Parishad, '...took off his shoes, entered a Hindu Temple, and participated in a two-and-a-half-hour service.' One suspects, however, that since the senator was neither Hindu nor Indian his participation did not extend much beyond him sitting and observing the proceedings.

In the 1970s and 1980s, Hindus began demanding more than just what resembled periodic attempts at pacifying Hindu concerns. Even during the religious languor of the early 1970s, forums to address the situation such as a 1974 symposium on 'The Struggle for Survival: The Hindu Youth in the Caribbean' (Siewah 1994, 201) were generated. Instead of being restricted to religious issues, the Hindu community began participating in debates on issues of national concern. Hindus aired their opinion on the government's proposed programme of national service. In a forum on the issue, reported in the *Trinidad Guardian*, November 21, 1989, a senior member of a growing Hindu youth organisation expressed the view that:

> ...while there are noble objectives formulated for the National Service...there were deep fears and concerns that the aspirations and values of Hindus in the society will not be considered.

Efforts at publicisation were both fuelled by and evident in the advent of performing artistes from India during that decade, including famous singers such as Manna Dey, Geeta Dutt, Mohammed Rafi, and Mukesh. Their performances were organised by various local promoters. *Bharat Natyam* dance performances by world famous Indian dancers Ram Gopal and Shrimal Gina (*Trinidad Guardian* October 29, 1955), and later on, by 'Indrani and Baliram' (*Trinidad Guardian*, September 1, 1960) were hosted, not within the confines of the community, but at the country's most popular cultural centres such as the Queen's Hall and the Globe Theatre in the capital, and the Naparima Bowl in San Fernando. According to reports in the *Hindu Times*, March 1966, along with the artistes from India, there was an increasing appearance of singing, dancing and music competitions, and what were called 'social evenings' featuring local performers. The *Trinidad Guardian* on August 19, 1962, reported on an 'Indian

Singing Exhibition and Dance Display' in commemoration of the country's independence. In 1964, there was both a 'Hemant Kumar imitation [singing] contest' with the artiste himself also performing during the second half of the programme (*Trinidad Guardian*, July 26, 1964), and an 'Indian Variety Show' with performers from Suriname (*Trinidad Guardian*, November 27, 1964). In 1966, what was to become the very popular 'Indian Ladies Singing Competition' was initiated.

Religious observances also transcended individual and communal boundaries to acquire a more structured, large-scale format, with Divali, the most prominent festival among Trinidad Hindus, being the forerunner in this turn of events. In 1964, all SDMS schools were closed in observance of both Divali and *Kartik Nahaan* (*Sunday Guardian*, November 1, 1964) and a 'Divali Show' was held at the Naparima Bowl in San Fernando (*Trinidad Guardian*, November 3, 1964). By 1965, large-scale celebrations in areas such as Caroni, St James, El Dorado, Warrenville, Aranjuez and the University of the West Indies stimulated the press to comment that for 'the first time Trinidadians were nationally aware of Divali the Hindu Festival of Lights' (*Evening News*, November 14, 1966). This awareness, however, can be better translated as a very superficial knowledge of only the most visible aspects of the festival such as the lighting of *deeyas*, a cultural programme, good food and, possibly, its association with the Goddess Lakshmi. The use of the term 'Trinidadian' suggested (somewhat unsurprisingly) the dominant, though often unvoiced, attitude of the non-Indian population until the 1970s: one that suggested an exclusion or distinction of Hindus from the national grouping. Despite the increasing, albeit yet few and rather simplistic press articles on Hindu religious observances, any real understanding of the significance and religious aspect of Hindu festivals and Trinidad Hinduism on the whole would almost totally elude the wider non-Hindu community for at least another decade. By the 1970s, there was an intensification of this publicisation in the religious sphere. Largely due to efforts of the SDMS, other festivals such as *Phagwa* and *Kartik Nahaan* were also being observed on comparably larger scales, very much in the public eye. According to a report in the *Trinidad Guardian*, November 9, 1965:

> ...the observation of *Kartik Nahaan* at the Manzanilla beach saw Sanatanists turn out as they never did before....More than five dozen religious services were held all over the beach by Pundits hailing from all over the country....SDMS schools were closed for the day....

A most notable aspect of this endeavour was the advent of *Divali Nagar* in 1986. This annual event owed its popularity to a combination of factors such as its affiliation to a number of the more nationally recognised Indian and Hindu organisations substantially comprising members of the middle or upper socio-economic strata. Land was granted by the state-owned Caroni (1975) Limited in 1989 especially (but not exclusively) for the observance of this event, and the site was named 'The Divali Nagar Site.' The Divali Nagar was associated with the major Hindu festival, Divali. It also provided the opportunity for individuals to enjoy various facets of Indian culture (the art forms, food, and dress) in one place. Its location outside the boundaries of any particular village or community augmented its appeal as a national rather than a communal event. Its location along one of the major highways in the country made it very accessible. In addition, with themes such as *Girmitiya Gaon* (Village of the Indentureds)), *Shri Raam Vijay* (Victory of/to Rama), *Jahaaji* (Indenture), and Hindu Festivals (1989), the '...thrust of *Divali Nagar*...introduced a much needed dynamism into the presentation and communication of Indian culture' (*Trinidad Guardian*, October 20, 1986). This has been the main argument in support of the *Divali Nagar*. One can speculate, however, on the connotation of this dynamism and also on to whom Indian culture was being presented and communicated. In fact, this dynamism was often interpreted as a tendency to overly commercialise the event, at the cost of its religious and cultural dimension. Such were the major arguments of the SDMS which did not support the thrust of the endeavour. The SDMS also did not approve of the fact that a Presbyterian was spearheading this commemoration of what was essentially a Hindu religious observance. Yet, one cannot deny that the *Divali Nagar* played a major role in promulgating some dimensions of both Hindu and Indian religion and culture.

In 1990 the Hindu Prachar Kendra inaugurated what was to become its annual Kendra Phagwa Festival. In the subsequent decade this event evolved into one of the most visible and controversial forums for the ventilation of issues affecting the Hindu community. Staged during the annual *Phagwa* festivities, it entailed the singing of social commentary songs (in various combinations of Hindi, Bhojpuri and English) which sometimes sought to refute calypsoes that were deemed offensive to Hindus and Hinduism, to highlight social ills and to air grievances within the Hindu community.

A more involved stance by the Hindu community was also evident in a seemingly reciprocal attitude by the wider society. At the beginning of the 1980s, the Hindu community, for the first time, benefited from an 'ecclesiastical grant' of $31,200 from the state, based on membership as received in the census of 1980.[19] By the 1990s several of the major socio-religious organisations for the observance of *Phagwa* and Divali were receiving government grants. However, the mere granting of financial aid cannot be interpreted as a definitive marker of either the state's or the wider community's more intrinsic attitude to Trinidadian Hinduism. In addition, there were always complaints about insufficient funding. According to a report in the *Trinidad Guardian*, April 24, 1987, as a method of addressing this and other concerns of the Hindu community, an 'agenda for action' was drawn up at the closing evaluation session of the 1987 Caribbean Hindu Conference, delineating several concerns relating to Hindu interaction in the wider society.

Hinduism and the Media

The number and nature of articles in the press reflected the society's attitudes and perception of Hinduism, and enhanced the Hindu community's level of visibility. Since the discontinuation of the 'Indian' pages by both the *Trinidad Guardian* and the *Port-of-Spain Gazette* during the Second World War, press coverage of Hindu affairs, until the 1960s, was restricted to very small, sporadic notices of private *yagnas,* pujas or other observances. These events were, more often than not, sponsored by wealthier Hindu individuals. During the 1960s, these notices became more frequent and more detailed, though still very much superficial in their exposition of Hindu festivals and observances. Some attempts at capturing the nuances of Hindu events in the language of the press (in other words, comprehensible by the wider society) often resulted in either awkward or erroneous representations. According to a report on *Phagwa* in the *Trinidad Guardian*, March 7, 1961:

> Village Hindu choirs added much colour to the merry-making, as they journeyed from house to house, singing songs of merriment for the occasion, and doing oriental dances.

Though not inaccurate in a literal sense, the reliance on Western classifications of 'choirs,' 'merry-making,' and 'oriental dances' overlooked the religious dimension of the festival. This was even more evident in a notice on Divali in the *Trinidad Guardian*, November 7, 1961, which read 'Hindus in the territory will celebrate the feast of Divali....Here several parties will be held and messages will be delivered.' 'Feasts' is the wrong word, and the reference to 'parties' totally misconstrued the nature of the events.

By the mid-1960s, entire pages were being dedicated to the recognition of the major religious observances such as *Divali, Shiv Ratri* and *Ram Naumi*. These included greetings to the Hindu community, articles on the significance of the events (from both Hindus and non-Hindus), and notices of celebrations. The mid-1980s, however, can be identified as the time when genuine sustained effort was made to present Hinduism on its own terms and as an integral dimension of Trinidad society. Many articles on the nature, tenets, rituals and observances of the religion were featured, especially around the time of the major religious observances. What was equally noteworthy was the transformation of these articles from just narrative reporting to pieces seeking to promote a deeper understanding of the dynamics of Hinduism. Such articles included 'Hindu woman – an evaluation' (*Sunday Express*, March 2, 1986), 'A Hindu Youth Speaks Out' (*Sunday Express*, March 2, 1986), 'Understanding Hindus in Trinidad and Tobago' (*Sunday Guardian*, October 29, 1989), 'Divali and Trinidad Society' (*Sunday Guardian*, October 29, 1989), and 'Coming in from the Cold' (*Sunday Guardian*, May 27, 1990). By 1986, entire supplements dedicated to the major Hindu festivals could be found in the country's main daily newspapers. Drawing from both the transformation in the attitude of Hindus and the fact that most of these articles were written by Hindus, it can be surmised that this development was largely a result of the upsurge in education among Hindus in the 1950s.

In addition to the more probing nature of the articles, the more commercial aspect of these supplements also revealed several salient transformations. That these supplements and articles were often sponsored by Hindu members of the business community confirmed the increasing inclination for promoting Hinduism on a more national, large-scale level. Such active attempts at taking aspects of Hinduism beyond its communal boundaries reflected a significant degree of confidence as Hindus within a multicultural society, an attitude that was barely discernible just one decade ago. That such supplements were also sponsored by non-Hindu members of the business community echoed Hinduism's growing visibility within the larger society. However, during the 1990s, the input of the business community would generate debate and lamentation on the commercialising of the religion, that is to say, the subjugation, or at least the diluting, of the religious dimension of Hindu festivals and observances by an excessive capitalising of the business community on such events. It would be fair to add that similar sentiments were not absent from the annual festivities at Christmas.

The emergence of a vibrant Indian press gave added impetus to the religio-cultural renaissance of the 1980s. Spearheaded by a group of young Hindu academics, publications such as *Sandesh* (Message), *Jagriti* (Awakening), and *Jagaran* (Watch), addressing social, political and religious issues, provided a previously lacking avenue for the articulation of Hindu opinion and concerns. This group initially comprised university students who, from the mid-1980s onwards, sought to highlight issues facing the Hindu community and to generate a deeper understanding and awareness of Hinduism both on and off the St Augustine campus. During this period also, The Indian Review Committee produced frequent special publications in observance of the major festivals and Hindu events. This group of 'young university level Hindus' defined itself as '...a society of activists dedicated to Indian Research, studies and causes' (*The Indian Review*, August, 1981). Articles in their journal *The Indian Review* included 'The Indian Dilemma,' 'The Indians and the Elections of 1981,' 'The Hindus in Trinidad,' and 'The Passive Indians.' The establishment of the Chakra Publishing House saw an increase in the number of publications by both Hindu and non-Hindu authors on various aspects of the Hindu/Indian experience in Trinidad. Professor John La Guerre viewed the 1980s' removal of the taboo surrounding discussions of the separate experience of the Indian community as an undeniable indication of the socio-economic and political changes of both the Indian community and the wider society (La Guerre, xviii). This was in contrast to the initial response of suspicion which met both the first edition of his publication *Calcutta to Caroni* in 1974, and the First Conference on East Indians in the Caribbean hosted by the University of the West Indies in 1975.

Formal Education

The dissemination of English education among Indians in Trinidad has been much studied.[20] Hence, rather than any detailed examination of the actual process, only some of the major related issues will be highlighted. As shown in Appendix V, there was a steady rise in the education of Hindus between 1952 and 1990. The desire for social mobility instigated a marked increase in English education among Hindus, while the acquisition of education resulted in transformations in both the religious and more general spheres of life. The approaches to and focus of religion were reworked to cater to varying levels of probing of more inquiring minds. Hindu religious and social forms were increasingly influenced by non-Hindu systems and tenets which were often filtered through the education system.

One of the most prominent Hindu concerns was the religious education programme, or a lack thereof. From as early as 1948, the Director of Education's Report acknowledged that:

> The religious education of the large number of Hindus and Muslims presents considerable difficulty. Qualified pundits and imams are extremely scarce. They would be permitted to enter Government schools and some assisted schools on request but few if any do so. They would not be admitted to Roman Catholic schools.[21]

It can be speculated that rather than reluctance, the failure to appoint teachers for Hindu religious instruction can better account for the situation. This was due to lack of unanimity among the

Hindu religious bodies on who should be appointed as teachers of Hindu religious instruction.[22] Also, in the light of the numerous village *pathshalas* whose main purpose was religious education, it is possible that Hindu leaders did not perceive the need for conducting additional classes, and that too in a setting that was quite alien from the traditional Hindu mode of instruction. There was also the problem of ideological conflict. For example, reciting a mantra or verses from the sacred texts in a classroom where all types of meat were consumed (assuming that students ate in the classrooms, or had eaten just before coming into the classroom) bordered on sacrilege. In addition, the high level of ridicule and scorn with which Hindu practices and beliefs were regarded discouraged Hindu individuals from venturing to promote their religion in a public, non-Hindu setting. Nevertheless, in 1951, Religious Instruction was included as a compulsory subject on the primary school curriculum.[23]

With the establishment of the SDMS, Arya Samaj and KPA Hindu schools, this issue was further highlighted. While both the general ambience and orientation of those new schools promoted education in Hindu religious matters, by 1965 there was an emphasis on establishing a formal Hindu religious programme. Thus, in his commendation of the Draft Education Act, the leader of the SDMS emphasised, in an article in the *Trinidad Guardian*, October 15, 1965, that '...Government should go further and provide that our pundits must be allowed to give religious instructions to the Hindu children in all Government schools...' and that the curriculum should include provisions for religious instructions. Such agitation seemed to have been somewhat successful for during that same year, religious bodies were granted permission to conduct religious instructions in government secondary schools to the two lowest forms.[24] By that time the preoccupation with formal education in English had somewhat superseded the concern with sacrilege perceived in the transporting of Hindu religious elements into the classrooms of government-run schools. In addition, the actual transposing of the religious into the secular spaces of the school and the curriculum further reduced the concern with ideological conflict. The religious revitalisation of the 1980s generated intensified efforts at providing Hindu religious education, especially at the secondary school level.

This preoccupation with establishing Religious Instruction as an integral part of the formal education system eventually led to the birth of two major school-based programmes: the Secondary Schools' *Sanskritic Sangam* (Secondary School's Cultural Meeting) in 1979, and the *Baal Vikaas* Festival in 1986. These were structured along the lines of inter-school competitions in several categories and aimed at both SDMS and non-SDMS schools. The primary schools' *Baal Vikaas* programme, with its emphasis on the study of the *Ramayana*, Hindi and the performing arts, had as its founding principles:

> ...the propagation of knowledge of the scriptures...the inculcation of moral values,...the fostering of [a] high quality of education... and the development of the latent talents of our students and the creativity of our teachers.[25]

By 1990, the Secondary Schools' *Sanskritic Sangam* included activities such as song, dance, art, craft, debate, poetry, play and essay writing, public speaking, drama, fashion, and quizzes on the *Ramayana* and the *Mahabharata* (*Trinidad Guardian*, October 2, 1981). Regular workshops and seminars with themes such as 'The Teaching of Religion and Ethics in Our Schools in Trinidad and Tobago' also assisted in enhancing Hindu religious instructions in both the primary and secondary school systems. Student exposure to all the basic teachings and elements of Hinduism at Hindu schools was ensured by the presence of images of Hindu Gods and Goddesses, especially of Saraswati (the goddess of knowledge), the steadfast observance of all the major Hindu festivals and events, the performance of pujas before the Common Entrance examinations, the daily recital of mantras and bhajans, and the presence of predominantly Hindu teachers.

In addition to the attempts at integrating Hindu religious education into the formal school curriculum, the propagation and dissemination of the many threads of Hindu religion and culture within the Hindu community was always a major concern. Before the 1960s, the two primary such structures were the *pathshala* and the more formalised but not dissimilar, in terms of form and syllabus, Hindi/Hindu schools. In his Annual Report of 1948, the Director of Education identified 49 such Hindi evening schools which taught Hindi and religious instruction out of school hours.[26] The frequent donation of land and accommodation for such schools, and the willingness by members of the community to teach without expecting any payment attested to the importance placed on this type of education. The structure of both the *pathshala* and Hindi/Hindu schools revolved around one or more learned, usually older male villagers schooling the village children in Hindi, mantras, religious belief and practice, Hindu mythology, bhajan singing and, sometimes, the reading of the *Ramayana*.[27] During the 1970s, however, the general socio-religious laxity, and the preoccupation with both English education and socio-economic mobility led to a marked decline in the number of such institutions. Even during the 1980s religious renaissance of sorts, this traditional system of education was not revived.

From the 1960s there was a noticeable increase in the influx of Hindu missionaries into Trinidad, all of whom contributed to (and sometimes confused) the scope and depth of Hindu knowledge. According to a report in the *Trinidad Guardian*, December 18, 1962, Swami Permananda, an Indian poet and lecturer, lectured at various venues across Trinidad on topics such as 'World Peace,' 'The Message of India,' 'Vedanta,' 'Unity of Mankind in a Divided World,' 'Religion in the Age of Science,' and 'Human Integration.' In 1966, Swami Chinmayananda conducted a 12-day *Gita Yagna*, along with a series of lectures throughout the country (*Trinidad Guardian*, October 1, 1966). They were, during the following two decades, succeeded by Swami Shuddha Chaitanya, Swami Ganapati, and Sant Keshavdas. Swami Satchidananda, Swami Chinmayananda and Swami Ganapati succeeded in establishing the Divine Life Society, the Chinmaya Mission and the Dattatreya Yoga Centre respectively.

Two of these organisations took up this cause on a larger, more visible scale. By 1966, the Divine Life Society had 50 units throughout the island which, through a programme of Hindi, philosophy, textual exposition, and music, sought to realise its aim of '...meeting the needs of Hindus of today and in particular, the young educated college students who do not respect traditions and always ask the question 'why' before doing anything' (*Hindu Times*, March 1966). This representative of the DLS was aware of the need to address, rather than ignore, the transformation or risk losing young Hindus to Christian proselytisers who were extremely aggressive during this period. In this sense, the attitude of this organisation can be interpreted as a technique of both meeting the requirements of young Hindus and in curbing the efforts of Christian proselytisers. This attitude on the part of Hindu socio-religious organisations and leaders was especially crucial since ignorance, confusion and consequently, a lack of respect for Hindu rites and traditions were the major push factors of conversion among Hindus during this period. In that same year a number of 'Hindi centres' were established by the DLS which offered structured teaching of Hindi in preparation for formal examination in 'junior and senior' level Hindi, and in Hindi orals (*Hindu Times*, July 1966). In addition, a Hindu Theological Examination (College) was established where a set list of books such as *All About Hinduism, Fasts and Festivals, Bhagwat Gita,* and *Hinduism* were studied (*Hindu Times*, August 1966).

In 1967, Professor H.S. Adesh was appointed Indian Consul for Cultural Relations for the Government of India in Trinidad (*Trinidad Guardian*, February 2, 1967). This commenced what was possibly the most structured, large-scale and sustained endeavour by any one individual at the dissemination of Indian religious and cultural knowledge in Trinidad. Professor Adesh founded the Bharatiya Vidya Sansthaan, which, by 1972, comprised thirteen centres and about one thousand students. Classes in Hindi, Urdu, Sanskrit, Indian music (sitar, tabla, violin, flue and mandolin) and vocal training were held on Saturdays to accommodate working individuals and school children (*Trinidad Guardian*, May 21, 1972). Formal examinations in these areas were also conducted. Examinations in the languages were conducted in association with the University of London. Residential camps were an annual event. These camps were essentially week-long retreats held in the coastal area of Blanchisseusse, and designed to facilitate maximum focus on the various cultural forms taught by the BVS within a more relaxed ambience. Indeed, throughout the 1970s and early 1980s, this organisation was acknowledged as '...the teaching body for Indian culture in this country' (*Trinidad*

Guardian, May 21, 1972). By the 1980s, many senior students of the BVS proceeded to extend the organisation's programme to village temples. Thus, by the 1990s, an overriding portion of the increasing number of persons under the age of 40 with formal education in Hindi, Indian music and vocals had had some degree of contact with the BVS.

Throughout the 1980s, the BVS continued to make the most substantial contribution to Hindu religious and cultural education. During this decade, however, Hindu socio-religious worker Raviji embarked on a programme of socio-religious mobilisation, but this time, unique in its focus and tenor. What can be labelled as the first phase of this effort involved the reworking of an already existent organisation, the Hindu Seva Sangh, which had as its focus the mobilisation of the Hindu youth. This comprised annual residential camps, weekly interactive sessions and other group activities which sought to instil a sense of religious pride among young Hindus through creative arts, sports and discourses on the scriptures, Hindu philosophy and Hindu leaders. The more formal focus on education began with Raviji's second project; the establishment of the Hindu Prachar Kendra. This programme entailed two six-month formal Hindu missionary training sessions during the 1980s and sustained activities such as *yagnas*, Sunday morning worship sessions and the observance of the major Hindu festivals.[28] What was outstandingly unique about the Kendra was its emphasis on appreciating and developing Hinduism within the context of Trinidadian society through its proposal of a Caribbean/Trinidadian Hinduism or, in other words, Hinduism in its specific location and evolution in Trinidad and the Caribbean.

Cremation

The issue of cremation was, between 1950 and 1980, a major preoccupation of the Hindu community, with the crux of the matter residing essentially in the conflict between the Hindu and Western methods of disposal of the dead, and the associated ideological differences. Although the issue was taken up much earlier, there was an intensification of efforts to address the situation during this period. This was on account of the mobilisation of the SDMS and the increased number of Hindu Members of Parliament. However, the Hindu population's growing awareness of and discontent with not being able to perform the last rites of their loved ones in accordance with Hindu religious prescription was the most powerful impetus in this issue. In order to fully grasp the gravity of the situation, however, one has to consider the implications of not disposing of the dead according to Hindu religious prescription.

Firstly, Hindus subscribe to the belief that the human body comprises five elements – fire, water, earth, space and ether – and that cremation was the most effective way of returning the body to its origin, that is, to the five elements (Brockington 1981, 37). Secondly, Trinidad Hinduism was, during that time, strongly centred upon the major life cycle rituals with the death rituals being possibly the most stringently observed. The purpose of these final rituals revolves around the detachment of the soul from the body, and rendering the soul's journey to the celestial region and then to a subsequent birth as trouble-free as possible. Thirdly, in the major Hindu religious texts, gods and other deified persona were seen to perform these rituals in a certain way. Inevitably, the Hindu population saw this pattern as the ideal that would guarantee maximum benefit for the departed soul. Finally, it was also an opportunity for offspring and relations to pay homage and service to the departed. Thus, failure to perform these death rituals was more than just a contravention of religious prescription; it carried with it deep-seated moral, emotional and social ramifications.

These concerns, however, were met with indifference, ignorance and opposition at the administrative and official levels. In 1953, the Minister of Agriculture and Lands the Hon. V. Bryan declared that government was prepared to '...agree to cremation of the dead in accordance with accepted modern methods and in suitable crematoria.'[29] This decision was in spite of the administration's knowledge of the requirements of the Hindu community. According to the Hon V. Bryan:

> ...what they [Hindus] wanted was not cremation on western lines, but cremation in accord with orthodox Hindu rites, which were understood to include the pyre system – burning of corpses in public, and casting of the remains into the nearest flowing river.[30]

Thus commenced another lengthy struggle of Hindu forms trying to find a place in Trinidadian society. The government proceeded to refute the requirements of Hindus with the argument that such a method would '...offend the sensibilities of the majority of the population and [that] there was also the danger of pollution of rivers by casting the remains in them.'[31] The Hindu refusal to relent on the issue was based on several factors. Firstly, the pyre system alone was enunciated in the religious texts. Secondly, the highly systematised performance of the series of rituals, accompanied by specific mantras could not be accurately performed in the system proposed by the government. And thirdly, possibly the most important ritual of placing the first flame at the departed's mouth, through which the soul was believed to exit the body, would be impossible in a crematorium. For the Hindu community, cremation, unaccompanied by the necessary rites and rituals performed in the prescribed manner, would be absolutely meaningless and unacceptable.

In 1955, after much debate, a Cremation Ordinance was passed. However, when the regulations appeared by Notice in 1956, several difficulties emerged. The major points of argument included the requirements for the grant of a cremation licence. The conditions that the cremation site be situated at least one mile from the nearest dwelling house, not less than 75 yards from any road '...where it is not likely to be a nuisance,' and '...properly fenced and screened from any animals or birds and from the public view'[32] provided other points of contention. The complicated nature of the forms (especially for those unable to read and write English), and the requirement that it be countersigned by a District Medical Officer and by a police officer, both often difficult to locate,[33] also compounded the problems.

The Cremation Ordinance, which also prescribed punishment for those who ventured to cremate a dead body without a valid licence, created a situation where state law seemed directly to contradict the application of a Hindu religious prescription. Thus, until the disparities were resolved, the Hindu community had no choice but to continue to bury their dead. So disenchanted were some Hindus with the countless fruitless committees looking into the matter that they eventually took it upon themselves to start '...setting up areas like the Caroni Savannah Extension Road, and the Caroni bank, on the Highway' to cremate their dead.[34] The fact that they were essentially breaking the law in a very public manner and were risking punishment demonstrated just how strongly they felt. Such illegal cremations continued at several sites until the 1980s under the most deplorable physical conditions. In 1969, Member of Parliament for Siparia, R. Rambachan, confirmed that in the Godineau cremation area there were no parking facilities and, hence, people often had to cross the highway to get to the proceedings. In addition, there was no running water or electricity, no shelter from the rain and the sun, and no seating accommodation. There was not even a permanent base upon which the pyre could rest.[35] The SDMS made persistent offers to the government to construct the required pyre system or crematoria, provided that they were reimbursed afterwards.[36] The government, however, ignored these offers.

During the 1970s, debate on the matter continued. However, the nature of these debates suggested an increasing awareness and consideration of the Hindu requirements of such facilities by the relevant offices. According to the 1970 Cremation Regulation Amendments, the disposal of the ashes of the dead into a river was now permitted and Justices of the Peace were added to the list of those with statutory powers to approve cremation forms. The minimum distance of the cremation site was reduced from one mile to one half of a mile, and the stipulation that the site be screened from birds was removed.[37] Six years later, the Cremation Amendment Act of 1976 saw the simplification of the procedure into four basic steps: the making of an application by a relative of the deceased, obtaining a death certificate from the attending doctor, obtaining a confirmatory certificate from a District Medical Officer, and procuring the cremation licence from any police officer with the rank of inspector or above.[38]

In addition to the struggle for cremation facilities, changes were also taking place in the death ceremonies themselves. Many of these changes were related to non-Hindu influences, as well as to the paradox of standardisation and factional activity within Trinidad Hinduism. The specification of time with regard to the various associated rituals was possibly the most confusing variant in the

Hindu death ceremony. Primarily due to the growth in the number of Hindu sects, each with its own spiritual leader, the time span of the ceremonies immediately following the death became increasingly varied. The 12-month mourning period was variably shortened. This was due to mundane considerations, a generally more lax and practical approach of many of the pundits to this issue, and the multiplicity in textual prescriptions and interpretations. Similarly, the ritual shaving of the head, ideally by five close male relatives of the deceased, was also transformed. While it was still the ideal that five persons perform the rituals, it was no longer mandatory for all − except for the main participant − to have their heads shaved. By the 1980s, shaving of the beard and a low haircut were becoming increasingly popular alternatives to a full shaving of the head, the main reason being that of having to go to school or work. This seemed to suggest the still dominant discomfort of Hindus at the idea of displaying certain aspects of their religion in the larger society.

The overall aura of fear, superstition, awe and trepidation that surrounded the domain of death and the associated rituals had, by the late 1980s, diminished considerably. Thus, the notion that the dead would harass its family if the ceremonies were not performed properly, and the concern − if not fear − of the malevolent potential of lingering spirits were being replaced by a more practical, informed outlook. It should be noted though, that while the awe and fear had somewhat diminished, great emphasis was still placed on performing the rituals in what was perceived of as the right way. Of course, as was evident in almost all spheres of Hinduism, there remained the question of what was the 'right way,' which takes us back to the impact of multiple groups and sects.

Religious Conversion

By the 1960s, the previous decade's spurt in Hindu socio-religious enthusiasm had ebbed considerably. Together with the considerable internal organisational problems among members of the SDMS, this generated an overall languor in Hindu socio-religious activity, and created an ideal situation for the emergence of the second phase of Christian proselytising among Hindus, this time by newer evangelical churches. This phase was characterised by a more aggressive and overt approach that relied heavily on charismatic appeal and the public, indiscriminate condemnation of Hindu practices and beliefs as essentially heathen. In addition to this shift in strategy, Haraksingh situated the success of this effort largely in the failure of Hindu leaders to respond to the situation. As he argued:

> The swift response of orthodoxy to the earlier Arya Samaj challenge was missing this time....The contrast between the vigorous reaction to the Arya Samaj and the quiet response to Christian conversion efforts also indicates the difficulty which Hinduism has in meeting outside challenges as compared to internal schisms. While on the one hand leaders can be bold, forthright and even aggressive, on the other they are tentative, vacillating even accommodating (Haraksingh 1984, 15).

He also cited the diametrically opposed natures of Hinduism and Evangelism as another source of this impotence:

> Ordinary Hindu villagers, if confronted, would admit there was good in all religions, but the evangelical crusaders were not as generous...the fact that in the Trinidad environment Hinduism as a non-proselytising religion was placed in close proximity to continued evangelical zeal...did mean that defensiveness would be part of the Hindu experience (Haraksingh 1984, 15).

While these would continue to be the major underlying factors of conversion right up until the 1990s, other, more personal factors came into play. One of the most recurrent reasons given for conversion was the relief from illnesses, physical disabilities or 'supernatural' ailments where both medicine and Hinduism had failed. In the village of Bejucal one such individual who was supposedly healed during the first Evangelical crusade in the village in the early 1960s, proceeded to become a staunch convert, emphatically denouncing Hindu principles and practices. Interestingly enough, all of his children refused to convert, setting the stage for some oftentimes hilarious conflicts.[39] In the village of Felicity, where proselytising efforts were quite intense during the 1960s, one individual converted, as he claimed, because the 'vision of Christ' cured him of his blindness, and also because his mother was relieved from possession by an 'evil spirit.'[40] The person who was suspected of casting the spell on his mother 'mysteriously' died on the day she was baptised. Social problems including poverty, unemployment, alcohol and marijuana abuse, domestic violence, or more so, the apparent nonchalance and ineptitude with which these problems were met by the various Hindu socio-religious bodies, also seemed to push the victims into the waiting arms of proselytising agents. In fact, according to oral sources, the success of such proselytising efforts resided in their readiness always to provide, if not direct solutions, then at least an avenue through which troubled individuals could vent their frustration and gain some sort of comfort and confidence to deal with their conditions.

By the 1970s, the perceived overemphasis on rites and rituals, often incomprehensible to Hindus themselves in terms of the language (Hindi), the intricacies and contradictions, was also a prominent push factor into the less complicated English-medium domain of the evangelists. Many, mainly young Hindus, often complained about not understanding the nature and significance of Hindu rites and rituals. This was largely because of the predominance of the Hindi and Sanskrit languages in the realm of religion, neither of which, by the 1970s, was spoken in the daily lives of younger Hindus. The decline in the number of *pathshalas* which formally taught the Hindi language further compounded the problem. The diversity in practice and interpretation of rituals and religious scripture would have been another source of confusion for the young Hindu. In addition, the numerous and multifaceted preparations involved in most Hindu socio-religious events and their lengthy durations would, in the light of the relative simplicity of Christian procedures, seem cumbersome.

The search for credible, effective and informed leadership,[41] and what one interviewee called the '...burden of being Indian, along with a general lack of identity and pride in Hinduism'[42] were also cited as reasons for turning away from Hinduism. Since such issues were general throughout the country, the evident variation in the success rate of proselytising efforts across districts could more readily be found in another factor, namely, the degree of religious fervour – at the levels of both the family and the community – with which Hindu principles and practices were met. The presence of local agents and Hindu missionaries within Hindu communities did, however, diversify the degree of conversion among the various communities. Such agents included the level of communal socio-religious activity, temples, Hindu primary schools, communal relations among fellow villagers, and resident pundits and sadhus. The efforts of Hindu missionaries at reworking, explaining and energising Hinduism also helped to curb the level of conversion in some areas.

There were also some small-scale efforts in the late 1980s by organisations such as the Hindu Prachar Kendra and even the Hindu Seva Sangh at reworking the face of Hinduism. By the end of the 1980s, however, such attempts remained only minimal, suggesting a junction of sorts where Hindu leadership vacillated between adhering to the traditional mode of a defensive, semi-fatalistic inaction – or at the most minimal indirect counteractive methods – and the adoption of a new, more aggressive approach in defence of Trinidad Hinduism and its followers.

The 'reclaiming of the lost sheep' or, in other words reconversion, provided an interesting debate in Hinduism. On the one hand it is claimed that the issue does not apply in Hinduism since one is born a Hindu, and hence, will always be a Hindu. The Secretary General of the SDMS invoked the laws of karma, moksha and reincarnation to highlight the inextricable and intricate nature of the relationship that exists between a Hindu and his religion, from birth to death (*Newsday*, June 19, 1999). Even if one were to denounce Hinduism and re-enter the fold, he simply has to resume the observance of the rites and tenets of Hinduism; there is no formal ceremony for reconversion back into Hinduism. Of course, the diversity within Hinduism makes it almost impossible to identify which aspects of the religion a person must adopt to be classified as having reconverted.

Yet, there was quite a number of conversions and reconversions to Hinduism during the twentieth century in Trinidad. According to a report in the *Port-of-Spain Gazette*, March 4, 1937, of a seven day *Bhagwat* in Caigual, Manzanilla in March 1937, nine persons 'were admitted to the folds of Hinduism.' In 1940, the Hindu Maha Sabha hosted an eight-night *Ramayana yagna* which ran through the festival of *Divali*. On *Divali* night, 'a mass baptism was carried out... thirty persons, formerly Christians, collected before the altar and were received back into the eternal faith of the Sanatan Dharma' (*Hindu Maha Sabha*, November 1940). The proceeding was described as a '*sanskar* ceremony' ('purification' ceremony; in this context carrying undertones of an essential life cycle ritual). Ironically, the use of the term 'baptism,' an essentially Christian concept, detracts from the fundamentally Hindu procedures and aura of the event. That is to say, to the non-Hindu public, the term 'baptism' conjures up images of a Hindu counterpart to the Christian ceremony. Such an interpretation, of course, would be erroneous since, in terms of both their respective procedures and ideologies, a Hindu *Shuddhi* and a Christian baptism are quite divergent.

The *Shuddhi* ritual was also used by the Arya Samaj to either convert non-Hindus to Hinduism, or to readmit those who had denounced Hinduism back into the Hindu fold. In his study of the Arya Samaj in Trinidad, anthropologist Richard Huntington Forbes argued that the Arya Samaj's subscription to the *Shuddhi* instigated the Sanatanist application of the ritual to readmit converted Hindus back into Hinduism; a practice which was previously 'unheard of' among Sanatanists (Forbes 1984). This trend of reconversion continued later on in the century. The impact of the second phase of Christian proselytising among Hindus, begun in the 1960s, was one of the most debated issues during the late 1980s socio-religious revitalisation among Trinidad Hindus. During the 1990s, reconversion was also used by the SDMS (*Trinidad Guardian*, October 10, 1998), the Hindu Prachar Kendra,[43] and SWAHA[44] as a measure of reclaiming the lost sheep. This involved either simply a recognition of the former Christian converts' personal reclamation of Hinduism, or the performance of a formal ceremony.

The reasons for reconversion to Hinduism were varied. In the first phase of conversion during the indenture and early twentieth century, the conversion was often a selective process on the part of the converts. The more innate essentially Indian or Hindu notions, values and practices in the sphere of the family and community were still observed. Thus, Hindu women continued wearing their *orhnis* and saris to the church, and caste continued to play a decisive role in marriage and other inter-personal interaction. In fact, Indian elements were worked into Presbyterianism to the extent that one could have argued for the 'Indianising' of Presbyterianism. This was apparent in the composition of a choir at a Presbyterian church in Monkey Town in 1942 which included eight men sitting cross-legged with a variety of Indian instruments. Whereas the response to the English hymns was 'meagre' there was 'manifest absorption of the congregation in their old musical inheritance.'[45] One can surmise that, notwithstanding the pull of the greater possibility of socio-economic and occupational amelioration, the persistent subscription to Hindu values and practices would have facilitated such reconversion. Also, as discussed in chapter one, given the flexible and assimilative nature of Hinduism, it was possible that many of the converts would have seen themselves as adopting Christianity but not necessarily denouncing Hinduism. This was suggested in the presence of both Hindu and Christian deities at many family altars and shrines, and the retention of Hindu middle names by converts and their children.

During the latter half of the twentieth century, the reasons were more diverse. Since the second wave of conversions thrived on the growing disenchantment and confusion among younger Hindus with Hinduism, the later attempts by Hindu organisations to rework the religion and present it in a more appealing and comprehensible manner partly accounted for the pull back into Hinduism. Also, as during the first half of the century, many were what can be termed 'half-way' conversions, often done because the proselytising religion was offering emotional comfort and assistance in areas that were ignored by Hindu religious leaders and organisations. Thus, when several Hindu organisations began focusing their energies on the Hindu community – rather than on the Hindu religion – there was the added incentive of a sustained source of comfort and advice on issues that were not necessarily religious in nature.

New Observances

In both Trinidad and the wider world, Hinduism constantly acquired new dimensions and elements. According to Brockington such innovations are

> ...not the enemy of tradition but that by which it [Hinduism] maintains its relevance. Hinduism does not reject the old in favor of the new but blends the two, expressing new dilemmas in traditional language and accommodating fresh insights to established viewpoints (Brockington 1981, 209).

Before the 1970s this was primarily on account of the innate Hindu tendency to sanctify almost anything associated with religion. For example, the *lota* and *thali* used in pujas, though essentially just brass vessels and performing the practical function of vessels in pujas, were, in Trinidad, treated as 'religious' items to be used exclusively for religious purposes. There would be a similar reluctance to use the *sohari* leaf (upon which food at Hindu socio-religious events is served) when consuming any kind of meat. This sanctifying tendency was most evident in the consecration of sites where rocks were claimed to have emitted blood or milk, most popular of which was the Patiram Trace Mandir in Penal in the late nineteenth century.[46] The incorporation of the Christian figure of La Divina Pastora into the Hindu pantheon as an aspect of the Mother Goddess was another prominent example of this tendency. Both subsequently provided the earliest Hindu pilgrimage sites in Trinidad. A Protector of Immigrants Report confirmed the church of La Divina Pastora as a popular pilgrimage site for Hindus by 1893.[47] According to Surendranath Capildeo, grandson of Pundit Capildeo of Chaguanas, even the famous 'Lion House' also popularly referred to as 'the Hanuman House,' (because of its Hanuman-like statues of monkeys), was treated as a '...pilgrimage for people to come from the deep south, all the way into Chaguanas, and to sit at the feet there... to talk....'[48] This pilgrimaging tendency was evident in yet another practice initiated during the late nineteenth century – visiting the most prominent Hindu temple during that time, the Green Street Hindu Temple in Tunapuna, especially for the observance of *Shiv Ratri* (*Port-of-Spain Gazette*, February 18, 1920). Brockington explained the Hindu preoccupation with pilgrimages as:

> ...a popular way to remove sins and accumulate merit; the merit acquired in visiting them was commonly reckoned in terms of the performance of so many Vedic rituals, but unlike the sacrifices that

they thereby replace, the sacred sites were open to all (Brockington 1981, 196).

Brockington added that in as much as many pilgrimage sites are associated with water and its purifying function, they invoke the universal Hindu concern with purity and pollution, the latter of which is held to be washed away by bathing in such places (Brockington 1981, 198). This can partially account for the rise in the observance of *Kartik nahaan* (ritual bath during the eighth lunar month of the Hindu calendar), and the post-1990 consecration of many local rivers and beaches as Hindu pilgrimage sites.

After the 1970s, however, the appearance of such pilgrimage sites and new observances could be classified as more contrived, deliberate phenomena, almost always the work of some socio-religious organisation. Notwithstanding the possible motives of reworking Hinduism to more tangibly situate it in the Trinidadian context and to generate contemporary appeal, such developments had a mobilising, revitalising and cohesive effect on both the Hindu community as a whole and within the various socio-religious sects. This was precisely the objective of the organising of *sankirtans* or processions, which first occurred in 1985. The leading figure explained that '...apart from the providing of a high visibility activity to help motivate Hindus and bring them together, *sankirtan* has strong spiritual and scriptural backings' (*Sunday Express*, March 2, 1986). The initiation of the *Divali Nagar* in 1986 both served as a new age annual pilgrimage of sorts, and provided the context for the promotion of Hinduism as situated within Trinidad, rather than solely in relation to its Indian origin. The advent of the first national *pradakshina* in 1987 also served the latter purpose by declaring Trinidad '...a *janmabhoomi* or a sacred motherland....' (*Express*, August 23, 1996).

The Sacred and the Secular

In multicultural societies conflict among different religious denominations or with elements of the secular sphere is, for the most part, inevitable. The pervasive nature of Hinduism, together with its lack of any categorical definition between the sacred and secular renders it more prone to such religio-ideological conflicts than the other Semitic religions with relatively clear-cut distinctions between the sacred and the secular. The perception widely held by the Christian population, until as late as the 1980s, of Hinduism as a subordinate religion rooted in superstition and idolatry and essentially heathen also substantially accentuated such conflicts. This was evident in many campaigns waged by Hindus for official recognition of their beliefs and practices, the most prominent of which were those related to the Hindu Marriage Bill and the Cremation Bill. As discussed in previous chapters, the heart of the conflict was situated largely in the wider society's failure to comprehend the nature and nuances of Hindu practices and belief systems.

Trinidad's annual Carnival revelry had, until the 1980s, been viewed as morally and ideologically in opposition with the tenets of Hinduism (as practised in Trinidad), and Hindu participation in Carnival was therefore more of the exception than the norm. The major points of contention resided in the free interaction of semi-nude male and female bodies, and the sexually provocative public dancing and behaviour. Calypsoes which ridiculed Hindu beliefs and practices and the almost annual coinciding of Carnival with the Hindu religious observance of *Shiv Ratri* also intensified the dissension. Against this backdrop emerged vigorous objections to the use of aspects of Hinduism, especially its gods and goddesses, in calypsoes and Carnival bands. Given the extremely low level of participation by Hindus in Carnival activities, it can be argued that the inclusion of Hindu religious elements into the portrayals was almost solely the initiatives of non-Hindu artistes such as band leaders and costume designers. In 1965, the attempt to portray both Hindu deities and practices in two Carnival bands, namely 'Gods and Worshippers of India' (*Evening News*, February 9, 1965) and 'Vishnu's Kingdom' (*Evening News*, February 8, 1965) evoked intense objection from Hindus. In addition to individual protests, the issue was taken to Parliament in 1965, where the Member for Caroni South, Surendranath Capildeo, claimed that three delegations of Hindus aired their grievances over the Carnival band which proposed '...to portray the Great Hindu God, Hanuman, the coronation of Ram Chanda, the Hindu God, and an authentic portrayal of the unblemished love of Lord Krishna and his wife Radha.'⁴⁹ His argument against this portrayal echoed the sentiments of the Hindu population. As he said:

> These adherents of the Hindu religion, like myself, believe that this is going to be a mockery of a living religion...do not believe that they intend to offend anybody. This is merely a thoughtless act which is going to offend the Hindu people if it is allowed to continue....I myself cannot see that this protest that I am making will cause the Government to intervene to stop these people, but...the religious susceptibilities of 200,000 Hindus would be deeply affected if the Carnival revellers, drinking, singing rude songs, parading the streets in half dress, should be allowed to portray the living god and goddess of a religion which has continued in the unchallenged tradition from the earliest time until today.⁵⁰

Seemingly insensitive and sensationalising newspaper headlines such as 'Two Days When Ancient India Will Come to Trinidad' (*Daily Mirror*, February 4, 1965), and the justification of '...playing history, not religion' (*Evening News*, February 8, 1965) by one of the bandleaders just added to Hindu indignation. According to a report in the *Evening News*, February 9, 1965, the leader of the SDMS subsequently formally asked the bandleader to shelve the band, a move which proved successful, but only after much vacillation on the part of the bandleader.

Calypsoes were also a constant source of aggravation. This was due to the projection of Indians as clannish, racist, backward and miserly. The persistent ridicule of what was perceived as the rather clumsy adoption of Western mannerisms and style by Indians and their use of language served to further alienate the Indian community from both the art form and its context. Some Hindus were deeply offended by the inclusion of the Hindu ritual incantation '*Om Shanti Om*' in a calypso sung by Ras Shorty I. This was deemed as blasphemous as the portrayal of Hindu Gods in Carnival bands. Sparrow's rendition 'Marajin' not only hit at the core of Hindu religious authority – the Brahmins – but also embodied what was probably the most inflammatory Indian theme in calypsoes, namely the pursuit of Indian women by men of African descent.

The term '*Marajin*' referred to the wife of a man belonging to the Brahmin caste, usually one with the surname 'Maharaj.' Being of the priestly class, Brahmin women would, in effect, be imbued with all the notions of ritual purity and the behavioural norms and taboos that were evoked by their socio-religious station. In contrast, persons of African descent were deemed 'a low nation' with undesirable and offensive habits, many of which were considered ritually polluting. Thus, placing – even vicariously – a *marajin* in a sexually suggestive relationship with a man of African descent would have been a virtual defiling, almost 'raping,' of the Hindu priestly caste and, by extension, the religion itself, through the receptacles of its seeds, the women. One can even recognise constructions of blasphemy in the association. In addition, the title of *marajin* was quite often assigned to an older Brahmin woman, usually over the age of 50. Thus, referring to an elderly Brahmin woman in such an overtly sexual way, and that too by a man of African descent, compounded the level of offence experienced by Hindus. This did not imply, though, that liaisons between men of African descent and other non-Brahmin Hindu women were any less unacceptable; they just did not invoke as substantial a level of religious indignation as in the case of women of the Brahmin caste.

In addition to these sustained carnival-related conflicts, isolated events further revealed this religio-ideological conflict between Hinduism and the wider society. During the general elections of 1986, the absence of the *Bhagvadgita* and the *Quran* at polling stations for required oath-taking was interpreted as a '...gross insult to Hindus and Muslims' (*Sandesh,* January 23, 1987). The absence of any Hindu religious texts at the official residence of the President of the Republic, where the formal swearing in of the new government in 1986 was taking place, added injury to this insult: it resulted in a mad rush to find a text when a Hindu minister refused to take his oath until one was provided.

The conflict between the sacred and the secular was also very much at play within the Hindu community. A most vivid example is the presence of both temple(s) and rumshop(s) in every predominantly Indian village in Trinidad. The importance of alcohol as an ingredient in many folk rituals further complicates the situation. The popular resolutions to the situation (both reflections of the community's ambiguity on the issue) usually involve the closing of those rumshops that are in very close proximity to the *yagna* just before the nightly proceedings commence at the expense of quite a few hours of business. Those that are not as physically close to the *yagna* often conduct business at their usual times, but if within the earshot of the proceedings will do so in a notably subdued manner.

Conclusion

It is evident that during the period 1945–90, both the private and public spheres of Trinidadian Hinduism were influenced by a number of factors, stimulating transformations in Hindu socio-religious practice, ideology and attitude. Feeding on the overriding desire and need for visibility and acceptance as both a valid socio-religious grouping and as individual citizens of Trinidad and Tobago, modernisation and secularisation could be identified as the most prominent of such factors. Thus, their impact was discernible in almost all areas – from the most intimate aspects of Hindu family life, to the most official interaction with the wider society. Given the intensity of the foregoing, the deconstruction of many of the traditional practices and ideology was not a remote impossibility. This, however, was intercepted by Hinduism's flexibility and dynamism.

Both secularisation and its antithesis, deification, were ongoing, simultaneous processes which, operating within the assimilative nature of Hinduism, would not demand any complete break with the traditional. Rather, any perceived contradictions were neutralised by another major operative within Caribbean Hinduism – compartmentalisation. On an individual level compartmentalisation '...shows the operation of the values of tolerance and reconciliation...' and as an adaptive process '...serves both as a mechanism for stability and change' (Haraksingh 1985, 169). Thus, the Hindu tendency to compartmentalise, rather than constrict, seemed to underscore its accommodating and flexible disposition. The resultant framework, then, allowed for the infiltration and harmonious co-existence of the influences of modernisation, Christianisation and secularisation with the more traditional aspects of Hindu existence. That is not to say that these traditional elements were left in an undiluted condition. In fact, within the persistent interplay of change and continuity it was almost impossible to identify such a condition. There was, rather, a simultaneous reworking of traditional ideas, attitudes and practices, which were largely determined by the nature and extent of the Hindu community's interaction with the non-Hindu element and also by the dictates of time, space and circumstance. Conflict was primarily evident in deliberate efforts at contesting and controlling the natural flow of Hindu socio-religious change.

By the 1970s, Trinidadian Hindus were being forced to recognise the need to transgress the boundaries of community, and to assert themselves as an integral part of Trinidadian society. This was collectively instigated by the economic and educational amelioration during that period, the remnants of only ancestral (rather than patriotic) ties to India, the threat of both conversion and the persistent ascription as second-class citizens. A full-fledged integration, however, demanded the renunciation of those fundamental aspects of Hindu religion and culture that were not in accordance with those of the wider society. What occurred, rather, was the drive to establish itself as a community within a nation, a process which can be safely described as multilayered, arduous, oftentimes misinterpreted or disregarded, and by no means uniform. Thus, the success of this venture, on both a personal and communal level, resided in the ability to strike a balance between being and belonging, that is to say, being Hindu but also belonging to the Trinidadian society. It is within this dialogue that one can identify the crux of Hindu socio-religious change in Trinidad until 1990.

CONCLUSION
Theory of Change

As we have seen, social mobility within the Hindu community was, to say the least, a relatively complex phenomenon, and neither the frame of reference provided by Srinivas's theory of Sanskritisation nor Verene Shepherd's concept of Selective Creolisation could, on its own, accurately capture the dynamics of the process. The crux of Srinivas's theory resided in a low caste group changing its customs, ritual ideology and way of life in the direction of a high and frequently 'twice-born' caste. While the overarching idea of a low group modifying its customs and lifestyle to climb the social ladder was partially applicable to Trinidad, the study has demonstrated a number of specific divergences. It was evident that, until the 1970s, aspirations at social mobility could be said to be operating on two levels. Within the boundaries of the Hindu community they operated on a sort of microcosmic level. This movement fell somewhat along the lines of Srinivas' concept of mobility where caste seemed to be the defining principle. The second movement occurred at the macrocosmic level; that is to say, within the context of the larger Trinidad society. The movements on this level were closely related to Shepherd's concept of selective creolisation. After the 1970s, the distinction was not as clear-cut.

On the internal, microcosmic level the very basis of Srinivas' theory – caste – had, by the beginning of the twentieth century, been substantially diluted. What persisted was a very loose, indistinct and diverse collection of sentiments and fragments of caste ideology. Far from the distinct, overarching system of power relations that obtained in India, the selection and sustenance of caste sentiments in Trinidad was varyingly conditioned by the social, economic and political milieu of Trinidad, which functioned on an altogether divergent set of principles and structures from that of the traditional caste system. However, until the 1970s the relative isolation from the wider society of Hindu religious practice and belief allowed for a persistence of caste sensibilities, though in an increasingly diluted and fluid form. This consequently placed those individuals recognised as Brahmins at the top, albeit precariously, of the socio-religious ladder. Their authority, however, was limited to almost exclusively the religious sphere. Within this framework, as the oral evidence made clear, there occurred attempts at mobility which, in principle, resembled those outlined by Srinivas but overridingly conditioned by the diversity, fluidity and adulteration that surrounded caste sensibilities in Trinidad.

Attempts at mobility though, unlike those in Srinivas's model, occurred on an individual rather than group level. As shown in chapter one, such individual attempts at socio-religious mobility were characterised by the relinquishing of practices and ideology deemed undesirable, and by the adoption of those that were closer to Brahminic values. By the 1920s, there were already collective attempts at both standardising religious elements and establishing the principles of Sanatan Dharma as the overarching stamp of Hinduism in Trinidad. This both conditioned and was conditioned by movements on the individual level. Yet, what was evident was the impotence and ambiguity that defined the position of the Brahmins in Trinidad. Because of the highly circumscribed nature of their dominance, and the decentralised and constricted nature of their power, there was little that the Brahmins could do, given the diversity inherent in the Hindu community, to curtail the attempts by non-Brahmins at socio-religious authority. Thus, whereas in Srinivas's theory the 'twice-born' caste occupied a position of marked control and power, in Trinidad Brahmins seemed to assign themselves some sense of pseudo authority which was in fact contingent more on the adherence of Hindus to respect for traditional authority than on the Brahmins' own religious merit.

Because of the localised and tenuous nature of these attempts at mobility among Hindus, transformations conditioned by developments in the larger society were inevitable. By the 1960s, a steep rise in the number of Hindus with varying degrees of Western schooling could be discerned. This rise in schooling served to diversify the scope of occupations among Hindus and highly increase their level of contact with the policies and power relations of the wider society. It was clear that social mobility within Trinidadian Hinduism was being defined in its relation to the larger society. This process was deepened in the 1970s following the economic windfall of that decade. The rapidly increasing depth and scope of the dialogue between Hindus and the larger Trinidadian society functioned to further dilute and severely restrict the sense of Brahmin authority exclusively to the religious realm. However, this too would be even more diluted notwithstanding the religious revitalisation of the 1980s.

Within this context one can situate Shepherd's theory of selective creolisation but, as in the case of Srinivas's theory, not in its wholesale application. The major point of divergence resided in the high level of selection that characterised the Trinidad situation. In contrast with Jamaica, the numbers, level of mobilisation, and the retention of elements of Indian religion, tradition and culture were substantially higher in Trinidad. By the 1950s, Hindus in Trinidad had established a sense of religious and cultural communalism highly susceptible to the influences of the larger society but too sound to be completely eroded. Instead of a creolisation of their values, norms and practices Indians invoked the processes of compartmentalisation and selection in their interaction with the larger society. What resulted was a situation where Hindus could define and regulate the nature and extent of the assimilation of the norms, values and structures of the wider society. This consequently resulted in an astute balance of both the new and the traditional. With the overriding preoccupation with social and economic mobility within the context of the larger society, considerations of the 'ritually purer' state of the higher caste were entertained primarily in religious observances.

It is evident then that social change among Hindus in Trinidad fell somewhere between Srinivas's and Shepherd's respective theories. The pertinence of both theories to the local situation resided more in their respective broad underlying principles rather than in their specific applications. Thus, one can use them as just general guidelines or points of contestation on the formulations of a theory of socio-religious change among Hindus in Trinidad. In other words, any attempt at constructing a theory of socio-religious change among Hindus in Trinidad demands the positioning of the specific experiences and the context of Hindus in Trinidad at the core of the exercise.

Socio-Religious Change

During the period 1917–90, Hinduism in Trinidad underwent tremendous transformation. The factors responsible for these transformations were extremely multidimensional, often intimately and intricately interwoven and thus, spun a socio-religious web wherein no one element could function in absolute isolation from the others. In its characterisation as a way of life, any examination of Trinidad Hinduism inevitably extends beyond the religious to encapsulate almost all dimensions of life. In other words, an examination of the religious implies an examination of the social. By the end of Indian indenture in 1917, Trinidad Hindus were already heavily involved in the process of socio-religious transformation. On a most cursory level, one could discern a tussle between retention of what could loosely be termed the 'traditional' and the need for modification. The sometimes overriding proclivity for retention of the traditional and the familiar was largely rooted in the community's deep concern with – or even fear of – the dissipation of those elements which defined their very existence in Trinidad, an attitude which is an inherent aspect of the early stages of community reconstitution in diasporic communities. On the other hand, the modification of elements of tradition and custom was generated largely by the changing economic, social and political milieus. This ongoing struggle between change and continuity underscored Hindu socio-religious transformation throughout the entire period under study.

Religious Trends

Throughout the period, transformations in religious thought and trends constantly mirrored economic, social and intellectual trends. Until the late 1970s Hindus in Trinidad were deeply immersed in tradition, in the more ritualistic aspects of Hinduism and in the Bhakti tradition. In approaching the religious scriptures, emphasis was placed on the storyline, exalting the gods, and the triumph of good over evil. The applicability of the teachings of the texts to daily life formed the bulk of analytical explorations. The 1980s saw the intensification of possibly the most monumental transformation in the attitude of Hindus towards religion. Economic and educational achievement along with influences of the religious attitudes and trends of the wider non-Hindu community generated increasingly more probing into religious matters. Hindus became increasingly preoccupied with the innate significance of rites and rituals, the more spiritual dimensions of the religion and the philosophy of Hinduism. Pundits and other religious figures had to change their approach to religious presentation to cater to these new demands. The steady flow of swamis and other religious teachers from India who spent extended periods in Trinidad contributed substantially to this change in the approach to religion. All along, new elements were added to the spectrum of Trinidad Hinduism, many of which carried distinctly local features. This 'Trinidadianising' of the religion could be located partially in the desire of Hindus in Trinidad to anchor themselves in and to stake a claim to their birthplace. Of course, the nature of Hinduism as a way of life without any clear-cut boundaries between the sacred and the secular rendered it substantially prone to the development of such new elements and observances.

One cannot ignore the impact of non-Hindu, essentially Christian elements, on Trinidad Hinduism. Factors such as the syncretic nature of Hinduism, the persistent often uncomfortable awareness of the divergences between Hindu practices and observances and those of the more mainstream religion, and the growing need for recognition as equal members of Trinidad's citizenry collectively facilitated transformations that very visibly bore the stamp of Christianity. This inevitably evoked the issue of balance and calls into question the line between influence and encroachment. Indeed, it was the fear of the dilution of Hinduism through its potentially overly accommodating nature that drove many Hindu socio-religious leaders and organisations to embark upon studied and intensified efforts to revert to what was conceived of as 'pure' Hinduism.

The major Hindu religious and life cycle rituals underwent notable degrees of transformation. This was evident in the materials used for these rituals, and in the timing, duration, structure and sequence and the social dimensions of the rituals. However, the notion of the significance and indispensability of many of these rituals was simultaneously affirmed. There was an overriding concern about what would happen if the most pertinent aspects of the rituals were not performed, and performed 'in the right way.' Yet, 'the right way' was often based on the interpretations of different ritual specialists, religious preceptors and philosophers, generating a high level of multiplicity even on this point. This situation continued up to the 1990s but with a significant refinement. By this time, it was evident that rituals were assuming a more symbolic role wherein, rather than being intrinsically understood, they were increasingly being perceived as necessary religious elements. It can also be argued that Hindu rituals were then functioning, to a notable degree, as identity markers of one's claim to Hinduism.

An overriding factor in the shaping of religious trends, practices and attitudes in Trinidad was the prominence of elements of the Little Tradition. Thus, despite the gradual move away from some aspects of Hindu popular practice (especially those involving the sacrifice of animals), both the sheer number of immigrants belonging to the lower castes and the internal social dynamics of the Hindu community generated a retention of many elements of popular Hindu practice. While it can be argued that until the 1990s the Hindu socio-religious elite in Trinidad was dominated by descendents of the Brahmin and Kshatriya castes, their comparatively smaller number together with the power relations of the larger society arrested the dominance of Brahminic culture. Thus, a situation developed where the most viable aspects of both the Brahminic and the popular tradition were worked into the religious life of Trinidad Hindus. Despite the further dilution or demise of some aspects of popular practice due to the influence of Western and Christian values, popular practice by the 1990s was still a visible force in Trinidadian Hinduism.

The *Ramayana* Tradition

Socio-religious transformation was also amply reflected in the accretions, additions and deletions in the *Ramayana* tradition. Such trends form the core of the argument of the *Ramayana* as mirror and metaphor of Hindu social and religious change. Within the entire tradition, the delicate balance of continuity and change indicated the larger Hindu challenge of balancing these two processes, both of which were fundamental to the survival and growth of Hinduism within the Trinidad context. As an enduring dimension of the *Ramayana* tradition that had been saturated with the Hindu socio-religious experience, the *Ramleela* provided an apt example of this interplay of change and continuity in the *Ramayana* tradition. The persistent addition of new elements to the *Ramayana* tradition, especially those that seemed to be attempting to 'Trinidadianise' the tradition, reflected the larger Hindu attempts at claiming their space as Hindu citizens of Trinidad and Tobago. Such new elements widened the scope of the *Ramayana* tradition, and rendered it more viable in fulfilling the needs of the Hindu society, especially within the constantly evolving Trinidad context. Thus, this dimension of the *Ramayana* tradition encapsulated the transforming social and religious milieu. Changes in the perception and treatment of the tradition echoed the ongoing changes in the value systems and social structures of the Hindu community, more often than not influenced by elements of the wider non-Hindu society. The change since the 1980s of the aura surrounding the *Ramayana* tradition from one of unquestioning devotion and deference to a more informed, probing and even practical approach indicated the general trends that were evolving in Trinidad Hinduism during that period.

The various dimensions of the *Ramayana* tradition encapsulated the form and innate values and attitudes from the most public to the most private aspects of Hindu life, which further endorsed its function as a mirror of society. Its enduring function as doctrine within the spheres of family and communal life, and internal politics in the face of substantial and diverse social transformation indicated both the tradition's flexibility and its indispensability to Trinidad Hinduism. That most of the later socio-religious organisations that disputed the divinity and primacy of the *Ramcharitmanas* had to at least acknowledge and often exploited both the tradition and the text for their own purposes, reiterated the foregoing point. The multiplicity of the manifestations of the *Ramayana* tradition and the high emphasis on the varying facets of its oral manifestation continuously fed upon the Hindu experience, thereby imbuing the processes of change and continuity, accommodation and rejection, and tradition and modernity. This, in turn, validated the *Ramayana* tradition as a pregnant metaphor of the Trinidad Hindu experience.

Texts

Transformations surrounding Hindu religious texts entailed the major processes of Christianising, de-ritualising, iconising and textual navigation, each of which continuously pointed to the fluidity and viability of Hindu religious texts and Hinduism. The primary notions along which the texts operated – namely text without boundaries, intertextuality, text as encyclopedia and text as living document – all drew heavily on the lived experience of Trinidad Hindus. This, in turn, supported the argument that Hindu religious texts mirror Hindu social and religious change. In almost each instance the modifications were variously conditioned by both the influences of the non-Hindu community and by changes within the Hindu community. The often close relationship between these changes and such intimate areas of Hindu life as the family, the community, life cycle rituals, marriage, and personal relations indicated the text's intimate relationship with the Hindu community in Trinidad. The *Ramcharitmanas* in Trinidad as encyclopaedia underscored the fundamental role of that text in the formation and function of the Trinidad Hindu community. Yet, despite its importance, the text underwent constant reworking to increase its relevance. The constant reworking of the treatment, content and presentation of the text mirrored the fundamental nature of the larger socio-religious transformation within the Hindu community. The developments in terms of language and the variety of Hindu religious texts were just two examples of the dynamism of this movement. What was outstanding was the tendency on the part of both Hindus and non-Hindus to overlook the unique processes and notions that surrounded Hindu religious texts which may have been divergent from those of Christianity but not any less substantive or pertinent in their application in the Hindu context. That Hindus also promoted such notions and analogies indicated the absorptive tendency of Trinidad Hinduism, the undeniable degree of Christianising among Trinidad Hindus, and a response to the pressure and criticism heaped unto Hindu social and religious beliefs and practices.

The occasions for readings from the texts provided some level of elucidation on what the community held as important enough to warrant association with the Divine, on dimensions of its evolving social and religious life, and on the changing boundaries and relations between the sacred and the secular. The efforts at the dissemination of knowledge of the texts echoed the indispensable nature of the texts to Hindus. Transformations in textual presentation reflected the changing social milieu and the texts' fluidity. It also suggested the awareness of pundits and other textual expounders of the need to rework the texts and of their changing role as socio-religious leaders. The preoccupation with the 'cracks in the mirror' in the texts – that is to say, the points of ambiguity, inconsistencies and contradiction in the texts – revealed the growth of a more intellectual and practical approach to religion. It reflected, from the 1970s, both a growing propensity to go beyond (yet not to question) the divinity of the text, and by extension, other aspects of Hinduism. It also echoed the diversity in approaches to religion among the rapidly increasing number of Hindu religious sects and groups.

Village/Community

Throughout this period both the concept of village and community, and the village itself underwent substantial transformation in terms of both structure and ideology. Until the 1950s, the structure, social systems, relationships and interaction, values, and communal activities in villages that were predominantly Hindu echoed the values and constructs of Indian villages (in India). Yet from the turn of the century, the structures and values of the wider society were gradually but persistently influencing both the idea of village and community, and the village itself in terms of its structure, process and role. Regulating this impact was the extent and nature of the interaction of Hindus with the wider society. This hinged on the question of whether their feelings of nationalism resided with India or with Trinidad, since this largely determined from whence they preferred to draw their psychological sustenance and socio-cultural systems. But, by the 1940s, Hindus were becoming considerably aware of the fact that some degree of integration was necessary in their aspirations of social mobility within the Trinidad context, since the traditionally inward-looking approach would only deter social and economic amelioration.

Each progressive generation brought with it an intrinsically higher degree of affiliation and more comfortable interaction with the larger Trinidad community. The economic windfall of the 1970s cemented this process since Hindus, now armed with educational skills, had to have their slice of the economic pie. The changing structure and nature of community was very evident in the rapid disintegration of the fictive kin ideology and terminology that permeated village life until as late as the 1970s. Thus, the idea of neighbour – devoid of kinship sentiments – replaced the feeling of family that defined Hindu village life before the 1970s. The dilution and eventual demise of traditional social systems such as the panchayat, *bhaiyachaarya* and *daheja,* and of village-based activities such as the *pathshalas* and *panchoutie yagnas* was also indicative of such transformation.

Family

In terms of its structure, function, values and power relations, the Hindu family was increasingly susceptible to the infiltration of norms and values of the wider non-Hindu society. However, due to the intimate nature of many of the practices, relationships and beliefs surrounding Hindu family life, transformations therein were very gradual and were underscored by a high degree of selectivity. In addition, the degree, nature and timing of the transformations were highly divergent. This divergence was substantially determined by economic and social conditions, geographic location and personal convictions. The acquisition of formal education in English, and the resultant transformations in occupation and economic status were the major determinants of both the degree and nature of the changes within the Hindu family. In as much as transformations within Hindu family life occurred at a much slower pace than in other less private areas as occupation, education, recreation and even religion, one can identify shades of compartmentalisation at work. This process invested individuals with a considerable level of control over the degree and nature of the ingress of newer elements into their established way of life.

Education

Transformations in education were both on account and reflective of transformation within the Hindu community. During the 1920s and '30s, the rise of formal institutions of Indian/Hindu education in the form of 'Hindu/Hindi schools' and *pathshalas* was a key component in the continuous process of community reconstitution and definition. The major processes at work in community reconstitution such as mobilisation, rejuvenation, retention and assimilation were discernible in the community's choice of approach, methods and material in this form of education. Until the 1930s, the inward-looking tendencies were also evident in the exclusive focus on Hindi and matters of Hindu religious and cultural import. However, the growing awareness of the importance of English education was evident in the establishment in 1930 of the first Indian secondary school. Yet, the lack of cohesion among Hindu and Indian organisations and the ambiguous attitude of the government towards Indian educational institutions were major deterrents in the formulation of any long-term, large-scale, effective effort at formal education in English among Hindus.

Large-scale formal education among Hindus was realised only during the 1950s in the form of primary schools established by the SDMS. These institutions performed the dual function of disseminating both English and Hindu religious and cultural education among Hindus. Notwithstanding the adoption of the national education syllabus, SDMS, along with the fewer Arya Samaj and Kabir Panth schools played a key role in the maintenance of Hindu religious and cultural life throughout the religious languor of the 1960s and 1970s. That these were essentially Hindu institutions dispelled most of the suspicion and fear that had surrounded the earlier Hindu encounter with education through non-Hindu efforts. From their very inception, the emphasis on English education over Hindi was evident in both the schools and in the attitudes of Hindu parents. This was reinforced by the heightened socio-economic prospects of the 1970s. Yet, judging from the continuous debates over such issues as the inclusion of Hindi on the formal syllabus and the teaching of Hindu religious instructions at both the primary and secondary levels, it can be argued that Hindus were eager to engage both aspects of education. By the 1950s, other such developments as the debates surrounding the granting of adult franchise to Hindus, the Hindu Marriage Bill and the (non) granting of capitation grants to Hindu educational institutions further sensitised Hindus to the need for schooling in English.

India

The Hindu community's dialogue with India was also a very valuable indicator of transformation. Until the 1940s, the passionate loyalty and almost reverential attitudes towards what was still heavily conceived of as the 'Motherland' was not unexpected. In its focus on community reconstitution during the first half of the twentieth century, Hindus in Trinidad could only intermittently draw from the larger Trinidad culture which was significantly divergent from theirs. However, due to a number of factors, a gradual change in this attitude was visible by the second half of the century. Indians in Trinidad became increasingly aware that the Indian government was paying mere 'lip service' to the conditions of Indians in Trinidad. The persistent reminder of prominent Indian political, social and religious figures to the Trinidad Indian population of their Trinidadian citizenship together with a growing attitude of nonchalance and distance confirmed such suspicions. Yet, there was an intensification of the cultural and religious dimensions of this dialogue with the constant influx of Indian performers and socio-religious figures. This, together with the greater assimilation of Hindus into the social and economic life of Trinidad, saw, by the 1970s, a situation where India, in its capacity as wellspring of Hindu practice and belief in Trinidad, was fast becoming more of a romanticised destination than the 'Motherland' in its connotations of patriotism, kinship and other deep-seated affective ties.

Organisation

Since the beginning of the twentieth century, efforts at mobilisation and organisation have both yielded to and reflected transformation within the Indian community. Until the 1940s, the location of the village as the nucleus of Hindu life was echoed in the localised nature of such organisational efforts as the *pathshalas*, Hindu schools and village panchayats. In addition, the still ingrained though considerably diluted sentiments of caste, the guru-chela and the patron-client relationships saw the emergence of a number of groups and organisations revolving around pundits, Brahmins and other individuals of high socio-economic status, and often significantly autocratic in nature. The appearance during the 1930s and 1940s of a number of large-scale Hindu and Indian organisations led to Hindu organisations operating on two levels. On one level there were the numerous village-based groups and sects, and on the other, the larger less localised bodies such as the SDBC and the SDA.

The lack of unity among the number of Hindu organisations exemplified clashing personalities and egos as well as agendas, and the contradiction between the Indian/Hindu and the Western concepts of organisational structure and function. Yet, Hindu organisational efforts functioned as both mediators and as the representatives of the Hindu community in matters of official import that threatened to either challenge Hindu sacred precepts and practices, or to overlook the Hindu community in one way or the other. This demonstrated their capacity to move beyond the discord – albeit only temporarily. With minimal Hindu participation in the national politics of the country throughout the first half of the twentieth century, this level of internal mobilisation and formal organisation was the major indicator of Hindu political sensibilities.

By extension, the determinants and functions of Hindu leadership also experienced significant change throughout this period. Until the 1960s, the major criteria for Hindu leadership included age, caste affiliation, economic status and religious credentials. With the economic transformations of the 1970s, the rise in formal education among Hindus and the consequent dilution or demise of the more traditional systems and values of Hindu organisation, there was an increasingly new approach to the question of Hindu leadership.

This development was underscored by an increasing shift from unquestioning deference to the leader to the concern with how effectively the individual could function as a representative of the Hindu community. The changing requisites and functions of Hindu leaders reflected the general more critical engagement with religious issues. The community was no longer satisfied with individuals whose credentials rested largely on their lineage, knowledge of the sacred mantras, and on their aura of pseudo-divine mysticism. Instead, the onus now resided heavily on the leaders, to prove themselves capable and worthy as leaders of the Hindu community.

Yet, by the 1990s, what was happening with Hindu organisation and leadership can more aptly be described as selective transformation rather than demise. While the structure, procedures and, to some extent, the ideology of Hindu organisations were analogous to those of the Western concept of organisation, certain traditional values and attitudes were still discernible. Thus, outstanding religious, socio-religious and wealthy figures continued to function as the nuclei of many Hindu organisations. The difference however resided in the emphasis – or sometimes the veneer of emphasis – on the democratic principles and structure of the organisation. Along similar lines, it can also be argued that the *Shankarachaarya* tradition which took root in Trinidad during the 1960s with the DLS was in fact a more glorified and contemporaneous packaging of the guru-chela system. The establishment of Indian centres of learning during the 1960s and 1970s further enhanced the guru-chela ideology, but yet again with more contemporary appeal. However, right up to the 1990s, the element of loyalty that defined the traditional Indian systems of power relations such as the guru-chela and patron-client relationships was still deeply entrenched in the Hindu psyche.

National Life

Interaction with the larger non-Hindu society occurred at two levels: at the official, policy making level and at the popular more mundane level, both of which yielded constant pressures towards change. The contestation for and of policies and regulations that had specific bearing on Hindu religious life revealed several currents. During the first half of the twentieth century, contestations at the official level were reflective of and fundamental to the Hindu community's gradual but persistent transgression out of the psychological and more palpable restrictions of its position at the bottom of Trinidad's socio-economic ladder. Fuelled by increasing public demonstrations of communalism, Hindu engagements with the state during this period served to boost Hindu communal morale. It also suggested varying degrees of amenability on the part of the state towards the Hindu community or, at least, an awareness of the latter as a section of the Trinidad citizenry that could no longer be ignored. However, much official perceptions and interpretations of, and attitudes towards Hindu socio-religious matters indicated varying degrees of ignorance, and socio-religious and socio-economic biases. By the 1950s, the presence of Hindus in Trinidad's House of Representatives and the large-scale mobilisation of Hindus spearheaded by the SDMS enhanced both the intensity and scope of Hindu interaction at the official level. What gradually evolved was an increasingly more aggressive, less apologetic tone in the official debates. The change in political power in 1985 together with the considerable academic and socio-economic achievements by Hindus saw, by the 1990s, the group no longer asking but demanding that their status as equal citizens of the country be reflected in the state's policies and practices. On its part, there seemed to be an effort by the state to develop a more informed, sensitive and inclusive approach in dealing with not just the Hindu community but religious and cultural issues on the whole.

Possibly the most sound indicator of the level and tenor of Hindu interaction with the larger society was through its festivals and socio-religious observances. The pre-1960s, relatively inward-looking tendencies of the Hindu community were evident in the communal nature of even the major festivals of Divali and *Phagwa*. The more sporadic observances on a national level indicated somewhat of a testing of the waters by Hindus; the publicising of Hindu religious festivals and observances was heightened during the 1960s. This was generated by the amalgam of academic and economic growth, a progressively – though extremely protracted – less derisive and dismissive treatment of Hinduism by the non-Hindu community, and a steady decline in the trepidation and suspicion with which

Hindus regarded the wider society, especially with regard to its religious practices. The increasing dialogue with and influences from the Indian sub-continent, and the simultaneous though seemingly paradoxical transferring of feelings of patriotism from India to Trinidad also contributed to this development.

The situating of Hindu religious rituals and observances in an essentially non-Hindu space raised a number of issues. Firstly, this move generated levels of de-ritualising or de-sanctifying of certain elements. The preoccupation with ritual purity and the overarching aura of sacredness that characterised both the preparations and the actual procedures could not be as fastidiously observed. For example, in a public neutral space, a fundamentally sacred act of the lighting of *deeyas* during Divali celebrations could not be guaranteed the level of sanctity which it invoked when conducted within an exclusively Hindu setting. In addition, there was little control over the proceedings in public settings. This further diluted the sacred aura of the event since not just non-Hindus, but also Hindus could overlook what they may perceive as troublesome religious nuances surrounding the observance.

Hindus also tended to sometimes overlook the transgressing of some of the sacred prescriptions. This attitude could be situated in the flexible nature of Hinduism. However, on a more fundamental level, it reiterated the Hindu community's growing preoccupation with national recognition of both themselves as equal citizens, and as a socio-religious group at the national level. Yet, this does not suggest that Hindus condoned the dilution of the most fundamental aspects of their religious observances. Conversely, they opted to counteract rather than fight the transgressions through the religious revitalisation initiated in the late 1970s. Drawing on the process of compartmentalisation, this involved a seemingly subconscious selection of those elements which could be 'sacrificed' for the cause of recognition and integration. Simultaneously, the more important dimensions were preserved and enhanced through sustained, strategic and effective efforts. Thus, Hindus were able to strike a balance between what could have been two very dichotomous yet equally fundamental issues for the community.

Processes

Throughout the period under study it was evident that a number of processes were at work in Hindu social and religious transformation, several of which, when placed in perspective, often seemed contradictory. Yet considering the diverse nature of Hinduism such discordance is not totally surprising. The attempts at homogenisation and standardisation can be viewed largely as a perceived necessity in Hinduism's location within the Trinidadian context. Both these processes were generated by the community's bid to adapt to life in Trinidad. They can be deemed as sensible mediators to the alternatives – expunction on the one hand, and rigid retention on the other. Conditioned by the wider society's considerably more definite and homogenised portrait of religion, both processes were major tools in the campaign by socio-religious organisations for recognition on both the official and popular levels. Yet, the inherent diversity, antiquity and fundamental nature of Hindu practice, structures, philosophy and values deterred any substantive success in the bid for standardisation. What resulted were sporadic, temporary veneers of standardisation and unity among Hindu socio-religious organisations, almost exclusively in situations where it was perceived that Hinduism was being threatened or compromised in one way or the other. Notwithstanding the trend of eliminating some of the more 'dubious' dimensions of popular Hindu practice, variance in Hindu practice and belief persisted. The equally numerous threads of uniformity were substantially rooted in Hinduism's defining trait of unity in diversity, rather than in the comparably studied efforts at homogenisation.

This does not deny the impact that the process of Christianisation and the infiltration of Western and modern elements had on Trinidadian Hinduism. Yet, a careful examination would reveal that the impact of these processes, though far-reaching and visible, were fairly unsuccessful in atrophying the more fundamental Hindu beliefs and practices. Rather, such influences were evident in what can be termed the more 'cosmetic' aspects of Hinduism. Thus, the analogy of the Hindu *Dharmachaarya* to the Catholic Archbishop did not transform the existing concept, function or importance of either the Hindu *Dharmachaarya* or other Hindu socio-religious leaders. The application of the essentially Christian structure of 'Sunday services' failed to modify the more fundamental procedures of the Hindu *satsang* format such as bhajan singing, reading from the scriptures, the performance of *havan* and the *satsang's* deep entrenchment in the Bhakti tradition. Indeed, the converse could be argued in the Canadian Mission's adoption of Hindu terminology, language, forms and Indian musical instruments into their missionary activity.

The arguments surrounding the infiltration of Western and modern elements were more complex and diverse. The impact of this movement was evident in almost all dimensions of Hindu life since it underscored the integration of Hindus into the social, economic and political life of the country. Thus, the public aspects of Hindu life that inevitably came into contact with these processes such as Hindu organisation and leadership, the more cosmetic aspects of Hindu life cycle ceremonies, occupation and education served as harbingers of this type of transformation. Even some of the most intimate dimensions of Hindu life such as family structure and values, conjugal relationships and language could not escape the infiltration of Western and modern systems and values. In fact, by the 1990s, one could argue that there was a preponderant subsumption of the traditional elements in Hindu family life by Western and modern elements. These factors also had a more far-reaching impact on Hindu religious practice and belief than did the efforts at Christian proselytisation. Since modern and Western elements did not directly juxtapose Hinduism with another religion (as did efforts at proselytisation), there was not the perceived threat of loss of religion. Thus, Hindus were less suspicious of the impact of these two processes. Also, the general perception of Western and modern elements in the daily lives of Hindus as 'positive' transformations also heightened their impact on the religious sphere of Hinduism. Thus, Hindu life cycle rituals, pujas, *yagnas, satsangs* and festivals were varyingly affected by modern and Western elements. A mixture of subconscious and concerted efforts, this trend served to rework elements of religion to suit the contemporary framework. Yet, it must be noted that the underlying principles of the most inherent aspects of Hindu practice and belief were not considerably transformed by Western and modern influences. For example, variations in the time frame surrounding the Hindu death ceremonies did not detract from the emphasis on performing the rituals 'in the right way.' Transformations in the *yagna* and *satsang* settings could not atrophy the Bhakti orientation of the events or the texts' function as doctrine.

Secularisation, wherein essentially religious elements are variously divorced of their religious interpretation, was a persistent process in Hindu socio-religious transformation. It was most commonly observed when elements of Hindu thought and practice were placed in a secular or neutral context, as was the case with Hindu religious texts and festivals. By overlooking their religious invocations secularisation facilitated the smoother, less problematic integration of such elements into the working of the national community. This process eventually, though at a markedly slower pace, was evident even within the Hindu community, in events such as weddings, funerals, some festivals, and to a lesser extent, *yagnas*. Yet, by the 1990s, none of the more fundamental religious beliefs and practices had undergone absolute secularisation. This conceivable paradox hinges on the process of compartmentalisation which facilitated multiple levels of, not just secularisation, but almost all of the other major processes. Compartmentalisation contributed to and accommodated the coexistence of change and continuity in Hindu thought and practice by functioning as a major tool through which Hindus could regulate the degree, nature and scope of transformation and retention. Thus, the benefits of change in selected areas could be enjoyed without the threat of it diluting those elements of tradition which were held as viable and necessary to Hindu life in their existing conditions. This process was highly responsible for the capacity of Hindus to function within the context of the larger non-Hindu society, even imbibing many of its values and practices, and still subscribe to the essentially divergent beliefs, practices and values of Hinduism in their more intimate life.

Other processes inherent in Hindu social change were those of synthesis, accommodation, assimilation, dilution, rejection, reconstitution and preservation. Through these, Hinduism invoked its flexibility to rework social and religious elements into a more temporally and spatially viable package. Hence, the outcomes of these processes were direct indicators of society and social change. Rejection allowed for the demise of those elements which seemed either distasteful or at least questionable, and which threatened negatively to colour the wider society's perception of the Hindu community. Reconstitution allowed for the 're-facing' rather than rejection of elements of tradition which, in the original Indian forms, could not apply to the Trinidad context. This was most evident with the Hindu social systems and family life.

This study has analysed socio-religious change among Hindus in Trinidad from 1917 to 1990. The amalgam of processes that collectively evoked and facilitated such transformations have highlighted Trinidadian Hinduism's propensity for change. That such change permeated all dimensions of life among Hindus depicted the veracity of the assignations of 'way of life,' 'unity in diversity' and 'change and continuity' to Hinduism in Trinidad. The *Ramayana*, in its function as both a metaphor of such change and as the major lens through which socio-religious transformation was examined, exhibited a high degree of fluidity, variety and viability – traits which also defined the larger sphere of Trinidadian Hinduism. By 1990, Trinidadian Hinduism was at another important juncture. The political ethos was more cognizant of and sensitive to the religious diversity of the country. Hindus had economically, politically, socially and psychologically entrenched themselves as equal citizens into the workings of the country. Hinduism was experiencing fundamental changes in terms of its interpretation, presentation and applicability. However, this was now infused with a discernibly less defensive, more progressive, practical and confident outlook. Given the level of transformation that characterised the religion's foregoing 165 years of existence and development in Trinidad, one is assured of its unremitting capacity to further evolve in accordance with the exigencies of time, place and circumstance, itself a time-worn Hindu formula. In other words, the stage was fully set for the transportation of Trinidadian Hinduism into the new millennium.

APPENDICES

APPENDIX I

Religious Composition of Trinidad's Population in 1990

Denomination	Number
Roman Catholic	330,655
Hindu	267,040
Anglican	122,194
Pentecostal	84,066
Muslim	65,732
Adventist	41,631
Presbyterian	38,740
Baptist	33,689
Jehovah's Witness	14,713
Methodist	13,448
Other	98,936
None	13,691
TOTAL	1,125,128

Source: Republic of Trinidad and Tobago Annual Statistical Digest, 2000.

APPENDIX II

Growth of Hindu Population in Trinidad

YEAR	TOTAL POPULATION	HINDU POPULATION
1931	412,783	93,889
1946	557,970	126,345
1960	827,957	190,403
1970	931,071	230,209
1980	1,055,763	262,917
1990	1,125,128	267,040

Sources:
– Census of the Colony of Trinidad and Tobago 1931.
– Census of the Colony of Trinidad and Tobago, 1946.
– Trinidad And Tobago Annual Statistical Digest, 1935-1991.

APPENDIX III

SHORT SYNOPSES OF THE MAJOR HINDU RELIGIOUS TEXTS IN TRINIDAD HINDUISM

The Bhagvadgita

The *Bhagvadgita* is an episode in India's Great Epic, the *Mahabharata*. The main story of the *Mahabharata* is the war between two sets of cousins of the solar dynasty, the *Kauravas* and the *Pandavas*. At the onset of the great war, Krishna – cousin to both factions and believed to be God incarnate – is faced with the task of instilling the will to fight in Arjuna, the Pandavas's most valiant warrior, who loses his nerve and the desire to fight his kinsmen and many others equally dear to him.

Though this thread runs throughout the entire poem/dialogue, its major concern is not with war and peace, but with philosophical and spiritual issues such as the nature of the self, man's existence and function in the world, the pathways to God, achieving spirituality, and expositions on the notions of karma (action, inaction and reaction), dharma (sense of duty), *jnana* (knowledge), Brahman (cosmic unity), bhakti (devotion), and nirvana (liberation). The climax of the *Bhagavadgita*, however, is when Krishna reveals himself in all his divine majesty to Arjuna. More philosophical probing continues at the end of the vision, which leads ultimately to Arjuna's readiness to engage in battle. While no firm date can be established, one can place the *Bhagvadgita* between the fifth and second centuries B.C. (Zaener 1969, 7). However, the work in its present forms indicate considerable revision (Stutley 1977, 40).

The Puranas

The Puranas are essentially recastings of older works of religious and didactic content (Winternitz 1927, 519–20) such as the Vedas and the Upanishads, composed in the simpler prose form with the intent of conveying the teachings of those works to the largely unlettered masses. The Puranas drew freely on the Vedic gods and demons, which were re-mythologized in new legendary settings. Puranas usually expounded five subjects: the creation of the world; its destruction and recreation; the genealogy and deeds of the gods, patriarchs, heroes and saints; the reigns and periods of the Manus, and the history of the Solar and Lunar royal dynasties. Many of the later versions include accretions such as geography, astrology, chronology, anatomy and medicine. Much of the information is in dialogue, in some of which a divinely inspired sage is the principal narrator who answers the questions of a disciple. Puranic literature comprises two groups: the primary or major *Mahapuranas*, and the secondary or minor *Upapuranas*, with each group consisting of 18 works. Since the Puranas cannot be placed earlier than circa 300 AD, the earliest events therein related (some having occurred more than two thousand years before) are likely to have undergone considerable re-editing. In addition, the traditional account contained in the *Puranas* is vitiated by exaggeration, mythological details, pronounced religious bias, and the divergences in the texts of the different Puranas. They nevertheless are the sole source of information relating to the early post-Vedic period, and hence, cannot be dismissed (Stutley 1977, 236).

The Bhagvadpurana

This is indisputably the work of Puranic literature that is most famous both in India and in Trinidad. Dated at around the tenth century AD (Winternitz 1927, 556), it is the one Purana which, more than any of the others, bears the stamp of a unified composition and deserves to be appreciated as a literary production on account of its language, style and metre. The incarnations of Vishnu are described in detail. Cosmogonic myths and legends glorifying Vishnu are numerous. The work is divided into 12 books, of which the tenth, detailing the biography of Krishna, is the most popular.

The *Ramcharitmanas*

This is Tulsidas's version of the *Ramayana* story. It tells the story of Rama, believed to be a Divine incarnation, who has assumed human form in order to rid the earth of social and religious menaces.

This text is infused with the Bhakti orientation of worship and love of God, and has been used since its appearance as a social, religious, political and moral doctrine. A brief synopsis of the *Ramcharitmanas* is as follows. After many barren years Dashratha, king of Ayodhya, and his three queens have been blessed with four sons: Rama by senior queen Kaushalya, Bharat and Lakshmana by Kaikeyi, and Shatrughana by Sumitra. The four young princes are sent by the king with sage Vishwamitra to rid the sages living in the forest of the atrocities of the *rakshasas* (demons). Mission accomplished, Vishwamitra proceeds to Mithila with the princes where the king Janaka is staging a bow-breaking ceremony for the marriage of his daughter, Sita. Rama succeeds in breaking the bow, and marries Sita, while his three brothers are wed to three of her immediate relatives.

Back in Ayodhya, Dashratha prepares to install Rama as Prince Regent. However, perverted by her personal maid, Manthara, Queen Kaikeyi recalls two boons promised to her by the king and demands that her son Bharat be installed as Prince Regent, and that Rama be banished to the forest for 14 years. Bound by his word, the king is forced to accede to her demands. Thus Rama, honouring his father's oath, graciously leaves for the forest accompanied by his wife, Sita and his brother, Lakshmana. The king, overcome by grief, expires, and Bharat, refusing to accept the kingship, proceeds to the forest in search of Rama. Rama, however, citing his duty to fulfill his father's promise, refuses to return. An adamant Bharat returns only after acquiring Rama's sandals which he enthrones at Ayodhya, then acquiescing to rule in Rama's name from his austere abode at Nandigrama. During their sojourn in the forest, Rama and Lakshmana destroy numerous demons and meet with various saints and sages. Incited by his cousin – the demoness Surpanakha – the demon king Ravana abducts Sita. During their search for her, the brothers encounter and form alliances with the monkey king Sugriva and Hanuman. In return for Rama slaying his brother Vali, king Sugriva and his army of monkeys and bears assist Rama in the search for his wife, who is eventually discovered at Ravana's palace garden in the city of Lanka.

Despite a series of appeals from his kinsmen, Ravana refuses to return Sita. After a raging battle, which leads to the destruction of almost all of his kinsmen, Ravana is killed by Rama. Rama then coronates Ravana's righteous brother Vibhishana as the new king of Lanka. However, he refuses to accept Sita on account of her having lived at another man's home, thus being defiled. After undergoing a fire test to prove her chastity, Sita is accepted by her husband and the party returns to Ayodhya where Rama is installed as king. Marital bliss, however, is sacrificed for the sake of the state when Rama opts to banish his pregnant wife to the forest when a citizen questions her chastity (since she lived at Ravana's home). Sita gives birth to twin sons Lava and Kusha at the abode of the sage Valmiki, where they are brought up as ascetics, yet skilled in the arts of warfare. Meanwhile, Rama performs the horse-sacrifice to acclaim himself as a supreme ruler. His sons capture the roaming horse and defeat Rama's army, and later, Rama himself. Eventually, their identity is revealed and Rama attempts to take his family back to Ayodhya with him. This time, however, Sita refuses and opts instead to take refuge in her mother – the Earth. Rama thus returns to his city with his two sons and continues his very illustrious reign.

Biographical Sketches of the Main Characters in the Ramayana

Bharat: Rama's other brother whose mother, Kaikeyi, demands the throne on his behalf. Bharat, however, refuses to accept kingship.

Dashratha: Rama's father.

Hanuman: A monkey with divine powers who plays a crucial role in finding Sita and eventually becomes Rama's most dedicated servant.

Kaikeyi: Dashratha's third wife who asks that Rama be banished to the forest and that her son, Bharat, be made Crown Prince.

Kowshalya: Rama's mother and Dashratha's eldest queen.

Lakshmana: Rama's younger brother who accompanies him to the forest.

Rama: In the story of the Ramayana, Rama is the exiled Crown Prince of Ayodhya. Within the context of Hinduism, Rama is believed to be an incarnation of the god Vishnu, the Preserver of the universe.

Ravan: The demon king who kidnaps Sita; anti-hero of the *Ramayana*.

Sita: Rama's wife who is kidnapped by the demon king, Ravan.

Sugriva: The king of the monkeys who helps Rama to find Sita and to defeat Ravan's army.

Surpanakha: Ravan's cousin who attempts to seduce Rama.

Vali: Sugriva's brother who steals Sugriva's kingdom and wife, and who is eventually slain by Rama.

Vibhishana: Ravana's righteous brother who allies himself with Rama.

APPENDIX IV

Ramayana Aarti: (*Sri Ramcharitamanasa*. Gorakhpur: Gita Press, 1999)

Transliteration
*Aarti Shri Ramayana jee kee,
keerati kalita lalita siya pee kee.*

*Gaavat Brahmaadika muni Naarada,
Vaalmeeka vigyaana vishaaarada.
Suka Sanakaadi Shesha aru Shaarada,
varani Pavana suta keerati neekee.*

*Gaavat Veda Puraana ashtadasa,
chha-o Shaastra saba granthana ko rasa.
Muni jana dhana sanatana ko saravasa,
saar ans sammat sabahee kee.*

*Gaavat santata Shambhu Bhavaanee,
aru ghatsambhava muni vigyaanee.
Vyaasa aadi kavivarja bakhaanee,
Kaakbhusundi Garuda ke hee kee.*

*Kali mala harani vishaya rasa pheekee,
subhaga singaara mukti yuvtee kee.
Dalana roga bhava mooree amee kee, taata maata saba bidhi Tulasee kee.*

Translation (by Madhava Sarana)
Soft lights we wave, soft lights, display before this Lord of Sita's lay –
The Ramayana, so sweet and dear,
So beautiful, without a peer,

Which gods like Brahma, Narada sing,
The ant-hill sage, soul-seers' king,
Suka, Sarada, Sesa, boy sages four,

The wind-god's son recount this lore
With great delight and voices gay.

The holy books their music mix
To sing this gist of <u>Sastra</u> six,
Of all good works, of all good thought;
The wealth of sages; yet what not
Of all the saints?—their mainstay,

Uma and Shankara e'er intone,
As well as the wise Agastya pot-grown.
The crow's, Garud's it heart indwells.
The poets great like Vyasa and else
In ecstasies this song relay.

Shuns sensuous joy, sins' abluent,
The dame of Mukti's ornament;
Ambrosial herb of rebirth to cure,
And parents both, 'tis only sure,
For Tulasidasa in everyway.

Ramayana Sumiran: (*Sri Ramcharitamanasa*, Descent I-*Balakanda, Sortha* 1-5)

Transliteration
Jo sumirata siddhi hoi,
Gana naayaka karivara vadana.
Kara-u anugraha soi,
Buddhi raasi shubha guna sadana.

Mooka hoi vaachaala,
Pangu charhai girivara gahana.
Jaasu kripaa so dayaala,
Dravau sakala kali mala dahana.

Neela saroruha syaam,
Taruna aruna vaarija nayana.
Karau so mama ura dhaama,
Sadaa ksheerasaagar sayana.

Kunda indu sama deha,
Uma raman karunaa ayana.
Jaahi deen para neha,
Karau kripaa maradana mayana.

Bandau Guru pada kanja,
Kripaa sindhu nararupa Hari.
Mahaamoha tama punja,
Jaasu vachana ravikara nikara.

Translation

May Lord Ganesha, the leader of Shiva's retinue, whose every thought, ensures success, who carries on his shoulders the head of a beautiful elephant, who is a repository of wisdom and an abode of blessed qualities, shower his grace.

May that merciful Lord, whose grace enables the dumb to wax eloquent and a cripple to ascend an inaccessible mountain, and who burns all the impurities of the Kali age, be moved to pity.

May the Lord who ever sleeps on the ocean of milk, and who is swarthy as a blue lotus and has eyes resembling a pair of full-blown red lotuses, take up His abode in my bosom.

May the crusher of Cupid, Bhagvan Shiva, whose form resembles in colour the jasmine flower and the moon, and who is the consort of goddess Parvati and an abode of compassion and who is fond of the afflicted, be gracious.

I bow to the lotus feet of my Guru, who is an ocean of mercy and is no other than Sri Hari Himself in human form. And whose words are sunbeams as it were for the dispersing the mass of darkness in the form of gross ignorance.

Bhagvata Aarti

(Taken from *Smarana. A Collection of Traditional Bhajans in Hindi and English*. Compiled by Kamla Ramlakhan. (Trinidad: Master Print, 1992).

Transliteration

Bhaagavata bhagvaana kee hai aarti,
Paapiyo ko paap se hai taarti.

Ye amar grantha ye mukti pantha
Ye panchama veda niraalaa.
Nava jyoti jagaanewaalaa.
Hari gaana yahee, vardaana yahi,
Jaga ke mangala kee aarti.

Ye shaanti geeta paavana puneet,
Shraapo ko mitaanewaalaa.
Hari darasha dikhaanewaalaa.
Hai sukh karanee, hai dukh harani.
Ye madhusoodan kee aarti.

Ye madhur bol, jaga phanda khol,
Sanmaarga dikhaanewaalaa.
Bigaree ko banaanewaalaa,
Shree Raam yahee ghanshyaam yahi.
Prabhu kee mahimaa kee aarti.

Translation

This is the aarti of Lord Bhagavat,
Which saves all people from sins.

This is the immortal book, the path of salvation. This is the unique fifth Veda.
It kindles new lights.
This is the prayer of Lord Hari.
This is a great boon for us.

This is the song of peace, pure and purifying. It is the remover of curses.
Granting the vision of Lord Hari, it gives us happiness and removes our pains. This is the aarti of Lord Madhusudhan which saves sinners from sins.

It has sweet words which untie the knots of the world. It shows us the righteous path. It restores us when we are ruined.
It is Shri Rama. It is the cloud, cloud-like Shri Krishna. It is the aarti of the great of the greatness of the Lord.

Verses from Two Popular Bhajans Sung at Ramayana Yagnas and Satsangs

(Taken from *Smarana. A Collection of Traditional Bhajans in Hindi and English*. Compiled by Kamla Ramlakhan. (Trinidad: Master Print, 1992).

Bhajan I: Mujhe Apanee Sharana Mein Lelo Raam

Transliteration

Mujhe apanee sharana mein lelo Raam
Lochana man mein jagaha na ho to
Yugal charana mein lelo Raam.

Jeevana de ke jaal bichhaayaa
Racha ke maayaa naacha nachaayaa
Chintaa meree tabhee mitegee
Jaba charano mein lelo Raam.

Tumne laakho paapee tare
Meree baaree baazi hare
Mere paasa na punya kee pujaa
Pada pujan mein lelo Raam.

Translation
O Rama, take me into Your shelter.
If there is no room in Your eyes or heart for me, then please give me shelter at Your feet.

You have entrapped me by giving me life. By creating *maya* (illusion) You confuse me. I will only be free of all worries when You shelter me at Your feet.

You have uplifted millions of sinners.
But You have lost the wage when my turn came. I do not have a wealth of virtues. Still draw me to the worship of Your feet.

Bhajan II – Jina Ke Hridaya Shree Raam Base

Transliteration
Jina ke hridaya Shree Raam base,
Una aur ko naam liyo na liyo.

Koee maange kanchan see kaayaa,
Koee maanga rahaa prabhu se maayaa.
Koee punya kare, koee daan kare,
Koee daan kaa roza bakhaan kare.
Jina kanyaadhana ko daan diyo,
Una aur ko daan diyo na diyo.

Koee ghar mein baithaa namanu kare,
Koee hari mandir mein bhajan kare,
Koee Gangaa Jamunaa snaan kare,
Koee Kaashi jaa ke dhyaan dhare,
Jina maata pitaa kee sevaa kee,

Una teerth snaan kiyo na kiyo.

Translation
In whichever heart that Rama resides,
Whether they remember any other name or not, it hardly matters.

Some ask for a beautiful body. Some ask for wealth. Some do good deeds, some give donations. Some talk every day about the *daan* (charity) they give. But for those who have done *kanyadaan*, if they give other *daan* or not, it does not matter.

Some offer salutations, sitting in their homes. Some sing *bhajans* in *mandirs*. Some bathe in the Ganga or Jamuna rivers. Some go to Kashi and do meditation. But those who serve their mother and father, if they bathe in sacred rivers or not, it does not matter.

APPENDIX V

Enrolment at Government Assisted Primary and Intermediate Schools

YEAR	TOTAL	HINDU	PERCENTAGE (%)
1952	121,427	431	0.35
1953	132,454	6,307	4.7
1954	137,625	8,507	6.1
1955	145,103	11,556	7.9
1956	153,362	12,080	7.8
1957	159,503	12,752	7.9
1958	167,294	14,315	8.5
1959	173,846	15,667	9.0
1960	181,745	16,667	9.1
1961	190,557	17,298	9.0
1962	195,685	17,801	9.1
1963	203,756	18,794	9.2
1964–65	209,366	20,043	9.5
1965–66	216,063	21,050	9.7
1966–67	219,679	21,409	9.7
1967–68	223,164	21,840	9.7
1968–69	224,343	21,121	9.4
1969–70	227,254	22,180	9.7
1970–71	228,319	22,246	9.8
1971–72	227,815	21,998	9.6
1983–84	166,739	16,851	10.1
1984–85	168,790	17,096	10.1
1985–86	172,424	17,422	10.1
1986–87	176,544	18,088	10.2
1987–88	182,764	18,870	10.3
1988–89	186,189	19,160	10.2
1989–90	189,752	19,525	10.2

Sources:
Central Statistical Office, Digest of Statistics on Education 1959, 1964–66, 1971–72.
Report on Education Statistics 1983–84, 1984–85, 1985–86, 1986–87, 1987–88, 1988–89, 1989–90.

NOTES

Introduction

1. A detailed description and analysis of the system of indenture can be found in K.O. Laurence, *A Question of Labour: Indentured Immigration into Trinidad and British Guiana 1875–1917* (Kingston: Ian Randle Publishers, 1994).
2. I.O.R. Official Series *V/27/820/10: Note on Emigration from India to Trinidad* by Surgeon Major W.D. Comins (Calcutta: Bengal Secretariat Press, 1893).
3. In Hinduism, the Little Tradition refers to those aspects which have evolved independently of the Great Tradition. These are usually embedded in orality, and are geographically localised and linguistically restrictive. The Great Tradition refers to the essentially Sanskritic/Brahminic strand of Hinduism which is embedded in the Vedas and other Sanskrit literature.
4. Republic of Trinidad and Tobago. Ministry of Planning and Development. Central Statistical Office, *Annual Statistical Digest* 45 (2000).
5. This has been debated in, among many others, works such as Arvind Sharma, *Hinduism and Its Sense of History*; A.L. Basham, *A Cultural History of India*; Heinrich Zimmer, *Myths and Symbols in Indian Art and Civilization*; and Romila Thapar, *Ancient Indian Social History: Some Interpretations*.
6. This theory of Brahmanical supremacy evolved gradually during the Vedic period of Indian history, and was further consolidated during the post-Vedic period (600 BC–300 AD). Accepted by the early Brahmin (and only) writers, they propounded this model of the caste system which placed them at the top and gave them the privilege of laying down the duties and rights of the other castes, even the King's. Srinivas promotes that the varna model became popular during the British period on account of a variety of factors.
7. Composed between 500 BC and 500 AD, the Puranas were essentially texts comprising elaborations of Hindu rites, rituals and philosophy in story form. Though mythical, they were not entirely so since they contain references to historical events.
8. Balkaran Jairam, interview by author, September 26, 2001.
9. Recitation and interpretation of verses from the *Ramayana* usually done within a congregational setting.

10. A sect that emerged around 500 BC in Indian response to the Brahmanic supremacy of the time. Its doctrine does not place much emphasis on the existence of God, but focuses instead upon the purity of the soul and its eventual release from the body into a state of eternal bliss as the purpose of life.
11. Also, in Russia, the world of Tulsidas's *Ramayana* in all its complexity was recreated by a Russian academician Alexey Brannikov, while simultaneously making it more intelligible to the Russian readers through the inclusion of his own conception and broad commentaries.
12. In Hinduism, there are four Vedas which are deemed as the most ancient scriptures in the world, and which collectively provide prescriptions and codes of operation for all dimensions of human existence. Thus, assigning the title of 'fifth Veda' to the *Ramcharitmanas*, would transfer onto that text the prestige and religious supremacy of the four Vedas.

Chapter 1

1. *Colony of Trinidad and Tobago Census Album*, 1948.
2. I.O.R. Public and Judicial Department Records *L/PJ/8/338: Royal Commission on the West Indies, Deputation of J.D. Tyson to the West Indies; Tyson's Report on the Condition of Indians in Jamaica, British Guiana and Trinidad; Labour Conditions in the West Indies (1938–1943)*, 27.
3. Some interviewees, mainly those in leadership positions, are still quite reluctant to accept this idea, due primarily to political purposes, or the desire to maintain 'purity and exclusivity.'
4. Crystallised towards the end of Rig Veda Samhitas, and fully developed between the Samhitas and Brahmanas.
5. Propitiation of the deity believed to be the protector of one's residential and agricultural property.
6. Moonsammy, interview by author, November 7, 2001.
7. Ramdial Boodram, interview by author, October 10, 1999.
8. Pundit Lutchmie Persad, interview by author, February 9, 2002.
9. Short definitions of each observance are provided in the glossary.
10. The works of Colin Clarke, Morton Klass, Arthur and Juanita Niehoff and Barton Schwartz all provide detailed examinations of caste in Trinidad.
11. A more detailed examination of caste and indentured labour is provided in K.O. Laurence, *A Question of Labour: Indentured Immigration into Trinidad and British Guiana 1875–1917* (Kingston: Ian Randle Publishers, 1994), 110–15.
12. *Emigration Certificates* 1866, 1872, 1882, 1902, 1912, 1917.
13. Hardeo Ramsingh, interview by author, October 7, 2001.
14. The surname was essentially a concept imposed on/adopted by Indians in their attempts at conforming to the policies and practices of the larger society.

15. See Morton Klass, *East Indians in Trinidad: A Study in Cultural Persistence* (Illinois: Waveland Press Inc., 1961); and Arthur and Juanita Niehoff, *East Indians in the West Indies* (Wisconsin: Milwaukee Public Museum, 1960).
16. Ramsingh, interview.
17. Soognia Bal, interview by author, October 15, 2001.
18. Dookani Soogrim, interview by author, June 7, 2002.
19. Gaitree Singh, interview by author, January 6, 2002.
20. This occurred even within the Arya Samaj (which, ironically, denounced the system), where a senior pundit and officer, Bhogi Dass, was stripped of both his religious and organisational privileges and duties on account of his appropriation of another man's wife. However, although his immediate chelas condoned the action taken by the Samaj, they would not allow anyone to ridicule him. Thus, Bhogi Dass still wielded influence based on the Guru-Chela system.
21. Dolly Rampersad, interview by author, January 6, 2002.
22. *Sri Ramcharitmanas*, Des. 3 Verse 5.
23. Gaitree Singh, interview.
24. Lutchmie Persad, interview.
25. Basdai Jagat, interview by author, November 16, 2001.
26. Narsaloo Ramaya, interview by author, December 12, 2001.
27. Cow dung/*Gobar* is an important element in many rituals in Hinduism. Here, it is used derisively in connotating both ritualism and animal excreta.
28. Hansard, *Trinidad and Tobago Debates of the House of Representatives Official Report* 1932, 279.
29. *Hansard* 1944, 434.
30. Lutchmie Persad, interview.
31. Jagat, interview.
32. *Hansard* 1941, 117.
33. *Colony of Trinidad and Tobago Census Album, 1948.*
34. *East Indian Weekly*, October 13, 1928. By the 1940s, it was acknowledged that Hindi was being taught at the Canadian Mission schools for 90 minutes each week. The government schools had very little or no Hindi at all.
35. Charles Grant, 'Observations on the State of Society among Asiatic Subjects of Great Britain.' Cited in Brinsley Samaroo, 'Women's Work in the Canadian Presbyterian Mission to Trinidad during the Century after 1868,' Paper presented at the *Conference on Religions of the New World*, January 7–9, 2002, The University of the West Indies, St Augustine, 3–4.
35. See Sarah Morton, *John Morton of Trinidad* (Toronto: Westminster Company, 1916); and K.G. Grant, *My Missionary Memories* (Halifax: The Imperial Publishing Company, 1923).
36. *Jubilee of the Trinidad Mission* cited in Samaroo, 'Missionary Methods and Local Responses,' 34.

37. I.O.R. Public and Judicial Department Records *L/P&J/8/319: Problems of Indians in Trinidad, 1941–1946*, 21.
38. Lutchmie Persad, interview.

Chapter 2

1. Barton Schwartz, 'Differential Socioreligious Adaptation,' *Social and Economic Studies* 16, 245.
2. *Sri Ramcharitmanas* (Gorakhpur: Gita Press, 1999) Des. I. Verses 7, 14D.
3. The most popular has been his black/dark colouring. However, certain paraphernalia associated with specific individuals, elements or situations have periodically been placed on the effigies.
4. Dr Kenneth Parmasad in discussion with author November 2001.
5. Ravindranath Maharaj (Raviji), interview by author, October 8, 2001.
6. This was perhaps also a reason why in the local process of selective sanskritisation, Kali worship would lose its appeal, and Kali herself would appear in some shrines as a pink figure.
7. It is interesting to note that at a *Ramleela* performance in Lopinot in 1995, all of the characters – both male and female – were portrayed by females; a possible metaphor of the increasing reversal in traditional gender roles among Hindus.
8. There were similar developments in the Indian film industry where, at first, female actors from 'respectable' families were not visible.
9. A major tenet of Hinduism promotes that the entire world and its creations are illusions (maya) with the only reality being God. Thus, the only way that one can become part of reality is oneness though that Supreme Divinty.
10. A 78-episode serialised adaptation of the *Ramayana*, based primarily on the *Ramcharitmanas*, produced and directed by Bombay film maker Ramanand Sagar, which premiered in India in 1987.
11. Literally, a Divali village. In, Trinidad, however, it refers to an annual event observed just prior to the Festival of Lights, showcasing various aspects of Indian culture in Trinidad.
12. This dance-drama tells the story of how Rama's father, king Dashratha unknowingly killed the only son and support of an old blind couple. The grief-stricken couple consequently cursed the king with the same pain of separation from his offspring that they were enduring.
13. The ancestral home of this author was thus named due to the imposing statue of Hanuman prominently displayed on its verandah. In the *Ramayana* tradition, Hanuman, who possessed the physical features of a monkey, was Rama's loyal servant and devotee.
14. Ramsingh, interview.
15. Ramaya, interview.

16. Ramaya, interview.
17. Boodram, interview.
18. Pundit Brahmanand Rambachan, interview by author, November 22, 2002.
19. Rambachan, interview.
20. Pundit Khemraj Vyas, interview by author, November 27, 2002.
21. Boodram Ramgoolam, interview by author, December 16, 2002.
22. Ramgoolam, interview.
23. Bhagwandai Sinanan, interview by author, December 17, 2002.
24. Vyas, interview.
25. *Sri Ramcharitmanas* Des.1 Verse 333.2.
26. *Sri Ramcharitmanas* Des.1 Verse 300–61.
27. Bhagwandai Sinanan, interview.
28. In this form, the marriage ceremony is performed with the couple and the pundit seated on chairs placed around a table instead of, as in the traditional ceremony, on the floor.
29. Ramgoolam, interview.
30. Ramgoolam, interview.
31. Boodram, interview.
32. Ramgoolam, interview.
33. Ameena Ali, interview by author, September 26, 2001.
34. A detailed examination of the relationship between Indian daughters-in-law and their mother-in-laws can be found in Shaheeda Hosein's PhD dissertation on 'Rural Indian Women in Trinidad, 1870–1945.' 351–59.
35. *Sri Ramcharitmanas* Des. 2 Verse 58.1.
36. *Sri Ramcharitmanas* Des. 2 Verse 74.4.
37. *Sri Ramcharitmanas* Des. 2 Verse 314.2.
38. *Sri Ramcharitmanas* Des. 3 Verse 5.
39. *Sri Ramcharitmanas* Des. 5 Verse 58.3.
40. *Sri Ramcharitmanas* Des. 4 Verse 14.3.
41. *Sri Ramcharitmanas* Des. 3 Verse 5.

Chapter 3

1. Night dedicated to the worship of the God Shiva.
2. Nine day period dedicated to the worship of the female aspect of Divinity.
3. This term, when used orally, referred not just to the text, but encapsulated the entire gamut of the socio-religious activity, which was usually a seven-, nine- or 14-day affair, with readings and all of the associated rituals being performed three times daily. This extension of the name of the text, in popular oral use, to connote the entire event with all its accoutrements exemplifies the intimate dialogue between text and tradition, and the textual tradition and society.

4. In Hinduism, the Almighty is perceived of as having 16 qualities (*kalas*) which are invoked according to the requirements of a particular time and purpose. The avatar of Rama in the *Ramayana* possessed 14 of those qualities, while Krishna, the avatar in the *Bhagvadpurana* possessed all 16. Hence Rama is viewed as a 'partial incarnation,' and Krishna as the 'complete incarnation' or the coming of God Himself.
5. Pundit Hardath Maharaj, interview by author, November 24, 2002.
6. Rambachan, interview.
7. Rambachan, interview.
8. Hardath Maharaj, interview.
9. Vyas, interview.
10. Rambachan, interview.
11. Pundit Prakash Persad, interview by author, October 5, 2001.
12. Brahmachari Prem Chaitanya, interview by author, November 23, 2001.
13. Lall Paladee, interview by author, November 22, 2001.
14. In Hinduism, non-Hindu religious icons such as Buddha and Mohammed, while not accepted as the Divine or as an avatar, are conceded as figures imbued with substantial levels of Divine attributes and capabilities, who act as agents of the Divine.
15. Sister Krishna Gupta, interview by author, November 22, 2001.
16. Ramlakhan Sukrit, interview by author, February 20, 2002.
17. Sukrit, interview.
18. Sankar Ramnarine, interview by author, February 21, 2002.
19. Boodram, interview.
20. Boodram, interview.
21. Hardath Maharaj, interview.
22. Rambachan, interview.
23. Vyas, interview.
24. *Sri Ramcharitmanas*, Des.1 Verse 34.5.
25. Pundit Doodnath Rampersad, interview by author, January 5, 2002.
26. Prakash Persad, interview.
27. Hardath Maharaj, interview.
28. Vyas, interview.
29. Sinanan, interview.
30. Sahadeo Sirju, interview by author, October 15, 2002.
31. Ramgoolam, interview.
32. The *nauni/nau* is a person who assists in the organisation and performance of many Hindu rites and rituals.
33. Vyas, interview.
34. Rambachan, interview.
35. Ramgoolam, interview.
36. Literally, a preceptor or instructor on the Hindu notion of Dharma (one's duty, righteousness and proper conduct).

37. Thomas B. Coburn, '"Scripture" in India: Towards a Typology of the Word in Hindu Life,' *Journal of the American Academy of Religion* 52 no. 3: 435–59.
38. Coburn 435–59.
39. Coburn 447.
40. Coburn 449.
41. *Sri Ramcharitmanas* Des. 7 Verse 128.3.
42. In the year 2001, *yagnas* were held for 'the political stability' of the country; and in 2002, in commemoration of the Sanatan Dharma Maha Sabha's fiftieth anniversary at various SDMS primary schools. In one instance, a *bedi* (consecrated altar) in the shape of the map of Trinidad was constructed and consecrated as the ritual altar for the duration of the *yagna*. Another prominent contemporary concept was the 'answer back *yagna*' which attempted to disseminate information to the adherents of Sanatan Dharma and to simultaneously combat the attacks launched against Hinduism.
43. Vyas, interview.
44. Vyas, interview.
45. Hardath Maharaj, interview.
46. *Sri Ramcharitmanas* Des. 7 Verse 120.14.
47. Doodnath Rampersad, interview.
48. Hardath Maharaj, interview.
49. Ramgoolam, interview.
50. Rambachan, interview.
51. Rambachan, interview.
52. Satnarayan Maharaj, interview by author, December 6, 2001.
53. Hardath Maharaj, interview.
54. Doodnath Rampersad, interview.
55. Lutchmie Persad, interview.
56. Rambachan, interview.
57. Lutchmie Persad, interview.
58. Prakash Persad, interview.
59. Rambachan, interview.

Chapter 4

1. A more detailed analysis of the twentieth century economy of Trinidad and Tobago can be found in Brereton, *A History of Modern Trinidad*.
2. In his study of the village of 'Amity' in central Trinidad, Morton Klass revealed such an internal geographic structure wherein the different settlements within the village were occupied by persons of specific varnas/castes.
3. Dolly Rampersad, interview.

4. It can also be argued that since each copy was somewhat of a 'carbon copy' of the other, there was no sustained urge for interaction since nothing new could be added to the experience.
5. See Morton Klass, *East Indians in Trinidad: A Study in Cultural Persistence*; and Arthur Niehoff and Juanita Niehoff, *East Indians in the West Indies.*
6. Seepersad Cassie, interview by author, November 19, 2001.
7. Chanardai Mahase, interview by author, January 6, 2002.
8. Pundit Balram Persad, interview by author, July 7, 2003.
9. Joyce Ramdass, interview by author, July 7, 2002.
10. Hardath Maharaj, interview.
11. Hardath Maharaj, interview.
12. Ramsingh, interview.
13. *Sri Ramcharitmanas.* Des. 3 Verse 33.1.
14. Boodram, interview.
15. Ramsingh, interview.
16. *Sri Ramcharitmanas.* Des. 3 Verse 34.3.
17. Jaggernath Bissoon, interview by author, June 5, 2002.
18. Vyas, interview.
19. Hari Preetam, interview by author, November 22, 2000.
20. Sonia Ramsumair, interview by author, June 4, 2002.
21. Ramsumair, interview.
22. Chanardaye Ramlagan, interview by author, November 10, 2000.
23. Basdai Jagat, interview by author, November 16, 2001.
24. I.O.R. Public and Judicial Department Records *L/P&J/8/317: Indians in Trinidad 1931–1940*, 485.
25. Preetam, interview.
26. These lines belong to two very popular local compositions by Indo-Trinidadian singer Sundar Popo.
27. For a detailed examination of the problems of second language acquisition, see Robert Bley-Vroman's article 'What is the logical problem of foreign language learning,' *Linguistic Perspectives on Second Language Acquisition*, eds. Susan H. Gass and Jacquelyn Schachter (Cambridge: Cambridge University Press, 1989), 41–68.
28. *Administrative Report of the Director of Education for the Year 1931*,16.
29. *Administrative Report of the Director of Education for the Year 1932*, 19.
30. It should be noted that the use and teaching of Arabic and Urdu among Muslims were undergoing transformations parallel to those of Hindi and Bhojpuri among Hindus.
31. Chaitram Gunness, interview by author, June 6, 2002.
32. Ramsingh, interview.
33. Nankissoon Mahase, interview by author, January 6, 2002.
34. Shaheeda Hosein provides a detailed examination of the working experience of Indian women between 1870 and 1945.

35. Satnarayan Maharaj, interview.
36. The introduction of handshaking into the Hindu repertoire of greetings also served to relegate the more traditional greeting of '*Sita Ram*' to the religious domain.
37. Indrani Rampersad, interview by author, June 12, 2002.
38. Balram Persad, interview.
39. Sanoutie Ramroop, interview by author, December 14, 2001.
40. Basdeo Jagdeo, interview by author, October 22, 2002.
41. Ramgoolam, interview.
42. Kamla Tewarie, interview by author, December 7, 2001.
43. Chanardaye Mahase, interview.
44. Balram Persad, interview.
45. Khamiya Jagdeo, interview by author, January 5, 2002.
46. Tewarie, interview.
47. Mungal Patassar, interview by author, June 7, 2002.
48. Pundit Buddharat Yankatesu, interview by author, June 9, 2003.
49. Doodnath Rampersad, interview.
50. Chanardaye Mahase, interview.
51. Chanardaye Mahase, interview.
52. Ramsumair interview.
53. Singh, interview.
54. Jagat, interview.
55. Thakur Ramdial, interview by author, September 26, 2002.
56. Sirju, interview.
57. Sirju, interview.
58. Khamiya Jagdeo, interview.
59. A detailed account of these activities is provided in chapters three and five of Hosein's 'Rural Indian Women in Trinidad, 1870-1945.'
60. Ramsumair, interview.
61. I.O.R. Public and Judicial Department Records *L/P&J/8/320: Trinidad: Constitutional Reforms, 1948*.

Chapter 5

1. This revitalisation predates the contemporary notion of Hindutva (Hindu nationalism) in both Trinidad and India. Interestingly, V.S. Naipaul, in an interview *in The Observor* (London), sees Hindutva as 'a necessary corrective to history and will continue to remain so.'
2. A more detailed analysis of the impact of the Black Power Movement on East Indians can be found in Mahin Gosine, *East Indians and Black Power in the Caribbean: The Case of Trinidad* (New York: Africana Research Publications, 1986).

3. Balram Persad, interview.
4. Ravindranath Maharaj (Raviji), interview by author, October 8, 2001.
5. Lalchan Ramroop, interview by author, October 18, 2002.
6. Nankissoon Mahase, interview.
7. Pundit Balram Persad, interview.
8. Bissoon, interview.
9. *Sri Ramcharitmanas* Des. 1 Verse 27.2.
10. *Sri Ramcharitmanas* Des. 7 Verse 20.1.
11. Raviji, interview.
12. Prakash Persad, interview.
13. *Hansard,* January 25, 1952.
14. Gupta, interview.
15. Chaitram Gunness, interview.
16. *Trinidad And Tobago Annual Statistical Digest* 29 (1982): 15.
17. Raviji, interview.
18. *Hansard,* December 14, 1962.
19. *Hansard,* September 10, 1982.
20. Some noteworthy works on the topic include Sarah Morton, *John Morton of Trinidad*; Carl C. Campbell, *The Young Colonials. A Social History of Education in Trinidad and Tobago 1834–1939*; E.B. Rosabelle Seesaran, *From Caste to Class*; Richard Huntington Forbes, *Arya Samaj in Trinidad. A Historical Study of Hindu Organisational Process in Acculturative Conditions*; Marianne D. Ramesar, *Survivors of Another Crossing*; and several articles by Professor Brinsley Samaroo.
21. *Administration Report of the Director of Education for the Year 1948*, 23.
22. *Administration Report of the Director of Education for the Year 1948:* 3a.
23. *Administration Report of the Director of Education for the Year 1951: 39.*
24. *Hansard,* December 8, 1965.
25. *Baal Vikaas Festival Syllabus* (St Augustine: Sanatan Dharma Maha Sabha Incorporated, 2003), 1.
26. *Administration Report of the Director of Education for the Year 1948*, 23.
27. Thakur Ramdial, interview by author, September 26, 2001.
28. Yankatesu, interview.
29. *Hansard,* May 8, 1953.
30. *Hansard,* May 8, 1953.
31. *Hansard,* May 8, 1953.
32. *Hansard,* October 22, 1965.
33. *Hansard,* October 22, 1965.
34. Cremation Ordinance 1953, 136.
35. *Hansard,* May 23, 1969.
36. *Hansard,* March 20, 1970.
37. *Hansard,* October 16, 1970.
38. *Hansard,* April 30, 1976.
39. Preetam, interview.

40. Jairam, interview.
41. Prakash Persad, interview.
42. Raviji, interview.
43. Yankatesu, interview.
44. Prakash Persad, interview.
45. J. Merle Davis, *Trinidad Report* (Toronto. 1942), 37. Cited in Brinsley Samaroo, 'Missionary Methods and Local Responses: The Canadian Presbyterians and the East Indians in the Caribbean,' 30.
46. Seeloch, interview.
47. I.O.R. Official Series *V/27/820/10: Note on Emigration from India to Trinidad* by Surgeon Major W.D.Comins, 38.
48. Siewah 1994, 56. Capildeo also claimed that both opium and ganja were sold at his grandfather's shop. They were used by some of the visitors. This seems to echo the ethos of some pilgrimage sites in India where not just narcotics, but alcoholic drinks and dancing girls were an integral part of this phenomena. It also, however, can be interpreted as an extension of what often took place when men congregated on evenings for both religious and non-religious fraternising.
49. *Hansard*, February 5, 1965.
50. *Hansard*, February 5, 1965.

GLOSSARY

aarti	Waving a lit lamp or camphor circularly around the object of worship.
ahimsa	non-violence
apanjat	literally, of your own kind
avatar	incarnation; usually of the Divine/God
baithak	Literally, a sitting down; within the Indian diaspora it refers to a union involving a man and woman living together as man and wife without having undergone any kind of formal ritual. It also refers to a group session where persons 'sit' together for purposes of discussion or *satsang*.
baal vikaas (festival)	A festival/competition showcasing children's skills and knowledge in various aspects of Hindu culture.
bania	merchant caste
baraat	bridegroom's procession at a Hindu wedding
barahi	twelfth day birth ritual
batwaan	Night before the Hindu marriage ceremony when the cooking for the wedding day feast is done, and which usually entails a lot of entertainment and revelry.
bedi	Altar used at Hindu religious ceremonies constructed of either mud or leaves of the banana tree.
bhang	The intoxicating hemp either smoked or consumed as a drink.
Bhagavadpurana	Hindu religious text based on the life story of Lord Krishna.
bhaiyachaarya	A cooperative brotherhood for building homes, cultivating crops and providing other forms of socio-economic and emotional support.

bhajan	devotional song
Bhakti	Hindu religious orientation of loving devotion to God, from the term *bhakta*.
bhakta	a devotee
Bhojpuri	Dialect originally of Western Bihar and Eastern Uttar Pradesh spoken in Trinidad.
brahmin	priestly caste within the Hindu caste system
chalisa	A 40-verse song composition usually dedicated to specific deities.
chamar	Low caste of leather workers within the Hindu caste system.
chhatti	sixth day Hindu birth ritual
chela	disciple or follower
chhand	six-line lyrical verse usually found in Hindu religious texts
chowpai	four-line lyrical verse usually found in Hindu religious texts
chowtaal	A type of song sung during the *Holi/Phagwa* period in which each line is sung four times.
chulha	earthen fireplace constructed either on the floor or on an elevated platform
daheja	System whereby members of a village assist each other at weddings by contributing money, foodstuff and manual assistance.
dhantaal	Percussion instrument consisting of a thin, long, steel rod and a smaller bent piece of steel.
dharma	Sense of duty or right action, morality and virtue; the Hindu complex of religious and social obligation.
Dharmaacharya	A senior, distinguished, learned person; a spiritual guide, or founder or leader of a sect.
Dharma Shastra	holy writ; code of law
Dharti Mata	Hindu Goddess of the Earth
dholak	hand drum
Dee	local deity believed to be the protector of one's personal property

Divali Nagar	literally, a 'Divali village.' In Trinidad, however, it refers to an annual event observed just prior to the Festival of Lights, showcasing various aspects of Indian culture in Trinidad.
doha	a lyrical couplet
ganja	marijuana
garara	An Indian dress worn by women comprising a full length skirt, waist length (or shorter) fairly form fitting bodice and a two and a half yard length shawl.
guru	preceptor or teacher or spiritual guide
havan	Ceremonial fire into which oblations are poured during Hindu religious ceremonies.
imam	Muslim religious leader
jahaji bandal	Refers to the sparse belongings that some of the indentured immigrants carried with them onto the ships, which were usually wrapped in cloth.
jahaji bhai	Relationships established aboard the Indian immigrant ships and usually sustained during and after the indenture period.
jati	An occupational sub-group within the Hindu caste system.
jhal	small cymbals
jhandi	consecrated flag on a bamboo pole
jura-jama	A long, flowing, gown-like garment sometimes worn by Hindu bridegrooms.
jutha	Pollution of food or drink by the touch of a person's mouth or saliva.
kaajal	Lampblack applied to the eyes for medicinal or cosmetic purposes.
Kali	Hindu Goddess; the 'terrible' form of the female force or *Shakti* responsible for the destruction of evil.
kangan	Literally, a thick bracelet. In the Hindu wedding ceremony it refers to a ceremonial thread attached to certain charms tied around the wrist of the bride and the groom to ward off 'evil forces.'
Kartik Nahaan	Ritual bath during the month of *Kartik*, the eighth lunar month of the Hindu calendar.

katha	ceremonial recitation of a sacred text
kicharee	A dish of rice and peas; also a ritual in the Hindu wedding ceremony involving – and thus named – the consumption of this dish.
Krishna janamashthami	birthday of Lord Krishna
Krishnaleela	drama depicting the life story of Lord Krishna
kshatriya	warrior caste
kujat	The state of outcaste pronounced upon an individual by the village panchayat for the most serious offences. This barred the offender – and sometimes his entire family – from having any form of contact with fellow villagers for varying periods of time.
kurta	A loose, flowing tunic-like top usually with long sleeves and varying from thigh to mid-calf length.
kutiya	small, hut-like structure usually made of rudimentary material
lawa	Hindu pre-wedding fertility ritual performed exclusively by women, which often includes very sexually suggestive singing and dancing.
lota	brass pot
majeera	very small cymbals
mala	flower garland
mandir	Hindu temple
mantra	sacred Hindu verse
maticor	Hindu pre-wedding fertility ritual paying homage to the earth usually done near to a water source which also involves sexually suggestive singing and dancing.
murti	image or small statue of a deity
nau	A man who assists in the organization and performance of many of the Hindu rites and rituals, especially the life cycle rituals.
nauni	female equivalent of a *nau*; the wife of a *nau*.
Nau Ratam	Nine-day period dedicated to the worship of the female aspect of the Divine.
neemakharam	ungrateful to the (person whose) salt you have eaten.

neota	Traditional form of Hindu invitation to weddings, *yagnas* and pujas usually performed by the village *nau/nauni*. It consists of a verbal invitation accompanied by the ritual giving of rice to the invitees as a symbol of the invitation. The *nau/nauni*, in turn, is sometimes given a token sum of money, more in a ritual context than for any financial purposes.
pancham	fifth
panchayat	A group (usually five) of village elders which, based on a combination of intelligence and social, economic and religious status, is entrusted with the responsibility of resolving both family and communal disputes.
panchoutie yagna	communally sponsored and organized *yagna*
panth	religious sect or group
pathshala	Localized village school engaged in the teaching of Hindi and aspects of Hindu religion and culture.
Phagwa	Hindu festival commemorating the beginning of the spring season and good over evil, celebrated with much revelry and the dousing of persons with coloured water.
pradakshina	ritual circumambulation
praja	traditional Indian patron-client relationship
puja	Hindu prayer ritual, usually conducted by a pundit.
pundit	In Trinidad usage, a Hindu priest
punditai	the practice of Hindu priesthood
Purana	Sacred writings in Sanskrit on Hindu mythology and folklore.
raga	Indian musical mode or sequence
rakshas	demon
Ramayana	the story of Lord Rama
Ramleela	A drama depicting the life story of Lord Rama.
Ramnaumi	birthday of Lord Rama
Ramrajya	utopian rule of King Rama depicted in the *Ramayana*
rehal	Wooden book stand used to keep the Hindu religious texts open during recitation.
sadhana	worship

sadhu	Male religious mendicant. In Trinidad, the term refers to a man who is particularly devout and knowledgeable on certain Hindu matters.
sadhuain	The female equivalent or the wife of a sadhu.
Sanatan Dharma	The generalized, orthodox form of Hinduism which evolved in both India and Trinidad; literally translated as 'eternal religion.'
sandhya	twilight; the evening prayer
sati	A widow who has immolated herself on her husband's funeral pyre.
satsang	Domestic religious occasion involving recitation from the holy texts and the chanting of devotional songs, not necessarily conducted by a pundit.
sharam	shame or disgrace
Shiva lingam	symbolic stone representation of Lord Shiva
Shiva Raatri	night dedicated to the worship of Lord Shiva
shloka	two- or four-line lyrical verse
shrota	literally, an audience; but popularly perceived to be the person taking an active part in the performance of sacred rituals.
sherwani	Indian suit for men comprising pyjama style trousers worn tight from the knee down, a knee length (or longer) flowing kurta, a sleeveless long (as the kurta) coat worn over the kurta, and sometimes accompanied by a narrow long scarf.
singhasan	literally, throne; but in the *yagna* setting it refers to the consecrated, elevated area upon which the pundit conducts the readings.
sindoor	Vermillion applied in the parting of a woman's hair as a symbol of a married woman.
smriti	Developed, expounded by men, and preserved and transmitted through memory.
sortha	type of lyrical couplet
stuti	two- or four-line prayer
sudra	lowest of the four Hindu castes
taal	rhythm

ulaaraa	A type of vigorous folk song sung during the *Phagwa* season.
vaishya	Merchant or farmer caste; third in the orthodox Hindu caste system.
vanvaas	exile
varna	each of the four major Hindu castes
Vedas	Hindu sacred scriptures comprising four volumes considered to have been divinely revealed.
Vyas	Title given to the pundit presiding at a *yagna* – after Vyasadeva, the legendary compiler of the Vedas.
yagna	A series of religious rites and ceremonial readings spanning five to 14 days.

BIBLIOGRAPHY

ARCHIVAL SOURCES

A. India Office Records (IOR), The British Library, London

Economic Department Records

Indians in Trinidad: Immigration Reports, 1922. L/E/7/1283.
Kunwar Maharaj Singh's Report on Indian Community in Trinidad, 1925. L/E/7/1425.
League of Nations, 1926. L/E/7/1455.
Marriage and Divorce Act, 1925. L/E/7/1385.
Rules of Emigration Act, 1922. L/E/7/1354.
Status of Aliens Act, 1927. L/E/7/1518.
Trinidad Visit of the British Guiana's Deputation from India, 1922 L/E/7/1248.

Public and Judicial Department Records

Colonial Development and Welfare Act, 1940. L/P&J/8/340.
Direct Correspondence between India and British Colonies on the Appointment of Agents, 1935–1945. L/P&J/8/179.
Indians in Trinidad, 1931–1940. L/P&J/8/317.
Indians in Trinidad: Immigration (Restriction) Ordinance, 1936, and Memorandum of Evidence for Royal Commission to the West Indies (New Delhi, 1939) *Tyson's Report.* L/P&J/8/318.
Problems of Indians in Trinidad, 1941–1946. L/P&J/8/319.
Report on the Condition of Indians in Jamaica, British Guiana and Trinidad; Labour Conditions in the West Indies (1938–1943). L/P&J/8/338.
Royal Commission on the West Indies, 1940–1948. L/P&J/8/339.
Royal Commission on the West Indies; Deputation of J.D. Tyson to the West Indies; Tyson's Trinidad: Constitutional Reforms, 1948. L/P&J/8/320.

Official Series c.1760–1950

Events Affecting Indians in the Empire. V/24/1190.
Note on Emigration from India to Trinidad by Surgeon Major W.D. Comins (Calcutta: Bengal Secretariat Press, 1893). V/27/820/10.

B. Colonial Office Records (CO), Public Record Office, London

SERIES 295: Original Official Correspondence between the Colonies and England

Annual General Report, 1926. CO/295/562/14.
Activities of Krishna Deonarine. CO/295/563/1.
Annual General Report, 1928. CO/295/565/13.
Colour Bar at State Functions. CO/295/600/2.
Condition of Indian Population. CO/295/594/1.
Despatches, 1845–1846. CO/295/146–150.
Despatches, 1850. CO/295/170–171.
Despatches, 1921–1926. CO/295/534–558.
Development Plans, 1949. CO/295/642/5.
Dietary and Constitutional Conditions of East Indian Labourers. CO/295/590/13.
Disturbances on Sugar Estates. CO/295/581/11.
Education Ordinance (No. 27 of 1951). CO/295/650/7.
Education Report, 1930 (for 1929). CO/295/569/7.
Immigration Restriction. CO/295/618/4.
Indians in Trinidad (1928). CO/295/545/5.
Indian National Party. CO/295/565/10.
Muslim Marriages and Divorce Regulation Ordinance. CO/295/583/14.
Ordinance no. 15 of 1932 – Incorporation of the Hindu Sanatan Dharam Association of Trinidad. CO/295/575/9.
Ordinance no. 36 of 1932 – Incorporation of the Kabir Association of Trinidad. CO/295/575/17.
Petition by E. Jawahir, 1940. CO/295/617/3.
Petition of Sankar – Gratuity for Injuries. CO/295/596/7.
Trinidad Riots. CO/295/599/14.
Trinidad Riots Commission of Enquiry Report. CO/295/600/6–7.

SERIES 298

Annual Reports, 1920.	CO/298/117.
Annual Reports, 1925.	CO/298/133.
Annual Reports, 1930.	CO/298/150.

Annual Reports, 1935. CO/298/168.
Trinidad Administration Reports, 1939–1945. CO/298/183.
Trinidad and Tobago Administration Reports, 1950. CO/298/193.
Trinidad and Tobago Administration Reports, 1952. CO/298/205.
Trinidad and Tobago Administration Reports, 1955. CO/298/208.
Trinidad and Tobago Administration Reports, 1961–63. CO/298/216.
Trinidad and Tobago Administration Reports, 1964–65. CO/298/217.

SERIES 318

Coolie Immigration. CO/318/165 (1845).
Coolie Immigration. CO/318/167 (1846).
Coolie Immigration. CO/318/171 (1847).
Coolie Immigration. CO/318/176 (1847).
Coolie Immigration. CO/318/185 (1850).

C. National Archives of Trinidad and Tobago

Colonial Emigration Passes

Years 1866, 1872, 1882, 1892, 1902, 1912, 1917.

Newspapers

Caroni News, Trinidad, 1966.
The East Indian Weekly, Trinidad, 1928–32.
Express, Trinidad, 1967–2003.
Port-of-Spain Gazette, Trinidad, 1915–55.
Sandesh, Trinidad, 1985–87.
Trinidad Guardian, Trinidad, 1919–2003.

Journals and Magazines

The *Hindu Times,* Trinidad, 1966.
India News, Trinidad, 1955.
The *Indian,* Trinidad, 1940–55.
The *Observer,* Trinidad, 1949–67.

D. The Library, University of the West Indies, St Augustine Campus, West Indiana Division

Official Records and Reports

Administration Report of the Director of Education for the years 1927, 1930, 1931, 1932, 1937, 1945, 1946, 1947, 1948, 1950, 1951, 1952, 1953, 1954, 1955, 1956, 1957.

Colony of Trinidad and Tobago Census Album 1948.

A Digest of Statistics on Education for the years 1959, 1964–1966, 1971–72, 1983–90. Central Statistical Office, Government of Trinidad and Tobago.

Education Report of 1959 of Committee on General Education.

Report on Education Statistics (1983–1984). Republic of Trinidad and Tobago Statistical Office.

Trinidad and Tobago Annual Statistical Digest for the years 1935-1990: Nos. 11, 21, 23, 29, 33, 38, 39, 41, 44. Central Statistical Office, Government of Trinidad and Tobago.

Trinidad and Tobago Debates of the House of Representatives Official Report (Hansard) 1917–50.

Trinidad and Tobago Debates of the Legislative Council (Hansard) 1950–90.

Contemporary Published Works

Collens, J.H. *A Guide to Trinidad: A Handbook for the Use of Tourists and Visitors.* 2nd edn. London: Elliot Stock, 1888.

Grant, Kenneth James. *My Missionary Memories.* Halifax: The Imperial Publishing Company, 1923.

Kirpalani, M.J., et al. *Indian Centenary Review. 100 Years of Progress 1845–1945.* Port-of-Spain: Indian Centenary Review Committee, 1945.

Morton, Sarah, ed. *John Morton of Trinidad.* Toronto: Westminster Company, 1916.

ORAL SOURCES: PERSONAL INTERVIEWS

Adhar, Basdeo (male, 58 years, petrol pump attendant). Interview by author. January 6, 2002, Sangre Chiquito.

Ali, Ameena (female, 76 years, retired agricultural labourer). Interview by author. September 26, 2001, Felicity.

Bal, Rampartap (male, 68 years, Ramleela actor/gardener). Interview by author. October 3, 2001, Felicity.

Bal, Soognia (female, 64 years, housewife/gardener). Interview by author. October 15, 2001, Felicity.

Baldeo, Jintie (female, 70 years, retired gardener). Interview by author. December 3, 2001, Bejucal.

Balgobin, Durjan (male, 40 years, President of Felicity Ramleela Committee/ electrician). Interview by author. October 8, 2001, Felicity.

Beepath, Nehru (male, 44 years, former President of the Kabir Panth Association). Interview by author. July 8, 2003, Freeport.

Bissoon, Jaggernath (male, 78 years, retired school principal). Interview by author. June 5, 2002, Chaguanas.

Boodram, Ramdial (male, 72 years, *Ramayana* reader/gardener). Interview by author. January 11, 2003, Bejucal.

Cassie, Seepersad (male, 57 years, retired prisons officer). Interview by author. November 19, 2001, Tunapuna.

Chaitanya, Prem (male, 37 years, Spiritual Head of the local branch of the Chinmaya Mission, an international Hindu religious order). Interview by author. November 23, 2001, Couva.

Gajai, Parag (male, 75 years, retired taxi-driver). Interview by author. November 21, 2000, Bejucal.

G., Mr S. (male, 61 years, retailer of clothing and household goods). Interview by author. January 20, 2003, Chaguanas.

G., Mrs V. (female, 50 years, retailer of clothing and household goods). Interview by author. October 30, 2002, Chaguanas.

G., Mrs K. (female, 36 years, primary school teacher). Interview by author. September 15, 2001, Chaguanas.

Gunness, Chaitram (male, 54 years, retired postman). Interview by author. June 6, 2002, Barrackpore.

Gunness, Pauline (female, housewife). Interview by author. June 6, 2002, Barrackpore.

Gupta, Sister Krishna (female, Spiritual Elder of the local branch of the Brahma Kumari Yoga Center, an international Hindu religious order). Interview by author. November 2, 2001, Tunapuna.

H., Mrs R. (female, 38 years, secretary). Interview by author. June 18, 2002, El Dorado.

Jagat, Basdai (female, 68 years, midwife/masseuse/*nauni*, retired gardener). Interview by author. November 16, 2001, Tunapuna.

Jagdeo, Basdeo (male, 57 years, office clerk). Interview by author. October 22, 2002, Bejucal.

Jagdeo, Jasodra (female, 78 years, retired cane farmer). Interview by author. November 18, 2000, Bejucal.

Jagmohan, Dolly (female, 53 years, housewife/gardener). Interview by author. June 6, 2002, Barrackpore.

J., Mrs D. (female, 37 years, housewife). Interview by author. July 1, 2002, Tunapuna.

Jairam, Balkaran (male, 70 years, farmer). Interview by author. September 26, 2001, Felicity.

Lachman, Motilal (male, 70 years, retired engineer). Interview by author. September 24, 2001, Chaguanas.

L., Mr D. (male, 45 years, *Ramayana* reader/office clerk). Interview by author. July 3, 2003, Bejucal.

Maharaj, Hardath (male, 73 years, pundit). Interview by author. November 24, 2002, Cumuto.

Maharaj, Rabindranath (male, religious and cultural activist). Interview by author. October 8, 2001, Chaguanas.

Maharaj, Satnarayan (male, Secretary General of the Sanatan Dharma Maha Sabha). Interview by author. December 6, 2001, Tunapuna.

Mahase, Chanardai (male, 52 years, housewife). Interview by author. January 6, 2002, Sangre Chiquito.

Mahase, Nankissoon (male, 57 years, bus driver). Interview by author. January 6, 2002, Sangre Chiquito.

Moosammy (male, 80 years, retired estate cart driver). Interview by author. November 7, 2001, Tunapuna.

M., Mrs R. (female, 50 years, typist). Interview by author. November 18, 2000, Sangre Grande.

Nazim, Sultan (male, 92 years, retired agricultural labourer). Interview by author. November 7, 2001, Tunapuna.

Paladee, Lall (male, 66 years, businessman, executive member of the Shri Sathya Sai Organization, Trinidad and Tobago). Interview by author. November 22, 2001, Tunapuna.

Patassar, Mungal (male, 56 years, Cultural Officer, sitar player, composer, music teacher). Interview by author. June 7, 2002, Chaguanas.

Persad, Balram (male, 51 years, pundit/secondary school teacher). Interview by author. July 7, 2003, Aranjuez.

Persad-Bissessar, Kamla (female, 50 years, politician/lawyer). Interview by author. July 12, 2002, Mayaro.

Persad, Lutchmie (male, 74 years, pundit). Interview by author. February 9, 2002, Tunapuna.

Persad, Dr Prakash (male, university (senior) lecturer, engineer, pundit). Interview by author. October 5, 2001, St Augustine.

Persad, Rajie (female, 72 years, housewife). Interview by author. November 21, 2001, Tunapuna.

P., Mr R. (male, 40 years, police officer). Interview by author. September 10, 2001, Sangre Grande.

Preetam, Hari (male, 50 years, supervisor). Interview by author. November 4, 2000, Bejucal.

R., Mr T. (male, 33 years, technician). Interview by author. February 16, 2002, Barrackpore.

Ramaya, Nasaloo (male, 82 years, violinist, pioneer of Indian music in Trinidad). Interview by author. December 12, 2001, San Juan.
Rambachan, Brahmanand (male, 44 years, pundit). Interview by author. November 22, 2002, San Juan.
Ramdass, Joyce (female, 49 years, housewife). Interview by author. June 7, 2002, Barrackpore.
Ramdass, Kalawatee (female, 55 years, school principal). Interview by author. October 5, 2001, Felicity.
Ramdial, Thakoor (male, 52 years, primary school teacher). Interview by author. September 26, 2002, Bejucal.
Ramgoolam, Boodram (male, 61 years, *Ramayana* reader/ watchman). Interview by author. December 16, 2002, Diamond.
Ramlagan, Chanardaye (female, 70 years, retired gardener/ housewife). Interview by author. November 10, 2000, Bejucal.
Ramnarine, Sankar (male, 63 years, importer and retailer of Indian goods and Hindu religious texts). Interview by author. February 21, 2002, Caroni.
Rampersad, Dolly (female, 67 years, retired labourer). Interview by author. January 5, 2002, Sangre Chiquito.
Rampersad, Doodnath (male, 42 years, pundit). Interview by author. January 5, 2002, Sangre Chiquito.
Rampersad, Indrani (female, pundit). Interview by author. June 12, 2002, Chase Village.
Ramroop, Lalchan (male, 51 years, agricultural labourer). Interview by author. October 18, 2002, Bejucal.
Ramroop, Sanoutie (female 68 years, retired agricultural labourer). Interview by author. December 14, 2001, Bejucal.
Ramroop, Savitri (female, 49 years, housewife). Interview by author. December 14, 2001, Bejucal.
Ramsingh, Hardeo (male, 72 years, retired school principal). Interview by author. October 7, 2001, Felicity.
Ramsumair, Sonia (female, 75 years, housewife). Interview by author. June 4, 2002, Barrackpore.
R., Mrs P. (female, 49 years, Indian folk song singer). Interview by author. December 15, 2001, Cunupia.
Santokee, Omapatee (female, 70 years, retired gardener). Interview by author. January 5, 2002, Sangre Grande.
Seeloch, Rampersad (male, 90 years, retired agricultural labourer). Interview by author. June 6, 2002, Barrackpore.
Sieukumar, Anil (male, 30 years, President of Warren Road Shiva Mandir). Interview by author. December 12, 2001, Bejucal.
Sinanan, Bhagwandai (female, 77 years, Indian folk song singer). Interview by author. December 17, 2002, El Dorado.

Sinanan, Churaman (male, 49 years, labourer). Interview by author. October 8, 2001, Bejucal.
Singh, Gaitree (female, 62 years, retired labourer/*nauni*). Interview by author. January 6, 2002, Sangre Grande.
Sirju, Sahadeo (male, 44 years, policeman/*Ramayana* reader). Interview by author. October 5, 2002, Bejucal.
Soogrim, Dookhani (female, 70 years, retired agricultural labourer). Interview by author. June 7, 2002, Barrackpore.
Sookdeo, Sandra (female, Indian dance instructor). Interview by author. March 14, 2002, Cunupia.
Sukrit, Ramlakhan (male, 89 years, importer and retailer of Hindu religious texts and Indian goods). Interview by author. February 20, 2002, Claxton Bay.
Tewarie, Kamla (female, 52 years Administrative Assistant). Interview by author. December 7, 2001, Tunapuna.
Vyas, Khemraj (male, 52 years, pundit). Interview by author. November 27, 2002, St Augustine.
Yankatesu, Buddharat (male, 36 years, pundit). Interview by author. July 9, 2003, Valsayn.

SECONDARY SOURCES

A. Books

Agarwal, Satya P. *The Social Role of the Gita. How and Why.* Delhi: Urmila Agarwal, 1993.
Aggarwal, Devi Dayal. *Protocol in Sri Ramcharitmanas.* New Delhi: Kaveri Books, 1998.
Allchin, F.R. *The Petition to Ram: Hindi Devotional Hymns of the Seventeenth Century.* London: George Allen & Unwin Ltd, 1966.
Altekar, A.S. *The Position of Women in Hindu Civilisation.* Delhi: Motilal Banarsidass Publishers Private Limited, 1962.
Babb, Lawrence A., and Susan S. Wadley, eds. *Media and the Transformation of Religions in South Asia.* Philadelphia: University of Pennsylvania Press, 1995.
Babineau, Edmour J. *Love of God and Social Duty in the Ramcharitmanas.* Delhi: Motilal Banarsidass, 1979.
Bahadur, K.P. *Ramcharitmanas: A Study in Perspective.* Delhi: Ess Ess Publications, 1976.
Barthes, Roland. *Mythologies.* London: Vintage, 1993.
Beals, Alan R., and George and Louise Spindler. *Culture in Process.* New York: Holt, Rinehart and Winston Inc., 1967.
Benedict, Burton. *Indians in a Plural Society: A Report on Mauritius.* London: Her Majesty's Stationery Office, 1961.

Bhandarkar, D.R. *Some Aspects of Ancient Hindu Polity*. Benares: Benares Hindu University, 1929.
Bharadwaj, Ramdat. *The Philosophy of Tulsidas*. New Delhi: Munshiram Manoharlal Publishers Pvt. Ltd., 1979.
Birbalsingh, Frank, ed. *Indenture and Exile: The Indo-Caribbean Experience*. Toronto: TSAR in association with the Ontario Association for Studies in Indo-Caribbean Culture, 1989.
Bisnauth, Dale. *The Settlement of Indians in Guyana 1890–1930*. England: Peepal Tree Press, 2000.
Boodhoo, Sarita. *Bhojpuri Traditions in Mauritius*. Mauritius: Mauritius Bhojpuri Institute, 1999.
Brassington, F.E. *The Politics of Opposition*. Trinidad: West Indian Publishing Co., n.d.
Brathwaite, Edward. *Contradictory Omens: Cultural Diversity and Integration in the Caribbean*. Mona, Jamaica: Savacou Publications, 1974.
Brereton, Bridget. *A History of Modern Trinidad 1783–1962*. USA: Heinemann International, 1981.
———. *Race Relations in Colonial Trinidad 1870–1900*. Cambridge: Cambridge University Press, 1979.
Brockington, J.L. *Righteous Rama: The Evolution of an Epic*. Delhi: Oxford University Press, 1985.
———. *The Sacred Thread: A Short History of Hinduism*. New Delhi: Oxford University Press, 1981.
Campbell, Carl C. *Colony and Nation: A Short History of Education in Trinidad and Tobago*. Kingston: Ian Randle Publishers, 1992.
———. *The Young Colonials: A Social History of Education in Trinidad and Tobago 1834–1939*. Barbados, Jamaica, Trinidad and Tobago: The Press University of the West Indies, 1996.
Campbell, Joseph. *The Power of Myth*. New York: Anchor Books Doubleday, 1988.
Carter, Marina. *Lakshmi's Legacy*. Mauritius: Editions de L'Ocean India, 1994.
———. *Servants, Sirdars and Settlers: Indians in Mauritius*. Delhi: Oxford University Press, 1995.
———. *Voices From Indenture: Experiences of Indian Migrants in the British Empire*. London: Leicester University Press, 1996.
Chackalackal, Saju. *Ramayana and the Indian Ideal*. Bangalore, India: Dharmaram Publications, 1992.
Chandra, Rajesh. *Maro. Rural Indians of Fiji*. n.p.: South Pacific Social Sciences Association, 1980.
Chaudhuri, Nirad. *Hinduism. A Religion to Live By*. London: Oxford University Press, 1979.
Chauduri, Pushpendu. *History Revealed by the Ramayana Astronomy*. Calcutta: Firma KLM Private Limited, 1998.

Chennakesan, Sarasvati. *A Critical Study of Hinduism*. New Delhi: Munshiram Manoharlal Publishers Pvt. Ltd., 1998.
Dabydeen, David, and Brinsley Samaroo, eds. *India in the Caribbean*. London: Hansib Publishing Ltd, 1987.
Dalmia, Vasudha, et al. *Charisma and Canon: Essays on the Religious History of the Indian Subcontinent*. New Delhi: Oxford University Press, 2001.
Dalmia, Vasudha, and H. von Stietencron, eds. *Representing Hinduism: The Construction of Religious Traditions and National Identity*. New Delhi: Sage Publications, 1995.
Dasgupta, Subhayu. *Hindu Ethos and the Challenge of Change*. India: Arnold Heinemann Publishers, 1977.
Dawson, John. *A Classical Dictionary of Hindu Mythology*. London: Routledge and Kegan Paul Ltd., 1972.
Day, Martin S. *The Many Meanings of Myth*. New York: University Press of America Inc., 1984.
Deen, Shamshu. *Solving East Indian Roots in Trinidad*. Freeport, Trinidad: n.p., 1994.
De Verteuil, Anthony. *Eight East Indian Immigrants*. Port-of-Spain: Paria Publishing Co. Ltd, 1989.
Dharma, P.C. *The Ramayana Polity*. Bombay: Bharatiya Vidya Bhavan, 1989.
Dimock, Edward C. Jr. *The Literatures of India: An Introduction*. Chicago: The University of Chicago Press, 1974.
Doniger O'Flaherty, Wendy. *Hindu Myths*. London: Penguin Books, 1975.
———. *Other Peoples' Myths*. New York: Macmillan Publishing Company, 1988.
Doty, William G. *Mythography: The Study of Myths and Rituals*. Alabama: The University of Alabama Press, 1986.
Dundes, Alan, ed. *Sacred Narrative: Readings in the Theory of Myth*. Berkeley: University of California Press, 1984.
Eliade, Mircea. *Myth & Reality*. New York: Harper & Row Publishers, 1975.
Etzioni, Amitai, and Eva Etzioni. *Social Change: Sources, Patterns and Consequences*. New York: Basic Books Inc., 1964.
Farquhar, J.N. *The Crown of Hinduism*. New Delhi: Munshiram Manoharlal Oriental Publishers & Booksellers, 1971.
Gillion, K.L. *The Fiji Indians: Challenge to European Dominance 1920–1946*. Canberra: Australian National University Press, 1977.
Goldman, Robert P. *The Ramayana of Valmiki Vol. I – Balakanda*. New Jersey: Princeton University Press, 1984.
Gosine, Mahin. *East Indians and Black Power in the Caribbean: The Case of Trinidad*. New York: Africana Research Publications, 1986.
———. *The Legacy of Indian Indenture: 150 Years of East Indians in Trinidad*. New York: Windsor Press, 1995.
Gould, Harold A. *The Hindu Caste System. Vol. 2: Caste Adaptation in Modernizing Indian Society*. Delhi: Chanakya Publications, 1988.
———. *The Hindu Caste System. Vol. 3: Politics and Caste*. Delhi: Chanakya Publications, 1990.

Gowen, Herbert H. *A History of Indian Literature: From Vedic Times to the Present Day.* Delhi: Seema Publishers, 1975.

Gray, Louis Herbert. *The Mythology of All Races: Vol. VI Indian/Iranian.* New York: Cooper Squares Publishers Inc., 1964.

Gupta, R.C. *Hindu Society and Influence of the Great Epics.* Delhi: B.R. Publishing Corporation, 1991.

Guruge, Ananda. *The Society of the Ramayana.* New Delhi: Abhinav Publications, 1991.

Hackin, J. et al. *Asiatic Mythology.* London: George G. Harrap & Co. Ltd., 1932.

Hamilton, Malcolm B. *The Sociology of Religion. Theoretical and Comparative Perspectives.* London: Routledge, 1995.

Hastings, James. *Encyclopedia of Religion and Ethics Vol. 10.* England: Morrison & Gibb Limited, 1952.

Hazareesingh, K. *History of Indians in Mauritius.* London: Macmillan Education Limited, 1977.

Henige, David. *Oral Historiography.* London: Longman Group Limited, 1982.

Hobsbawm, Eric, and Terence Ranger. *The Invention of Tradition.* New York: Cambridge University Press, 1983.

Holm, Jean, and John Bowker, eds. *Myth and Meaning.* London: Pinter Publishers, 1994.

Iyengar, K.R. Srinivasa, ed. *Asian Variations in Ramayana.* New Delhi: Sahitya Akademi, 1983.

———. *Sitayana.* Madras: Samata Books, 1987.

———. *The Epic Beautiful: An English Verse Rendering of the Sundar Kanda.* New Delhi: Sahitya Akademy, 1983.

Iyer, Paramsiva. *Ramayana and Lanka.* Bangalore: Bangalore Press, 1940.

Jain, Ravindra K. *Indian Communities Abroad: Themes and Literature.* New Delhi: Manohar Publishers and Distributors, 1993.

Jatava. D.R. *Indian Society: Culture and Ideologies.* Jaipur, India: Surabhi Publications, 1998.

Jayaram, Raja. *Caste and Class: Dynamics of Inequality in Indian Society.* Delhi: Hindustan Publishing Corporation, 1981.

Kanuga, G.B. *Immortal Love of Rama.* New Delhi: Lancer Publishers, 1993.

Kapadia, K.M. *Marriage and Family in India.* Bombay: Oxford University Press, 1955.

Kapur, Anuradha. *Actors, Pilgrims, Kings and Gods: The Ramlila at Ramnagar.* Calcutta: Seagulls Books, 1990.

Karve, Irawati. *Hindu Society: An Interpretation.* Poona: Deccan College, 1961.

———. *Kinship Organisation in India.* Poona: Deccan College Post-Graduate and Research Institute, 1953.

Khan, Benjamin. *The Concept of Dharma in Valmiki Ramayana.* Delhi: Munshi Ram Manoharlal Oriental Booksellers and Publishers, 1965.

Klass, Morton. *East Indians in Trinidad: A Study of Cultural Persistence.* Illinois: Waveland Press Inc., 1961.

———. *Singing with Sai Baba: The Politics of Revitalisation in Trinidad.* San Francisco: West View Press, 1991.

Kosambi, D.D. *Myth and Reality.* Bombay: Popular Prakashan Pvt. Ltd., 1983.

Krishna, Daya. *The Problematic and Conceptual Structure of Classical Indian Thought about Man, Society and Polity.* Delhi: Oxford University Press, 1996.

Kulkarni, V.M. *The Story of Rama in Jain Literature.* Ahmedabad, India: Saraswati Pustak Bhandar, 1990.

La Guerre, John, ed. *Calcutta to Caroni: The East Indians of Trinidad.* St Augustine: Extra Mural Studies Unit, University of the West Indies, 1985.

Lal, Brij V. *Girmitiyas. The Origin of the Fiji Indians.* Canberra: The Journal of Pacific History, 1983.

———. *Politics in Fiji.* Sydney: Allen & Unwin Australia Pty Ltd., 1986.

Lannoy, Richard. *The Speaking Tree.* Bombay: Oxford University Press, 1971.

Lauer, Robert H. *Perspectives on Social Change.* Boston: Allyn and Bacon, Inc., 1977.

Laurence, K.O. *A Question of Labour: Indentured Immigration into Trinidad and British Guiana 1875-1917.* Kingston: Ian Randle Publishers, 1994.

Leslie, Julia. *Roles and Rituals for Hindu Women.* Delhi: Motilal Banarsidass Publishers Pvt. Ltd., 1992.

Levi-Strauss, Claude. *Myth and Meaning.* London: Routledge Classics, 1978.

Lutgendorf, Philip. *The Life of a Text.* Berkeley, California: University of California Press, 1991.

Macdonell, Arthur A. *A History of Sanskrit Literature.* New York: Haskell House Publishers Ltd., 1968.

Maharaj, Ashram B. *The Pundits in Trinidad: A Study of a Hindu Institution.* Trinidad: Indian Review Press, 1991.

Maharaj, Devant, et al. *Bhadase Sagan Maraj: Hostile and Recalcitrant.* Trinidad: Sanatan Dharma Maha Sabha, 2001.

Malik, Yogendra K. *East Indians in Trinidad: A Study in Minority Politics.* London: Oxford University Press, 1971.

Mandelbaum, David G. *Society in India: Volume One. Continuity and Change.* Los Angeles: University of California Press, 1972.

Manikar, T.G. *The Vasistha Ramayana: A Study.* New Delhi: Oriental Booksellers & Publishers, 1977.

Mansingh, Laxmi, and Ajay Mansingh. *Home Away From Home: 150 Years of Indian Presence in Jamaica 1845–1995.* Kingston: Ian Randle Publishers, 1999.

Marwick, Arthur. *The Nature of History.* London: Macmillan Press Ltd., 1989.

Matilal, Bimal Krishna. *Moral Dilemmas in the Mahabharata.* Delhi: Indian Institute of Advanced Study in association with Motilal Banarsidass, 1989.

McGuire, Meredith B. *Religion: The Social Context.* Belmont, California: Wadsworth Publishing Company, 1997.

Mishra, Dhira. *Political Role of Women in the Ramcharitmanas*. Delhi: Neha Prakashan, 1986.
Misra, L.K. *The Dynamics of the Ramayana: A Mid-Twentieth Century Version*. Bhagalpur: L.K. Misra, 1966.
Mishra, Vijay, ed. *Rama's Banishment: A Centenary Tribute to the Fiji Indians 1879–1979*. London: Heinemann Educational Books, 1979.
Mohammed, Patricia. *Gender Negotiations among Indians in Trinidad, 1917–1947*. New York: Palgrave, 2002.
Mohammed, Shamoon. *Mastana Bahar and Indian Culture in Trinidad and Tobago*. Trinidad and Tobago: Mastana Bahar Thesis Publication Committee, 1982.
Moore, Dennison. *Origins and Development of Racial Ideology in Trinidad: The Black View of the East Indian*. Trinidad and Tobago: Chakra Publishing House, 1995.
Moore, Wilbert E, and Robert M. Cook. *Readings on Social Change*. New Jersey: Prentice-Hall Inc., 1967.
Morgan, Kenneth W., ed. *The Religion of the Hindus Interpreted by Hindus*. New York: The Ronald Press Company, 1953.
Mukherjee, Prabhati. *Hindu Women: Normative Models*. New Delhi: Orient Longman Limited, 1978.
Munasinghe, Viranjini. *Callaloo or Tossed Salad: East Indians and the Cultural Politics of Identity in Trinidad*. Ithaca: Cornell University Press, 2001.
Muslim-Christian Research Group. *The Challenge of the Scriptures: The Bible and the Quran*. New York: Oasis Books, 1989.
Naipaul, Seepersad. *Adventures of Gurudeva and Other Stories*. London: Andre Deutsch Limited, 1976.
Naipaul, V.S. *A House for Mr Biswas*. London: Penguin Books, 1969.
———. *The Mystic Masseur*. London: Penguin Books, 1964.
———. *Reading and Writing: A Personal Account*. New York: New York Review Books, 2000.
Narula, Joginder. *Hanuman: God and Epic Hero*. New Delhi: Manohar Publications, 1991.
Navlekar, N.R. *A New Approach to Ramayan*. Jabalpur, India: N.R. Navlekar, 1957.
Niehoff, Arthur and Juanita. *East Indians in the West Indies*. Wisconsin: Milwaukee Public Museum Board of Trustees, 1960.
Parker, Andrew et al., eds. *Nationalisms and Sexualities*. New York: Routledge, 1992.
Pearsall, Judy. *The Concise Oxford Dictionary*. New York: Oxford University Press, 1999.
Persaud, Lakshmi. *Butterfly in the Wind*. Leeds: Peepal Tree Press, 1990.
Prasad, R.C. *The Ramayana of Tulsidasa*. Delhi: Motilal Banarsidass, 1978.
Premdas Ralph R., ed. *Identity, Ethnicity and Culture in the Caribbean*. St Augustine: The University of the West Indies School of Continuing Studies, 1999.
———. *The Enigma of Ethnicity: An Analysis of Race in the Caribbean and the World*. St Augustine: University of the West Indies, School of Continuing Studies, 1993.

Radhakrishnan, S. *The Hindu View of Life*. London: Unwin Papers, 1960.
Raghavan, V., ed. *The Ramayan Tradition in Asia*. New Delhi: Sahitya Akademi, 1980.
Raglan, Lord. *The Hero: A Study in Tradition, Myth and Drama*. New York: Vintage Books Inc., 1956.
Ramakrishna Mission Institute of Culture. *The Cultural Heritage of India. Volume II: Itihas, Puranas, Dharma and Other Sastras*. Calcutta: Sri Gouranga Press Private Ltd., 1962.
Rambachan, Anantanand. *Rama Darshan: The Valmiki-Rama Dialogue*. Minnesota: Vijnana Publications, 1995.
Ramesar, Marianne D. Soares. *Survivors of Another Crossing: A History of East Indians in Trinidad, 1880–1946*. St Augustine: University of the West Indies, School of Continuing Studies, 1994.
Richman, Paula. *Many Ramayanas: The Diversity of a Narrative Tradition in South Asia*. Berkeley: University of California Press, 1991.
———. *Questioning Ramayanas: A South Asian Tradition*. Berkeley: University of California Press, 2001.
Ross, Aileen D. *The Hindu Family in its Urban Setting*. Canada: University of Toronto Press, 1961.
Ryan, Selwyn. *Pathways to Power: Indians and the Politics of National Unity in Trinidad and Tobago*. St Augustine: Institute of Social and Economic Research, University of the West Indies, 1996.
———. ed. *The Independence Experience 1962–1987*. St Augustine: Institute of Social and Economic Research, University of the West Indies, 1988.
Sanatan Dharma Maha Sabha. *Master and Servant: Bhadase Sagan Maraj*. Trinidad: Sanatan Dharma Maha Sabha, 1991.
Sankalia, H.D. *The Ramayana in Historical Perspective*. Delhi: Macmillan India Limited, 1982.
Sarkar, Amal. *A Study on the Ramayanas*. Calcutta: Rddhi India, 1987.
Sastri, V.S. Srinivas. *Lectures on the Ramayana*. Madras: S. Vishwanathan Pvt. Ltd., 1949.
Schwartz, Barton M., ed. *Caste in Overseas Indian Communities*. California: Chandler Publishing Company, 1967.
Seecharan, Clem. *'Tiger in the Stars': The Anatomy of Indian Achievement in British Guiana 1919–29*. London: Macmillan Education Ltd., 1997.
Shah, A.M. *The Family in India: Critical Essays*. London: Sangam Books Limited, 1998.
Shapiro, Harry L., ed. *Man, Culture and Society*. London: Oxford University Press, 1971.
Sharma, Arvind. *Hinduism and Its Sense of History*. New Delhi: Oxford University Press, 2003.
———. *The Concept of Universal Religion in Modern Hindu Thought*. New York: Palgrave, 1998.

Sharma, Ramashraya. *A Socio-Political Study of the Ramayana.* Delhi: Motilal Banarsidass, 1971.

Shepherd, Verene. *Transients to Settlers: The Experience of Indians in Jamaica 1845–1950.* England: University of Warwick and Peepal Tree Books, 1993.

Siewah, Samaroo. *The Lotus and the Dagger: The Capildeo Speeches (1957–1994).* Trinidad: Chakra Publishing House, 1994.

Singh, K.K. *Patterns of Caste Tension: A Study of Intercaste Tension and Conflict.* London: Asia Publishing House, 1967.

Sinha, Raghuvir. *Family to Religion: A Theoretical Exposition of Basic Social Institutions.* n.p.: National Publishing House, 1980.

Smith, Bardwell L. *Hinduism. New Essays in the History of Religions.* Leiden: E.J. Brill, 1982.

Smith, M.G. *Culture, Race and Class in the Commonwealth Caribbean.* Mona, Jamaica: Department of Extra Mural Studies, University of the West Indies, 1984.

Smith, W.L. *Ramayan Traditions in Eastern India.* Stockholm: Department of Indology, University of Stockholm, 1988.

Srinivas, K.S. *Ramayanam As Told by Valmiki and Kamban.* New Delhi: Abhinav Publications, 1994.

Srinivas, M.N. *Caste. Its Twentieth Century Avatar.* New Delhi: Penguin Books India (P) Ltd., 1996.

———. *Social Change in Modern India.* Los Angeles: University of California Press, 1969.

———. *The Cohesive Role of Sanskritisation and Other Essays.* Bombay: Oxford University Press, 1989.

Stone, Merlin. *Ancient Mirrors of Womanhood: A Treasury of Goddess and Heroine Lore from Around the World.* Boston: Beacon Press, 1984.

Stutley, Margaret and James. *Harper's Dictionary of Hinduism.* New York: Harper & Row Publishers, 1977.

Strasser, Hermann, and Susan C. Randall. *An Introduction to Theories of Social Change.* London: Routledge & Kegan Paul, 1981.

Subbamma, Malladi. *Hinduism and Women.* Delhi: Ajanta Books International, 1992.

———. *Women: Tradition and Culture.* New Delhi: Sterling Publishers Private Limited, 1985.

Subramani, ed. *The Indo-Fijian Experience.* Queensland: University of Queensland Press, 1979.

Swarup, Hemlata, and Sarojini Basaria, eds. *Women, Politics and Religion.* Etawah, India: A.C. Brothers, 1991.

Thakur, Upendra. *Some Aspects of Ancient Indian History and Culture.* New Delhi: Abhinav Publications, 1974.

Thapar, Romila. *Cultural Pasts: Essays in Early Indian History.* New Delhi: Oxford University Press, 2000.

———. *Exile and the Kingdom: Some Thoughts on the Ramayana*. Bangalore: The Mythic Society, 1978.

———. *Narratives and the Making of History: Two Lectures*. New Delhi: Oxford University Press, 2000.

Thiel-Horstmann, Monika, ed. *Ramayana and Ramayanas*. Wiesbaden: Otto Harrasowitz, 1991.

Uberoi, Patricia, ed. *Family, Kinship and Marriage in India*. Delhi: Oxford University Press, 1993.

Vaidya, C.V. *The Riddle of the Ramayana*. Delhi: Oriental Publishers and Booksellers, 1972.

Van der Veer, Peter. *Religious Nationalism. Hindus and Muslims in India*. Berkeley: University of California Press, 1994.

Vertovec, Steven. *Hindu Trinidad: Religion, Ethnicity and Socio-Economic Change*. London: Macmillan Education Ltd., 1992.

Vyasa, Lallan Prasad. *Ramayana: Its Universal Appeal and Global Role*. New Delhi: Har-Anand Publications, 1992.

Walcott, Derek. *The Antilles: Fragments of Epic Memory: The Nobel Lecture*. New York: Farrar, Straus and Giroux, 1993.

Whaling, Frank. *The Rise of the Religious Significance of Rama*. Delhi: Motilal Banarsidass, 1980.

Williams, Joanna. *The Two-Headed Deer: Illustrations of the Ramayana in Orissa*. Berkeley: University of California Press, 1996.

Winternitz, M. *A History of Indian Literature*. New York: Russel and Russel, 1971.

Yardi, M.R. *The Ramayana, Its Origin and Growth: A Statistical Study*. Poona: Bhandarkar Oriental Research Institute, 1994.

Yelvington, Kevin A., ed. *Trinidad Ethnicity*. Knoxville: The University of Tennessee Press, 1993.

Zaener, R.C. *The Bhagvadgita*. London: Oxford University Press, 1969.

Zimmer, Heinrich. *Myths and Symbols in Indian Art and Civilisation. Bollingen Series VI*. Delhi: Princeton University Press, 1972.

B. Articles

Anand, Vidya Sagar. 'The Ramayana and the Modern World.' In *The Ramayana: Its Universal Appeal and Global View*, edited by Lallan Prasad Vyas, 84–99. New Delhi: Har-anand Publications, 1992.

Bhatia, Tej K. 'Trinidad Hindi: Its Genesis and General Profile.' In *Language Transplanted: The Development of Overseas Hindi*, edited by Richard K. Berz and Jeff Siegel, 179–96. Weisbaden: Otto Harrassowitz, 1988.

Bulcke, C. 'Ramcaritmanasa and Its Relevance to Modern Age.' In *The Ramayan Tradition in Asia*, edited by V. Raghavan, 58–75. New Delhi: Sahitya Akademi, 1980.

Chaitanya, Krishna. 'Man, Myth and Meaning: Mircea Eliade and Indian Perceptions.' In *Indian Horizons* 32 no. 1 (1983): 5–12.

Coburn, Thomas B. 'Scripture in India: Towards a Typology of the Word in Hindu Life.' *Journal of the American Academy of Religion* 52 no. 3: 435–59.
Haraksingh, Kusha. 'Aspects of the Indian Experience in the Caribbean.' *Calcutta to Caroni: The East Indians of Trinidad*, edited by John La Guerre, 155–69. St Augustine: University of the West Indies Extra Mural Studies Unit, 1985.
———. 'Indian Leadership in the Indenture Period.' *Caribbean Issues* 11 no. 3 (1976): 17–38.
———. 'Indians and Socio-cultural Aspects of Assimilation: The Trinidad Experience.' *L'inde en Nous* 9 (1989): 131–37.
———. 'Structure, Process and Indian Culture in Trinidad.' *Immigrants and Minorities*, edited by Colin Holmes and Kenneth Lunn, 113–22. London: Frank Cass, 1988.
Jain, Ravindra K. 'The East Indian Culture in a Caribbean Context: Crisis and Creativity.' *India International Centre Quarterly* 13 no. 2 (1986): 153–64.
James, C.L.R. 'West Indians of East Indian Descent.' Port-of-Spain: Ibis Publications, 1965.
Jha, J.C. 'Indian Heritage in Trinidad.' *Journal of the Ganganatha Jha Kendriya Sanskrit Vidyapeetha* 31 (1975): 201–39.
Kishwar, Madhu. 'Manu and the Brits.' *Hinduism Today* 28 (February 2001): 56–60.
La Guerre, John. 'The Indian Response to Black Power: A Continuing Dilemma.' In *The Black Power Revolution 1970* edited by Selwyn Ryan, 273–306. St Augustine: Institute of Social and Economic Research, University of the West Indies, 1995.
Lutgendorf, Philip. 'Monkey in the Middle: The Status of Hanuman in Popular Hinduism.' *Religion* 27 (1997): 311–32.
Maharaj, Niala. 'Going Ramayan.' *Caribbean Beat* (March–April 2000): 43–47.
Misra, Pramode Kumar. 'Cultural Design in Identity Formation in Trinidad.' *The Eastern Anthropologist* 48 no. 3 (1995): 201–26.
Mohammed, Patricia. 'The "Creolization" of Indian Women in Trinidad.' In *The Independence Experience 1962–1987* edited by Selwyn Ryan, 381–97. St Augustine: Institute of Social and Economic Research, University of the West Indies, 1988.
Naidoo, M.B. 'The East Indian in Trinidad: A Study of an Immigrant Community.' *Journal of Geography* 59 no. 4 (1960): 175–81.
Naravane, V.S. 'The Role of Mythology in the Indian Cultural Tradition – 1.' *Indian Horizons: Indian Council for Cultural Relations* 32 no. 1 (1983): 5–18.
———. 'The Role of Mythology in the Indian Cultural Tradition – 2.' *Indian Horizons: Indian Council for Cultural Relations* 32 no. 2 (1983): 29–41.
Nevadomsky, Joseph. 'Changes in Hindu Institutions in an Alien Environment.' *Eastern Anthropologist* 33 (1980): 39–53.
Nicholls, David. 'East Indians and Black Power in Trinidad.' *Race* 12 no. 4 (1971).
Parekh, Bhikhu. 'Some Reflections on the Hindu Diaspora.' *New Community* 20 no. 4 (1994): 603–20.

Rampersad, Indrani. 'The Role of the Ramayana in the Lives of the Early Indentured Labourers in the Caribbean.' *Jagriti* 3 (1986): 10–11.

Schwartz, Barton. 'Differential Socio-religious Adaptation.' *Social and Economic Studies* 16.

Singaravelou, 'Indian Religion in Guadeloupe, French West Indies.' *Caribbean Issues* 11 no. 3 (1976): 39–51.

Tewarie, Bhoendradath. 'Hinduism, Nation-Building and the State.' In *The Independence Experience 1962–1987* edited by Selwyn Ryan, 207–16. St Augustine: Institute of Social and Economic Research, University of the West Indies, 1988.

Thapar, Romila. 'Traditions Versus Misconceptions.' *Manushi* 42–43 (1987).

———. 'Origin Myths and the Early Indian Historical Tradition.' *History and Society* edited by Debiprasad Chattopadhyaya, 271–95. Calcutta: K.P. Bagchi and Company, 1978.

Tiwari, Badri Narayan. 'Bidesia: Migration, Change, and Folk Culture.' *International Institute or Asian Studies Newsletter* (March 2003): 12.

C. Unpublished Papers and Theses

Ali, Shameen. 'A Social History of East Indian Women in Trinidad since 1890.' MA diss., University of the West Indies, St Augustine, 1993.

———. 'Africans, Indians and the Press in Trinidad, 1917–1946.' PhD diss., University of the West Indies, St Augustine, 2000.

Basdeo, Sahadeo. 'Indian Participation in Labour Politics in Trinidad 1919–1939.' Paper at the Conference on East Indians in the Caribbean: A Symposium on Contemporary Economic and Political Issues, University of the West Indies, St Augustine, September 16–23, 1979.

———. 'Mitra Sinanan and Political Consciousness among Indians in Trinidad in the Thirties.' Paper presented at the Conference on East Indians in the Caribbean – Beyond Survival, University of the West Indies, St. Augustine, August 28–September 5, 1984.

Bush, Ratimaya Sinha. 'Festivals, Rituals and Ethnicity among East Indians in Trinidad.' PhD diss., Ohio State University, 1997.

Forbes, Richard Huntington. 'Arya Samaj in Trinidad: An Historical Study of Hindu Organisational Process in Acculturative Conditions.' PhD diss., University of Miami, 1984.

———. 'Arya Samaj as Catalyst: The Impact of a Modern Hindu Reform Movement on the Indian Community of Trinidad between 1917 and 1939.' Paper presented at the Conference on East Indians in the Caribbean: A Symposium on Contemporary Economic and Political Issues, University of the West Indies, St Augustine, September 16–23, 1979.

Haraksingh, Kusha. 'Hindu Legal Thought in Trinidad.' Paper presented at the Conference on the Hindu Presence in Trinidad and Tobago, University of the West Indies, St Augustine, October 25–27, 2002.

―――. 'The Hindu Experience in Trinidad.' Paper presented at the Conference on East Indians in the Caribbean – Beyond Survival, University of the West Indies, St Augustine, August 28–September 5, 1984.

―――. 'Trouble in the Kutiya: Popular Expression and the Indian Intellectual Tradition in the Southern Caribbean.' Paper presented at the Conference on Caribbean Intellectual Traditions, Mona, Jamaica, October 1988.

Hosein, Shaheeda. 'Rural Indian Women in Trinidad, 1870–1945.' PhD diss., University of the West Indies, 2002.

Johnson, Judith. 'The Changing Cultural Context of the Neonatal Period in an East Indian Rural Community of South Trinidad.' Paper presented at the Conference on East Indians in the Caribbean: A Symposium on Contemporary Economic and Political Issues, University of the West Indies, St Augustine, September 16–23, 1979.

Koss, Joan D. 'Hindus in Trinidad: A Survey of Culture and Cultural Continuity.' PhD diss., University of Pennsylvania, 1959.

Mahabir, Kumar. 'Poetry in Song: Literary Devices in East Indian Folk Songs of the West Indies.' Paper presented at the Twentieth Anniversary Conference on West Indian Literature, University of the West Indies, St Augustine, March 1–3, 2001.

Parmasad, Kenneth. 'Break a Vase…Indian Folk Tales of Trinidad.' Paper presented at Twentieth Anniversary Conference on West Indian Literature, University of the West Indies, St Augustine, March 1–3, 2001.

Persad, Prakash. 'Puja and Politics.' Paper presented at the Conference on The Hindu Presence in Trinidad and Tobago, University of the West Indies, St Augustine, October 25–27, 2002.

Prorok, Carolyn. 'Hindu Temples in Trinidad: A Cultural Geography of Religious Structures and Ethnic Identity.' PhD diss., University of Pittsburgh, 1988.

Ramesar, Marianne. 'The Impact of the Indian Immigrants on Colonial Trinidad.' Paper presented at the Conference on East Indians in the Caribbean: Colonialism and the Struggle for Identity, University of the West Indies, St Augustine, June 1975.

Rampersad, Krishendaye. 'The Growth and Development of Indo-Trinidadian Literature 1850 to 1950.' PhD diss., University of the West Indies, 2000.

Samaroo, Brinsley. 'Missionary Methods and Local Responses: The Canadian Presbyterians and the East Indians in the Caribbean.' Paper presented at the Conference on East Indians in the Caribbean: Colonialism and the Struggle for Identity, University of the West Indies, St Augustine, June 1975.

―――. 'Reconstructing the Identity: Hindu Organization in Trinidad during Their First Century.' Paper presented at Conference on the Hindu Presence in Trinidad and Tobago, University of the West Indies, St Augustine, October 25–27, 2002.

―――. 'Women's Work in the Canadian Presbyterian Mission to Trinidad during the Century after 1868.' Paper presented at the Conference on Religions of the New World, University of the West Indies, St Augustine, January 6–8, 2002.

Sharma, Kailash Nath. 'Changing Forms of East Indian Marriage and Family in the Caribbean.' Paper presented at the University of the West Indies, St Augustine, n.d.

Singh, Odaipul. 'Hinduism in Guyana: A Study in Traditions of Worship.' PhD diss., University of Wisconsin, 1993.

Singh, Simboonath. 'Ethnic Association and the Development of Political Consciousness: The Indo-Caribbean Experience in Canada.' Paper presented at the International Conference on Asian Migration to the Americas, University of the West Indies, St Augustine, August 11–17, 2000.

Tewarie, Laxmi Ganesh. 'Singing the Story of Ram: The Ramayan among Trinidad Indians.' Proceedings of Conference on Challenge and Change: The Indian Diaspora in its Historical and Contemporary Contexts, University of the West Indies, St Augustine, August 11–18, 1995.

Tikasingh, Gerard I.M. 'The Establishment of Indians in Trinidad, 1870–1900.' PhD diss., University of the West Indies, 1973.

———. 'The Representation of Indian Opinion in Trinidad, 1900–1921.' Paper presented at the Conference on East Indians in the Caribbean: A Symposium on Contemporary Economic and Political Issues, University of the West Indies, St Augustine, 1975.

Vertovec, Steven. 'Hinduism and Social Change in Trinidad.' PhD diss., University of Oxford, 1987.

INDEX

Adesh, Professor, H.S.: and Hindu religious instruction, 218

Adventures of Gurudeva and Other Stories: and theme of personal sanskritisation, 32, 78; women in, 96, 165

Ahisma: Ghandi and, 30

Alcohol: and Hindu rituals, 233–34; and the Hindu wedding ceremony, 170–71

Animal sacrifice: in Hindu rituals, 150–53

Arts: and the *Ramayana*, 78

Arya Samaj: and primary education, 155, 246; and sanskritisation of Indians, 49–51, 224; and the Shuddhi, 227; and the wedding ceremony, 87, 168

Baal Vikaas programme: and the *Ramayana*, 216

Backward Classes Movement: and social mobility, 15

Bahadoorsingh, Jang: and the SDMS, 201

Baithana: and common-law unions, 168–69

Banking system: Hindu mistrust of, 181–82

Baptism: and religious conversion, 226–27

Beharry, Harry Persad: and the SDMS, 201

Bhagvadgita: christianising the, 123–27; and death rituals, 128; as religious icon, 112, 113, 122; synopsis of the, 259

Bhagvapurana: and the dissemination of knowledge, 36, 102–103, 111–13, 114; synopsis of the, 260

Bhagvata: Aarti, 267–68

Bhaiyachaarya: socio-religious change and the decline of the, 145

Bhakti: in India, 2; and the *Ramcharitmanas*, 67–69; in Trinidad, 31, 33

Bharatiya Vidya Sansthaan, 204, 218–20

Bhojpuri language, 155–57, 159–60

Bidesia tradition: Hindu religious texts and the, 101

Biracial marriages: in the Hindu community, 47, 173–76

Births: and the *Ramayana*, 84–86

Bisnauth, Dale: and Indians in Guyana, 35

Black Power: and Hindu revitalisation, 191

Brahma Kumari Raja Yoga Center: and Rama, 108, 204

Brahminic supremacy: challenge to the, 33, 34, 148–50

Brahminisation: concept of, 14

Brahmins: and education, 129; conflict with Kshatriya, 45; and marriage, 148; and the performance of

Sanatanist rituals, 34; and political leadership, 194-99; and the priesthood, 148; and the *Ramayana*, 116-20; and *Ramleela*, 75-76; and Ravan, 73; and religious Hindu texts, 104-105; and social mobility, 37-39, 48; status of, 237; in Trinidad, 31-32, 33, 37-39; and women, 233

Brathwaite, Edward: and creolisation of Indians, 15-16

Business community: media and the Hindu, 213-14

Butterfly in the Wind: and the *Ramayana*, 78

Canadian Mission Schools: and the use of English language, 155

Canadian Presbyterian Mission (CM): Christian influence of the, 61, 253; and Hindu education, 56-62

Capildeo, Rudranath: and political leadership, 194, 201

Capildeo, Simboonath: and political leadership, 194, 207

Caribbean Hindu Center, 165

Caribbean Hindu Conference: and the Hindu community, 211; and women, 166

Caribbean Hinduism: concept of, 7

Carnival: and Hindu deity, 231-32

Caste system: evolution of the, 36-37, 144-45, 147-50, 236-39; marriage and the, 42-43; and respectability, 45-46; in T&T, 1, 3, 15; *Ramcharitmanas* and the, 69-70, 116, 129-30

Chaitanya, Bramachari Prem: and Vedantic philosophy, 108

Chaitanya, Swami Shuddha: visit to Trinidad, 217

Chakra Publishing House, 214

Challenge and Change: The Indian Diaspora in its Historical and Contemporary Contexts: UWI, 17

Children's literature: the *Ramayana* and, 77

Chinmaya Mission: and Hindu religious instruction, 108, 217

Chinmayananda, Swami: and Vedantic philosophy, 108, 217

Christianisation: of the Hindu community, 56-62, 223-28. *See also* Conversion and Westernisation

Christof, Martin: and the *Bhagvadpurana*, 112-13

Chutney music: the *Ramayana* and, 82-84

Codes of conduct: *Ramcharitmanas* and Hindu, 92

Colour: and the *Ramayana*, 113

Common-law unions: among Hindus, 168-69

Compartmentalisation: in Trinidad Hinduism, 234, 251-52, 254

Conferences on East Indians in the Caribbean: University of the West Indies (UWI), 17

Conversion: of Hindus to Christianity, 131-33, 223-28, 229-31

Cremation: and the Hindu community, 219-23

Cremation Act, 1976, 222

Cremation Ordinance: Hindu community and the, 221

Cremation Regulation Amendment, 1970, 222

Dance: the *Ramayana* and, 77

Dattatreya Yoga Centre: and Hindu religious instruction, 217

Death ceremonies: and cremation, 219-23; the *Ramayana* and, 88; *Ramcharitmanas* and, 128; westernisation of, 254

Dee puja: and animal sacrifice, 150–52
Democratic Labour Party (DLP): and the Hindu revitalisation, 218; and political leadership, 194, 194–95, 201, 249
Development of the East Indian Community in British Guiana 1920–1950, 69
Devi, Deokie: initiation of, 33, 118
Dharmachaarya: and the christianising influence, 124, 251
Director of Education's Report: and the Hindu community, 214
Dissemination: of the *Ramayana* story, 128–30
Divali Nagar: and Hindu festivals, 210; and religious conversion, 230
Divali celebrations: as a national holiday, 207, 209–10, 250; and the *Ramayana*, 77–78;
Divine Life Society: and Hindu religious instruction, 204, 217
Divorce: and the Hindu community, 176–78
Divorce Bill: and the Hindu religion, 54, 55
Dow Village Hindu Youth Organisation: and Divali, 207
Draft Education Act, 215

East Indian Advisory Board, 51
East Indian National Congress (EINC), 47–48
East Indian National Association (EINA), 47–48
East Indian Weekly, 12
East Indians in Trinidad. A Study of Cultural Persistence, 8
East Indians in the West Indies, 8
Economic development: and socio-religious change, 139–55
Education: Brahmins and, 129; Hindus and English, 214–19, 237–38, 246–47; Hindu women and, 161–65; among Indians, 55–60, 65, 66; SDMS and, 155, 157, 206. *See also* Primary schools and Schools
English language: Hindu education in, 59–62, 155–60; in the *Ramayana*, 109–12; in religious texts, 103–104; and social mobility, 158, 192
Entertainment: at weddings, 171–72
Establishment of Indians in Trinidad 1870–1900, 9
Ethics: *Ramcharitmanas* and Hindu, 92–93
Evangelism: and religious conversion, 224–28
Extended family: decline of the, 93–94, 160

Family: definition of, 40
Family life: Hindu, 5, 39–47, 51–62, 93–95; socio-religious change and, 143–44, 160–78, 245–46
Family planning: and family size, 161–62
Felicity: religious conversion in, 224–25
Fiji: Hinduism in, 124; *Ramayana* yagna in, 115
Folk music: the *Ramayana* and Hindi, 82–84
Folk tradition. *See* Oral culture
Format: of Hindu religious texts, 109–12
From Caste to Class. Social Mobility among Indo-Trinidadians, 9

Ganapati, Swami: and religious instruction, 217
Gandhi, Mahatma: and *Ramcharitmanas* as doctrine, 92
Gandhi Seva Sangh, 204
Ganja: and Hinduism, 91
Garud Purana: and death rituals, 128

Guadeloupe: *Ramayana* tradition in, 131
Gender: and Hinduism, 33; and the Hindu family, 41–45
Gender Negotiations among Indians in Trinidad, 10
God: Hinduism and the concept of, 30–31
Group worship: among Hindus in Trinidad, 35
Guru Granth Sahib: in Sikhism, 115
Guyana: Hindus and group worship in, 35; Kali worship in, 152; *Ramayana* tradition in, 69

Hanuman worship, 131
Haraksingh: and the *Ramayana*, 104–105
Hindi films: and identity, 46–47, 156; *Ramayana* and, 76–78, 80–81
Hindi language: demise of the, 155, 156; and identity, 158; as a second language, 158–60
Hindi Nidhi Foundation: and the preservation of Hindi, 158, 205
Hindi prose, 109–12
Hindi Religious education: in primary and secondary schools, 214–19, 246–47
Hindu community: and the business community, 213–14; and the caste system, 144–45; and citizenship[p, 250; and the CM, 55–60; conflict within the, 200–206; and cremation, 219–23; and death, 88; and education, 55–62, 65, 66; and the family feeling, 142–44, 244–45; and India, 184–88; and land ownership, 178–80; and monogamy, 87; and national life, 249–52; religious conversion in the, 223–28; socio-religious change and westernisation of the, 145–55; organisations in the, 48–49; population statistics, 29; and wealth creation, 180–84
Hindu culture, 6, 208–10, 212–14, 218–20; westernisation of, 253–55
Hindu family: adultery and the, 178; divorce and the, 176–78; the father in the, 162; features of the, 39–45; males in the, 161, 162; and marriage, 42–44, 47, 51–56, 167–76; *Ramayana* and the, 93–95; women in the, 41, 161–65
Hindu festivals, 6; and the wider Trinidad society, 212–14, 250–52
Hindu leadership, 191–99, 248–49; and politics, 194–99; and religious conversion, 225–26, 249
Hindu Mahasaba, 48
Hindu Marriage Act: and divorce, 54, 55
Hindu Marriage Bill, 52–53, 54, 231, 247
Hindu organisations, 47–56, 65, 147; 199–206, 248–49
Hindu Prachar Kendra: and Hindu religious instruction, 219; and Hindu revitalisation, 226; and political leadership, 205, 210; and women, 118
Hindu priest: role of the, 48
Hindu religious texts, 100–38; *Bhagvadgita* as, 112–13, 122, 123–28, 259; Bhagvadpurana as, 260; Christian influence on, 123–27, 240; de-ritualising of, 120–22; dissemination of, 128–30; Hindi language and, 156; language in, 102–12; Puranas as, 259–60; and purpose, 127–29; questioning of the, 90–91, 102, 114, 115, 119–20, 127, 131–33, 135; readings of, 130–33; reinterpretation of, 134–38, 198–99, 240, 243–44;

Ramcharitmanas as, 260–62; and socio-economic change, 130–33
Hindu revitalisation: christianity and the, 131–33, 146–47, 153–55, 157, 190–91, 215–19, 226–28, 251–52
Hindu rituals, 35–36, 150; socio-religious change and the decline of the, 145, 225–26, 240–41, 251; westernisation of, 253, 254
Hindu Sabha; organisations, 48
Hindu Seva Sangh: and Hindu revitalisation, 226
Hindu Swayamsevak Sangh, 165
Hindu temple: transformation of the, 153–54
Hindu women: and divorce, 176; and education, 161–62; and marriage, 41–44, 53–55; and the priesthood, 117–19; *Ramayana* and, 95–97, 117–19, 135–38; Westernisation of, 165; and work, 161–63
Hindu Trinidad: Religion, Ethnicity and Socio-economic Change, 10
Hinduism. *See* Trinidad Hinduism
Historical Vision of an Afro-American People: by Price, 17
History: the *Ramayana* as, 21–22, 106–107
House for Mr Biswas, A: the, *Ramayana* and, 78

Identity: Hindi language and, 155, 158; Hindi films and, 46–47; the *Ramayana* and, 26
Indentured Indians: social diversity of, 9
India: bond between Trinidadian Indians and, 57, 156–57, 184–88, 247, 251
Indian, 12
Indian artistes, 208
Indian diaspora: *Ramayana* and the, 26; Sanskritisation in the, 32–39
Indian indenture: T&T statistics of, 1
Indian family: features of the, 39–45
Indian organisations, 47–56
Indian press: in Trinidad, 211–14
'Indian Renaissance': in Trinidad, 30
Indian Review, The, 213
Indians: in Trinidad (1940–46), 12 17; 29
Intermarriage. *See* Biracial marriages
Invitations: the yagna, 120–22

Jagaran, 213
Jagriti, 213
Jahaji bhai relationships: and family feeling, 144
Jaimini, Pundit: and the *Ramcharitmanas* as doctrine, 92
Jhal Ramayana style, 80
Jutha: definition of, 159

Kabeer Phunt: features of the, 2
Kali puja: and animal sacrifice, 150–52
Kali worship: in Trinidad, 152–53
Kartik nahaan: rise of the observance of, 230
Katha: and the oral tradition, 126, 127
Kelly, John: on Hinduism in Fiji, 124
Kendra, Shankar Kala: Ramayana ballet, 77
Keshvadas, Swami: visit to Trinidad, 217
Khan, Youseff: and the jhal Ramayana style, 80
Klass, Morton: and the caste system, 147; and Hindu leadership, 193; and the history of Trinidad, 8
Kshatriya: conflict with Brahmins, 45–46; model of sanskritisaion, 14: and the *Ramayana* tradition, 75–76
Kutiya: and the dissemination of religious education, 128–29

La Divina Pastora deity: acceptance in the Hindu pantheon, 35–36, 229
Ladoo, Harold Sonny: and the *Ramayana*, 78
La Guerre, Professor John: and the Hindu community in Trinidad, 214
Land: Hindu relationship with, 178–80
Language: and the Hindu community, 155–60; in the Ramayana texts, 109–12
Life cycle rituals: the *Ramayana* and, 84–90
Literature: the *Ramayana* in Trinidad, 78–79
Little Tradition: and animal sacrifice, 131, 151, 241
Love: *Ramayana* and, 94–95
Lutgendorf, Philip: and narrative style of *Ramayana* readings, 131; and the reinterpretation of the *Ramcharitmanas*, 135

Madrassis: rituals practised by Trinidad, 31
Mahabharata, 106–107
Mahabirsingh, T.R.: and Hindu political leadership, 198
Maharaj: and upward social mobility, 38–39
Male: in the Hindu family, 161
Maraj, Bhadase, Sagan: death of, 65, 151; and the SDMS, 201; and Trinidad politics, 140–41,193, 194, 195
Marriage: and the Hindu family, 42–44, 47, 51–56, 95, 143–44, 161, 163, 166, 167–78. *See also* Baithana, Biracial marriages, Common-law unions, Monogamy and Polygamy
Mauritius: Hinduism in, 129
Media: and Hindu community, 211–14
Mobility. *See* Social mobility

Mohammed, Haniff: and the jhal *Ramayana* style, 80
Mohammed, Patricia: and biracial marriages, 173; and East Indians in Trinidad, 10; and the Indian family, 40
Monogamy: among Hindus, 43, 87; and the *Ramayana*, 137–38
Music: and the *Ramayana*, 79–84
Myth: and history, 23; the *Ramayana* and, 22–23, 65–92

Naipaul, Seepersad: and issue of personal sanskritisation, 32; and the *Ramayana*, 78; and women, 96, 165
Naipaul, V. S.: and the *Ramayana* tradition, 63, 78
Naming: of Hindi schools, 57; and upward social mobility, 38–39
Narrative style: of the *Ramayana*, 131, 132
National Council for Indian Culture: and the *Ramayana*, 77–78, 205, 207
National Council of Hindu Organisations, 205
Neemakharam: definition of, 159, 160
Niehoff, Arthur and Juanita: and the caste system, 147; and the history of Trinidad, 8
Niyoga: tradition, 95
Non-Brahmin rites and rituals: and Trinidad Hinduism, 150–51
Nuclear family: Hindus and the emergence of the, 161

Observer, 12
Oral sources: on Hindus in Trinidad, 17–19
Oral tradition: and Hindu religious texts, 100–101; and katha, 126
Oral Tradition. A Study in Historical Methodology: by Vansina, 17;

Organisations: Hindu, 199–206, 248–49; Indian, 47–56, 65
Oughur Phunt: features of the, 2

Panchayat system: evolution of the, 61, 195–96; socio-religious change and the decline of the, 145
Panday, Basdeo: and political leadership, 194–95
Panday, Pundit Lutchmie Narine: and the DMS, 201
Parent-child relationships: Hindu, 162–63
Parents: role of Hindu, 161
Pathshalas: and Hindi religious education, 216–19; and Hindu education, 56–57, 128–29, 157, 158, 248
Peoples Democratic Party (PDP): and the Hindu community, 140–41
People's National Movement (PNM): and the Hindu Community, 64, 140–41, 207
Permananda, Swami: and Hindu religious instruction, 217
Personal sanskritisation: in Trinidad, 32
Persaud, Lakshmi: interpretation of the *Ramayana*, 78
Phagwa celebrations: and the Hindu community, 211, 250; *Ramayana* and, 83–84
Pilgrimages: religious conversion and, 230
Poetry: the *Ramayana* in, 78–79
Political development: and socio-religious transformation, 140–42, 250
Polygamy: and the Hindu community, 87; and the *Ramayana*, 137–38
Population: Hindu (1930–90), 258; religious composition of Trinidad 1990), 257

Port-of-Spain Gazette: and the Hindu Community, 211
Praja: definition of, 159; socio-religious change and the decline of the, 145
Presbyterians: and the Hindu education, 56–60; Indianising of the, 228
Press: Indians in the, 10–12. *See also* Indian press and Media
Price, Richard: and the oral tradition, 17
Primary schools: Hindu community and, 155; Hindi religious instruction in, 215–19; SDMS and, 155, 157, 199, 203. *See also* education and Westernisation
Puja, 127–28; and the marriage ceremony, 168
Punditai: criticism of the, 192–94; and education of Brahmins, 129; and wedding ceremonies and, 169–71
Puranas: synopsis of the, 259–60

Questioning of Hindu religious texts, 90–91, 102, 114, 115, 119–20, 127, 131–33, 135

Race: and politics, 141
Rama: and the banishment of Sita, 135–38; and leadership, 195, 196–97; and the *Ramayana* tradition, 75, 112; and the Ramleela, 76; religious interpretation of, 106, 108, 135–38; and sibling loyalty, 94
Rama Rajya: and the principles of good government, 195
Ramanund Phunt: features of the, 2
Ramasami, E.V.: interpretation of Ravan, 24–25
Ramayana: Aarti, 115, 264–65; and the Arts, 76–84; and Brahmins, 116–18; characters in the, 262–63;

Christianising the, 123–27; de-ritualising of the, 120–22; diversity of the, 242–43; and education, 129–30; and Hindu family life, 93–95; as Icon, 112–20; and Indians, 92–93; language in the, 109–12; and music, 79–84; narrative style, 131–33; and the oral tradition, 18–19, 70–76, 127–34; questioning of the, 131–32, 135; readers, 116–20, 132–33; readings, 127–34; reinterpretation of the, 134–38, 243–44; rituals, 121–22; satsang sessions, 90–91, 102, 114, 115, 116, 119–22; in schools, 130; story, 260–62; Sumiran, 115, 265–66; text, 36, 109–12; tradition, 3, 5, 7, 20–27, 63–99, 241–42; and the wedding ceremony, 85–88; women and the, 95–97, 117; yagnas, 88–90, 102, 114, 115, 116, 120

Ramayana yagna. See Yagna

Ramcharitmanas: and the caste system, 69–70, 116, 129–30; editions of the, 109–12; and Hindi films, 80, 81, 103; as katha, 126–27; and political leadership, 195–97; as religious icon, 113; and music, 79–82; reinterpretation of the, 134–38; as religious text, 103–109, 116–20, 242; as social doctrine, 92–93; synopsis of, 260–62; in Trinidad, 3, 5, 7, 25, 66–70; and the wedding ceremony, 85–88

Ramesar, Marianne: and Indians in Trinidad, 9

Ramleela: Brahmins and, 75–76; and the oral tradition, 18–19, 25, 70–76

Ramnamis: and the Ramayana, 25

Ravan: and corrupt leadership, 195, 197; in the *Ramayana* tradition, 24–25, 71–74;

Readers: *Ramayana*, 116–20
Readings: *Ramayana*, 127–32
Rehal: and the *Ramayana*, 113–14
Religion: of Indentured Indians, 1, 2
Religious conversion. *See* Conversion
Religious icon: *Ramayana* as, 112–20
Religious texts: de-ritualising of the, 120–22; Hindu: 100–38; reinterpretation of, 134–38, 198–99
Rice: symbolism of, 121
Rienzi, Adrian Cola: and political leadership, 194

Saddhu of Couva, The: interpretation of the *Ramayana*, 78–79
Sadharan Ramayana, 80
Samajists: and Western influences, 61
Sanatan Dharma: and Trinidad Hinduism, 29, 237
Sanatan Dharma Association (SDA): establishment of the, 48, 50–51; leadership by the, 199; and political change, 141: and the revitalisation of Hinduism, 153–54
Sanatan Dharma Board of Control (SDBC), 48, 50; leadership by the, 199; and religious education, 129–30
Sanatan Dharma Maha Sahba (SDMS): and cremation, 219–23; and the Hindu community, 64, 65, 193; internal conflict in the, 200–204; leadership by the, 199, 206, 250; and primary education, 155, 157, 199, 203, 246; and religious conversion, 226–28; and temples, 203; and women, 165
Sanatanist organisations: in Trinidad, 48
Sandesh, 213
Sangha Shakti Sammelan: and Hindu women, 165

Sanskar ceremony, 227
Sanskritisation: and community, 45–48; Srinivas and the concept of, 13–16, 236, 238; of Trinidad Hinduism, 32–39, 153–54, 236
Sansthaan, Bharatiya Vidya: and Hindi classes, 158; and transformation of Hindu temples, 154
Saraswatee: in Hindu religious texts, 115
Satchidananda, Swami: and Hindu religious instruction, 217
Satsang sessions: and the Bhakti tradition, 253, 254; as political platforms, 197–98; and questioning of the doctrine, 90–91, 102, 114, 115, 119–20, 127, 131–33
Satya Sai Baba Organization: and the *Ramayana*, 108
Schools: religious education in, 130, 246–47
Schwartz, Barton: and the caste system, 147
Sects: Indian religious, 2
Secularisation. *See* Westernisation
Seesaran, E.B. Rosabelle: and East Indians in Trinidad, 9
Selective creolisation: Shepherd and the concept of, 13–14, 15, 236, 238
Sewarnian Phunt: features of the, 2
Shaktism: in India, 2, 152
Shankaraacharya tradition: Sanatan Dharma and the, 108, 249
Sharma, Kailas Nath: and the Indian family in the Caribbean, 160
Sharma, Dr Parasunam: and Hindu organisations, 199–200
Sharma, Pundit Jankie Persad: and the SDMS, 201
Shepherd, Verene: and the concept of selective creolisation, 13–14, 15, 236, 238

Shiva Purana: as icon, 113
Shri Goswami Tulsidaskrit Ramayana: edition of the *Ramyana*, 109
Shuddhi ritual: and Hindu revitalisation, 227
Sibling relations: *Ramayana* and, 94–95, 196
Sikhism: religious texts in, 115
Sinanan, Mitra: and political leadership, 194
Singh, K.B.: and the jhal *Ramayana* style, 80
Singh, Ram Surat: and the SDMS, 201
Singhasam, 115: and women, 117–18
Singing with Sai Baba. The Politics of Revitalization in Trinidad, 8
Siparia Mai: in Hindu worship, 36
Sita: banishment of, 135–38; and family loyalty, 94; as the ideal Hindu woman, 95–97; as wife, 97, 112, 163
Social doctrine: *Ramcharitmanas* as, 92–93
Social mobility: and the Backward Classes Movement, 15; economic development and, 140; English language and, 158; Hindus and, 35, 36–39, 236, 237; and internal organisation, 47–62; and political development, 250
Society Working for the Advancement of Hindu Aspirations (SWAHA): and the *Ramayana*, 107–108
Socio-religious transformation: the economic context of, 139–55; and the family, 160–89; Hindu, 4–6, 236–39; and public life, 190–235; the *Ramayana* tradition and, 20–27, 65–70, 130–31
Srinivas, M.N.: and the concept of Sanskritisation, 13, 15, 236, 238
'Struggle for Survival: The Hindu Youth in the Caribbean, The', 208

State: Hindu engagement with, 250
Superstition: and religious conversion, 224–25
Survivors of Another Crossing. A History of East Indians in Trinidad 1880–1946, 9
Swamis: and the caste system, 149

Teelucksing, Hon. Sarang: and the Hindu Marriage Bill, 52
Temple: transformation of the Hindu, 153; SDMS and the funding of, 203
Temple-based worship: Hindus and, 35
Textual presentations. *See* Readings
Thapar, Romila: and the *Ramayana* tradition, 63, 111
Tikasingh, Gerard: and East Indians in Trinidad, 9
Trinidad Academy of Hinduism: challenge to Brahminic supremacy, 149; and women, 118
Trinidad Government: and cremation issue, 220–22
Trinidad Guardian: and the Hindu community, 211; report on the Divali celebration, 212
Trinidad Hinduism, 1, 3, 10, 12, 14–16, 29–30, 65–70, 201–10; and the Bhagvadgita, 112, 113, 122; and Carnival, 231–32; in the Indian diaspora, 26–27; ganja and, 91; leadership in, 33–34; and politics, 198–99; in Mauritius, 129; questioning, 90–91; *Ramayana* tradition in, 20–27, 116–20, 241–43; *Ramcharitmanas* in, 3, 5, 7, 25, 66–70, 103–109, 242; Ramleela in, 18–19, 25, 70–76, 242–43; religious trends in, 239–41; revitalisation of, 4, 131–33, 146–47, 153–55, 190–91, 215–19, 226–28; Sanskritic, 31; socio-religious transformation of, 31–32, 61, 190–206, 239; Westernisation of, 131–33, 145–55, 223–28, 229–30; women and, 117–18
Trinidad population: religious composition of (1990), 257
Tulsidas: and the *Ramcharitmanas*, 105, 126, 260–62

United Hindu Organisation, 204
University of the West Indies (UWI): conferences on East Indians in the Caribbean, 17
Upanishads, 108

Vaishnavism: in India, 2
Vaishya: model of sanskritisation, 14
Valmiki Ramayana, 105, 106
Values: *Ramcharitmanas* and Hindu, 92–93
Vansina, Jan: and the oral tradition, 17
Vegetarianism: Hinduism and, 30
Vertovec, Steven: and Hinduism in Trinidad, 10, 12
Village concept: socio-religious change and the Hindu, 141–55, 244–45
Vishwa Hindu Parishad, 204

Walcott, Derek: and the Ramleela performance, 76, 78
Wealth creation: and the Hindu community, 180–84
Wedding ceremony: African guests at the Hindu, 175–76; alcohol and the, 170–71; entertainment, 171–72; money gift, 183–84; Ramayana and the, 85–86; Sanatanist, 167–68; socio-religious change and the Hindu, 167, 169–75. *See also* Marriage and Marriage Bill, 52–53, 54, 231

Western education: of Hindus, 237–38, 246–47
Westernisation: of Hindu worship, 35, 145–55; of Hindu organisations, 205, 253–54
Where Beards Wag All: by Evans, 17
Wife: the Hindu, 161; Sita as the ideal Hindu, 97, 196
Williams, Dr Eric: and the Hindu community, 140–41
Women: Brahmin, 233; and education, 161–63; Hindi, 33; and marriage, 41–44, 47, 51–62, 161, 163–64, 165, 166; and the *Ramayana*, 95–97, 117–19; and the *Ramleela*, 74–75; westernisation of Hindu, 164; and work, 161–63, 164
Work: Hindus and, 238

Yagna: socio-religious change and the *Ramayana*, 88–90, 102, 114, 115, 120–22; as political platform, 197–98, 211; westernisation of the, 254

www.ingramcontent.com/pod-product-compliance
Lightning Source LLC
Chambersburg PA
CBHW020637230426
43665CB00008B/209